MEDICAL ASTROLOGY

Discovering the Psychology of Disease using TRIANGLES

The Rays, the Signs, the Planets, the Chakras

All rights reserved

Copyright © Leoni Hodgson

No part of this publication may be reproduced, stored in a retrieval system, or transmitted in any form or by any means, electronic, mechanical, photocopying, recording or otherwise, without the prior written permission of the author.

ISBN: 978-0-646-98288-5

Using triangles to find disease patterns in the astrology natal chart is ground-breaking work; this book Medical Astrology is essential reading for every medical astrologer.

About the Author

Leoni Hodgson works professionally as a practitioner and teacher in several specialist areas in the esoteric arts - Astrology (DMNZAS - Diploma Member of the NZ Astrological Society 1982, and the PMAFA - Professional Member of the American Federation of Astrologers 1983), Esoteric Psychology (MA in Esoteric Psychology and Ph.D. in Esoteric Philosophy), Raja Yoga and Esoteric Healing (INEH Certificate).

About this Book

After years of studying medical astrology and books written on the subject by many excellent astrologers, I became really dissatisfied with the existing diagnosis methods because they were inconsistent. I could not find a reliable method that would accurately map disease in the chart.

So I decided to start from the beginning and devise my own method. To do so I fell back on my esoteric training. Esotericism is a science based on the notion that we are souls having an earthly experience. Having studied and taught Esoteric Astrology, Esoteric Psychology, Esoteric Healing and Raja Yoga for years, I went back and searched in these texts until I settled on the triangle.

The Tibetan Master Djwhal Khul (the real author of the Alice A. Bailey books), said *"The triangle is the basic geometric form of manifestation and is seen (by those who have eyes to see) underlying the entire fabric of manifestation, whether it is the manifestation of a solar system.. cosmic triplicities or the tiny reflection of this divine triple whole which we call man"* [1] - or a disease, I thought. This set me on an investigative study of hundreds of charts, using a triangulated method of disease diagnosis.

Another point I wanted to highlight is the link between psychology and disease. In Bailey's Esoteric Healing book, the Tibetan said that most diseases on an individual level are directly attributable to our inner states, mainly our disturbed emotions. I had been using that premise for years in my astrological counselling work and found it very accurate.

The results of my research are presented in this book, *Medical Astrology: Discovering the Psychology of Disease using Triangles*. It is a combination of Traditional and Esoteric Astrology, Eastern teachings on the Seven Rays and Chakras and modern medical and psychological notions.

It is my belief that this book is just one step towards a future goal where the sciences of psychology, medicine, astrology and the chakras are combined in the treatment and healing of disease. This the Tibetan predicted. Leoni Hodgson

---

[1] Bailey, Alice A; Esoteric Astrology, 429.

Acknowledgements

This book is dedicated to the world service work of the Tibetan Master Djwhal Khul.

Loving thanks to my husband Jim who supports me in every way in all my endeavours and many thanks to my dear friends - Jeanni Monks, Marion Child, Kay Hanan, Keryn Christensen and James Orchard, who assisted me in so many generous ways to help produce this book.

Appreciations to the online site www.astro.com for astrology chart data, for artwork from authors named in the book, and for free online clipart or photos. All other artwork by Hodgson.

MEDICAL ASTROLOGY

Discovering the Psychology of Disease using TRIANGLES

The use of a triangle is not accidental. It is "the basic geometric form of all manifestation and it is to be seen underlying the entire fabric of manifestation, whether it is the manifestation of a solar system, a man", or in this case disease.

- Djwhal Khul

Leoni Hodgson

Foreword

It is a pleasure to be writing the Foreword to this ground-breaking book on medical astrology written by my colleague Leoni Hodgson. For some reason, there are very few books on the esoteric aspect of medical astrology despite the great interest in what is essentially an esoteric subject. Given the huge interest in disease and health, you would think that astrologers over the decades would have already explored more fully the esoteric side of astrology.

Leoni Hodgson has made an impressive contribution to filling this gap, at the same time as including well-known models and formulas associated with astrological/medical diagnosis. Of especial note is how she has prepared the student with detailed information on those areas which she sees as necessary pre-requisites for the central issue of astrological diagnosis. The book begins with a description of our subtle constitution, so that we can understand where the astrological energies including those from the signs and planets are received by our vehicles of mind, emotions and physical body.

The next detailed section features the characteristics of the seven rays which form the basis of the energies that flow through the signs and planets, including their association with bodily parts and various diseases. She sees the study of the seven rays as vital to understanding medical astrology and has written and taught on this subject herself over the years. Following this section of the book, the astrological signs receiving the ray forces are described and related to bodily parts and possible health problems. There is then a natural progression to examining the planets associated with each sign.

Many people would not be aware that the planets are understood to fall into three types of influence on a person, depending on whether the planets concerned are classed as exoteric or esoteric. This particular philosophy comes from the writings of Alice Bailey whose work has been deeply studied by the author of this book together with other esoteric sources of wisdom.

The author then presents the subject of the human chakra system which forms the reception of the energies flowing through the signs and planets and which are finally received by the endocrine glands, tissues and body organs.

> After this hierarchical progression of energies which condition our health and disease, we come to the unique contribution of the book – triangulation of three planets related to each disease process. One planet will represent the cause of the disease problem; another represents the organ concerned or reception point, and a third planet shows the effects or actual disease such as blindness. Then follows many case histories illustrating this formula.

This book will be appreciated by all astrological students interested in health and disease whether physical or psychological, lay people interested to understand astrology, and all esoteric students who study the meaning of life. Leoni Hodgson has written a detailed, comprehensive, and lucid account of those energies that condition our health and wellbeing.

Judy Jacka, BH.Sc. Post Grad.Dip. HRE, N.D.

Leoni is my spiritual mentor and a beloved soul friend who I have known since the early 2000's when I undertook to study her two year esoteric psychology course about the seven rays and raja yoga meditation which revolutionized my life at that time. I continue our spiritual work together by attending her monthly Full Moon meditations and the Brisbane Goodwill Meditation & Friendship Group which meets on a monthly basis.

Leoni has worked professionally for over 20 years as an astrologer and as a teacher of esoteric psychology, esoteric healing, the science of the Seven Rays, the science of the Chakras and Raja Yoga meditation.

In her new ground-breaking book on *"Medical Astrology: the Psychological Link to Disease"*, Leoni combines exoteric and esoteric astrology in an easy informative way that takes us right to the core of how dis-ease inherent in the natal birth chart can be activated at any time by major transits, progressions or solar arc dynamic techniques throughout our life cycle.

Leoni's sensitive and enlightening way of pinpointing a particular illness and relating it to the astrological indicators in a horoscope with its underlying psychosomatic causes, makes this a unique and revolutionary book that every medical astrologer and healer needs to have on their book shelf. It delves into the deepest crevices of the astro-medical realm of cause and effect which our medical world and humanity in general can benefit from, at this very important stage of our Earth's evolutionary process. It was, after all, Hippocrates who stated that "a physician without a knowledge of Astrology has no right to call himself a physician".

In her book, Leoni succinctly examines how the astrological signs related to the energies of the seven rays, can be associated with the parts of the body they rule and health problems. Her presentation of the human chakra system and the etheric body via the flowing of energy through the zodiac signs, their planets, their rays and then on to the endocrine glands and organs of the body, takes us to a new level of understanding of esoteric healing on a cellular soul level. From this angle, esoteric healers will also benefit from a study of the book.

> Leoni's unique approach to finding disease in the body uses triangles; three planets at least that are related to each step of the progression of disease: one planet represents the Cause of disease, another the Organ that is targeted by the disease, and a third the ultimate Effect of the disease. This process is vividly demonstrated in her book with many examples of case studies and clear diagrams, which makes this book a vital teaching tool in the study of medical astrology and the esoteric healing arts.

I personally feel that all of humanity will benefit from this book, especially Leoni's unique insights and contribution to understanding how health and disease from a physical, emotional, mental, spiritual and psychological energetic level are interrelated. Thank you my dearest friend for writing this book which is so needed at this time, as it creates a new paradigm of miraculous wellbeing possibility for healing ourselves and each other in the future.

> "Today any astrological investigation done in the field of medicine has relation to physical disease within the physical body. In the future, it will concentrate upon the condition of the etheric vehicle." [1]

Namaste & Blessings, Jeanni Monks

> Active committee member of QFA (Queensland Federation of Astrologers); APA (Association of Professional Astrologers) and an examiner on the FAA Examination Board. BA Psych.; Master of Science in Esoteric Psych.; Post Grad. Education/Counselling Dip; FAA Practitioner's Diploma.

---

[1] Bailey, Alice A; Esoteric Healing, 277.

Table of Contents

1. Spirit, Soul and Body 1
2. Forces & Energies 9
2a. The Seven Rays 11
Ray 1 of Will and Power 14
Ray 2 of Love and Wisdom 16
Ray 3 of Intelligent Activity 18
Ray 4 of Harmony through Conflict 20
Ray 5 of Concrete Mind 21
Ray 6 of Devotion and Idealism 22
Ray 7 of Ceremony, Order and Magic 24

2b. Astrology Signs 27
1. Aries 28
2. Taurus 30
3. Gemini 32
4. Cancer 34
5. Leo 36
6. Virgo 38
7. Libra 40
8. Scorpio 42
9. Sagittarius 44
10. Capricorn 46
11. Aquarius 48
12. Pisces 50

2c. Astrology Planets 53
1. The Sun 54
2. The Moon 56
3. Mercury 58
4. Venus 60
5. Mars 62
6. Jupiter 64
7. Saturn 66
8. Uranus 68
9. Neptune 70
10. Pluto 72
11. The Earth 74
12. Vulcan 74

2d. The Etheric Web and Chakras 75
1. The Crown or Sahasrara Chakra 78
2. The Brow or Ajna Chakra 80
3. The Throat or Vishudda Chakra 82
4. The Heart or Anahata Chakra 84
5. The Solar Plexus or Manipura Chakra 86
6. The Sacral or Svadhisthana Chakra 88
7. The Base or Muladhara Chakra 90

3. Disease and its Diagnosis **95**
　　1. Disease and its cause - it is simply misuse of energy 96
　　2. Diagnosing Disease via Chakras and Psychology 100
　　3. Diagnosing Disease via Astrology 102
　　4. Find a Health-Triangle 108

4. Case Studies **115**

4a. Crown Chakra Diseases **116**
　　4a.1. The Brain 116
　　4a.2. Dementia 122

4b. Ajna Chakra Diseases **126**
　　4b.1. Ears 126
　　4b.2. Eyes 128
　　4b.3. Nose 133
　　4b.4. Nervous System 134
　　4b.5. Pituitary Gland 139
　　4b.6. 5th Ray Psychological Disorders 141

4c. Throat Chakra Diseases **144**
　　4c.1. Breathing Problems 144
　　4c.2. Thyroid Disorders 148
　　4c.3. Cancer in Throat Chakra Organs 149

4d. Heart Chakra Diseases **151**
　　4d.1. Blood Disorders 151
　　4d.2. Cardiovascular Diseases 153
　　4d.3. Immune System 157
　　4d.4. Lung Cancer 160

4e. Solar Plexus Chakra Diseases **161**
　　4e.1. Allergies 161
　　4e.2. Gallbladder and Stomach 163
　　4e.3. Liver 164
　　4e.4. Pancreas 166
　　4e.5. Intestinal, Bowel 168
　　4e.6. Cancer in the Solar Plexus Organs 170
　　4e.7. Psychological Disorders 173

4f. Sacral Chakra Diseases **178**
　　4f.1. Genetic Diseases 178
　　4f.2. Reproduction Problems 180
　　4f.3. Sexually Transmitted Diseases (STD's) 183
　　4f.4. Cancer in the Sacral Chakra Organs 184

4g. Base Chakra Diseases **185**
　　4g.1. Adrenal Glands 185
　　4g.2. Bladder, Kidney problems 186
　　4g.3. Skeletal, Spine, Joint, Muscle Diseases 188
　　4g.4. Skin and Hair 192
　　4g.5. Cancer in the Base chakra Organs 195

5. Steps to Good Health **197**
　　Appendix 203
　　Glossary 204

1. SPIRIT, SOUL AND BODY

The Triangle is the basic geometric form of God in manifestation - Spirit, Soul and Body; the Divine pattern on which man is modelled.

1. The Journey of the Soul - Evolution of Consciousness

This section answers questions like "who am I" and "why am I here?" This is important because disease is related to our struggle to understand the world and ourselves.

Esoteric teachings tell us that we are more than just a body, or emotions or a mind. These are our human parts that enable our true self - the soul, to manifest on earth. When describing the soul, most people say something like "the soul is the inner-self that is wise and loving" and they are correct. But it is more than that. It is our link with the Life ensouling the universe, known in different philosophies by names such as God or the Oversoul.

In a technical sense, God in manifestation is triune, appears as a three-fold energy influence we commonly know as "Spirit-Soul-Body", "Father, Son, Holy Ghost" (Bible), or as "Atma, Buddhi, Manas" in esoteric literature. Human beings reflect this triune model as the following drawings show.

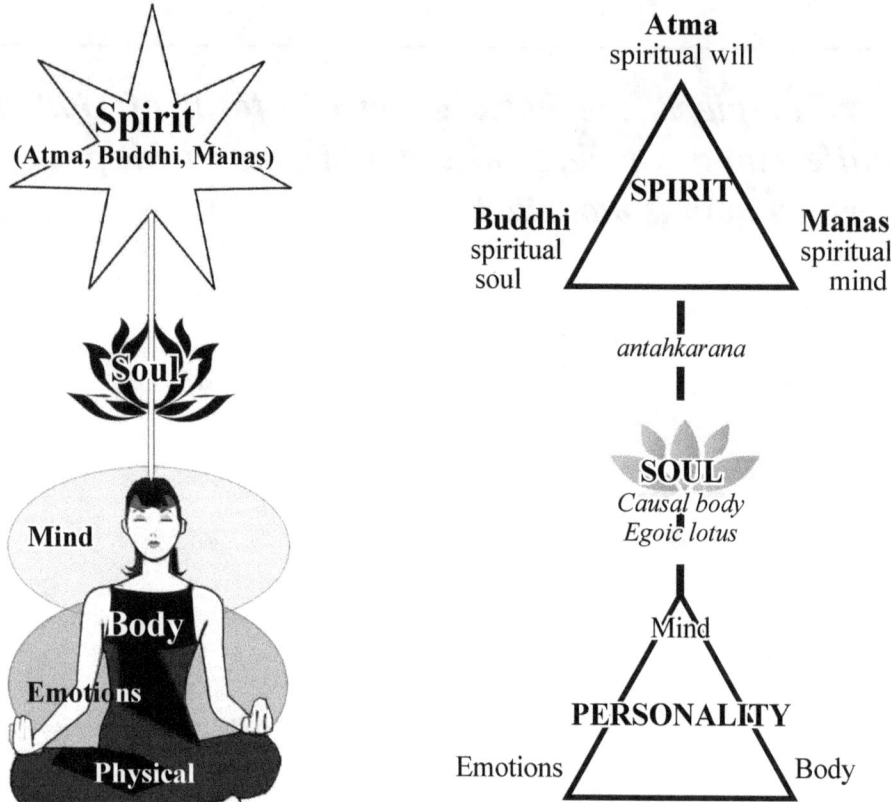

The soul - our human soul, is the bridge between our spiritual and human natures. It unfolds through experience on earth over many incarnations. A synonym of soul is "consciousness". As we acquire knowledge and apply it in our everyday lives, we learn to be more discerning and consequently our consciousness or soul expands. This proceeds across lives until union with Deity is achieved - in consciousness.

In the sketch, a dashed line is drawn from the mind to the soul and to spirit. Its Hindu name is "antahkarana" and it represents a stream of lighted consciousness that we must build to become spiritually aware and to reach the higher levels of existence. In most people, it has not been constructed. We build it through regular meditation, study of spiritual matters and by applying a holistic philosophy to the way we conduct our lives.

The "personality" consists of our human parts - the mind, emotions and the physical body. The soul uses the personality bodies to interact in the human world and to expand awareness and understanding.

"Who am I"?

If we are still identified with sexual desire, we might say "I am a passionate and sexual being". If we are still identified with intellectual cleverness, we might answer, "I am intelligent". Or, if we are identified with higher wisdom our response may be "I am a kind and loving soul". We express as much of the inner wisdom and love of the soul that we are able, and we answer the question differently depending upon our level of consciousness and the perspective from which we view life.

"Why am I here and where am I going?"

Our task is to live the most creative, fulfilling and productive life that we can manage. Across lives, this will take us through all the human departments in the world, from the very lowest to the highest.

Our task as a soul is to gain experience, to learn, to grow in character and expand our psychological understanding of the world. This will take us to the Spiritual Path. From that point on, our task is to climb to the heights of God wisdom, to become enlightened.

The term "enlightenment" as used in this book, refers to the stage when consciousness is filled with soul love and wisdom because all impediments that previously prevented this, have been removed. This occurs on the higher, Mental Plane. Here is a diagram to help explain things.

The Path and Consciousness

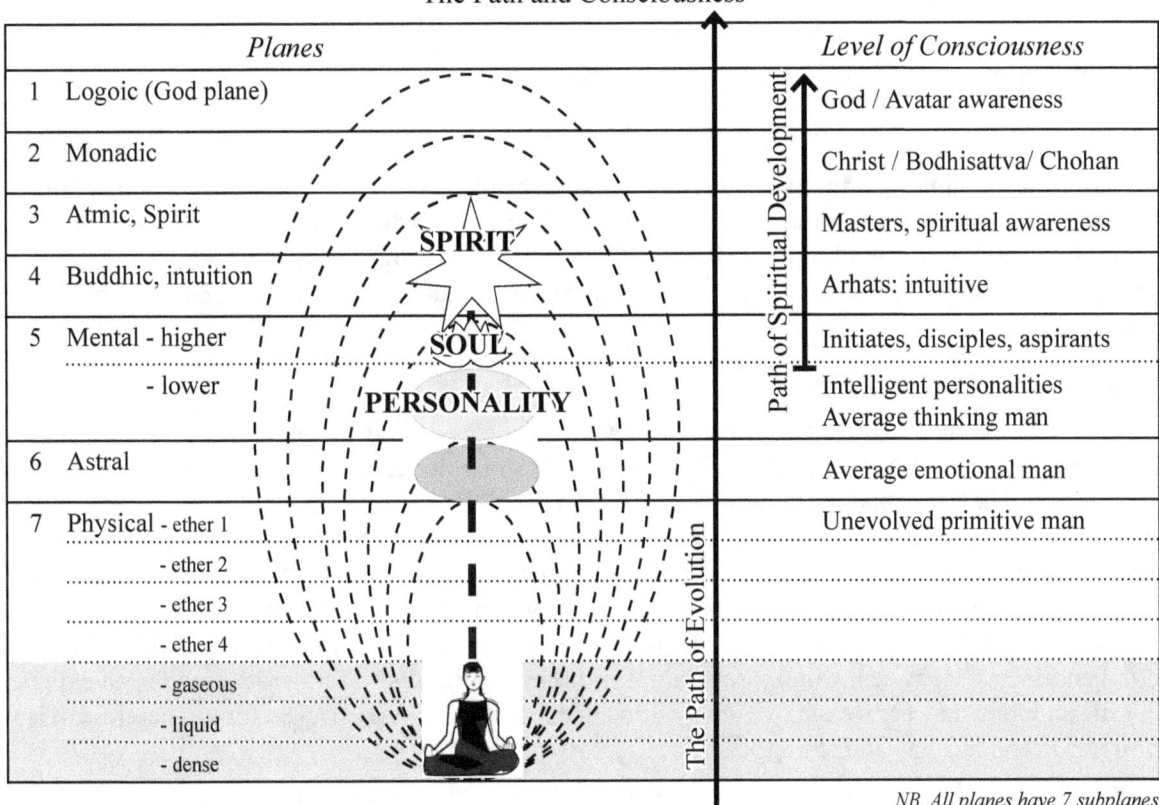

NB. All planes have 7 subplanes

The diagram depicts the 7 levels of consciousness in our solar system.

- The names of the planes or levels of consciousness are on the left-hand side. The lower 3 planes (5, 6, 7) are the human worlds. The higher four planes (1, 2, 3, 4) are the "spiritual worlds".
- Each of the 7 planes has 7 subplanes, but in the drawing they are shown only on the Physical Plane.
- On each plane, we have a seed-body which the soul uses when it has reached that plane.
- The names that are given to people who are stationed in consciousness on each plane are on the right-hand side of the chart.
- The Path of Spiritual Development, where we accelerate our progress, begins on the higher Mental Plane where the soul body (causal or egoic lotus) is located.
- The Monadic Plane is where our monads or the spiritual rays that connect us to God are located.
- A simple way to view the whole process - is like climbing a ladder.
    Each rung or plane symbolises both a plane of substance and a level of consciousness. When we move from one level to the next, it shows in our consciousness as increased wisdom and greater insight into ourselves, increased spiritual power and opportunity for service.
- Note that the arrow for the Path of Evolution goes off the chart at the top. There are six higher, equivalent universes above ours. We scale them all.

2. Consciousness ascends as our psychology expands

The whole emphasis of the evolutionary process is focused on the development of intelligent awareness and this is achieved on the Wheel of Rebirth, by incarnating through the astrological signs. We cycle round and round the zodiac through the twelve signs, all the time learning and expanding our psychological capabilities according to the sign we are travelling through. Each sign is responsible for developing and instilling certain positive qualities and values, though in the early stages, usually the negative traits are displayed.

Here is how Bailey describes the process.

> From point to point, stage to stage, and finally Cross to Cross, he fights for his spiritual life, in all the twelve houses and all the twelve constellations, subjected to countless combinations of forces and energies—ray, planetary, zodiacal and cosmic—until he is "made anew," becomes the "new man," is sensitive to the entire range of spiritual vibrations in our solar system and has achieved that detachment which will enable him to escape from the wheel of rebirth. [1]

Ascending the Ladder of Consciousness

As we evolve through the signs, gradually our consciousness ascends. "The Path and Consciousness" diagram on the previous page lays out in diagrammatic form, the levels through which consciousness rises. We start at the bottom, physical rung of the evolutionary ladder. Then, through the opportunities and growth challenges that incarnation provides, we gradually unfold our psychological faculties as we ascend or grow into the higher levels.

1. The Physical Plane and physical body

This is where our physical body is located. It has two levels - the etheric and dense, the latter consisting of the gaseous, liquid and dense subplanes. The etheric body is built from lighter etheric substance and is covered more fully in a later section. The dense body is built from heavier matter of the lower subplanes.

The consciousness of primeval man was focused in this body, at this level. He identified completely with the physical form, its instincts and physical survival. The physical body is like a robot that does what its owner tells it to do. If we are emotional people, the body will be used to search for happiness. If we are ambitious, the body will be used to pursue wealth and power. If we seek enlightenment, the body will be used for that. The physical body gives the human soul access to the physical world, providing it with the opportunity to further its growth and experience. Whatever our life ambition may be, we achieve it only through the medium of the physical form. Therefore, it is wise to look after it and keep it healthy and strong.

Astrology: dense physical - Moon, Mars, Saturn. The sign on the ascendant, its ruler and the sign it is in, and planets in the first house; all these colour the type of dense physical body we are born with and our appearance. The Moon represents all forms in nature, the physical containers that house the indwelling spiritual life, so it can be used to represent the physical form. Mars rules and controls the physical body when viewed as an animal form of blood and muscle. Saturn and Capricorn represent the dense skeletal structure and tissue of the body.

Astrology: the Etheric Body - Moon, Mercury, Uranus. Energy circulation through the etheric is governed by the Moon.[2] This means that any hard aspects to the Moon can be read as potential blockages in the etheric, the precursor to disease. Gemini (and Mercury), the custodian of conditioning energy and intermediary between soul and body is also related to the etheric. The 7th ray that Uranus carries, governs the etheric subplanes of the Physical Plane, so Uranus can also be used to represent the etheric condition in the body.

2. The Astral Plane and the astral/ emotional body - the Moon, Mars and Neptune

The Astral Plane is where our emotional body is located and where the consciousness of emotional people is focused. The emotional-desire body gives expression to emotions ranging from love and compassion to fear and hate; and desires ranging from the most gross to the most sublime. The astral body is definitely the most difficult vehicle to control and for many lives it keeps us trapped, swinging between the opposites of pleasure and pain.

---

1 Bailey, Alice A; Esoteric Astrology, 83.
2 Bailey, Alice A; Esoteric Healing, 143.

Most people on the planet at this time are stationed at this level and are primarily emotional in their psychology. An unstable emotional body has the greatest negative effect upon our health. Toxic emotions produce toxic chemicals in the body, which result in disease. The development of a harmonious astral nature through the development of a serene mind, improves health.

Astrology: the Moon, Mars and Neptune govern our emotional life. The Moon is closely linked with our astral bodies [1] and its sign represents "the prison of the soul" pattern, a powerful negative core belief that controls consciousness.

Mars is the lower ruler of the Emotional Plane and governs the coarser emotions such as anger, annoyance, irritation, lust, rage, suspicion, hate, avoidance, disgust and loathing. It governs also the desire emotions such as passion, yearning, thirsting and higher emotions such as courage and aspiration.

Neptune is the higher ruler of the Emotional Plane. It refines our emotional life, instilling in us the softer emotions such as sadness, sorrow, grief, hurt, anguish, anxiety, guilt and acceptance; and also admiration, joy, hope, serenity, ecstasy, bliss and devotion. Afflictions to these planets show troubled emotions.

3. The lower Mental Plane and the mind - Mercury, Venus and Uranus.

Mentally creative people have reached the lower mental plane.

People focused on the Mental Plane are definitely "mind" people and are not sometime thinkers who are dominantly astral. Due to widespread modern education, this is a fast growing group.

The mind is the individualizing principle that enables us to know that we exist, that we feel and know. It creates thoughtforms, concentrates, analyses, compares, deduces and memorises. It is not well organised in emotional people whose task is to develop the mind and mental discrimination. When this is achieved, when our psychology is firmly grounded on the Mental Plane, the soul (which is on the higher mental level) can begin to work through it.

Astrology: Mercury, Venus and their rays (4 and 5) influence the mind. Mercury's primary task is to unfold the discriminating and analytical powers of lower mind and to bring about its illumination. At a higher level, Mercury develops the intuition.

Venus carries the 5th ray of mind and works closely with Mercury to develop our mental powers. Its place in the chart shows where our thought life needs beautification and where we should endeavour to think and speak intelligently and with kindness.

Uranus is a representative of the scientific and abstract mind. Its place in the chart shows where we need to refresh the way we see life, shatter old concepts and develop new and freer ways of living.

The Personality **- the Sun and Leo.** When the mental body asserts itself, it integrates the forces of the emotions and physical body with itself into a composite entity called the "personality". Integrated personalities are powerful. They are the men and women who dominate the world and environment through the weight of their intelligence and power.

Astrology: our personality life is represented primarily by the Sun Sign. Aspects to the Sun show the level to which we have integrated our personality parts (mind, emotional, physical), and therefore the ability or inability of the personality to dominate the environment.

---

1 Bailey, Alice A; Esoteric Healing, 341.

Quotes from the Master Djwhal Khul

The Etheric Body

At present the etheric body is responsive to energies from:

1. The physical world.. the feeders and controllers of the animal appetites.

2. The astral world, determining the desires, emotions and aspirations which the man will express and go after upon the Physical Plane.

3. The lower Mental Plane, the lower mind, developing self-will, selfishness, separateness and the direction and trend of the life upon the Physical Plane.

4. The soul, the principle of individualism, the reflection in the microcosm of the divine intention. [1]

Opportunity of incarnation

For all of you this is an incarnation wherein the life focus becomes either irrevocably oriented toward the soul, as must be the case with newly accepted disciples, or powerfully expanded and inclusive as in the case of older disciples. [2]

---

1 Bailey, Alice, A: Telepathy and the Etheric Vehicle, 156.

2 Bailey, Alice, A: Discipleship in the New Age II, 546.

4. The Path of Spiritual Development on the higher Mental Plane

The Spiritual Path - sometimes just called "The Path", is the process that we embark upon when we begin the search for spiritual knowledge and illumination. This happens because at this level, the mind is coming under the illuminating effect of the soul.

In esoteric astrology, each sign functions at 3 levels, is represented by 3 planets, to cater for the three levels of our consciousness. Ordinary personality consciousness is represented by the *exoteric* planets, soul consciousness by the *esoteric* planets, and spiritual life by the *hierarchy* planets.

The presence of the soul in the chart is represented by the esoteric planets - the planets that rule each sign on the esoteric or soul level. They represent the purpose of the soul.

The esoteric planet ruler of the ascendant sign is the "ruler of the chart" as far as the goals and ideals of the spiritual life are concerned. The Hierarchy rulers that develop spiritual awareness are not used in this book. They are not relevant to disease, except perhaps at a mass level. Here is a chart showing these rulerships. [1]

Chart 1: Planet rulers of the Signs

Signs	*Exoteric Ruler*	*Esoteric Ruler*	*Hierarchy ruler*
	Personality	Soul	Spirit
Aries	Mars	Mercury	Uranus
Taurus	Venus	Vulcan	Vulcan
Gemini	Mercury	Venus	Earth
Cancer	Moon v. Neptune	Neptune	Neptune
Leo	Sun	Sun v. Neptune	Sun v. Uranus
Virgo	Mercury	Moon v. Vulcan	Jupiter
Libra	Venus	Uranus	Saturn
Scorpio	Mars, Pluto	Mars	Mercury
Sagittarius	Jupiter	Earth	Mars
Aquarius	Uranus, Saturn	Jupiter	Moon v. Uranus
Capricorn	Saturn	Saturn	Venus
Pisces	Jupiter, Neptune	Pluto	Pluto

The esoteric rulers start to influence us when we step onto the Path of Spiritual Development. So for instance, a Cancer Sun person prior to the Path is ruled by the conflicted Moon; but on the Path is ruled by esoteric Neptune, which begins its refining process. Another example is Scorpio. Prior to soul influence we can be destructive (Pluto) and highly aggressive (Mars). On the Path, we come under higher Mars, where the soul urges us to fight for the higher good. The following quote defines esoteric and exoteric astrology.

> Exoteric astrology deals with the characteristics and qualities of the personality and of the form aspects, and also with the events, happenings, circumstances and the conditioning environment which appear in the personal horoscope... Esoteric astrology concerns itself primarily with the unfoldment of consciousness, with the impacts which awaken it to the peculiar "gifts" of any particular sign and ray endowment and with the reaction of the man and his consequent enrichment through his response to the influence of a sign, working through the esoteric planets from the angle of humanitarian awareness, of discipleship and of initiation. [2]

Higher Venus represents the human soul and the Solar Angel, our spiritual guide and mentor. When we establish conscious contact with our souls, our character begins to transform and gradually, values that are more inclusive are demonstrated such as intelligent love. These are higher Venus qualities.

---

1 Bailey, Alice A; Esoteric Astrology, 68.
2 Bailey, Alice A; Esoteric Astrology, 145-146.

Discipleship and the Path

Going back to the ladder diagram (remembering it portrays levels of consciousness), the Path of Spiritual Development starts on the higher mental and spans the top three subplanes. It takes three steps, three expansions of consciousness to cross this higher way on the upper Mental Plane and to become enlightened.

- The higher Mental Plane, subplane 3: the 1st step - Aspirants.

This is the first stage of the Path, sometimes called the Probationary Path. Aspirants whose minds have become infused a little with soul love and wisdom have reached this level in consciousness. The impact of this upon their psychology is like an electric shock. They feverishly run around looking for information, books, groups and teachers who can explain more about the wonderful world which they have contacted. Their task is to bring their physical appetites into balance and when successful they pass *the 1st initiation*. The word "initiation" simply refers to an expansion of consciousness and enhanced soul influence.

At this mystical stage of our development, the cause of illness and disease may change. Where before negative thoughts and emotions primarily caused disease, now the movement of energy from lower to higher chakras starts to cause trouble.

Astrology: Vulcan and Pluto govern this stage. "The influence of Vulcan reaches to the very depths of his nature, whilst Pluto drags to the surface and destroys all that hinders in these lower regions." [1]

- The higher Mental Plane, subplane 2: the 2nd step - Disciples.

At this level are "older souls", those whose focuses lie beyond the normal attractions of the human material world. On the ladder, consciousness has reached the top of the Mental Plane and is beginning to move into the Buddhic/Intuitional Plane, the world of inclusive love and wisdom.

Astrology: Disciples are becoming decentralised at a personality level, have found their chosen group and are working in a profession to help their fellow men. Their first task is to purify the emotional nature, a process governed by Venus, Jupiter and Neptune. When successful they pass the 2nd initiation. Here is a description of a disciple.

> For what is a disciple? He is one who seeks to learn a new rhythm, to enter a new field of experience, and to follow the steps of that advanced humanity who have trodden ahead of him the path, leading from darkness to light, from the unreal to the real. He has tasted the joys of life in the world of illusion and has learnt their powerlessness to satisfy and hold him. Now he is in a state of transition between the new and the old states of being .. His spiritual perception grows slowly and surely as the brain becomes capable of illumination from the soul, via the mind. As the intuition develops, the radius of awareness grows and new fields of knowledge unfold .. As he perseveres and struggles, surmounts his problems and brings his desires and thoughts under control .. the Master is found; his group of disciples is contacted; the plan for the immediate share of work he must assume is realized and gradually worked out on the Physical Plane. [2]

- The higher Mental Plane, subplane 1: the 3rd step - Initiates.

The battle taken up by the soul for complete domination of the personality is managed through Mars and most likely Uranus. It is a tremendous fight but success gives entry to the higher levels of spirituality. With the 3rd initiation complete, consciousness moves to the top of the Mental Plane and onto the Buddhic Plane. Later, towards the Atmic or Spiritual Plane. The Path continues ever upwards, or inwards perhaps is a more correct term. From the Buddhic to the Atmic, then to the Monadic where great consciousnesses like the Christ and Gautama Buddha are stationed. Then beyond to the Logoic, God-conscious level; and later, even further into higher planes of the universe.

Evolutionary progress takes its toll on the body. Every step forward we take, subjects the atoms of the physical body to forces of a higher and faster vibration than they were previously used to. This places stress on the system and the body causing disease.

---

[1] Bailey, Alice A; Esoteric Astrology, 70.
[2] Bailey, Alice A; Treatise on White Magic, 58-59.

2. FORCES & ENERGIES

2a. The 7 Rays

2b. Astrology Signs

2c. Astrology Planets

2d. The Etheric Web and Chakras

2a. The Seven Rays

*From the One Life,
comes the Three - Spirit, Soul and Body;
From the Three come the Seven - the 7 Rays
- seven different energies, vibrations, colours and
characteristics that condition, shape and colour all that
is found in the universe.*

Overview of the Seven Rays

According to Eastern Wisdom, the Seven Rays are the seven basic forces of the universe from which all things are made. They are seven different energies, vibrations, colours and characteristics that condition our human nature on all levels.

The Seven Rays are not used in traditional astrology, but all astrologers who wish to understand the link between psychology and disease should include them in their astrological work. This is because these fundamental forces, just as they determine our psychology, they also determine disease.

> **The 7 rays give rise to seven different psychological and disease groups. The diseases or disorders in each particular group display the energy traits of the parent ray.**

Matching our psychology to a disease is made possible through the rays, which are the linking cause. For example, a violent 1st ray mind gives rise to a violent 1st ray disease such as a stroke; suppressed 6th ray emotions give rise to 6th ray psychological problems such as alcoholism or watery physical troubles such as oedema. We know which rays flow through the signs and planets making it easy to follow these streams of energy through the chart, linking planets, psychological states and disease. The rays knit together the various astrological forces we use, enabling us to study the arising of disease scientifically.

The Rays in our System

The seven rays originate from the heart of our galaxy, reaching us via the signs and planets. Here is a simple diagram, depicting the ray flow through the signs, the planets, to earth and to us.

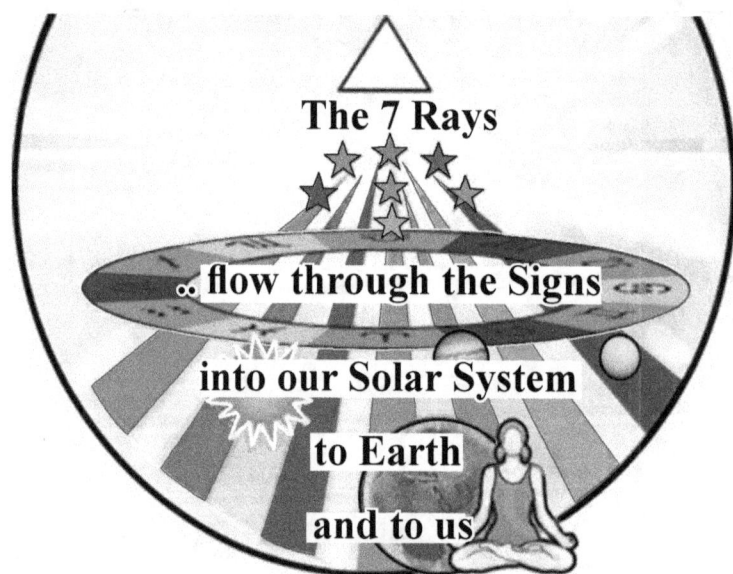

- Ray 1 of Will and Power (the red ray)
- Ray 2 of Love and Wisdom (the indigo blue ray)
- Ray 3 of Intelligent-Activity (the green ray)
- Ray 4 of Harmony through Conflict (the yellow ray)
- Ray 5 of Concrete Mind and Science (the orange ray)
- Ray 6 of Devotion and Idealism (the pale blue ray)
- Ray 7 of Ceremony, Order and Magic (the violet ray)

The rays form three groups

1. **Rays 1 and 7:** carry the will and power of God, give strength and will to our character.
2. **Rays 2, 4 and 6:** carry the love and wisdom of God, help us develop conscious wisdom.
3. **Rays 3 and 5:** carry the intelligence of God, they enhance our minds, our ability to think.

Chart 2: The Seven Rays and Astrology

The rays stream through space, through three constellations each and through one or two planets. The planets are the agents of the rays; each planet is a pure distillation of its ray's force. The chart shows how the rays connect to the body via the centres or chakras (wheels of force in the etheric body). This means that the signs and planets that carry each ray are also influential in the chakra and the organs the chakra rules. The drawing shows the rays that primarily govern each centre. But any ray can potentially flow through any chakra.

	Rays	Signs	Planets	Chakras
1	Will and Power	Aries, Leo, Capricorn	Pluto, Vulcan	Crown, Base
2	Love and Wisdom	Gemini, Virgo, Pisces	Sun, Jupiter	Heart
3	Intelligent Activity	Cancer, Libra, Capricorn	Saturn, Earth	Throat
4	Harmony through Conflict	Taurus, Scorpio, Sagittarius	Moon, Mercury	Ajna
5	Concrete Mind	Leo, Sagittarius, Aquarius	Venus	Ajna
6	Devotion and Idealism	Virgo, Sagittarius, Pisces	Mars, Neptune	Solar plexus
7	Ceremony, Order and Magic	Aries, Cancer, Capricorn	Uranus	Sacral

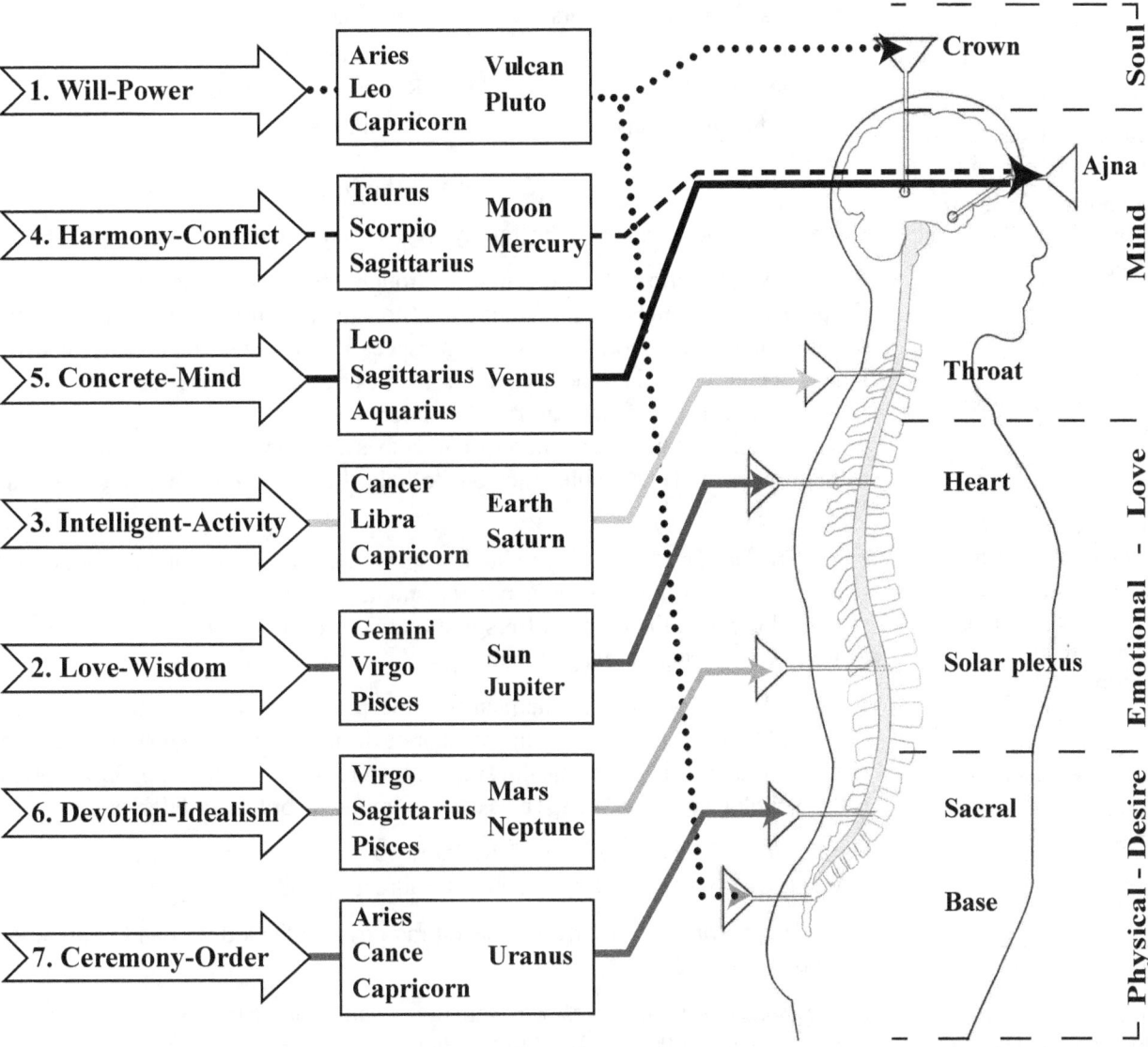

- **Chakra:**

  The Crown and the Base.

- **Planet agents:**

  Vulcan: higher spiritual will, the power to purify and build.

  Pluto: power to destroy - for the higher good or for selfish power and control.

  Saturn[1] and Uranus.

- **Sign agents:**

  Aries: power to lead and initiate for the greater good; or the arrogant use of power.

  Leo: power to rule for the greater good or arrogant displays of power. "I will because I can".

  Capricorn: executive power for the higher good or ruthless ambition.

  R1 virtues: strength, courage, steadfastness, truthfulness, fearlessness, power of ruling, capacity to grasp great questions in large-mindedness.

  Virtues to acquire: tenderness, humility, sympathy, tolerance, patience. [2]

---

1 Bailey, Alice A; Esoteric Astrology, 621.

2 Bailey, Alice A; Esoteric Psychology I, 201.

Ray 1 of Will and Power

"The will of God as it works through humanity"

The 1st Ray of Will and Power is the energy expression of the first aspect of God, the "spirit" aspect in the "Spirit-Soul-Body" trilogy. It is the most powerful force in the universe, ruling creation, life and death.

1. Ray 1 psychology

This ray as its number "1" suggests, initiates action, it urges us to be first and best, to pioneer change and go where no one has gone before. It invests us with the will to be, to do and to survive. 1st ray types (the ascendant or Sun conjunct Pluto, Uranus or Saturn or located in Aries, Leo or Capricorn) are leaders, managers and organisers on all levels. For instance, kings, union bosses or the family matriarch who rules domestic life with a steely will.

The function of ray 1 people is to rule, to organise, to administer the law, to control the masses and ensure people follow the rules.

When the 1st ray expresses imperfectly, we see hard people who use power ruthlessly. Here are some 1st ray traits that may lead to problems and disease.

Anger	Arrogance, pride
Desire to control others	Cruel, lacking pity
Destructive	Hard, insensitive
Obstinacy	Ruthlessly ambitious
Self-aggrandising	Wilfulness

2. Ray 1 in the Body

a. Crown and base chakras: the 1st ray works primarily through these centres.

b. Sutratma. The life of God reaches us through a thread of light called the sutratma. Other names by which it is known are the Monadic life stream, the silver cord or life-thread. The sutratma connects our spirit aspect with the soul, then the soul with the body - anchoring in the pineal gland, in the heart and in the base chakras. From the brain, it connects to the ajna and the alta major centres. Vital life energy flows through this thread into the heart, the bloodstream, the arteries and veins to vitalise every part of the organism. This enables the soul to hold the body coherently together during incarnation.

c. Respiration. The "breath" is related to spirit, the 1st aspect. The holy books tell us that God breathed life into man's nostrils and he became a living soul. The 1st aspect rules and controls the organs of respiration, working in conjunction with the throat chakra, whose organs manage breathing.

d. Sleep. The 1st ray governs the faculty of sleep. A good night's sleep is essential for good health - various body systems recuperate during sleep and if disturbances should occur for prolonged periods, health suffers. It increases the risk of high blood pressure and psychological disorders such as anxiety, mood disorders and depression.

e. The will to live and to survive. The 1st ray gives these vital instinctual traits to the physical body via the base chakra and the adrenal glands.

f. The kidneys and urinary tract. The 1st ray governs the kidneys and elimination of urine from the body.

g. The spinal column and skeleton. Both rays 1 and 7 govern the hard, mineral structure of the body and both are related to the skeleton.

3. Ray 1 in Disease

- Diseases that affect the brain (crown chakra), the adrenals and urinary tract (base chakra).
- Diseases that are relentless and unstoppable, that move inexorably towards death.
- Diseases that crystallise, harden, restrict, reduce, atrophy and age.

When ray 1 runs amok in our psychology, people use their personal power and influence to destroy people, relationships, groups and organisations when they cannot get their way. They launch a bullying and unrelenting onslaught to wear down all resistance. The same pattern occurs in ray 1 diseases, which wear down and destroy their hosts. They overpower all resistance through a relentless onslaught and pressure until death eventuates. This may be rapid or extend over many years.

Although cancer is primarily a ray 2, over-energising disease, ray 1 causes it when the will is used to suppress emotional or sexual expression causing congestion. For ray 1 diseases, look for afflictions to planets that carry ray 1 - Pluto, Saturn, Uranus, or to planets in Aries, Leo and Capricorn.

▲ **Psychology**
Egomania
Megalomania

▲ **Body**
Chemotherapy
Minerals

Crown
Cerebral cortex
Circadian rhythm
Death
Head
Melatonin
Neocortex
Pineal gland
Serotonin
Sleep

Throat
Breathing
Respiration

Heart
Life-thread/ stream, sutratma, silver cord

Base
Adrenal-cortex
Adrenaline
Adrenal-medulla
Aldosterone
Bladder
Catalysts, body
Cortisol
Enzymes
Fight or flight
Kidneys
Old age
Rigor mortis

Spinal column, spine
Survival instinct
Urea
Ureters
Urethra
Uric acid
Urinary tract
Urine
Vertebrae, all
Will to live, to exist

▲ **Disease**
Amputation
Lead poisoning
Mineral poisoning
Radiation poisoning

Crown
Alzheimer's
Arrested development
Ataxia
Blood pressure high, pineal
Brain cells overactive: cancer, tumour, abscess
Brain haemorrhage, inflammation
Cerebral-spinal meningitis
Coma
Concussion: head injuries

Convulsions
Dementia
Encephalitis
Head injuries
Huntington's disease
Hydrocephalus
Hypertension, pineal cause
Insanity, idiocy
Insomnia
Lewy body dementia
Lunacy
Meningitis
Multiple personalities
Possession
Senile decay
SIDS: sudden death infant syndrome
Sleep disturbance
Stroke

Ajna
Achondroplasia (dwarfism)
ALS: amyotrophic lateral sclerosis
Blindness
Cataracts
Deafness
Dwarfism
Glaucoma
Growth stunted
Guillain-Barre syndrome

Lou Gehrig's disease
Motor neurone disease
Multiple sclerosis
Myopia
Palsy
Paralysis
Paraplegic, quadriplegic
Parkinson's disease
Polio
Short sighted
Simmond's disease

Throat
Asphyxia
Drowns, drowning
Grave's disease
Hashimoto's disease
Hodgkin's disease
Lymphoma
Strangulation
Suffocation

Heart
AIDS
Autoimmune diseases
Ebola virus
Heart attack
Immune attack
Lupus
Myasthenia

gravis
Shock

Solar plexus
Cirrhosis, liver
Gallstones

Sacral
Karmic diseases

Base
Aches, intense
Addison's disease
Ageing unnaturally
Alopecia
Ankylosis spondylosis
Arthritis
Attrition
Back pain
Bone fractures: shoulders, arms, hands; hips, thighs
Bone: deformities, crippling
Bright's disease
Bursitis
Calcification
Cervical osteoarthritis
Chronic diseases
Constrictions
Crippled
Cushing's syndrome
Cystitis
Deformity

Fatigue: adrenal overload
Fractures, bones
Geriatric
Hardening, stiffening
Hyper-uricaemia
Joints stiff
Kidney infection
Kidney stones
Knee problems
Limping
Lumbago
Murder
Nephritis
Osteoarthritis
Osteoporosis
Paget's disease
Progeria
Rheumatic fever
Rheumatism
Rheumatoid arthritis
Sciatica
Scleroderma
Sclerosis
Scoliosis
Skull: injuries
Spina bifida
Spinal fractures
Stiffness
Stones
Toothache
Underactive, undeveloped organ
Urinary tract infections

Ray 2 of Love and Wisdom
"Christ-sensitivity as it works through man"

- **Chakra:**

The Heart and the Ajna.[1]

- **Planet agents:**

Jupiter: it is the main distributor of ray 2. It fuses and expands, manifests as brotherly love or exaggeration and wastefulness.

The Sun: it represents self-consciousness, the personality, which can radiate solar warmth and inclusiveness or egotistical selfishness.

- **Sign agents:**

Ray 2 flowing through the signs manifests as:

Gemini: a wise and loving messenger or an indiscriminate chatterer.

Virgo: the wise server or an indiscriminate criticizer.

Pisces: a wise and loving healer/ teacher or emotional naivety.

R2 virtues: calm, strength, patience, love of truth, faithfulness, clear intelligence, serenity.
   Virtues to acquire: love, compassion, unselfishness, energy.[2]

1. Ray 2 Psychology

The 2nd ray represents the "soul" aspect in the "Spirit-Soul-Body" trilogy, which means it deals with feelings and consciousness. Its job is to help us become sensitive, caring people - like our souls and like Christ.

The 2nd ray is the ray of consciousness, of sentiency. Under its influence, our senses are developed and refined, enabling us to become aware of ourselves as an "I", who we are as a human being and how we relate with others. "2" is the number of "relationships".

Through the cauldron of earthly experience, strife and striving, from our darkest and most shameful failures to our most amazing and self-sacrificing successes; Ray 2 helps us develop understanding and compassion for ourselves and for others. It is the ray of spiritual workers, teachers, healers and scholars.

There are two ray 2 types. "Love types" are more sensitive, feeling people. If they are advanced spiritually, they are anchored in the heart. If they are still working through their emotions, they are anchored in the solar plexus chakra - such people can be emotionally naive, fearful and impressionable, with no clear sense where personal boundaries begin and end. "Wisdom" types work through the ajna and negatively, they can be mentally cool. Below are some negative traits that may lead to 2nd ray type diseases.

Love, heart or solar plexus chakra types

Amoral (overactive thymus)	Excessive
Gluttonous, greedy	Impressionable
Love of comfort	Materialistic (excessive)
Wastefulness	

Wisdom, mind types

Coldness, indifference	Contempt of mental limitations in others
Over-absorbed in study	Self-love, extreme

2. Ray 2 in the Body

a. The heart chakra and thymus gland. Ray 2 governs this centre and gland - primarily the love aspect of the ray. The wisdom aspect of ray 2, of consciousness, is connected with the ajna, the centre of personality awareness.

b. The cardiovascular system, the heart. The 2nd ray flows through the Sun and the heart chakra, and the cardiovascular system is its physical plane means of distribution. All the organs governed by the heart chakra - such as the heart, the thymus, the blood and cell life are governed by this ray.

c. Vitalising of the body, prana and the immune system. Prana is the vitalising energy of the cosmos that gives life to all living creatures. Prana that vitalises our bodies flows from the Sun. We receive solar prana from golden devas (intelligent angels of nature). Entering the body via the spleen, prana rises to the heart and merges with the life stream as it enters the blood; contributing to the overall vitalising of the body.

A balanced and unhindered flow of prana via the etheric web into the body is the basis of good physical health. If vitalisation does not reach a particular part of the body because there is damage to the etheric, congestion in a chakra or a diseased or destroyed gland; then that part of the body becomes diseased.

---

1 Bailey, Alice A; Esoteric Healing, 210.
2 Bailey, Alice A; Esoteric Psychology I, 202.

d. The nervous system. The 2nd ray is the force that develops consciousness - of ourselves, of others and of the world around us. Its primary means of distribution in the body is the nervous system and sense organs. Ray 2 flows through Gemini, which is related to the ajna via ruler Mercury.

e. Sight and eyes. The Sun is the primary ruler of sight - the physical eye came into being in response to the light of the sun.[1] Sunlight is governed by the 2nd ray and so is sight.

f. Growth. The 2nd ray is the force behind our growth and development, physically and consciously. The Sun and Jupiter that carry this ray represent growth in the body.

3. Ray 2 in Disease

- Diseases that affect the cardiovascular system.
- Diseases of the eyes or ears
- Diseases caused through excessive cell building.

In our psychology when 2nd ray force goes awry, it demonstrates as excess on one level or another. In our psychology, it plays out as over-the-top emotional displays and uncontrolled consumption. This is the model also for 2nd ray diseases - excessive growth and expression. Ray 2's task in the body is to gather atoms together, causing them to cohere and vibrate in unison so that a form or physical body is produced. But when it malfunctions, excess energy pours into the body, more than it is able to handle. The result is an overstimulation of atoms causing multiplication, inappropriate growths such as tumours, cancer and extra body parts.

For ray 2 diseases, look for afflictions to ray 2 planets Jupiter and the Sun, or to planets in Gemini, Virgo or Pisces.

▲ **Psychology**

No emotional boundaries

▲ **Body**

Crown
Antahkarana

Ajna
Brow
Central nervous system
Cognition
Consciousness thread
Cornea
Ears
Eye lens
Eyes
Face
Hearing
Hypothalamus
Intelligent self-consciousness
Iris
Motor nerves
Nerve fluid
Nerve synapse
Neurons
Nose
Pituitary gland
Pupils
Retina
Sciatic nerve
Sclera
Self-consciousness
Sentiency
Sight
Spinal cord
Spinal fluid
Synapse
Vision

Throat
Ears
Hearing

Heart
Aorta
Arteries
Blood
Blood circulation, quality
Bloodstream
Capillaries
Cardiovascular system
Cell life
Constitution
Haemoglobin
Heart
Immune system
Iron in the blood
Leukocytes
Life-force, soul energy
Oxygen, oxygenation
Pericardium
Plasma
Prana
Pulmonary circulation
Recuperative power
Red blood cells
Spleen
Stem cells
Thymus
Vagus nerve
Valves - heart
Veins
Vena Cava
Venous system
Vitality (solar fire)
Vitamin A
White blood cells

Solar plexus
Enteric NS
Motor nerves
Sympathetic NS

Base
Body fat

▲ **Disease**

Ajna
Acromegaly
Conjunctivitis
Gigantism
Hypo-pituitarism
Keratitis

Throat
Carpal tunnel syndrome
Goitre

Heart
Allergic reaction from immune
Aneurism
Blood cancer
Blood circulation problems
Bruises
Cardio-myopathy
Fainting
Fever
High blood pressure
High temperature
Hypertension
Hypotension
Inflammation
Sunburn
Sunstroke

Solar plexus
Cancer: all body organs
Carcinoma
Cellulite, fatness
Cholesterol
Colitis
Cysts
Diseases caused by excess
Fatness, obesity
Flabbiness
Gluttony
Growths, abnormal
Hypertrophy
Metastases
Obesity
Overgrowth
Polyps
Sarcoma
Swellings
Tumours, growths
Weight gain

Base
Extra body parts
Melanoma

---
1 Bailey, Alice A; Treatise on White Magic, 213.

Ray 3 of Intelligent Activity
"The ray of intelligent versatility and adaptability"

- **Chakra:**

The Throat; also the Sacral and Base.

- **Planet agents:**

Saturn: the responsible use of power or selfish manipulation.

The Earth: global experience that develops group skills, the ability to work cooperatively and intelligently with others.

Mercury [1] and the Moon

- **Sign agents:**

Cancer: intelligent nurturing or crafty dishonesty.

Libra: intelligent balance in relationships or superficiality.

Capricorn: intelligent action or devious ambition.

R3 virtues: wide views on abstract questions, sincerity of purpose, clear intellect,.

Vices: intellectual pride, coldness, isolation, inaccuracy in details, dishonesty.

Virtues to acquire: sympathy, tolerance, devotion, accuracy, energy, common-sense. [2]

---

[1] Bailey, Alice A; Esoteric Astrology, 280.

[2] Bailey, Alice, A: Esoteric Psychology I, 204.

1. Ray 3 Psychology

The 3rd Ray of Intelligent Activity is the "body" aspect in the "Spirit-Soul-Body" trilogy. While ray 1 governs breathing and life and ray 2 governs consciousness and vitalisation; ray 3 generally governs digestion, reproduction and the body structure.

Ray 3 is the ray that is most closely associated with matter and form.

Ray 3 also represents the mind of God that gives all living forms "intelligence" whether this is the brilliance of an Einstein or the ability of an amoeba to survive and reproduce. Ray 3 rules creative intelligence and its highest expression is education, or progressive development through experience. Ray 3 people (the ascendant or Sun conjunct Saturn or located in Cancer, Libra or Capricorn), are very intelligent in the ways of the material world. They use their wits to survive economically and are effective in business and finance.

When ray 3 intelligence is misused, people become predators. They use their wits in devious ways to prey on people, to manipulate, to steal and take what they have. White collar crimes, cyber-crimes, fraud and theft come under its banner.

2. Ray 3 in the Body

a. Chakras and thyroid. Ray 3 works primarily through the throat chakra and the base. It also works through the sacral chakra for reproduction.

b. The physical body and body intelligence. Ray 3 governs the dense physical body and tissue - primarily through Cancer and Capricorn. This versatile force of Mother Nature, underlies the intelligent design of the body, giving it its instinctual ability to stay alive, reproduce and raise its young.

c. Endocrine system. Ray 3 governs the intelligence of the endocrine system as it balances and regulates our health through hormonal release.

d. Breathing apparatus. The throat chakra, therefore ray 3, governs the respiratory organs. The 1st ray manifests through these organs - it is the breath.

e. Digestion and the gastrointestinal (GI) tract. Ray 3 governs digestion and the GI tract is governed by the throat chakra, ruled by ray 3.

f. The lymphatic system. This is governed by the throat chakra, ruled by ray 3.

g. Reproduction. The 3rd aspect governs sex and reproduction generally.

h. Kundalini: this fire of matter is housed in the base chakra. It animates the atoms of the physical body and keeps the body warm. The base and crown are partners. When spirit emerges via the crown at a very advanced stage, kundalini cycles up the spine to unify with the fire of spirit in the higher centre.

3. Ray 3 in Disease

- Diseases that affect breathing and speech organs.
- Digestion, stomach and intestinal disorders; also reproduction difficulties.
- Sexually transmitted diseases.

Ray 3 is a highly active and versatile ray. When misused it manifests as manipulative and deceitful behaviours, manipulations that rebound upon digestion, causing intestinal and gastric disorders via the solar plexus. Cancer, the sign most associated with digestive trouble carries ray 3. This misused force can affect the throat, speech and breathing via the throat chakra and cause psychological trouble and fatigue via the thyroid.

2. Forces and Energies: a. The 7 Rays ▲ 19

When ray 3 manipulations play through the sacral chakra as sexual misconduct, sexually transmitted diseases such as syphilis arise. For ray 3 diseases, look for afflictions to Saturn or to planets in Cancer, Libra or Capricorn.

▲ Psychology
ADD: attention deficit disorder
ADHD: > hyperactivity disorder

▲ Body

Crown
Brain mass, tissue

Throat chakra
Adam's apple
Adenoids
Airways
Alimentary canal
Alta-major
Alveoli
Appetite
Brainstem
Bronchial tree
Carotid gland, arteries
Cerebellum
Diaphragm
Digestion
Endocrine system
Gastrointestinal tract
Glottis
Jugular vein
Larynx
Lips
Lungs
Lymph, nodes
Lymphatic system
Medulla oblongata
Metabolism
Mouth
Mucus
Neck
Palate
Parathyroids
Parotid glands
Peristalsis
Pharynx
Pons
Reptilian brain
Salivary glands
Sinuses
Speech
Submandibular glands
Taste
Thalamus
Thoracic duct
Throat
Thyroid
Thyroxine
Tongue
Tonsils
Trachea
Tubes, body
Uvula
Vocal cords
Windpipe

Solar plexus
Abdomen
Anus
Appendix
Bile
Bowel
Carbohydrates
Chyle
Colon
Defecation
Digestion
Duodenum
Excretion
Faeces
Gallbladder
Glucose, sugar
Ileum
Insulin
Intestines
Islets of Langerhans
Jejunum
Liver
Nutrition
Oesophagus lower
Pancreas
Pylorus
Rectum
Stomach
Sugar, glucose

Sacral chakra
Babies
Birth
Breasts
Cervix
Clitoris
Conception
Egg ovum
Embryo
Estrogen
Fallopian tubes
Fertility
Genitals
Gestation
Infancy
Lacteals,
Locomotion
Maternity
Menstruation
Mothers
Movement
Ovaries
Penis
Periods
Physical power
Placenta
Pregnancy
Procreation
Progesterone
Prostate gland
Reproduction
Semen
Sex hormones, organs
Sexual power
Sigmoid flexure
Sperm
Testes
Testosterone
Uterus
Vagina
Vans deferens
Womb

Base
Biceps
Birthmark
Body containers, sheaths
Body intelligence
Body warmth
Bone marrow
Buttocks
Calves
Cartilage,
Chin
Corpses
Dead things
Feet
Flesh
Gums
Hair
Hamstrings
Hands
Integumentary system
Joints
Knees
Kundalini
Ligaments
Membranes
Moles, skin
Nails
Peritoneum
Physical body
Pleurae
Protein
Secretions
Skin
Substance
Tears
Tendons
Thighs
Tissue, flesh
Toes
Wrist

▲ Disease

Throat
Allergies, breathing
Aphasia
Asthma
Bad breath
Bronchitis
Buboes, plague
Chicken pox
Cholera
Croup
Cystic fibrosis
Dengue fever
Diphtheria
Dyslexia
Emphysema
Epstein–Barr virus
Fatigue - thyroid
Glandular fever, swellings
Halitosis
Hormonal trouble
Hyperactivity
Laryngitis
Learning difficulties
Measles
Mononucleosis
Mucus
Mumps
Nasal congestion
Phlegm
Pleurisy
Pneumonia
Pulmonary tuberculosis
Rubella
Scarlet fever
Sinusitis
Sleep apnoea
Smallpox
Snoring
Stuttering
Tonsillitis
Weight gain or loss, thyroid

Solar plexus
Acid reflux
Acidosis
Allergies, digestive
Anal fissure
Biliousness
Bulimia
Coeliac disease
Dyspepsia
Eating disorders
Flatulence
Food allergies
Gastric disorders
Heartburn
Indigestion
Malnutrition
Nausea
Parasites, intestinal
Peptic ulcer
Reflux
Starvation
Tapeworm
Ulcers, gastric
Vomiting
Worms

Sacral
Barrenness
Chlamydia
Endometriosis
Fibroids womb
Genital disorders, warts
Gonorrhea
Herpes, genital
Infertility
Locomotive disorders
Miscarriage
Prostate trouble
Pubic, crabs
Social diseases
STD: sexually transmitted diseases
Sterility
Syphilis
Uterine troubles
Venereal dis.

Base
Baldness
Bunions
Cramps
Decay
Dysplasia of the hip
Feet problems
Fistula
Hereditary diseases
Hernia
Lesions
Prolapses
Scurvy
Warts
Wrinkles

Ray 4 of Harmony through Conflict
"The ray of music, dance and drama"

- **Chakra:**

The Ajna and Throat via Mercury.
The Solar Plexus via the Moon.
The Base via the Moon, the ruler of form.

- **Planet agents:**

Moon: balanced emotional expression or a conflicted astral life ruled by the "prison of the soul" pattern.
Mercury: mental harmony and balance or a conflicted, agonising mind.

- **Sign agents:**

Taurus: aspiration or conflict and unregulated desire.
Scorpio: the internally centred warrior or inner war and conflict.
Sagittarius: the balanced archer or dominated by the lower appetites.

R4 virtues: strong affections, sympathy, physical courage, generosity, devotion, quickness of intellect and perception.
Virtues to acquire: serenity, confidence, self-control, purity, unselfishness, accuracy, mental and moral balance.[1]

---
[1] Bailey, Alice, A: Esoteric Psychology I, 206.

1. Ray 4 Psychology

The 4th Ray of Harmony through Conflict is aligned with the 2nd Ray of Love and Wisdom, which means it deals with feelings and consciousness.

Ray 4 affects the mind and mental bodies on this ray are "right-brain", "feeling" minds - intuitive, artistic, picture making and colourful. Many artists and entertainers are on this ray. Affected intensely by discord they share what they feel through art, literature or music. Right-brain people have their brain cells coloured by Mercury since it carries the 4th ray.

Most people on the planet probably have a 4th ray mind, which means that as a whole we are colourful and expressive people. Ray 4 is the bridging ray. It makes connections between people who cannot reconcile their differences. This first connection leads to war and conflict, but later to harmony as a reconciliation to achieve peace unfolds.

Ray 4 oscillates, it moves back and forth, shuttling between opposites. When it does this vertically in our psychology, between the mind and an unstable emotional body, it leads to mood swings. Such people reach the highs of exhilaration only to suddenly drop into the lows of depression. People who are susceptible have the Sun or ascendant in Taurus or Scorpio or a heavily afflicted Moon or Mercury. Here are some 4th ray negatives that may result in psychological problems or disease.

Continuous agonising	Emotional instability
Extravagance	Indolence
Inner conflict, agitation	Lack of moral courage
Mood swings	Worrying, inner suffering

2. Ray 4 in the Body

Ray 4 affects mental development via Mercury and the ajna, and our moods via the Moon and the solar plexus chakra.

3. Ray 4 in Disease

- Mental and nervous disorders based on mood swings.
- Ray 4 debilitation as a consequence of conflict.
- Chronic pain and suffering

Fear, worry and continual conflict generated by ray 4 burns up energy, leading to debility, to a lowering of the vitality of the immune system and consequently, opening the body up to all manner of infections and contagious diseases. It also leads to pain and suffering, psychological and physical. For ray 4 problems, look for afflictions to the Moon, Mercury or to planets in Taurus, Scorpio or Sagittarius.

▲ Psychology		▲ Disease	*Throat*	Fatigue
Anti-social, dangerous brooders	depression	Contagious infections	Colds	Immunity low
	Mentally unstable		Influenza	Tissue, insidious changes
	Mood swings	Epidemics	Postpartum blues	
Anxiety	Trauma, psychological	Pain and suffering		
Bipolar			*Solar plexus*	
Depression		*Ajna*	Chronic fatigue	
Inner conflict		Neuralgia	Debilitation	
Manic		Shingles	Devitalisation	

Ray 5 of Concrete Mind
"The Ray of Scientific Mind"

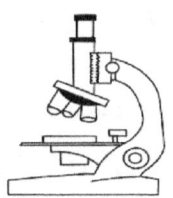

1. Ray 5 Psychology

The 5th ray is allied with Ray 3 of Intelligent Activity. It is the force of the lower concrete mind that is vital to our evolutionary development. This is because lower mind acquires knowledge about the world, helps us learn from our mistakes, thus teaching us discrimination. This intellectual movement towards improvement leads us from our own selfish truths and limited beliefs into wider and more inclusive understandings and eventually into the Mind of God.

Ray 5 minds are "left-brain". They are logical and pragmatic, preferring a fact based and scientific approach to life. Consequently, scientists, researchers and technicians often have their mental bodies on this ray. Left-brain people have their brain cells coloured by Venus since it carries the 5th ray.

People are more likely to be "left-brain" if the Sun, Mercury, Venus or ascendant are in Aquarius. If the 5th ray is too strong, we see "mind" people who are out of touch with their emotions. Ultra-rational, their view of life is narrow. Lacking compassion or empathy, rigid in thought and belief, they are separative and judgemental. Ray 5 people tend to suffer from mental disorders that involve illusion or a cleavage.

A cleavage occurs when we are torn in two directions - one part of us wants something, another part of us wants something else.

A cleavage can occur within our emotional nature with competing desires, between the mind wanting something and the lower bodies yearning for something else, between the soul and the personality or between a person and the environment. When it occurs within the personality, causing one part of the nature to be out of touch with another, serious mental health issues can arise. Here are ray 5 negatives.

Anti-social	Austere and cruel
Critical and judgemental	Dogmatic, a fixed, inflexible mind
Mental, clinical coldness	Misinterprets ideas
Sectarianism	Separativeness

2. Ray 5 in the Body

Ray 5 influences primarily our mental life and the intellectual ajna centre.

3. Ray 5 in Disease

- Mental disorders and migraine.

The separative action of the 5th ray lies behind many of our psychological troubles. It creates an energy gap or dissonance between the soul and personality, between the crown chakra and the ajna and between the pineal and pituitary glands. Migraine is a consequence. Mental inflexibility and a desire to force one's ideas on others can play out through the body as certain cancers, metabolic problems and hardening of tissue and joints. For ray 5 problems, look for afflictions to Venus or to planets in Leo, Sagittarius or Aquarius.

▲ Psychology			▲ Disease	
Asperger's	troubles	Drugs, medical	_Crown_	_Throat_
Autism	▲ Body	Medicine, modern,	Brain lesions	Metabolic disorder caused by emotionalism
Egomania	Chemical medicines, drugs	alternative and traditional	_Ajna_	
Insanities		Surgery	Headaches	
Megalomania	Chemotherapy		Migraine	
Psychological				

• **Chakras:**
The Ajna.

• **Planet agents:**
Venus: either the intelligent expression of love or a cold fact-finding mind.

• **Sign agents:**
Leo: an astute, intelligent leader or use of mental power to control people.

Sagittarius: an astute, intelligent director of men or an "I'm always right" expert

Aquarius: an astute and intelligent social reformer or the aloof and separative "expert".

Scientists and people who are purely mental and governed only by the [R5] mind.[1]

Ray 5 virtues: strictly accurate statements, justice (without mercy), perseverance, common-sense, independence, keen intellect.
  Virtues to acquire: reverence, devotion, sympathy, love, wide-mindedness.[2]

---

[1] Bailey, Alice, A: Discipleship in the New Age vol.1, xiii.
[2] Bailey, Alice, A: Esoteric Psychology I, 207.

- **Chakra:**
The Solar Plexus

- **Planet agents:**

Mars: the ardent devotee who fights for the higher good or the fanatical crusader who kills for his ideals.

Neptune: devotion to higher ideals or blinded by personal devotion and fantasy.

- **Sign agents:**

Virgo: the idealistic teacher devoted to healing and teaching, or devotion to the material world.

Sagittarius: the idealistic devotee, directing men and women to their higher good, or devotion to a hedonistic lifestyle.

Pisces: an idealistic and devoted server or a delusionary mystic, blinded by fanaticism.

R6 virtues: devotion, single-mindedness, love, tenderness, intuition, loyalty, reverence.

Virtues to acquire: strength, self-sacrifice, purity, truth, tolerance, serenity, balance and common sense.[1]

---

1 Bailey, Alice, A: Esoteric Psychology I, 208.

Ray 6 of Devotion and Idealism
"The force of human emotion"

The 6th Ray of Devotion and Idealism is closely aligned with the 2nd Ray of Love and Wisdom, which means it deals with emotions and consciousness. This is currently the most feeling-conscious force in humanity.

1. Ray 6 Psychology

The 6th ray governs our emotions and is the primary influencer of the astral/ emotional/ desire body. It gives expression to emotions ranging from love and compassion to fear and hate.

In advanced spiritual man the astral body anchors in the heart centre, giving expression to higher feelings of spiritual love, inclusiveness and compassion. At its highest, ray 6 is the force of spiritual idealism, aspiration and devotional service to the whole. Spiritual servers, healers and carers are on this ray.

In the average person, the astral body anchors in the solar plexus centre, controlling the physical body, driving it to satisfy its desire. Most people focus at this level, which means they are controlled by one desire or another. 6th ray force, emotion-desire, is the most powerful force driving humanity. It keeps us swinging between the opposites of pain and pleasure. Desire is the sensuous grasping after objects that give us pleasure. In man, desire can range from the grossest desires imaginable, to the natural desire for food, sex and companionship; up to an aspiration for spiritual union. Human love and desire without the inclusive influence of ray 2, is Mars-ruled, conditional, exclusive, intolerant and in extreme cases can be cruel and murderous. In the normal course of evolution, objects of desire change until ultimately the only desire remaining is a yearning to unite with the wholeness of Deity.

> **"Glamour" is a word used to describe how ray 6 distorts perception. Glamoured people refuse to see reality. They embellish situations with their hopes and wishes. Looking at life through rose coloured glasses, is a ray 6 phenomenon. Glamoured people live in delusion. They believe that the unreal is real, because they want to.**

The astral nature is ruled by Mars and the Moon in average man and by Neptune in the more advanced. Most people have a ray 6 emotional body, which means that Mars and Neptune rule the astral natures of most people on earth. Ray 6 influence increases in people who have the ascendant, Moon or Sun in Virgo, Sagittarius, Pisces, or conjunct Mars or Neptune. Here are some negative 6th ray traits that may lead to problems.

Addictive tendencies	Cruelty, fiery anger
Emotionalism, feelings of guilt	Fanaticism, sectarianism
Impressionable, lack of discernment	Jealousy, envy
One-eyed, blinkered perception	Over-leaning on others
Self-deception, glamour superstition	Selfish and jealous love
	Victim consciousness, martyr complex
Vindictive, revengeful	Warped, narrow ideals

2. Ray 6 in the Body

a. The solar plexus chakra and pancreas: the solar plexus is the entry point for ray 6 from the Astral Plane and from our astral nature.

b. Body fluids and waterways. Directly or indirectly, the three water signs are related to the astral, water-plane and therefore to the 6th ray that governs it. Neptune that carries ray 6 is the higher ruler of Cancer and it rules Pisces; and Mars, the other carrier of ray 6, co-rules Scorpio.

The water signs are related to body fluids. Cancer rules white, colourless or very pale fluids and with Neptune and Pisces the lymphatic system, the watery drainage system of the body. Neptune also rules the bloodstream. Scorpio governs thicker body fluids such as the blood via Mars, menstruation flow and semen.

3. Ray 6 in Disease

- Nervous and breathing disorders that arise from emotional trouble.
- Diseases that pervert cell life - such as viruses and carcinogenicity.
- Diseases and troubles in the digestive tract, due to a troubled solar plexus chakra

The 6th ray lies behind most disorders and diseases today because it is the force of the Astral Plane. The astral body is an outstanding cause of ill health because it has a potent a effect upon the etheric body. Most diseases arise from a disturbed emotional body as it affects the etheric.[1] Additionally, the basis of all nervous trouble lies hidden in the emotional body,[2] is caused by 6th ray emotionalism. Ray 6 is the force of desire and is connected with the misuse of sex and violent acts that some people do to satisfy desire - such as rape, paedophilia and sexual sadism.

Viruses and cancer. Not only does the glamorous light thrown by ray 6 fool people, it fools the body. Neptune that carries ray 6 is the primary symbol of viruses, which manage to invade the body by masking their activities before the immune system sees them and reacts. Ray 6 can also be connected with the development of cancer. This is because its force perverts, relating it to carcinogenicity, the ability or tendency to alter the genetic structure of healthy cells so they become cancerous.

Since most diseases today arise from a troubled emotional body, many health-triangles (minimum of three planets in a chart that symbolise a disease), will contain a ruler of the solar plexus chakra (Mars, Neptune or the Moon), or afflictions to a planet in Cancer, Scorpio or Pisces.

▲ **Psychology**
Alcoholism
Anti-social, dangerous brooders
Anxiety, worry
Astral maniac
Borderline personality disorder
Cuts, cutting
Delirium, delusory
Depression
Dreams, troubled
Gambling addiction
Glamour
Hallucination
Hypochondria
Hysteria
Incest
Masochism
Neurotics, neuroses
Obscure diseases due to

emotionalism
Obsessive compulsive
Paedophilia
Panic attacks
Paranoia
Phobias
Predatory behaviour
PTSD
Schizophrenia
Self-harm, self-injury
Serial killer
Sexual: rape, perversions, murder, sadism
Sleep-walking
Substance abuse

▲ **Body**
Anaesthetics

▲ **Disease**
Hidden, obscure disorders
Misdiagnosis
Plant poisons,

drugs
Poisonous gas

Heart
Blood poisoned
Viruses

Solar plexus
Acid reflux
Acidosis
Allergies, digestive
Anorexia
Appendicitis
Biliousness
Bulimia
Candida
Carcinogenic
Coeliac disease
Colic
Constipation
Crohn's disease
Diabetes
Diarrhoea
Diverticulitis
Drug addiction
Dysentery
Dyspepsia

Eating disorders
Flatulence
Food allergies
Gastric disorders
Haemorrhoids
Hallucinatory, recreational drugs
Heartburn
Hepatitis
Hyper-glycemia, Hypo-glycaemia
Indigestion
Irritable bowel syndrome
Jaundice
Narcolepsy
Nausea
Nightmares
Oedema
Pancreatitis
Peptic ulcer
Piles
Pus
Reflux
Septicaemia
Sluggish action

of organs
Ulcers, gastric
Vomiting
Water retention
Weight gain
Wind
Yeast infection

Sacral
Chlamydia
Genital disorders, warts
Gonorrhea
Herpes, genital
Pubic, crabs
Social diseases
STD: sexually transmitted diseases
Syphilis
Venereal disease

Base
Abscesses
Acne
Athlete's foot
Boils
Dermatitis

Eczema
Fungus, fungi
Gout
Impetigo
Leprosy
Pimples
Rashes
Ringworm
Scabies
Skin eruptions
Sores, weeping
Thrush
Tinea

---
1 Bailey, Alice A; Esoteric Healing, 3.
2 Bailey, Alice A; Esoteric Healing, 107.

Ray 7 of Ceremony, Order and Magic

Ray 7 is the lower extension of ray 1 - it carries power. Its higher function is to unite spirit and matter and part of this task is to bring our bodies into alignment with the soul. This forces them to evolve so they become more sophisticated and useful vehicles for the soul's expanding powers and service work on earth.

1. Ray 7 Psychology

Ray 7 is the "manifesting" ray and all ray 7 people have the power to get things done and to bring their projects to fruition.

When the "order" aspect of this ray dominates (Sun or ascendant in Aries, Cancer or Capricorn), people have determined wills and managerial, organising and leadership skills. They use the will to control life. Ray 7's can be:

Bigotry and pride	Controlling
Judges by appearances	Over-concerned with rules
Over-indulged	Perfectionists
Regimented, rigid, inflexible	Self-opinionated

A different ray 7 type expresses the "ceremony and magic" aspect. They are Uranian, freedom-loving (Uranus conjunct the ascendant or Sun). They shatter the past and bend rules and laws to create the world to their design. Ritualists are on this ray and the Magician card in the Tarot deck is an excellent symbol. Negative types on this ray can be:

- Black magicians who pervert and do evil
- Creators of chaos
- Destructively wild and violent

2. Ray 7 in the Body

a. Chakras: ray 7 is related to the sacral, throat and base chakras.

b. The etheric body. It is ruled by ray 7 via the sacral chakra.

c. Sex and reproduction. Ray 7 brings together negative and positive poles. It governs sex, the marriage relationship and associated problems such as sexual license, immorality, marriage problems and divorce. Together, ray 7 and the sacral govern reproduction, "the building of forms of expression".[1] The 3rd aspect is the overall ruler of sex and reproduction at the animal level.

d. DNA (deoxyribonucleic acid). The energy pattern of the physical body is recorded in the "physical permanent atom", a memory cell or atom located on the 1st etheric subplane of the Physical Plane. The 7th ray governs the ethers. Our patterns are replicated in our DNA, which is the carrier of genetic information inherited from our forefathers.

e. Blood and blood circulation. Although the Sun and Leo govern the heart and are the overall rulers of the cardiovascular system, Aquarius, Uranus, and the 7th ray govern the blood system and its circulation.

f. The ray 7 body type. Rays 3 and 7 govern our physical bodies. Ray 3 bodies are muscular and well-built. Ray 7 bodies are more delicate, smaller-boned and graceful. They like routine and though graceful, can be tough - the bodies of trained dancers such as ballerinas are usually on this ray. Graceful, dancing hands and the ability to move gracefully are ray 7 qualities.

- **Chakra:**
The Sacral; also the Throat and the Base.

- **Planet agents:**
Uranus: the white magician, manifesting for the greater good or the evil black magician.

The Moon: the builder of "forms" and relationships that are harmonious and nurturing, or that create conflict and cause trouble.

- **Sign agents:**
Aries: the highly organised pioneer or the regimented fanatic.

Cancer: the highly organised nurturer and provider or the family dictator.

Capricorn: power and professional success used for the higher good, or for selfish profit and gain.

Ray 7 virtues: strength, courage, perseverance, courtesy, extreme care in details, self-reliance.

Virtues to acquire: realisation of unity, wide-mindedness, tolerance, humility, gentleness and love.[1]

---

1 Bailey, Alice, A: Esoteric Psychology I, 210.

1 Bailey, Alice A; Esoteric Psychology I, 261

3. Ray 7 in Disease

- Bacterial and contagious diseases and infections.
- Sexual and reproductive disorders, genetic and congenital diseases.
- Diseases of blood circulation; also arrhythmia, fibrillation and spasms.

When ray 7 is misused, "order" types repress force, while "ceremony and magic" types pervert force, turn it to wrong use. In both types, the rhythm of life is upset and this is mirrored in disease. The 7th ray brings together spirit and matter at a cellular level. But when this process goes awry and cells do not conform to the healthy design of nature it results in cellular promiscuity, genetic mutations and aberrations. This ray is responsible for the breeding of virulent germs and bacteria that cause infectious and contagious diseases. It can cause bizarre effects in the body such as wild and uncontrolled growth or the stunting of growth. It is susceptible to the problems and diseases of the bloodstream [1] and heart disease [2]. The task of ray 7 is to establish beauty, balance and rhythm [3] but when this fails there is arrhythmia, seizures and spasms. Uranus, Aries, Cancer and Capricorn carry ray 7.

▲ **Psychology**
Perversions
Promiscuity

▲ **Body**
Chemotherapy
Minerals

Ajna
Balance, equilibrium via pituitary
Homeostasis
Regulation, balance

Heart
Blood circulation, quality
Cardiovascular system

Sacral
Birth
Breasts
Cervix
Chromosome
Clitoris
Conception
DNA
Egg ovum
Embryo
Estrogen
Etheric body
Fallopian tubes
Gene, genetics
Genitals
Gestation
Libido
Menstruation
Ovaries
Penis
Periods
Physical permanent atom
Placenta
Procreation
Progesterone
Prostate gland
Puberty
Reproduction
Semen
Sex hormones, organs
Sex life
Sex relations
Sexual development
Sigmoid flexure
Sperm
Testes
Testosterone
Urge to self-perpetuate
Uterus
Vagina
Vans deferens
Womb

Base
Ankles
Arms, hands, shoulders
Atlas axis
Bones
Calcium
Carpal and metacarpal bones
Clavicle
Coccyx - tailbone
Collagen
Cranium
Elbow
Enamel
Femur
Fibula
Fingers, phalanges
Hips
Humerus
Hyoid bone
Ilium
Ischium
Jaws
Leg bones
Limbs, lower
Patella
Pelvic girdle
Pelvis
Pubic bone
Pubis
Radius
Ribs
Sacroiliac joint
Sacrum
Scapula
215
Skeleton
Skull
Spinal column, spine
Teeth
Tibia
Ulna
Vertebrae, all

▲ **Disease**
Accidents
Bacterial infection
Contagious infections
Electrification
Epidemics
Poisoning: lead, mineral, radiation

Crown
Brain congenital disorders
Huntington's disease
Lewy body dementia

Ajna
Astigmatism
Balance, all problems of
Bells Palsy
Cerebral palsy
Epilepsy
Labyrinthitis
Meniere's disease
Middle ear problems
Muscle spasms, cramps
Nerve spasms
Neuro-degenerative diseases
Seizures
Spasms, nerves
Spasticity
Tinnitus
Tourette's syndrome
Tremors
Twitching, tics
Vertigo

Throat
Buboes, plague
Thyroid imbalance

Heart
Anaemia
Angina
Arrhythmia
Arteriosclerosis
Atrial fibrillation
Blood cancer
Blood circulation problems
Deep vein thrombosis
Gangrene
Germs
Heart fibrillation
Heart disease
Heart problem, congenital
Leukaemia: blood cancer
Myocarditis
Palpitations
Pathogens
Reynaud's disease
Varicose veins

Solar plexus
Enteritis
Food poisoning
Peritonitis
Typhoid fever

Sacral
Abortion
Barrenness
Castration
Congenital diseases
Endometriosis
Fibroids in womb
Frigidity
Gene mutation
Genetic diseases
Immorality
Impotency
Infertility
Miscarriage
Premature ejaculation
Prostate trouble
Sexual license
Social diseases
STD: sexually transmitted diseases
Sterility
Uterine troubles

Base
Ankle problems
Dental problems
Gingivitis, pyorrhea
Hip disease
Rickets
Vertebrae degeneration

---

1 Bailey, Alice A; Esoteric Healing, 128.
2 Ibid, 51.
3 Bailey, Alice A; Externalisation of the Hierarchy 668.

2b. Astrology Signs

Chart 3. Sign rulerships in the Body

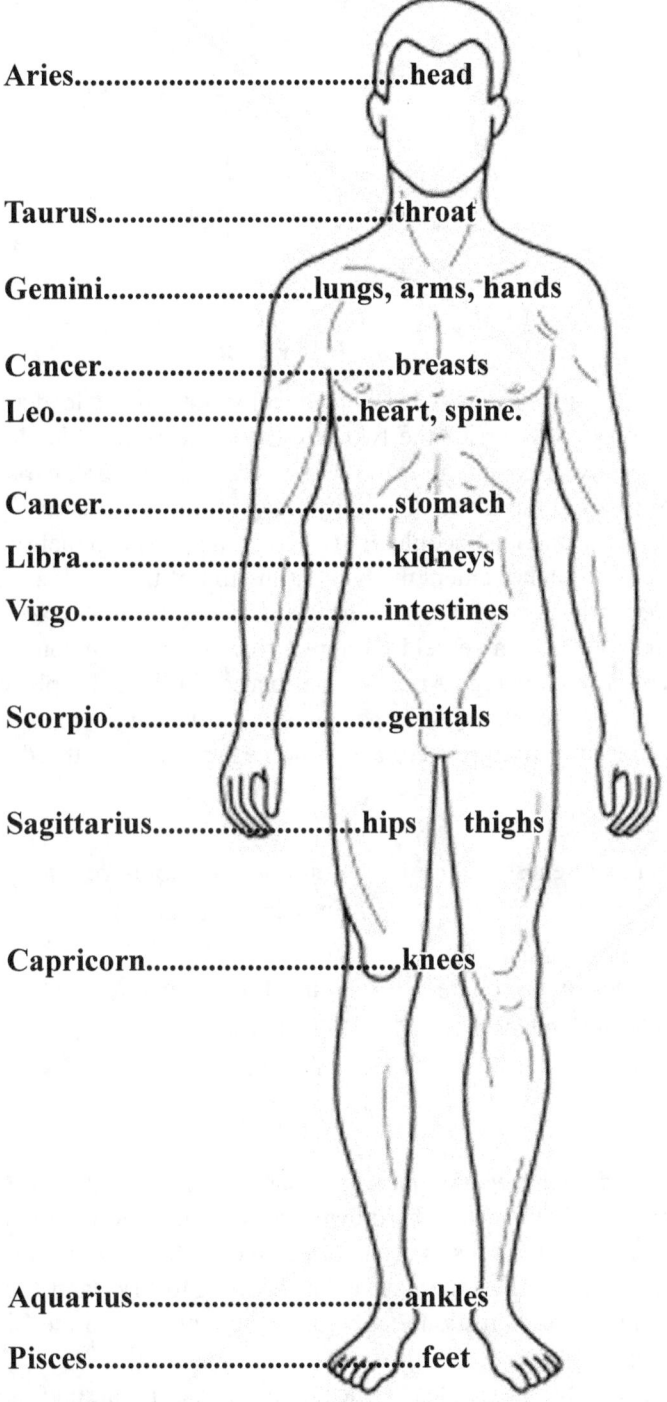

Aries..................................head
Taurus................................throat
Gemini..............................lungs, arms, hands
Cancer..............................breasts
Leo...................................heart, spine.
Cancer..............................stomach
Libra................................kidneys
Virgo................................intestines
Scorpio.............................genitals
Sagittarius........................hips   thighs
Capricorn.........................knees
Aquarius..........................ankles
Pisces..............................feet

- **Rays:** 1 and 7.

- **Chakra:**
The Crown.

- **Planet rulers:**
Exoteric: Mars.
Esoteric: Mercury.
Hierarchy: Uranus.

- **Personality Keynote:**
Let form again be sought.

- **Soul Keynote:**
I come forth and from the plane of mind I rule.

Aries, at different points along the Path of Life forces the soul on to the burning ground and subjects it to a purifying process. Through the lesser fire of mind, the "jungles of experience are set on fire and dissolve in flames and then the Path stands clear and unobstructed vision is achieved." Old Commentary

The rays which are expressing themselves through Aries are curiously balanced, Rays 1 and 7 are the highest and the lowest, and therefore demand a point of balance upon the wheel which is provided in Libra.[1]

---

[1] Bailey, Alice A; Esoteric Astrology, 101.

1. Aries

CROWN CHAKRA

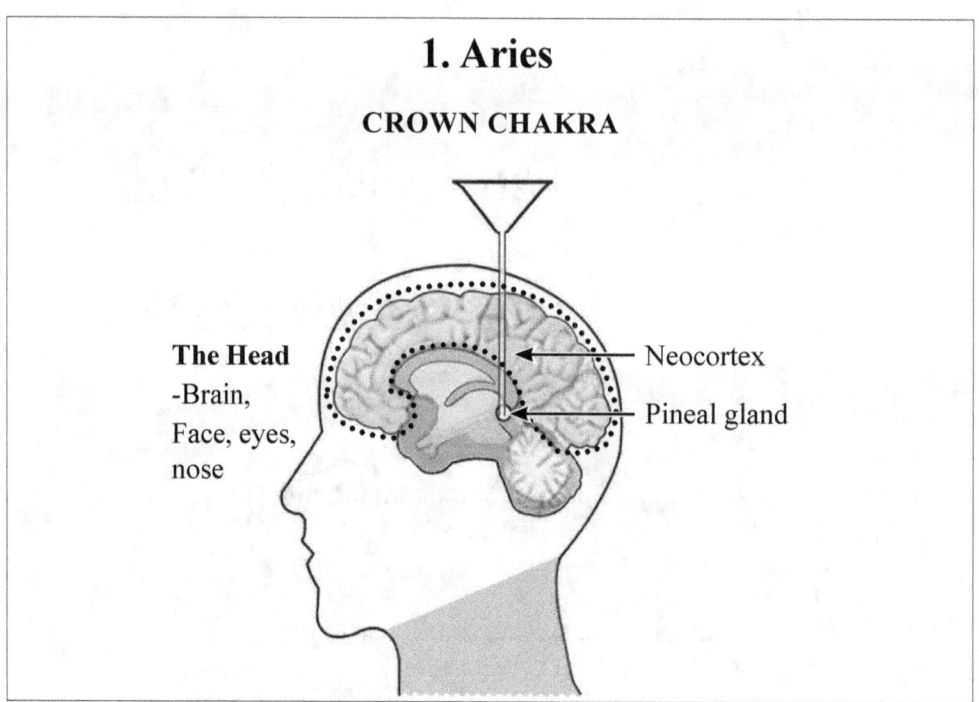

1. Psychology

The evolutionary task of Aries is to develop intelligent leaders who work for the higher good. Aries carries the two power rays to bring this about. The 1st Ray of Will-Power gives leadership skill and personal power and charisma. The 7th Ray of Ceremony and Order gives the ability to apply those skills in a practical and potent way to manage and lead people. It also gives the power to manifest.

The crown chakra enters the body at the top of the head, a region ruled by Aries. This centre is the portal for spirit. The exaltation of the Sun in Aries symbolises human consciousness that is a vessel for the radiance and glory of spirit.

However, the average Aries person focuses in the solar plexus or sacral chakras via Mars. At this level, the Aries person is hot, ardent and tempestuous, characteristics that get him into trouble. Here are some negative Aries attitudes that may result in disease:

Aggression	Arrogance
Combativeness	Emotionally impulsive
Fiery	Ferociously aggressive
Power hungry	Pride
Ruthless ambition	Self-pitying, the dramatic "I"
Self-aggrandising	Selfishness
Violence	Wilfulness

2. Body

a. Head, brain and pineal gland. Aries has general rulership over the head, the brain, the pineal gland (in which the crown anchors) and the cranium. The dividing line between Aries and Taurus is at the top of the neck. Some astrologers place it at the level of the mouth - the upper jaw and teeth going to Aries and Taurus ruling all below. Taurus is related to digestion that begins at the mouth and the Limbic System in the lower brain.

But generally, Aries rules the head, Taurus the throat, and the jutting out chin is more symbolic of Mars than it is of Venus.

b. The "Triune Brain" and the neocortex. The Triune Brian theory was presented by American neuroscientist Paul D. MacLean in the 60's. It divides the brain into three parts based on evolutionary development - the *neocortex* or thinking brain, the *limbic* or emotional brain, and the *reptilian* or action brain. Aries, Taurus and Gemini are associated with each of these three parts.

- *The neocortex (Aries)*. It is the latest part of the brain to evolve and is concerned with advanced cognition, language and planning. It is the seat of curiosity and asks, "What can I learn?" Aries, the sign that rules exploration and pioneering is the natural ruler of the neocortex.
- *The Limbic System or emotional brain (Taurus)*. It emerged in the first mammals and in man is the seat of the desire nature. Taurus, the sign of desire rules this system. It asks, "What do I want and how do I get it?"
- *The Reptilian or instinctual brain (Gemini):* this is the brainstem and the cerebellum, the oldest part of the brain that dominated in reptiles. It controls breathing and balance, vital functions associated with Gemini. It constantly monitors the environment asking, "Am I safe?"

c. The senses and the eyes, ears and nose. Mars rules the five senses according to Bailey [1] confirming that the sense organs are ruled primarily by Aries, which Mars rules.

The Triune Brain

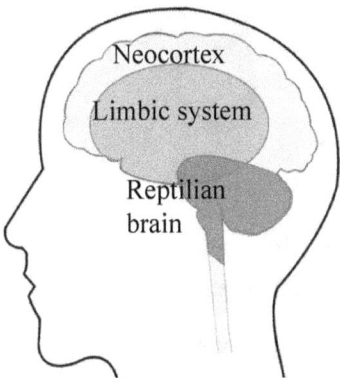

Although this triple division of the brain is largely discounted today by scientists, it fits comfortably with the esoteric practice of dividing all living organisms into three aspects that follow the spirit - soul - body model.

3. Disease

- Diseases of the head, brain and pineal gland.

Aries is a cardinal-fire sign. Of all the elements, fire is most conducive to good health because it represents the life force of God and vitality. This is a huge benefit for people who have their Suns or ascendant in Aries, Leo and Sagittarius. But when Aries' fire turns rogue, when negative traits like those in the previous list are expressed, the result can be inflammatory diseases that strike suddenly, without warning. This is emphasised because of the presence of the 1st ray in Aries, which is the most powerful and dynamic of all ray forces. Health problems associated with this type of force are strokes and head injuries.

Aries people fight their way through life, leading with their heads. They open themselves up to injuries or accidents to the head, especially to the nose, face and eyes. Aries is the natural ruler of the brain, so is associated with the many disorders that involve brain trouble, such as dementia.

▲ **Psychology**
Egomania
Megalomania

▲ **Body**
Crown
Brain mass, tissue
Cerebral cortex
Face
Head
Melatonin
Neocortex
Pineal gland

Serotonin

Ajna
Brow
Cornea
Eye lens
Eyes
Iris
Nose
Pupils
Retina
Sclera
Sight
Vision

Base
Chin
Cranium
Hair
Jaws
Skull

▲ **Disease**
Crown
Alzheimer's
Ataxia
Blood pressure high, pineal
Brain cells
overactive: cancer, tumour, abscess
Brain congenital disorders
Brain haemorrhage, inflammation
Cerebral-spinal meningitis
Coma
Concussion: head injuries
Convulsions
Dementia

Encephalitis
Head injuries
Huntington's disease
Hydrocephalus
Hypertension, pineal cause
Insanity, idiocy
Lewy body dementia
Multiple personalities
Possession
Stroke

Ajna
Astigmatism
Blindness
Cataracts
Conjunctivitis
Glaucoma
Keratitis
Myopia
Short sighted

Base
Alopecia
Baldness
Skull injuries

---
1 Bailey, Alice A; Esoteric Astrology, 215.

- **Ray:** 4.

- **Chakra:**
The Throat.

- **Planet rulers:**
Exoteric: Venus.
Esoteric: Vulcan.
Hierarchy: Vulcan.

- **Personality Keynote:**
Let struggle be undismayed.

- **Soul Keynote:**
I see, and when the eye is opened, all is illumined.

Carotid neck arteries and glands

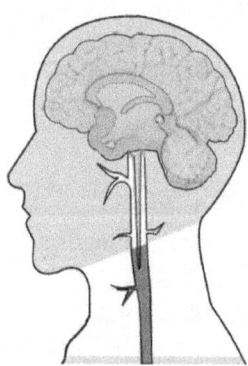

The mouth as the entry point of digestion.

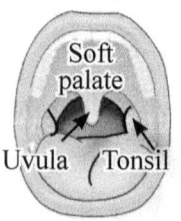

2. Taurus

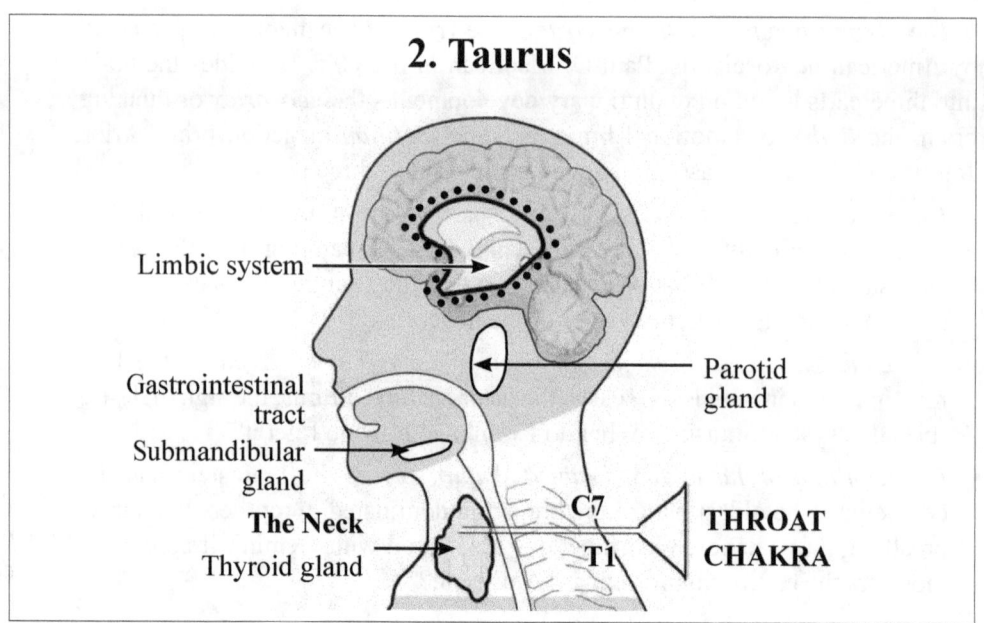

1. Psychology

Taurus and Scorpio are polar opposites and they both carry a single ray, the 4th of Harmony through Conflict. This makes them battleground signs. People born in Taurus often find themselves in conflict, within themselves or with others due to their powerful desires and wills. The evolutionary task of Taurus, is to teach us to "ride the bull" of desire rather than be ridden by it, to control our lower appetites rather than be ruled by them.

At the higher level, the 4th ray is the force of harmony and beauty and many great artistes have Taurus in their make-up. It is likewise the force of diplomacy and negotiation and integrated Taurus people make fine diplomats and counsellors.

Taurus is a fixed earth sign and its people are notorious for their stubbornness. Over time, this blocks the physical systems in the body and when chronic can lead to crystallisation, hardening and atrophying of organs. It can also lead to insanity - mental inflexibility is a precursor to mental disorders. Here are some negative attitudes that may cause trouble:

Bullheadedness, stubborn	Continual conflict
Emotional instability	Gluttony, greed
Sexual promiscuity	Uncontrolled desire

2. Body

a. Throat and ajna chakras. Taurus co-rules the throat centre with Gemini, which enters the body at the base of the neck on the borderline between the two signs. This centre is involved in both their functions - Taurus for food digestion and Gemini for breathing. Taurus people who are still emotional or sensual are focused primarily in the solar plexus or sacral chakras, not the throat. Their task is to raise their focus up to the throat. Taurus is also related to the ajna chakra, the centre of personality consciousness, through its ruler Venus.

b. The thyroid gland. The throat chakra anchors in the thyroid gland. This gland uses iodine from food to make two main hormones: Triiodothyronine (T3) and Thyroxine (T4). They regulate many functions including our metabolic rate, breathing, heart rate, muscle strength, menstrual cycles etc.

c. The neck. Taurus is the traditional ruler of the neck, with Aries ruling the head and Gemini the shoulders.

d. The upper digestive tract: Taurus rules the neck and throat, all its organs and parts. This includes the upper gastrointestinal or digestive tract, the mouth as the organ for food intake, the palate, salivary glands, the hyoid bone, taste sense etc.

e. Tonsils. Taurus rules the tonsils, which are part of the immune and lymphatic systems that fight infection. Latest studies show that immune T-cells develop in the tonsils. They are first line of defence and when they do their job and trap germs, we get a sore throat.

f. The limbic or emotional brain. This is the feel good recording part of the brain that asks "am I happy, am I appreciated, am I getting what I want, are my desires being satisfied?" Based on the answers it comes up with and records (it deals with memories), it influences our value judgements and future actions and behaviours. Every time we repeat a behaviour that brings us a reward we crave or cherish, the memory - behaviour - pay-off pattern is reinforced, and so is the urge to repeat the pattern to get the reward. The Limbic System influences our future choices, actions and habits and is at the root of any addictions we form. Here are its parts:

The Limbic System

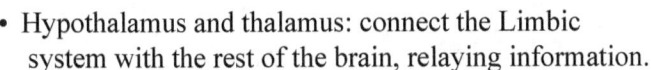

- Hypothalamus and thalamus: connect the Limbic system with the rest of the brain, relaying information.
- Nucleus accumbens: the pleasure centre in the brain.
- Olfactory bulb: processes odours
- Amygdala: integrative center for emotions, emotional behaviour, and motivation.
- Hippocampus - memories

Whether we call this system *limbic* or the *reward-pleasure* centre, the seat of desire as far as it relates to the brain is centred in this region, linking it to Taurus and Venus. Taurus is the sign that represents desire. Today physicians do not recognise this system, referring instead to "reward" or "pleasure" centres.

3. Disease

- Diseases of the throat and thyroid gland.

Attachment to desire is the cause of all sorrow according to Buddha. Stubbornness leads to stiffness and rigidity in body and mind. Gluttonous attachment to food and a hedonistic lifestyle are Taurus problems and its people often struggle with weight gain and associated diseases. Today scientists are claiming that our genes determine eating patterns, that DNA pre-programming causes us to eat in certain ways. This fits with the astrological theory that each sign invests our character with certain basic traits, qualities and behaviours. Taurus people - influenced by ruler Venus, like sweet or sugary foods and when laziness and a sedentary lifestyle is added it is a recipe for disease. One consequence is diabetes, a disease of wrong inner desires. [1]

▲ **Psychology**
Mental rigidity that leads to mental illness.
Ridden by desire.

▲ **Body**
Ajna
Amygdala
Dopamine
Hippocampus
Limbic system
Nucleus

accumbens, pleasure centre
Olfactory bulb

Throat
Adam's apple
Adenoids
Alimentary canal
Appetite
Carotid gland, arteries
Glottis
Jugular vein

Larynx
Lips
Metabolism
Mouth
Neck
Oesophagus upper
Palate
Parathyroids
Parotid glands
Pharynx
Salivary glands
Submandibular

glands
Taste
Throat
Thyroid
Thyroxine
Tongue
Tonsils
Uvula

Base
Gums
Hyoid bone

▲ **Disease**
Throat
Goitre
Grave's disease
Hashimoto's disease
Hormonal trouble
Metabolic disorder caused by emotionalism
Mumps
Postpartum blues

Snoring
Thyroid imbalance
Tonsillitis
Weight gain or loss, thyroid

Solar plexus
Diabetes
Obesity

---
1 Bailey, Alice A; Esoteric Healing, 311.

- **Ray:** 2.

- **Chakra:**
The Ajna and Throat.

- **Planet rulers:**
Exoteric: Mercury.
Esoteric: Venus.
Hierarchy: Earth.

- **Personality Keynote:**
Let instability do its work.

- **Soul Keynote:**
I recognise my other self and in the waning of that self I grow and glow.

Nervous system, shoulders, arms, hands, fingers

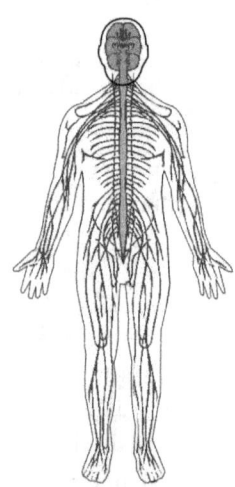

Bronchial tree

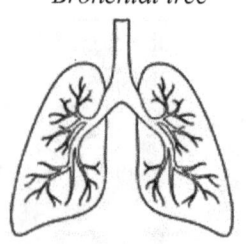

3. Gemini

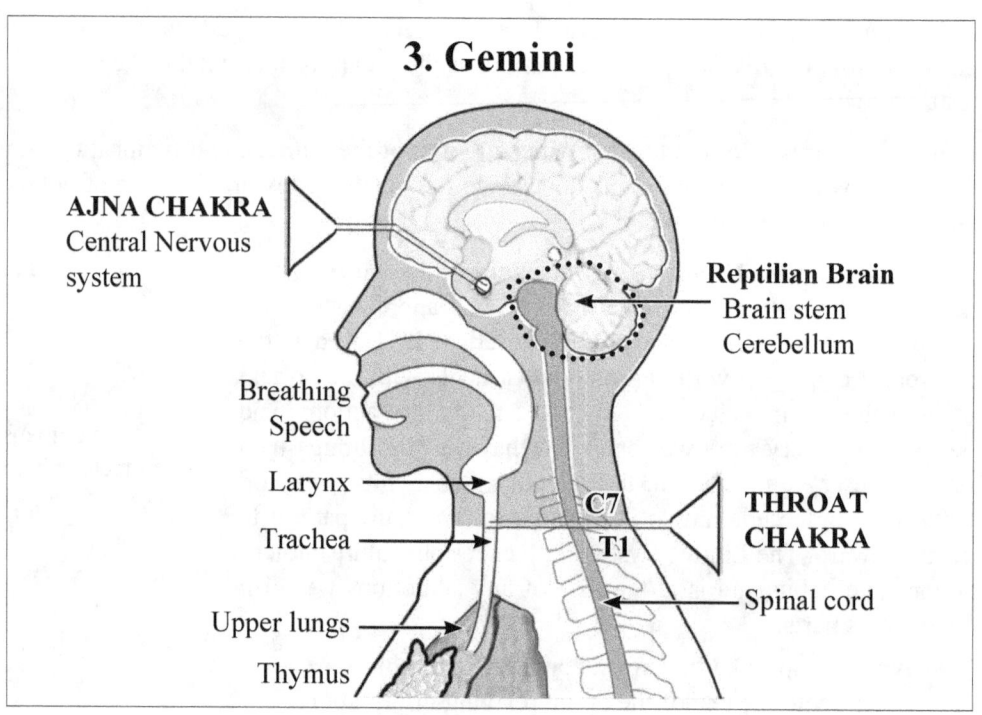

1. Psychology

Gemini is an air sign whose task is to develop the powers of the mind and to teach us to communicate intelligently. For this purpose it carries a single ray - the 2nd Ray of Love and Wisdom, the "consciousness" ray. This is why Gemini people are curious, cerebral people, with minds that are continually reaching out for new information and knowledge. However, when the mind is unstable, Gemini's force produces flitting minds that cannot concentrate, which are restless and superficial. Here are some negative Gemini attitudes that may result in problems or disease:

Changeability	Duality, unstable swings in consciousness
Mental instability	Shallowness
Two-faced	Superficial mental chit-chatter

2. Body

a. The ajna and throat chakras. The throat centre enters the body between Taurus and Gemini around vertebrae cervical 7 (C7) and thoracic 1 (T1).

b. The pituitary gland and endocrine system. The pituitary is governed by the ajna that is ruled by Venus and Mercury, relating this gland to Gemini. The pituitary is called the "master gland" because it controls the activity of most other endocrine glands. The intelligence of the endocrine messaging system as it balances and regulates our health through hormonal release suggests that Gemini and Mercury are appropriate rulers.

c. The thymus: this gland is governed by the heart chakra. Normally it atrophies in adults, but Gemini [1] re-activates it in people who are spiritually advanced and who are expressing inclusiveness through an opened heart chakra. This strengthens the immune system and resistance to disease.

d. The Central Nervous System. Gemini rules the nervous system and governs the fluid reactions of the entire nervous organism.

e. Speech and learning. Gemini and Mercury govern these vital functions, all ruled by the throat chakra. Mercury is the "Messenger of God".

---

1 Bailey, Alice A; Esoteric Astrology, 367.

f. Organs of respiration: Gemini governs the bronchial tract and the oxygenation of the blood.

g. Tubes in the body. Gemini rules tubes that transport substances in the body from one place to another. For instance, the nervous system that enables nerve messages to flow around the body, digestive tubes that transport food, fallopian tubes that transport ova and the urethra that transports urine and semen in men.

h. The Reptilian or Instinctual Brain: Gemini is related to the older parts of the brain, which we share with reptiles – the brainstem (pons, medulla oblongata) and cerebellum. They control Gemini-type automatic functions such as breathing and balance.

i. Shoulders, arms and hands and movement. Gemini traditionally rules the "grasping" and "balancing" parts of the body. Nerves that control these functions leave the spinal cord in the throat chakra region.

3. Disease

- Diseases of the nervous system and of breathing.
- Diseases and injuries that affect learning, speech and balance.

Ruler of Gemini, Mercury, carries the conflicted 4th ray. It creates turmoil in the lives of people who are mentally and emotionally unstable. This leads to debility and the easy taking on of germs. Because Gemini is a mutable-air sign its people are susceptible to air-borne pathogens, lung and breathing problems and to epidemics such as influenza. Known for being "nervy", Gemini people often have nervous system disorders.

▲ **Psychology**
ADD: attention deficit disorder
ADHD :> hyperactivity disorder
Asperger's
Autism
Imbecilities
Insanities
Mental instability
Psychological troubles

▲ **Body**
Crown
Antahkarana
Consciousness thread

Ajna
Central nervous system
Cerebellum
Cognition
Ears
Hearing
Intelligent self-consciousness
Motor nerves
Nerve fluid

Nerve synapse
Neurons
Spinal cord
Spinal fluid
Synapse

Throat
Airways
Alta-major
Alveoli
Brainstem
Breathing
Bronchial tree
Diaphragm
Ears
Endocrine system
Hearing
Lungs
Medulla oblongata
Pons
Reptilian brain
Respiration
Sinuses
Speech
Thalamus
Trachea
Tubes, body
Vocal cords

Windpipe

Heart
Oxygen, oxygenation
Pulmonary circulation
Thymus
Vagus nerve

Solar plexus
Sympathetic NS

Sacral
Etheric body
Locomotion
Movement

Base
Arms, hands, shoulders
Biceps
Carpal and metacarpal bones
Clavicle
Elbow
Fingers, phalanges
Hands
Humerus
Radius
Scapula
Ulna

Wrist

▲ **Disease**
Ajna
ALS: amyotrophic lateral sclerosis
Bells Palsy
Cerebral palsy
Deafness
Epilepsy
Guillain-Barre syndrome
Labyrinthitis
Lou Gehrig's disease
Meniere's disease
Middle ear problems
Motor neurone disease
Muscle spasms, cramps
Nerve spasms
Neuralgia
Neuro-degenerative diseases
Palsy
Paralysis

Paraplegic, quadriplegic
Parkinson's disease
Polio
Seizures
Shingles
Spasms, nerves
Spasticity
Tinnitus
Tourette's syndrome
Tremors
Twitching, tics

Throat
Allergies, breathing
Aphasia
Asthma
Bronchitis
Carpal tunnel syndrome
Chicken pox
Cholera
Colds
Croup
Deafness Dengue fever
Diphtheria
Dyslexia

Emphysema
Hyperactivity
Influenza
Labyrinthitis
Learning difficulties
Measles
Meniere's disease
Middle ear problems
Nasal congestion
Pleurisy
Pneumonia
Pulmonary tuberculosis
Rubella
Scarlet fever
Sinusitis
Smallpox
Stuttering
Tinnitus

Sacral
Locomotive disorders

Base
Bone fractures: shoulders, arms, hands; hips, thighs

- **Rays:** 3 and 7.

- **Chakra:**
The Solar Plexus.

- **Planet rulers:**
Exoteric: the Moon.
Esoteric: Neptune.
Hierarchy: Neptune.

- **Personality Keynote:**

Let isolation be the rule and yet the crowd exists.

- **Soul Keynote:**

I build a lighted house and therein dwell.

Motherhood, women and reproduction

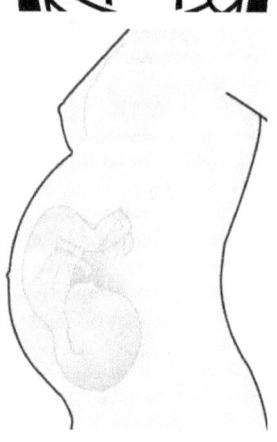

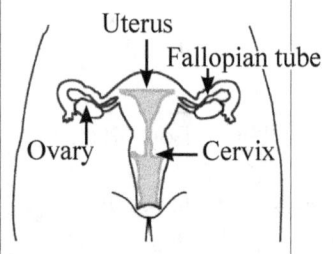

4. Cancer

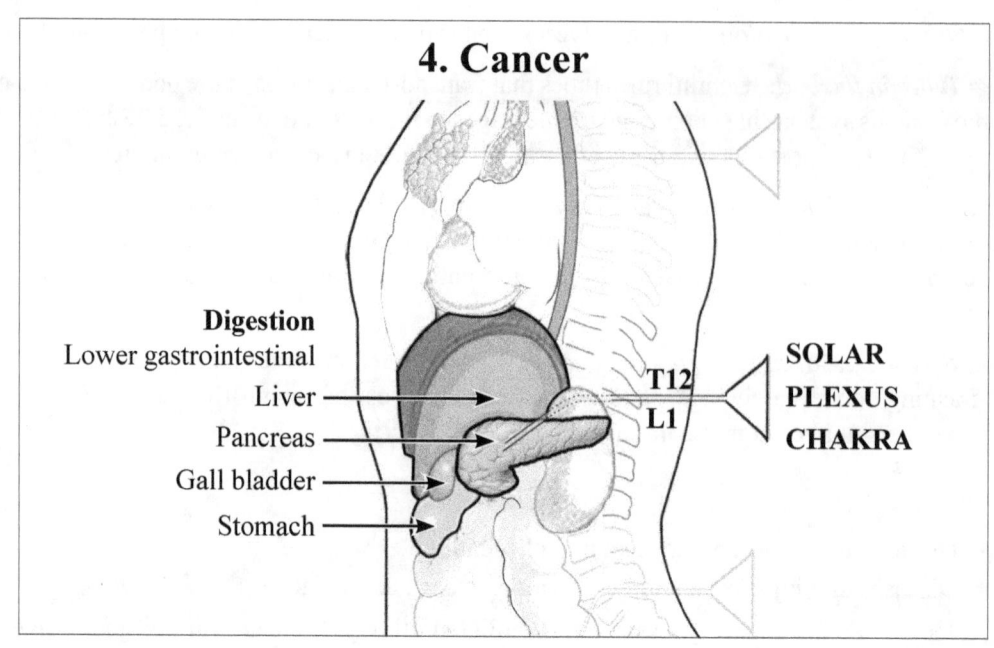

1. Psychology

Cancer is a water sign, the element ruling the emotional Astral Plane. Its evolutionary task is to help the emotional man or woman born in this sign develop their mental faculties. Two rays help achieve this. Ray 3 of Intelligent Activity gives Cancer people the intelligence to do what they need to do to feed and house the family and Ray 7 of Ceremony and Order gives them organising power. By doing their best for family or their own survival, Cancerian's develop their mental powers. Here are some negative Cancer attitudes:

Addictive tendencies	Emotionalism
Moodiness	Defensive, over-protectiveness
Glamour	Hyper-sensitivity

2. Body

a. *Solar plexus chakra:* this centre enters the body in the Cancer-ruled region around thoracic 12 (T12) and lumbar 1 (L1), and anchors in the pancreas.

b. *Digestion, the stomach, pancreas, gallbladder and liver.* Cancer is the ruler of mid-region digestion.

c. *Female gender and reproduction.* Cancer rules "women" generally, especially mature women and mothers. It supports the sacral chakra in childbearing, birth and babies, with prime rulership over female reproduction.

d. *Body fluids and the lymphatic system.* Cancer, Pisces, the Moon and Neptune are the primary rulers of fluids in the body. Cancer is related particularly to white body fluids such as lymph and mucus. When these become toxic, the result is pus, phlegm and congestion. Cancer and the Moon - the ruler of tidal activity on the planet, are also related to the cleansing housework carried out by the lymphatic system.

> The Crab, who clears the ocean of matter which flows around the soul of man. [1]

e. *The physical body, cells, tissue and flesh.* Cancer and its opposite pole Capricorn rule the dense physical body via ray 3, the ruler of matter-substance. While Capricorn rules the dense skeletal structure and cartilage that ties the structure together, Cancer rules soft tissue such as bone marrow and brain matter.

---

1 Bailey, Alice A; Esoteric Astrology, 62.

f. Containers. The protective quality of Cancer is seen in its rulership of all body "containers" that enfold organs such as the womb and provide the linings of tubes such as those for the thoracic duct.

3. Disease

- Psychological disorders caused through emotionalism.
- Diseases of the digestive system, reproduction organs, motherhood and body tissue.

The energy of Cancer is water-cardinal and just like its people can be weepy, moody and defensive, its diseases are seepy, watery, damp, lethargic and devitalising. Contaminated water is a breeding ground for germs and disease and so are the three water signs when there is emotional congestion. Of the water signs, Cancer is very susceptible to disease because it carries ray 7, which is related to the breeding of germs. Scorpio is more resistant to disease because ruler Mars carries heat which destroys them. Pisces is very susceptible to addictive type diseases, weight gain and cancer through ray 2.

Cancer, being the sign that rules family life, also represents diseases we inherit genetically, through our family line or because we are part of the human kingdom.

Cancer (the disease). Emotional repression is the underlying psychological cause of cancer. This causes congestion and over-activity in a chakra, which translates into over-activity in cells. Men born in Cancer often repress their feelings in order to present a more 'manly' front to the world. Now breast cancer rates are increasing amongst women, linking this to Cancer and the Moon, which rule the breasts. Professional women in particular, who compete in male-dominated fields are prone. The Moon carries the 4th ray and when people live in continual conflict, debilitating the immune system, they become susceptible to the indigenous diseases of the planet that include cancer.

▲ **Psychology**
Anxiety, worry
Borderline personality disorder
Cuts, cutting
Delirium, delusory
Dreams, troubled
Hallucination
Hysteria
Negative core beliefs
Neurotics, neuroses
Obsessive compulsive
Panic attacks
Past-life soul prison pattern
Paranoia
Phobias
PTSD
Schizophrenia
Self-harm, self-injury
Sleep-walking
Substance abuse

▲ **Body**
Body fluids
Watery systems
in the body

Throat
Lymph, nodes
Lymphatic system
Thoracic duct

Heart
Stem cells
White blood cells

Solar plexus
Abdomen
Bile
Chyle
Digestion
Gallbladder
Insulin
Islets of Langerhans
Liver
Nutrition
Oesophagus lower
Pancreas
Stomach

Sacral
Babies
Birth
Breasts
Cervix
Conception
Egg ovum
Embryo
Estrogen
Fallopian tubes
Fertility
Gestation
Infancy
Lacteals, lactation
Maternity
Menstruation
Mothers, mothering
Ovaries
Periods
Placenta
Pregnancy
Procreation
Progesterone
Reproduction
Uterus
Womb

Base
Body containers, sheaths
Body intelligence
Bone marrow
Flesh
Physical body
Secretions
Substance
Tears
Tissue, flesh

▲ **Disease**
Bacterial infection
Contagious infections
Epidemics

Throat
Buboes, plague
Epstein–Barr virus
Glandular fever, swellings
Hodgkin's disease
Lymphoma
Mononucleosis

Solar plexus
Acid reflux
Acidosis
Allergies, digestive
Anorexia
Biliousness
Cancer: all body organs, especially solar plexus organs
Carcinogenic
Bulimia
Candida
Coeliac disease
Cystic fibrosis
Cysts
Diabetes
Drug addiction
Dyspepsia
Eating disorders
Flatulence
Food allergies
Food poisoning
Gallstones
Gastric disorders
Hallucinatory, recreational drugs
Heartburn
Hyper-glycemia, hypo-glycaemia
Indigestion
Malnutrition
Mucus
Narcolepsy
Nausea
Nightmares
Oedema
Pancreatitis
Peptic ulcer
Peritonitis
Phlegm
Reflux
Sluggish action of organs
Starvation
Tissue, insidious changes
Ulcers, gastric
Vomiting
Water retention
Yeast infection

Sacral
Abortion
Barrenness
Endometriosis
Fibroids in womb
Hereditary diseases
Infertility
Miscarriage
Sterility
Uterine troubles

Base
Athlete's foot
Fungus, fungi
Ringworm
Thrush
Tinea

- **Rays:** 1 and 5.

- **Chakra:**
The Heart.

- **Planet rulers:**
Exoteric: the Sun.
Esoteric: the Sun veiling Neptune.
Hierarchy: the Sun veiling Uranus.

- **Personality Keynote:**
Let other forms exist. I rule.

- **Soul Keynote:**
I am That and That am I.

Vitality

Cardiovascular

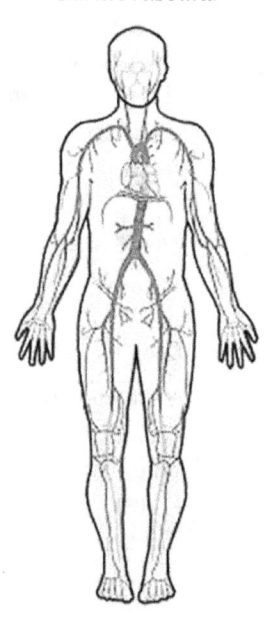

5. Leo

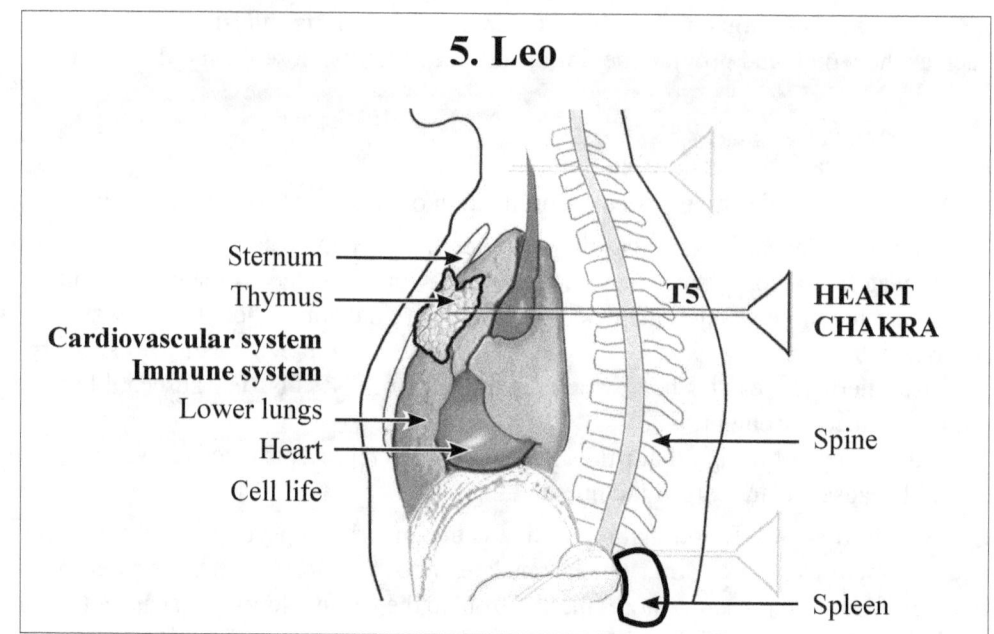

1. Psychology

Leo's evolutionary task is to produce a fully self-conscious, intelligent and integrated personality, who is fully aware of his individual and independent destiny. The 1st ray of Will and Power that flows through Leo helps to bring this about. At first such men and women are selfish and arrogant, serving only themselves and expecting all others to do so as well. Leo people are also exceedingly intelligent in the way they conduct their affairs, the gift of the 5th Ray of Scientific Mind. Both these forces are on the "will" line. If Leo people become wilfully hard-hearted and mentally rigid it leads to serious heart trouble. Here are some negative Leo attitudes that may result in disease.

Arrogance	Cruel, pitiless
Dogmatism	Fixed minded
Power hungry	Pride
Self-love, extreme	Self-pitying, the dramatic "I"
Self-aggrandising	Selfish use of power
Stubbornly self-willed	Urge to control others

2. Body

a. Heart centre: this centre enters the body in the Leo-ruled region around vertebrae thoracic 5 (T5) and anchors in the thymus.

b. Sutratma, the life stream. Leo is related to the life of God the Father and to the life aspect that reaches us via the sutratma. This stream of life energy emanates from the monad, flows through the crown and heart chakras and anchors in the heart organ. From there, life flows into the bloodstream vitalising the entire physical body. The soul utilises this thread and its force to hold the atoms of the body together during incarnation. All this Leo assists

c. The cardiovascular system and pranic vitalisation. Leo and the Sun rule the heart, the powerhouse of the cardiovascular system, the means through which the cells in the body are vitalised. The life-stream flowing in from the soul via the sutratma is the primary means of vitalisation. A second stream of vitality flows from the Sun. It enters the body via the spleen and flows to the heart where it merges with the life-stream as it flows into the cardiovascular system. Leo's opposite sign and partner Aquarius works with Leo to circulate blood. Together, these two signs rule the cardiovascular system.

d. The immune system and the thymus gland. Leo and the Sun govern the immune system, the body's natural defence system to fight off disease. The heart chakra anchors in the thymus gland, which trains and develops T-lymphocytes (T cells), white blood cells that kill disease.

e. Spinal column and vertebrae. The purpose of the spinal column is both structural and protective. It supports the head and protects the spinal cord and vital organs with the rib cage. The Leo qualities of uprightness and erectness are apparent in the spine.

3. Disease

- Diseases of the cardiovascular system and spine.

Self-pity is a trait to which all 1st ray people are prone. They are especially sensitive to any form of humiliation and play the injured victim well. Apart from affecting the heart, chronic self-pity may lead to brain cancer. Hard-heartedness, or at the other end of the spectrum - being heart centred and giving all that one has to others; both cause heart trouble.

The energy of Leo is fiery-fixed. In disease, this manifests as inflammatory heart diseases and conditions that are slow forming and consequently become chronic and hard to move. Because the heart organ is central to physical plane life, its diseases are dangerously life threatening.

The Cardiovascular System

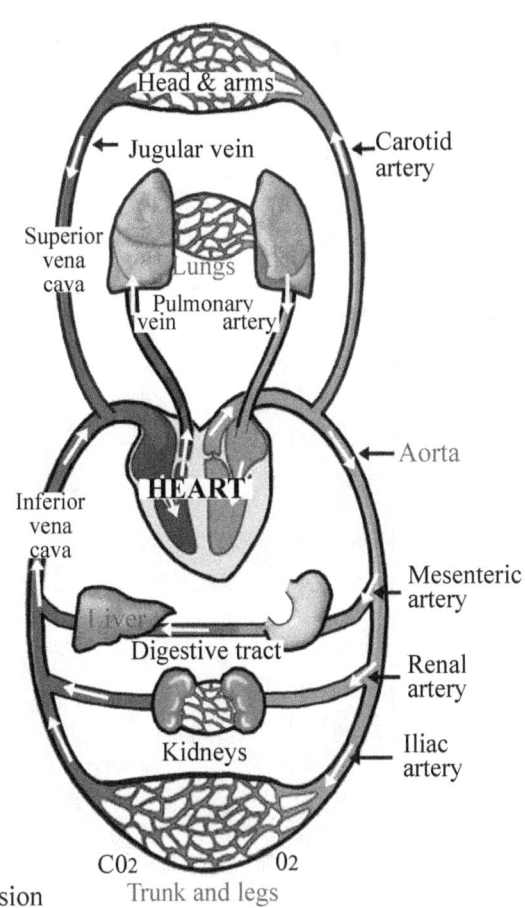

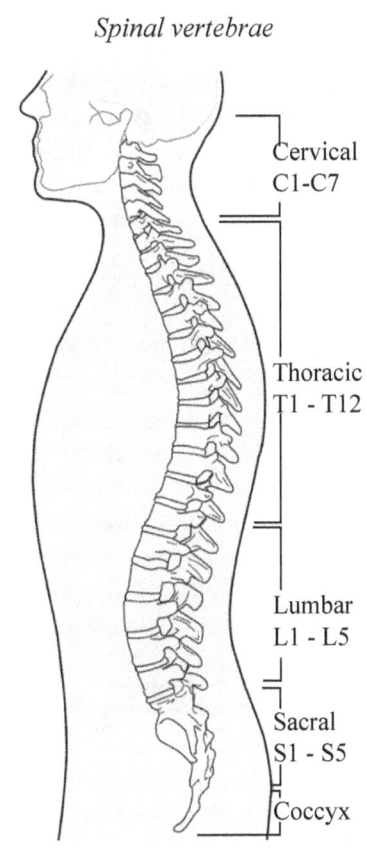

Spinal vertebrae

▲ **Psychology**
Egomania
Megalomania

▲ **Body**

Ajna
Self-consciousness

Heart
Aorta
Arteries
Blood
Blood circulation, quality
Bloodstream
Capillaries
Cardiovascular system
Cell life
Constitution
Haemoglobin
Heart.
Immune system
Iron in the blood
Leukocytes
Life-force, soul energy
Life-thread/ stream, sutratma, silver cord
Pericardium
Plasma
Prana
Recuperative power
Red blood cells
Spleen
Stem cells
Sternum
Thymus
Valves - heart
Veins
Vena Cava
Venous system
Vitality (solar fire)

Base
Spinal column, spine
Vertebrae, all

▲ **Disease**

Crown
Meningitis

Ajna
Multiple sclerosis

Heart
AIDS
Allergic reaction from immune
Anaemia
Aneurism
Angina
Arrhythmia
Arteriosclerosis
Atrial fibrillation
Autoimmune diseases
Blood cancer
Blood circulation problems
Bruises
Cardio-myopathy
Ebola virus
Fainting
Fever
Gangrene
Heart fibrillation
Heart attack
Heart disease
Heart problem, congenital
High blood pressure
High temperature
Hypertension
Hypotension
Immune attack
Inflammation
Lupus
Myasthenia gravis
Myocarditis
Overgrowth
Palpitations
Scoliosis
Shock
Sunburn
Sunstroke

Base
Ankylosis spondylosis
Back pain
Rheumatic fever
Rheumatoid arthritis
Spina bifida
Spinal fractures
Vertebrae degeneration

- **Rays:** 2 and 6.

- **Chakra:**
The Solar Plexus.

- **Planet rulers:**
Exoteric: Mercury.
Esoteric: the Moon veiling and Vulcan.
Hierarchy: Jupiter.

- **Personality Keynote:**
Let matter reign.

- **Soul Keynote:**
I am the Mother and the Child. I, God, I matter am.

Virgo, represented Eve, Isis and Mary, gives birth to the Christ child.

Eve, the symbol of the mind of man, took the apple of knowledge from the serpent of matter and started the long human undertaking of experiment, experience and expression. Eve has no child in her arms; the germ of the Christ life is as yet too small to make its presence felt. In Isis the quickening of that which is desired has taken place. Isis consequently stands in the ancient zodiacs for fertility, for motherhood and as the guardian of the child. Mary carries the process down to the Physical Plane, and there gives birth to the Christ child. [1]

---

1 Bailey, Alice A; Esoteric Astrology, 253.

6. Virgo

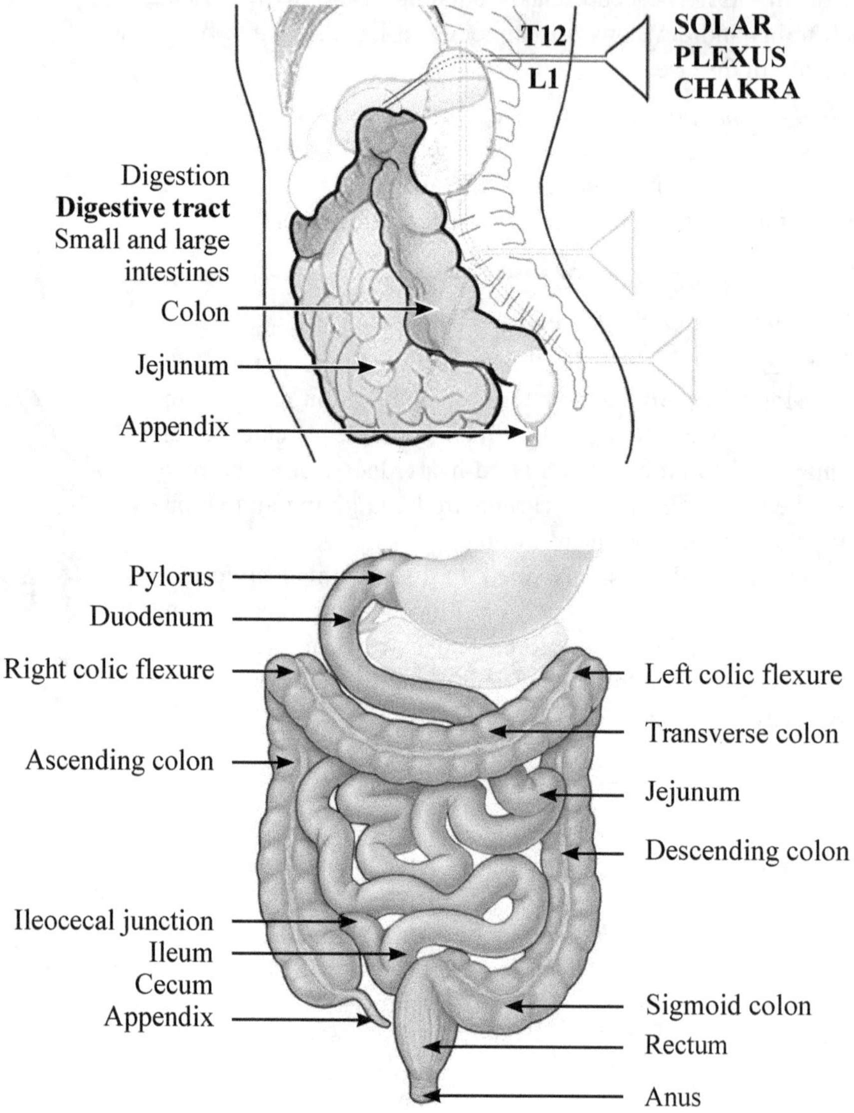

1. Psychology

Virgo's higher task is to bring about the "birth of the Christ spirit in the heart". This is a 2nd ray occurrence, a deeply momentous event on the evolutionary path when for the first time the personality turns away from its materialistic focus and responds to the inner call to aspire to something higher and finer. Here is a mystical description of that event.

> Later, upon the wheel of the disciple, the voice emerges from the Virgin Herself and she says: "I am the mother and the child. I, God, I, matter am." Ponder upon the beauty of this synthesis and teaching and know that you yourself have said the first word as the soul, descending into the womb of time and space in a far and distant past. The time has now come when you can, if you so choose, proclaim your identity with both divine aspects—matter and Spirit, the mother and the Christ. [1]

---

1 Bailey, Alice A; Esoteric Astrology, 284.

Signs in the earth element teach us to manage material life practically and pragmatically. In Taurus, the urge for material acquisition is powerful and its people avidly pursue their desires. In Virgo, we are taught to be more meticulous and discriminatory.

Discrimination is an aspect of the 6th Idealism Ray that flows through Virgo. In the early stages it is misused. The Virgo ego is highly critical and judgemental and obsessed with "being right". It strives for perfection, by finding imperfection in others. This misuse of the mind faculty - especially when egged on by mental and emotional irritation, leads to many troubles in the intestines and bowel. If fanaticism is also present, another 6th ray trait, this can lead to inflammatory conditions.

Ray 2 of Love and Wisdom flows through Virgo. Younger souls in Virgo love money and are engrossed with it. The love of money and the material comforts it can provide is a lower aspect of the 2nd ray. This is all as it should be in the normal course of evolution. But if the "love of money" should develop into avarice and an insatiable grasping after "things", it can lead to dense materialism. The keynote of lower Virgo warns us against this - "And the Word said, Let Matter reign." [1]

Virgo rules health and its people are particularly interested in diet and healthy lifestyle practices. Some become obsessed about health, which leads to hypochondria and other health complications. Health improves when Mercury loses its critical edge and when love infuses the mind and tongue. Here are some negative Virgo attitudes that may result in problems.

Picky criticism	Being judgemental
Fanaticism	Materialism
Narrow view of life	Nit picking
One-eyed	Extreme perfectionism

2. Body

a. Solar plexus centre. This centre governs the Virgo-ruled part of the body, the intestines, which are vital to the digestive processes that this centre rules.

b. Intestinal digestion. Digestion starts with Taurus and the consumption of food through the mouth, which then passes through the upper alimentary canal. Cancer represents the breaking down of food in the stomach, before chyme (gastric juices and partly digested food) is passed onto the intestines.

Then Virgo takes over. It rules the intestines and shares rulership of the bowel with Scorpio. The small intestine mixes food with digestive juices from the pancreas, liver and intestines, then Virgo decides which nutrients to absorb or to eliminate. Nutrients are absorbed through the intestine walls into the bloodstream, delivering nourishment to the rest of the body. Finally, muscles push the remaining products into the large intestine, which absorbs any remaining nutrients before waste is eliminated.

c. The enteric nervous system. This system is one of the main divisions of the nervous system and consists of a mesh-like system of neurons that governs the function of the gastrointestinal tract.

3. Disease

- Diseases and problems of the intestines.

When emotionalism (via the 6th ray) is added to its perfectionist and nit-picking tendencies, this directly affects the intestines, digestion and bowel health. Examples of this type of trouble are Crohn's disease and diverticulitis. Virgo is a mutable, changeable sign and through ruler Mercury, its diseases are adaptive and infectious.

▲ Body	Colon	Nutrition	Colic	Enteritis	Parasites,
Solar plexus	Digestion	Pylorus	Constipation	Food allergies	intestinal
Abdomen	Duodenum		Crohn's disease	Gastric disorders	Peritonitis
Appendix	Enteric NS	▲ Disease	Diarrhoea	Hypochondria	Tapeworm
Bowel	Ileum	*Solar plexus*	Diverticulitis	Indigestion	Typhoid fever
Chyle	Intestines	Appendicitis	Dysentery	Irritable bowel	Wind
	Jejunum	Coeliac disease	Dyspepsia	syndrome	Worms

---
1 Bailey, Alice A; Esoteric Astrology, 284.

- **Ray:** 3.

- **Chakra:**
The Base, also the Solar Plexus and Ajna.

- **Planet rulers:**
Exoteric: Venus.
Esoteric: Uranus.
Hierarchy: Saturn.

- **Personality Keynote:**
Let choice be made.

- **Soul Keynote:**
I choose the way that leads between the two great lines of force.

Libra occupies a unique place in the Great Wheel, for it is the energy coming from this constellation which controls the "hub of the wheel." This is that point in intermediate space where the twelve zodiacal energies meet and cross. Libra, therefore, controls the "moment of reversal of the wheel" in the life of every aspirant, for there comes a moment in the cycle of lives wherein a point of balance is reached and a relative equilibrium is attained, and over this event Libra presides. [1]

---
1 Bailey, Alice A; Esoteric Astrology, 183.

7. Libra

Diagram showing kidneys, adrenals, lumbar vertebrae, S5, coccyx, BASE CHAKRA, and urinary tract with kidneys, ureter, bladder, urethra — Regulation, the Urinary tract.

1. Psychology

The evolutionary task of Libra, the second of the air signs, is to take the development of the mind achieved in Gemini to a higher level. In Libra, through Venus and the ajna chakra, we are taught judicious balance and discernment. We learn to weigh things carefully before making decisions and to be mentally dexterous and flexible. Wise King Solomon from the Bible story is an example of this higher type. Libran's are potentially very clever, because this sign is a channel for the two rays that govern the Mental Plane - ray 3 and ray 5 via Venus.

On the negative side, Libran's procrastinate. They find it hard to come to a definite conclusion or make a fuss because they do not want to make a mistake or upset people. This can have a weakening effect on the body and cause imbalance. Libran's can also be manipulative via the 3rd ray and manoeuvre people around to get what they want. This psychological trickery makes a negative impact in the gut, in gastric and intestinal disorders. Here are some Libra attitudes that may result in problems:

Fear of upsetting people	Imbalance
Indecisiveness	Inaction to keep the peace
Manipulation	Procrastination
Self-doubt	Selfish and self-indulgent
Superficial and vain	

2. Body

a. Solar plexus, sacral and base chakras. Libra governs the belt area of the body, close to where the solar plexus chakra enters the body. It supports the work of four chakras - the ajna, solar plexus, sacral and base.

b. Homeostasis. Libra, the great sign of balance governs homeostasis. This is the body's natural ability to maintain internal balance of all its functions, bringing it naturally under Libra's rulership. The pituitary gland is the control centre for homeostasis, relating Libra to the ajna centre via Venus. If mental indecision becomes chronic, it upsets homeostasis. Energy follows thought, and self-doubt and other mental negatives can upset balance in the system.

c. Digestion, the pancreas gland and the Islets of Langerhans. Libra supports the work of the solar plexus chakra through the pancreatic endocrine glands. They secrete insulin to maintain blood sugar balance. The balancing function in the body ruled by Libra is upset when people are excessive in their consumption of sugary foods and carbohydrates. A serious consequence of this process going wrong is diabetes, a disease that is caused by wrong inner desire. Libra's ruler Venus represents the emotional craving for pleasure and love, which can manifest as a love of sweet foods if this desire is thwarted. Venus rules sugar, all sweet foods and carbohydrates. If we "comfort-eat", stuff ourselves with sweet or fatty food to try to alleviate feelings of emotional emptiness and upset, it is evidence that the astral nature has hijacked the natural balancing systems in the body.

d. Adrenal cortex. Libra rules the adrenal cortex, the outer part of the adrenals, which are governed by the base chakra. This gland secretes hormones such as cortisol and aldosterone to help regulate metabolism and maintain the body's salt - water balance. The inner, combative part of the gland, the adrenal medulla, is linked to Scorpio.

e. The urinary tract, kidneys and bladder: they are governed by Libra and the base chakra. Through them, water levels are balanced and blood pressure and acid levels are regulated. The kidneys are the waste-disposal system of the body, filtering toxins from the blood and storing urine in the bladder prior to its elimination.

f. Sex and reproduction. These are sacral chakra functions. Libra rules sex from the point of view that it governs relationships and the balancing of the opposites. Libra via Venus is also related to the female reproductive system, co-ruling organs and functions such as menstruation, the ovaries, ovum, the vagina etc. Genital infections and sexually transmitted diseases caught through unbalanced sexual activities and promiscuity are related particularly to Venus and Mars.

3. Disease

- Diseases of the urinary tract - the kidneys, bladder and urine disturbance.

The indecisive and procrastinating traits of this sign, if they should become chronic in expression, will have a weakening effect on the body and organs. Libra and Venus rule poor muscle tone, including weak internal muscles, so that organs prolapse. There are many types of prolapse, which differ according to which organ is affected. For example, when the walls of the vagina become lax, the organs that they should be supporting bulge into the vagina. As an air-cardinal sign, Libra diseases are adaptive, infectious and acute and may strike suddenly and painfully, like cystitis.

▲ Psychology	balance	Uric acid	balance problems	Hyper-uricaemia
Mental imbalance and manipulations	*Sacral*	Urinary tract	Tinnitus	Kidney infection
	Sex relations	Urine	Vertigo	Kidney stones
	Base	▲ Disease	*Solar plexus*	Lumbago
▲ Body	Adrenal-cortex	*Ajna and Throat*	Diabetes	Nephritis
Ajna	Aldosterone		*Base*	Prolapses
Balance, equilibrium via pituitary	Bladder	Balance, all problems of	Addison's disease	Sciatica
Homeostasis via pituitary	Cortisol	Labyrinthitis	Bright's disease	Urinary tract infections
	Kidneys	Meniere's disease	Cushing's syndrome	
Regulation,	Urea	Middle ear	Cystitis	
	Ureters			
	Urethra			

- **Ray:** 4.

- **Chakra:**
The Sacral and Base.

- **Planet rulers:**
Exoteric: Mars, Pluto.
Esoteric: Mars.
Hierarchy: Mercury.

- **Personality Keynote:**
Let Maya flourish and let deception rule.

- **Soul Keynote:**
Warrior I am, and from the battle I emerge triumphant.

In Scorpio, the personality is humbled and brought to grips with the soul; in that sign the personality is "occultly killed and then resurrected into air and light," in order to become from that moment the servant of the soul. [1]

---

[1] Bailey, Alice A; Esoteric Astrology, 145.

8. Scorpio

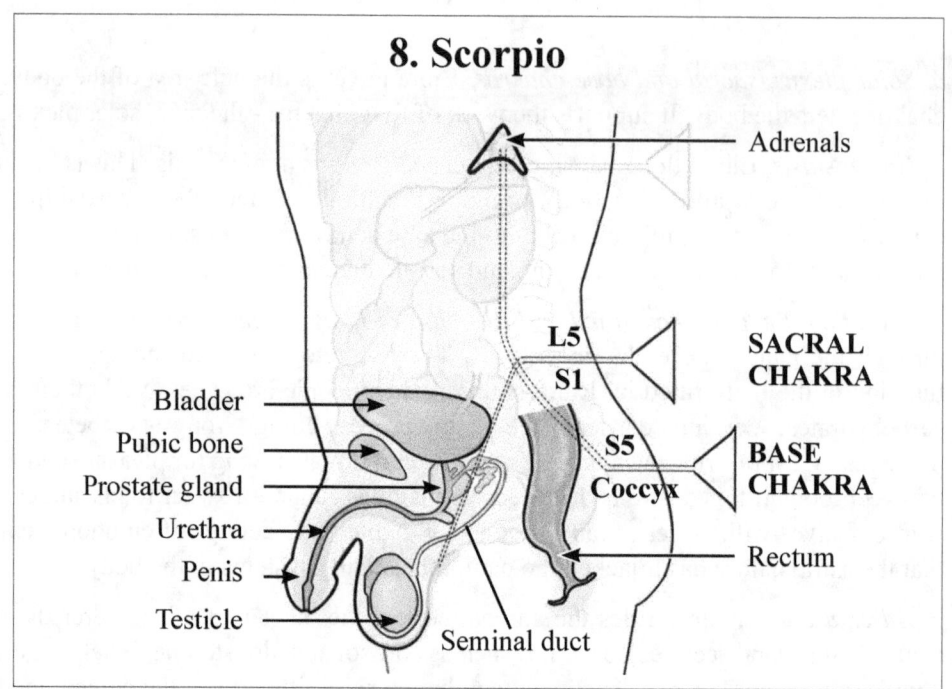

1. Psychology

Scorpio is a fighting sign and for this purpose, it carries only one energy stream - the 4th Ray of Harmony through Conflict, the force that rules warfare. In Scorpio, we are trained to be warriors, because in this sign we are pitted against the deadliest foes we face on the Path of Evolution - astral delusion and lower desire. In Scorpio, we are forced to rise above delusion into the clear light of mind if we are to survive. There we learn to transmute desire into a higher form such as spiritual aspiration.

Hercules, the mythical warrior, portrayed this great test in his battle with the Lernean hydra. The beast had many heads, representing the fact that desire has many forms. Hercules defeated the hydra by lifting it up into the air. The message for us is, when we are confused or feel angry, lift the mind up into the cool light of clear mind and from there assess a situation before acting or speaking. Otherwise, we get mired into the bloodiness and detritus of vindictive combat. Here are some negative Scorpio attitudes that may result in debility and disease:

Aggression, anger, hate	Combativeness
Continual conflict	Holding onto past grievances
Jealousy, envy, covetousness	Maya, self-deceitfulness
Vindictiveness, revengefulness	Violence

2. Body

a. Sacral chakra: it enters the spine around lumbar 5 (L5) and sacral 1 (S1) and is partially ruled by Sagittarius. Scorpio rules its reproductive function.

b. Reproductive glands - the ovaries and testes.
The sacral governs sex and reproduction. Scorpio is the overall ruler of sex, the sex glands and the organs and processes of reproduction. Sagittarius generates the physical force powering sex.

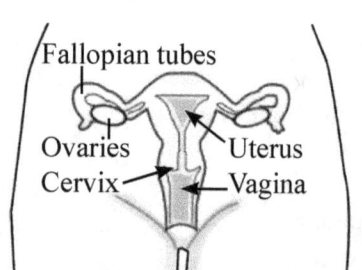

c. Adrenal medulla and the "fight or flight" reaction. The medulla, the inner part of the adrenal gland gives us the urge to live and to survive. This is a ray 1 attribute carried by Scorpio's rulers Pluto and Mars. It produces the hormone adrenaline in response to stress, which increases our heart rate and blood flow to the muscles and brain so that we can respond quickly to perceived danger, physical or non-physical.

d. Elimination of body waste. Scorpio is the traditional ruler of the excretory organs and of excretion - the elimination of waste from the body; particularly solid waste, faeces, which is the end of the gastrointestinal process. Scorpio is also a back-up ruler of the urinary system after Libra.

3. Disease

- Diseases of sexual performance, reproduction and excretion.

Scorpio natives who lack inner stability are riddled with inner conflict. This is a consequence of the 4th ray. Its force oscillates, causing mental and emotional swings. Over time, this conflict grinds down vitality, undermining the immune system and rendering the body open to attack from any passing epidemic. Influenza is a primary example.

Promiscuity and licentiousness in early primitive man gave rise to sexually transmitted diseases and the syphilitic miasm is imprinted in our DNA. In some cases, this may emerge as dementia because there is a connection between the sex organs and the brain. Even if we have not contracted a syphilitic disease in this incarnation, given the right circumstances and because of karma, dementia could manifest due to this taint.

> .. the breaking down of brain tissue [many such diseases] are definitely syphilitic in origin.. the physical sex organs are a lower correspondence of the negative-positive relation existing in the brain between the two head centres and the pituitary and pineal glands.[1]

Scorpio is a fixed-water sign, bringing sluggish and damp conditions that are slow moving, chronic and hard to move. If we hold onto the past, old issues and hurts, the reflex action upon the body thickens body fluids causing phlegm and problems with other body fluids. If we harbour anger and vengeance, it poisons the blood, erupting as nasty skin conditions.

▲ **Psychology**
Incest
Masochism
Paedophilia
Serial killer
Sexual promiscuity, addiction
Sexual: rape, perversions, murder, sadism

▲ **Body**
Crown
Death

Solar plexus
Anus
Bowel
Colon
Defecation
Excretion, solid waste
Faeces
Intestines
Rectum

Sacral
Clitoris
Conception
Cowper's glands
Epididymis
Fertility
Genitals
Labia
Libido
Menstruation
Penis
Procreation
Prostate gland
Puberty
Pubis
Reproduction
Scrotum
Semen
Seminal vesicle
Sex hormones, organs
Sex life
Sexual development
Sigmoid flexure
Sperm
Testes
Testicles
Testosterone
Vagina
Vans deferens
Vulva

Base
Adrenal-cortex
Adrenaline
Adrenal-medulla
Aldosterone
Bladder
Cortisol
Fight or flight
Kidneys
Pubic bone
Survival instinct
Urea
Ureters
Urethra
Uric acid
Urinary tract
Urine
Will to live, to exist

▲ **Disease**
Crown
Death

Throat
Asphyxia
Strangulation
Suffocation

Solar plexus
Anal fissure
Colitis
Constipation
Crohn's disease
Diarrhoea
Diverticulitis
Dysentery
Haemorrhoids
Irritable bowel syndrome
Piles

Sacral
Abortion
Castration
Chlamydia
Frigidity
Genital disorders, warts
Gonorrhea
Herpes, genital
Immorality
Impotency
Infertility
Miscarriage
Premature ejaculation
Prostate trouble
Pubic, crabs
Sexual license
Social diseases
STD: sexually transmitted diseases
Sterility
Syphilis
Venereal disease

Base
Addison's disease
Bright's disease
Cushing's syndrome
Cystitis
Fatigue: adrenal overload
Fistula
Hernia
Hyper-uricaemia
Kidney infection
Kidney stones
Murder
Nephritis
Urinary tract infections

---
1 Bailey, Alice A; Esoteric Healing, 316.

- **Rays:** 4, 5, 6.

- **Chakra:**
The Sacral and Base.

- **Planet rulers:**
Exoteric: Jupiter.
Esoteric: the Earth.
Hierarchy: Mars.

- **Personality Keynote:**
Let food be sought.

- **Soul Keynote:**
I see the goal. I reach the goal and see another.

Hips, thighs, buttocks

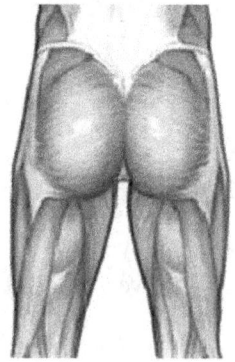

Sagittarius - the ordinary man demonstrates one-pointed selfishness and though he may be, friendly and kind, it is through a desire for popularity. The lessons of life are being learned..

[On the higher cycle] This is now the sign of the one-pointed disciple. The arrow of the mind is projected unerringly towards the goal. [1]

---

1 Bailey, Alice A; Esoteric Astrology, 121.

9. Sagittarius

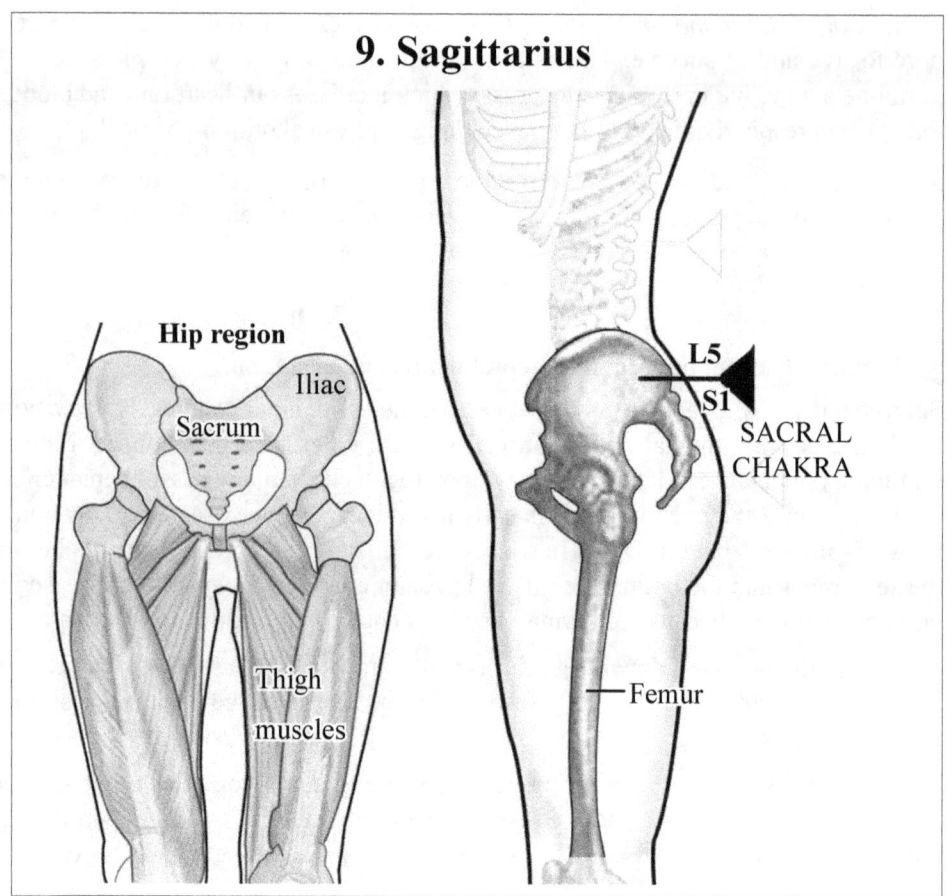

1. Psychology

Three rays flow through Sagittarius and the most powerful to influence the sign is the 6th Ray of Idealism and Devotion. It engenders a desire to find and follow our very highest ideals and consequently, Sagittarius people have an inner urge to "travel far" - physically, mentally or spiritually.

Ray 4 of Harmony and Ray 5 of Concrete Mind also flow through Sagittarius, which accounts for the artistic ray 4 flair demonstrated by many in this sign and their superb ray 5 intellects.

Sagittarius people are friendly and good humoured thanks to ruler Jupiter. But in its lower aspect, it represents their tendency to excess. Here are some negative Sagittarius attitudes that may result in problems or disease.

Exaggeration, extravagance, excess	Gambling addiction
Greed, hedonism	Irresponsible life choices
Pleasure seeking to excess	Predatory behaviours
Rashness, recklessness	Self-gratification
Thoughtlessness	Wastefulness

The first eight signs govern the development of the human psyche or personality - then Sagittarius takes over. It is the sign of discipleship (a process started in Scorpio), and its evolutionary task is to direct those who have reached this level towards the higher spiritual way ruled by the final three signs.

|| *NB. Being born in Sagittarius does not mean we are spiritually advanced. We could be of course, but it takes many cycles around the zodiac, with several incarnations in each sign per cycle, to reach enlightenment. The final three signs represent the tests and trials required to achieve this and all born in these signs receive an aspect of this training as a preparation.*

2. Body

In the physical body, Sagittarius marks a dividing point between the first eight signs, which rule the upper body organs found in the head and torso, and the final three signs - Capricorn, Aquarius and Pisces, which rule parts of the legs. With Sagittarius, these three signs are related to physical movement and locomotion. Esoterically, they symbolise moving forward in time and space, and climbing the Path of Spiritual Evolution.

a. Sacral chakra. This centre is ruled by Sagittarius. It enters the spine around lumbar 5 (L5) and sacral 1 (S1).

b. Physical power and reproduction. A vital function of the sacral centre is to generate physical power and strength for locomotion and sex. Sexual desire is ruled by Scorpio, while Sagittarius generates the physical power that is required to see the sex act through. In this regard, these two signs work together. Sexual performance issues or problems in reproduction could indirectly be a Sagittarius or Jupiter problem. For example obesity, linked to excesses that are associated with this sign and its ruler Jupiter, has a degrading effect upon sexual performance, fertility, semen and egg ovum health.

c. Hips, thighs, buttocks and locomotion: these parts of the body when strong and healthy give us ease of movement.

Greek sculpture depicting movement

3. Disease

- Diseases of excess.
- Diseases or problems with movement, mobility.

Ruler Jupiter continually wants to expand and include and this works positively in relationships via the heart chakra. But when it works through the solar plexus and sacral chakras, the lower appetites are stimulated. The keynote for average man struggling in this sign is "Let food be sought". This can manifest as over-eating and drinking at one end of the scale, to serious criminal, sexual abuse at the other. There is a predatory side to Sagittarius when its energy is misused, due to its association with the sacral chakra.

Afflictions to Jupiter or to planets in Sagittarius can represent problems with mobility. Psychologically, a fear of moving forward in life may contribute to impairment in movement. This sign also rules horses and horse riding, and horse-riding accidents come under Sagittarius.

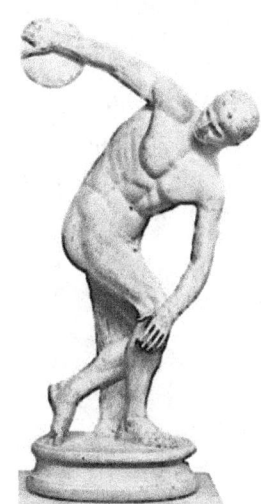

Pegasus, mythical flying horse

A centaur archer

▲ **Psychology**
The mind and life actions being controlled by the lower appetites, especially sexual desire.

▲ **Body**
<u>Throat</u>
Tubes, body

<u>Sacral</u>
Locomotion
Movement
Physical power and strength.
Protective power
Sexual power

<u>Base</u>
Buttocks
Coccyx - tailbone
Femur
Gluteus muscles
Hamstrings
Hips
Ilium
Ischium
Pelvic girdle
Pubis
Quadriceps muscles
Sacroiliac joint
Sacrum
Sciatic nerve
Thighs

▲ **Disease**
Horse riding injuries.

<u>Sacral</u>
Locomotive disorders

<u>Base</u>
Bone fractures: shoulders, arms, hands; hips, thighs
Crippled
Dysplasia of the hip
Hip disease
Limping
Sciatica
Thigh injuries

- **Rays:** 1, 3, 7.

- **Chakra:**
The Base.

- **Planet rulers:**
Exoteric: Saturn.
Esoteric: Saturn.
Hierarchy: Venus.

- **Personality Keynote:**
Let ambition rule and the door stand wide.

- **Soul Keynote:**
Lost am I in light supernal, yet on that light I turn my back.

Skeleton, knees

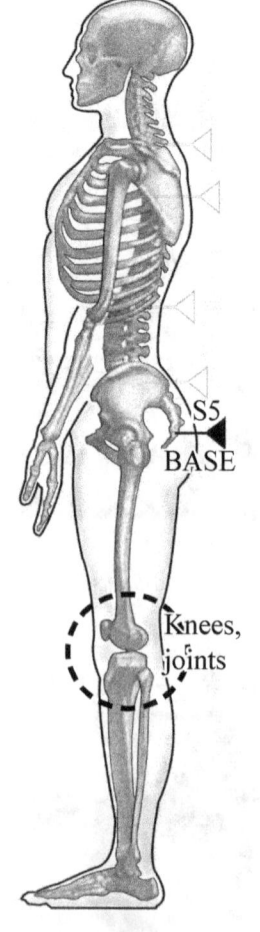

10. Capricorn

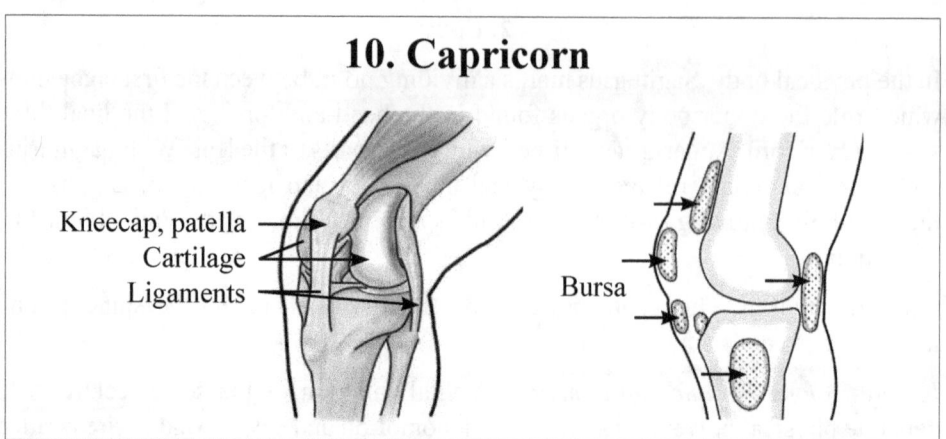

1. Psychology

Capricorn culminates the work of the previous two earth signs Taurus and Virgo. It teaches us to use desire (Taurus) and discrimination (Virgo) to realise ambition (Capricorn). In Capricorn, we acquire power and influence, then later we learn to handle power wisely and with humility.

Psychologically, integrated Capricorn people are very strong in character due to their rays. The two power rays 1 and 7 give a strong will, ambition and manifesting power. The 3rd ray gives intelligence and a native cunning, and through ruler Saturn, stability and an outlook of life that is prudent.

The lower man is ruled by the injunction "Let ambition rule and let the door stand wide". The 3rd ray tendency to manoeuvre and manipulate for profit and gain leads him straight through the doorway of deep materialism. Amongst all the twelve signs, the deepest venality is seen amongst people born in this sign. In some cases, this produces white collar criminals, people who are highly skilled at defrauding and cheating others. Here are some negative Capricorn attitudes that may result in trouble or physical disease:

Ambition that is ruthless	Arrogance
Avarice and greed	Cruelty, lacking pity
Insensitivity, coldness, hardness	Manipulation, deviousness
Overwhelming pride	Power hungry
Rigid orderliness	Ruthless ambition
Self-aggrandising	Wilfulness

In this sign, we climb the mountain of materiality, then very much later after many cycles around the zodiac we climb the mountain of spirituality. Capricorn is the sign of initiation and after having passed all the tests of karma, eventually we reach enlightenment where consciousness is fully illumined with soul love and light. This Jesus portrayed on the Mount of Transfiguration.

2. Body

a. The base chakra: it enters the spine between sacral 5 (S5) and the top of the coccyx or tailbone. Capricorn supports the base chakra's task of building and maintaining the entire dense physical body. However, remember that each chakra has first rulership over the organs in the region it rules.

b. Dense physical body, skeleton, bones, joints and knees. Ray 3 governs the dense physical body, rays 1 and 7 govern the skeleton and Capricorn carries these three rays. It governs the main-frame rigid skeleton and bony structure of the body, and the tendons, ligaments, cartilage and muscles that tie it together and give it its durability and strength.

Capricorn's specific area of rulership is the knee. When healthy, the knees give flexible rotation between the upper and lower leg. They are essential for ease in walking, running, sitting and standing. A stiff, unbending attitude (a negative Saturn attitude), will eventually manifest as stiffness in the knees and an inability to move without pain. A spiritual goal in Capricorn is to learn to kneel in humility.

> .. with his knees upon the rocky mountain top [his job is] to offer his heart and life to the soul and to human service. [1]

c. Skin and hair: Capricorn's rulership of the physical body includes the integumentary system - the teeth, skin, hair, nails and exocrine glands that protect the body from various kinds of external damage, wear and tear.

Knee muscles, tendons

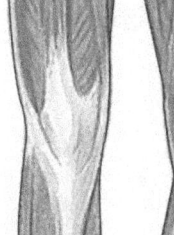

Arthritic knee

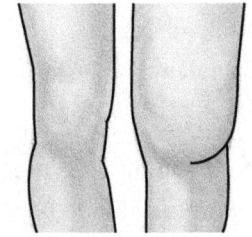

3. Disease

- Diseases of the body structure, the skin and knees.

Unbending pride, hard thoughts and attitudes lead to crystallisation, to a hardening in the body generally, to the atrophying of organs and joints. The body ages prematurely, organs shrivel, movement is restricted, bones dry out and the skin wrinkles. Any problems or diseases with the structure of the body and the parts that tie it together such as ligaments, membranes and skin are associated with Capricorn and Saturn.

Mean-spiritedness affects the heart, hardens its walls and causes failure of its function. Selfish manoeuvring and manipulating via ray 3, leads to gastric and intestinal disorders, certain brain disorders and low vitality.

▲ **Psychology**
A mind and life controlled by avarice.

▲ **Body**

Base
Birthmark
Body intelligence
Bone marrow
Bones
Calcium
Cartilage, connective tissue
Coccyx - tailbone
Collagen
Enamel
Flesh
Hair
Integumentary system
Joints
Knees
Leg bones
Ligaments
Membranes
Moles, skin
Nails
Old age
Patella
Peritoneum
Physical body
Pleurae
Protein
Ribs
Rigor mortis
Sacroiliac joint
Skeleton
Skin
Substance
Teeth
Tendons
Tissue, flesh
Vertebrae, all

▲ **Disease**

Crown
Meningitis

Ajna
Achondroplasia
Dwarfism
Growth stunted

Solar plexus
Hypochondria

Base
Aches intense
Ageing unnaturally
Arthritis
Attrition
Back pain
Bone: deformities, crippling
Bursitis
Calcification
Cervical osteoarthritis
Chronic diseases
Constrictions
Crippled
Deformity
Dental problems
Dermatitis
Eczema
Fractures, bones
Geriatric
Gingivitis, pyorrhea
Hardening, stiffening
Impetigo
Joints stiff
Knee problems
Leprosy
Lesions
Limping
Osteoarthritis
Osteoporosis
Paget's disease
Progeria
Rashes
Rheumatism
Rickets
Scabies
Scleroderma
Sclerosis
Scoliosis
Scurvy
Skin eruptions
Spina bifida
Stiffness
Stones
Toothache
Underactive, undeveloped organ
Vertebrae degeneration
Warts
Wrinkles

Capricorn crystallises.. it is an earth sign, and in it we the densest point of concrete materialisation of which the human soul is capable.. When crystallisation has reached a certain "hardness," it is easily shattered and destroyed and man, born in Capricorn, then brings about his own destruction due to his fundamentally materialistic nature, plus the "blows of fate" which are the enactments of the law of karma.

Effort, strain, struggle, the fight with the forces native to the underworld, or the strenuous conditions entailed by the tests of discipleship or initiation—these are distinctive of experience in Capricorn. [1]

---

1 Bailey, Alice A: Esoteric Astrology, 169.

1 Bailey, Alice A; Esoteric Astrology, 158

11. Aquarius

- **Ray:** 5.

- **Chakra:**
The Sacral and Base.

- **Planet rulers:**
Exoteric: Uranus.
Esoteric: Jupiter.
Hierarchy: Moon veiling Uranus.

- **Personality Keynote:**
Let desire in form be ruler.

- **Soul Keynote:**
Water of life am I, poured forth for thirsty men.

Lower legs and ankles

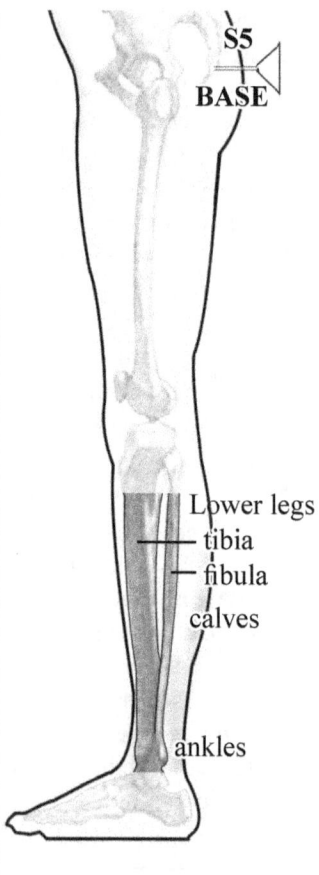

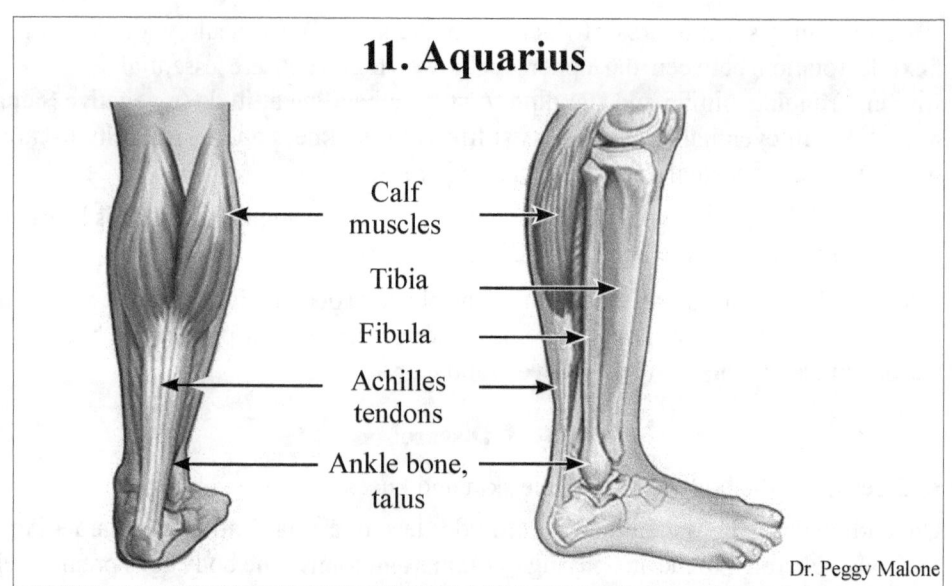

Dr. Peggy Malone

1. Psychology

The 5th Ray of Concrete Mind and Science flows through Aquarius. Its people are the purest examples of the developed concrete mind, the fact finding, knowledge gathering mind. People who have their Sun, ascendant, Mercury or Venus in this sign are often cerebral thinkers.

The higher evolutionary task of Aquarius, the Water-Bearer (another name for the Christ), is to teach us to combine the activities of the mind with the heart, to use the mind as a vessel for love and wisdom. When successful, we see great scientific and social reformers such as Abraham Lincoln who had an Aquarian Sun. On the negative side, Aquarius produces people who use their mental powers for their own personal and selfish gain. Here are some Aquarius attitudes that may result in disease:

Coldly unsympathetic	Dogmatic
Fixed, inflexible mind	Ultra-critical
Lacking emotional warmth	Mentally aloof, isolated
Narrow, closed mind	Selfish individualism
Sense of alienation	Separativeness

2. Body

a. The heart chakra. Aquarius is related to the heart centre via its opposite sign and partner Leo. It is also related to the base chakra, through its rulership of the lower legs and ankles.

b. Etheric body. The physical etheric web anchors in the sacral chakra, which is governed by Uranus. Aquarius rules the ethers, relating it also to the etheric body. Both the etheric body and Aquarius have as their goal the free distribution of energy: the etheric web is the medium that connects us into the whole and Aquarius represents universal consciousness. Consequently, Aquarius shares rulership of the web with Gemini.

c. DNA (deoxyribonucleic acid). The basic energy pattern of the physical body is recorded in the physical permanent atom, which is etheric in nature and located on the 1st subplane of the Physical Plane. This pattern is replicated in our DNA, which science has proven to be the carrier of genetic information inherited from our forefathers - and from our own previous incarnations.

Aquarius is connected with the physical permanent atom, which is on the etheric level, [1] giving it rulership over DNA.

There is an obvious connection between DNA and karma. Karmic law brings forward our past imperfections for resolution in the present. So any physical body imperfections that we have to deal with are recorded in our DNA. There are equivalent permanent (DNA) atoms on the emotional and mental planes that record our psychological patterns.

d. Blood circulation. Aquarius rules the circulation of blood and blood quality. When these are amiss, Aquarius and Uranus are often involved.

e. Nervous system. Aquarius - through the 5th ray, supports the work of the ajna chakra in its management of the nervous system. It is often implicated when there is nerve damage. Nervous disorders usually involve Aquarius' 5th ray, in conflict with the 6th emotional ray - Venus and Aquarius in conflict with Mars and Neptune. All nervous disorders have at their basis, emotional discord.

f. Calves, ankles. Aquarius rules the calves and ankles, which enable stretching and bending. They also propel the body forward into space and this forward progress is a physical correlation with the forward progression of the spiritually mature Aquarian who is a world server – the Water Bearer.

3. Disease

- Diseases of the lower legs and nervous system.

The Aquarius trait that most often lies at the root of their troubles and diseases is their habit of "living in an ivory tower". This refers to their tendency to separate themselves off from others by dwelling singularly in a world of thought they have created. In such isolation, amongst the concepts and ideals they hold to be most worthy, they judge other people for failing to measure up. This separation in thought is a cleavage problem, a lower 5th ray trait that underlies many modern "dissociative" disorders that occur today. Aquarius is not the only sign that generates this problem. Anyone who has the discriminating 5th ray mind can succumb if they do not love their fellow men.

Cleavage causes physical trouble. Organs and systems that should work harmoniously together begin to break down. For instance, the endocrine glands may start to send incorrect messages so that glands malfunction or release toxic chemicals. Another 5th ray problem is migraine, which is caused by a lack of relationship between the energies of the pineal and pituitary glands.

▲ **Psychology**
Cleavages, dissociative disorders

▲ **Body**
Heart
Blood circulation, quality
Cardiovascular system

Sacral
Chromosome
DNA

Etheric body
Gene, genetics
Physical permanent atom

Base
Ankles
Calves
Fibula
Limbs, lower
Tibia

▲ **Disease**
Crown
Brain lesion

Ajna
Headaches
Migraine

Heart
Anaemia
Angina
Blood cancer
Blood circulation problems
Deep vein thrombosis
Gangrene
Leukaemia: blood cancer

Reynaud's disease
Varicose veins

Sacral
Congenital diseases
Gene mutation
Genetic diseases

Base
Ankle problems
Calf problems

DNA

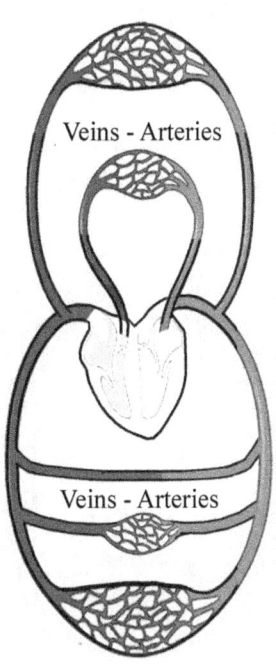
Blood Circulation

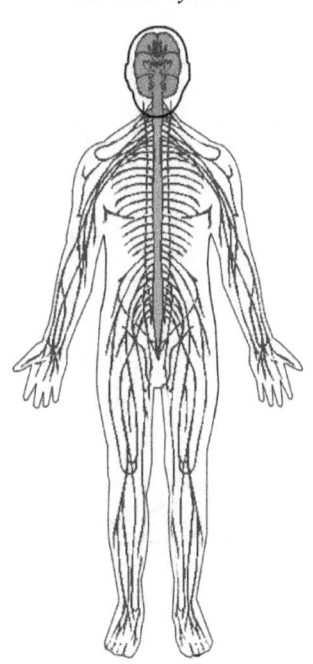
Nervous system

---
1 Bailey, Alice A: Esoteric Astrology. 303.

- **Rays:** 2 and 6.

- **Chakra:**
The Base.

- **Planet rulers:**
Exoteric: Jupiter and Neptune.
Esoteric: Pluto.
Hierarchy: Pluto.

- **Personality Keynote:**
Go forth into matter.

- **Soul Keynote:**
I leave the Father's Home and turning back, I save.

Pisces rules the feet

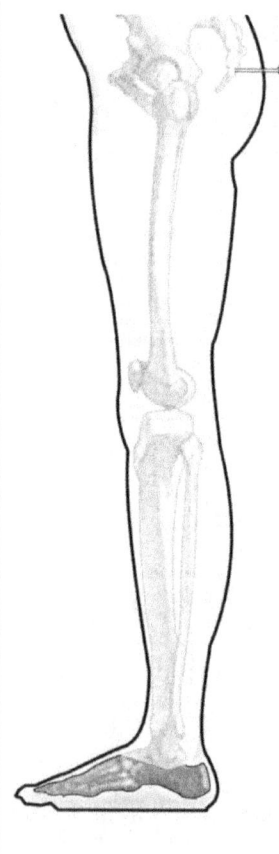

12. Pisces
Bones

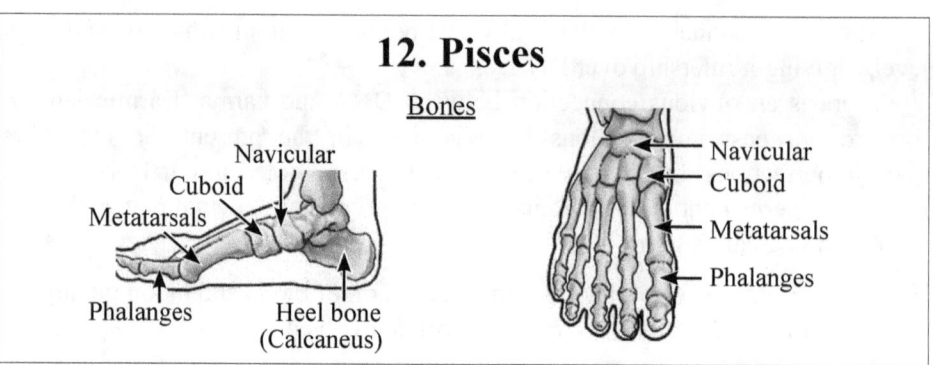

1. Psychology

The average person born in a water sign is very susceptible to the psychological condition called glamour. This arises from the effects of the 6th Ray, the force of the Astral Plane, which Pisces happens to carry. The astral world is called the plane of delusion, because when its force dominates and discrimination has not been developed, its hazy or glamorous effect distorts perception. Those who are affected see and believe whatever they want to see and believe.

Pisces also carries the 2nd ray. In average man, it pours out through the solar plexus chakra as a boundless desire for feel-good experiences. This can lead to over-eating, uncontrolled drinking and all manner of over-indulging so that the body gets fat or unhealthy. Here are some negative Pisces attitudes that may contribute to disease:

Addictive susceptibility	Emotionalism, glamour
Escapism	Fanaticism
Hyper-sensitive, impressionable	Martyr complex
Naivety, guilelessness	One-eyed
Self-deception	Victim consciousness

The higher evolutionary task of Pisces is to transmute emotion into inclusive love, a 2nd Ray quality; then to radiate love-wisdom out into the world in service. This is the ultimate goal in this sign of the World Saviour.

2. Body

a. The base chakra. Pisces is related mostly to the base centre, which rules the feet. But it is also related to the heart chakra via Neptune, which rules the bloodstream and to the throat chakra, which rules the lymphatic system.

b. Feet. Pisces rules the lowest part of the body, the feet and toes. Metaphorically, there is a parallel between world saviours and the feet. Just as the feet or Pisces carry the heavy load of the entire human body, world saviours carry the heavy load of human suffering and karma.

c. Body fluids. Water signs Cancer, Scorpio and Pisces are related to the secretions and liquids in the physical body. Neptune has general rulership over body fluids with the Moon and may for instance show up in the chart for problems like oedema or excess phlegm.

d. Sleep state. In the hours of sleep, consciousness slips away to the Astral Plane, which is ruled by Neptune. This relates the sleep state to Pisces.

f. Cyclic waterways in the body, the lymphatic systems. This system is the body's sewerage system. It is governed by the throat chakra, which rules excretion generally as the end part of digestion. The lymphatic system includes the tonsils, adenoids, bone marrow, spleen, thymus, appendix, lymph nodes and vessels.

The cleansing of dead cells and tissue waste from the body by washing clear watery fluid (lymph) through its tubes is the vital task carried out by the lymphatic system. Helped by valves and muscular contractions, this flow moves directionally always towards the heart. The system interacts with blood circulation by draining plasma from tissue and cells and returning interstitial fluid to the blood via the subclavian veins beneath the base of the neck. In the accompanying diagram, this point is shown in the small circle at the base of the neck. The main central "drain" of this system is the thoracic duct. Cancer, Pisces, Neptune and the Moon rule the lymphatic system.

To assist the immune system, white blood cells circulate through the lymphatic system. Some are stored in the lymph nodes and as lymph passes through, they attack and destroy any germs that may be present. Cancer and the Moon rule white blood cells and the lymphatic system in its cell-breeding and immunity aspect.

3. Disease

- Psychological troubles caused by emotionalism.
- Diseases of the feet and toes.
- Diseases of the lymphatic system and bloodstream.

Pisces rules the oceans via Neptune, which in our psychology represents the world of the emotions. Trying to escape emotional pain through mind-altering substances such as alcohol or drugs is prolific in Pisces and Cancer. When Pisces people play "the victim" and drown in self-pity, this leads to excess phlegm, colds, flu and problems with body fluids like oedema. Stagnant and contaminated water is a breeding ground for germs.

The 2nd ray flows through Pisces and when dysfunctional can cause overstimulation of cells so that they pile together and overbuild, resulting in fatness and more insidiously, tumours and cancer.

The deceiving action of ray 6 is implicated in carcinogenicity, which undermines cell life. Neurodegenerative diseases such as dementia and Alzheimer's that are due to brain fluid atrophy may be indicated by serious Neptune or Moon afflictions.

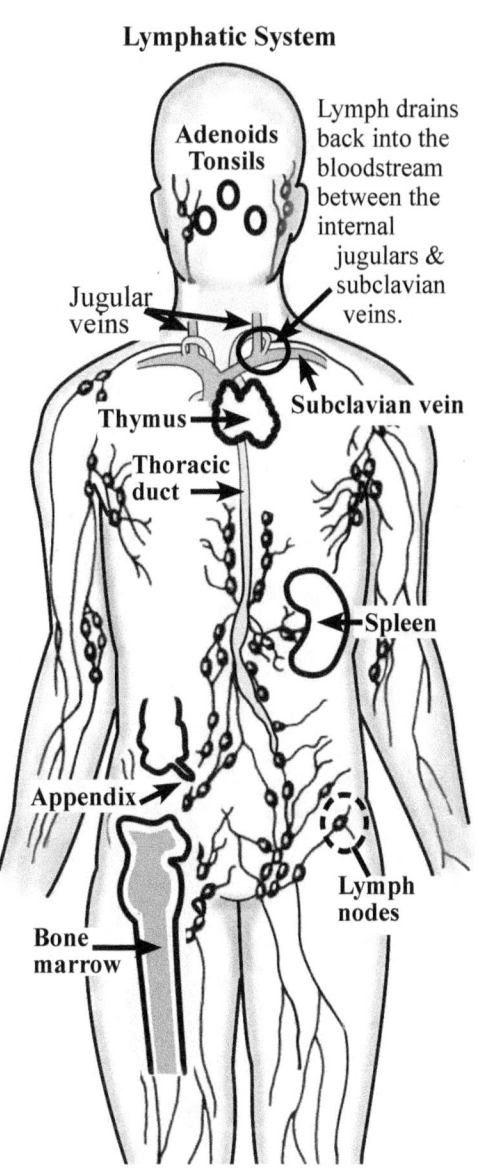

Lymphatic System

▲ **Psychology**
Alcoholism
Borderline personality disorder
Cuts, cutting
Delirium, delusory
Dreams, troubled
Glamour
Hallucination
Hysteria
Neurotics, neuroses
Obscure diseases due to emotionalism
Obsessive compulsive
Panic attacks
Paranoia
Phobias
PTSD
Schizophrenia
Self-harm, self-injury
Sleep-walking
Substance abuse

▲ **Body**
Anaesthetics
Body fluids
Watery systems in the body

Throat
Lymph, nodes
Lymphatic system
Thoracic duct

Base
Feet
Toes

▲ **Disease**
Hidden, obscure disorders
Misdiagnosis

Throat
Buboes, plague
Drowns, drowning
Epstein–Barr virus
Glandular fever, swellings
Hodgkin's disease
Lymphoma
Mononucleosis

Solar plexus
Carcinogenic
Cystic fibrosis
Cysts
Diseases caused by excess
Drug addiction
Fatness, obesity
Flabbiness
Gluttony
Growths, abnormal
Hallucinatory, recreational drugs
Hypertrophy
Mucus
Narcolepsy
Nightmares
Obesity
Oedema
Phlegm
Polyps
Sluggish action of organs
Swellings
Water retention
Weight gain

Base
Bunions
Feet problems
Gout

2c. Astrology Planets

The planets are the transmitting agents of the Seven Rays.

- **Ray:** 2.

- **Chakra:**
The Heart.

- **Sign rulerships:**
Exoteric: Leo.
Esoteric: Leo.
Hierarchy: Leo.

Solar vitality

Cell life

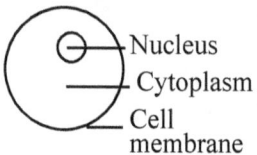

Immune System

Heart and cardiovascular system

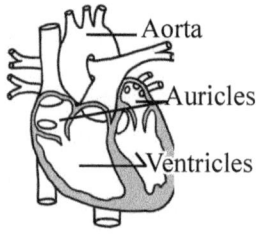

Spine, eyes

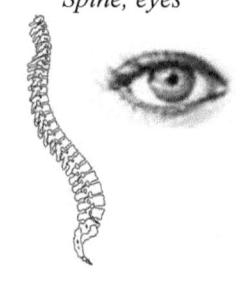

1. The Sun

1. Psychology

The Sun carries the 1st ray of assertiveness via Leo and the 2nd ray of Wisdom. Ray 2 is the "consciousness" or sentient ray that enables us to develop a sense of self, or "I-ness". The Sun represents personality consciousness, the power of the individual "I" and its ability or inability to dominate the environment. Personality power hinges upon the level to which we have integrated our personality parts - mind, emotional, physical; and have brought them under the control of the central "I" self. When the personality is fully developed the soul fights to bring our consciousness under its control. When successful, the Sun then represents the expression of radiant soul love and wisdom.

Developing a strong and healthy ego is an important milestone on our spiritual journey. It is represented by the arrogant, proud and strutting lion, the symbol of Leo. Here are some negative attitudes that cause trouble:

Egomania	Extreme self-will
Pride	Narcissism, egoism, extreme self-love

2. Body

a. The Heart chakra. It enters the body in the Leo-Sun ruled region of the body, anchoring in the thymus gland.

b. The thymus gland. Its main function is to support the immune system. To this end it develops T-lymphocytes, powerful killer immune cells.

c. Vitalising of the body and the immune system. Two major streams of energy vitalise the physical body. The first is the dynamic stream of life we receive from the soul via the sutratma that anchors in the heart. A smaller pranic stream from the Sun enters via the spleen where it rises to the heart and merges with the life stream as it enters the blood.

The Sun's energy is prophylactic - it kills all germs and frees from disease. This activity is reflected in the body by the immune system, which the Sun governs. It is a subset of the cardiovascular system and uses blood vessels to send out its army of white defender cells to fight infection.

d. The spleen, the organ of vitality. The spleen chakra and its physical counterpart the spleen organ are the primary receivers and distributors of pranic vitality. The spleen chakra receives vitality from the Sun, sends it to the spleen organ, which then sends it to the heart. A second important function of the spleen is to support the immune system by filtering dead cells and waste from the blood and storing white blood cells to fight disease. The spleen serves the physical form and is not included in the list of major seven chakras because it is not connected with the evolution of consciousness.

e. Cardiovascular system: it includes the heart organ, arteries, capillaries, veins, blood and bloodstream. The heart plays a similar role in our physical system as the sun does in the solar system. It distributes life, vitality and nourishment to every cell in the body through blood circulation. When considered esoterically, the two types of blood channels (arteries and veins) are reflections in the body of the involutionary Path of Outgoing and the evolutionary Path of Return. All souls travel these paths, go out to explore desire on the red path and return to the Source on the blue path.

Mars represents the prodigal son who, full of blood and life, leaves the father's house to experience the sensual pleasures of the material world. Mars' colour is red, it governs red blood cells, passion and desire. Venus is Mars' opposite and its colour is indigo blue. It rules the blue Path of Return and the less muscular veins that return deoxygenated blood to the heart. At its highest, Venus represents the human soul who, having exhausted lower desire returns to its spiritual source.

f. The eyes: we are able to see because of the light of the Sun. It is related to vision, to the eyes - particularly the right eye, and to eye health.

3. Disease

A well placed and well aspected Sun in the natal chart promotes a positive psychological outlook on life and is the most positive indicator of good health. It indicates a heart that has an excellent ability to absorb prana, thus vitalising cell life and boosting the power of the immune system. Easy aspects to the Sun from Mars and Jupiter boost vitality. This is because the brute animal strength of Mars and the expansive power of Jupiter, support, promote and strengthen the Sun's power. Even hard aspects (square, semi-square, opposition, conjunction) are better than none. In this case, energy is available, though if misused can lead to burn-out.

Afflictions to the Sun indicate heart and circulation problems, depletion of vitality and lowered resistance to disease. The Sun sign often points to a part of the body that will suffer if vitality or immunity should falter. Sometimes solar function is potentially impaired if the Sun is in Virgo, Pisces, or the sixth and twelfth houses, which govern illness and hospitalisation. This does not mean that illness naturally follows such placements; there may be other compensating factors in the chart. What it does mean is that attention should be given to diet, exercise and living a moderate lifestyle to help strengthen vitality and health.

In disease, the 2nd ray that flows through the Sun produces overstimulation and an over-production of atoms that show as growths, tumours, cancer, organs that are too big etc.

Interestingly, germs are living organisms that find their way into the human mechanism through the medium of the life force, which in its turn, uses the heart and the bloodstream as its agents of distribution.

▲ **Psychology**
Egomania
Megalomania

▲ **Body**
Ajna
Cornea
Eye lens
Eyes
Iris
Pupils
Retina
Sclera
Self-consciousness
Sentiency
Sight
Vision

Heart
Aorta
Arteries
Blood
Blood circulation,
quality
Bloodstream
Capillaries
Cardiovascular system
Cell life
Constitution
Haemoglobin
Heart.
Immune system
Iron in the blood
Leukocytes
Life-force, soul energy
Life-thread/ stream, sutratma, silver cord
Pericardium
Plasma
Prana
Recuperative power
Red blood cells
Spleen
Stem cells
Thymus
Valves - heart
Veins
Vena Cava
Venous system
Vitality (solar fire)
Vitamin A
Vitamin D3, sunshine vitamin

Base
Spinal column, spine
Vertebrae, all

▲ **Disease**
Crown
Arrested development
Meningitis

Ajna
Astigmatism
Blindness
Cataracts
Conjunctivitis
Glaucoma
Keratitis
Multiple sclerosis
Myopia
Short sighted

Heart
AIDS
Allergic reaction from immune
Anaemia
Aneurism
Angina
Arrhythmia
Arterio-sclerosis
Atrial fibrillation
Autoimmune diseases
Blood cancer
Blood circulation problems
Bruises
Cardio-myopathy
Ebola virus
Fainting
Fever
Gangrene
Heart fibrillation
Heart attack
Heart disease
Heart problem, congenital
High blood pressure
High temperature
Hypertension
Hypotension
Immune attack
Inflammation
Lupus
Myasthenia gravis
Myocarditis
Overgrowth
Palpitations
Shock
Sunburn
Sunstroke

Solar plexus
Cancer: all body organs
Tumours, growths

Base
Ankylosis spondylosis
Back pain
Extra body parts
Rheumatic fever
Rheumatoid arthritis
Scoliosis
Spina bifida
Spinal fractures
Vertebrae degeneration

- **Ray: 4.**

- **Chakra:**

The Solar Plexus; the Moon is also related to the Sacral for reproduction

- **Sign rulerships:**

Exoteric: Cancer.
Esoteric: Virgo.
Hierarchy: Aquarius.

Women

Motherhood, babies

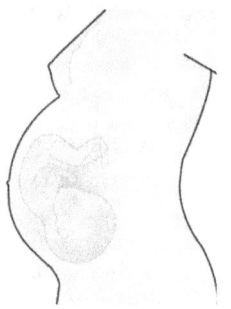

Ovaries, womb

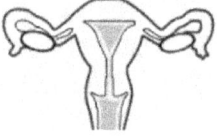

Body tissue

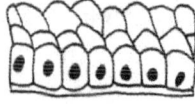

Body fluid

2. The Moon

Esoterically, the Moon is considered a dead planet with no life of its own. However, it retains a powerful influence over humanity because it orbits within the Earth's atmosphere and continually sweeps its force over us affecting our astral nature. It carries the 4th ray and in the chart represents conflict, internal and with the environment.

1. Psychology

In our psychology, the Moon represents unresolved emotional baggage that we have brought from past lives into the new incarnation. These are hidden in the unconscious as negative core beliefs. The most important task we can do in our personal development is to transform the Moon sign negatives because they keep us locked to the past and prevent us from moving forward. These negative beliefs emerge automatically when we feel afraid, causing us to defend ourselves as we would if we were a child, in irrational and inappropriate ways. For this reason, always examine the Moon for potential emotional disturbances that could lead to a health issue. Here are some negative attitudes associated with the Moon that can lead to disease.

Agonising over issues	Conflicted, torn within
Anxiety, emotionalism	Fear, deep and primeval
Living always in the past	Worry, agitation, inner suffering

When the lunar pattern has been healed, then the Moon in the chart represents our ability to harmonise, to balance and to bring peace to troubled waters.

2. Body

a. The solar plexus chakra: this centre enters the body in the Cancer ruled region, relating the Moon to the function and organs ruled by this chakra.

b. The physical body, flesh and tissue. The Moon is the "mother of form" and with Cancer and ray 3, governs body substance and tissue generally. It governs brain substance and is often prominent when brain tissue breaks down.

c. Digestion. The Moon is related to digestion and all mid-region digestive organs, via Cancer. Afflictions to the Moon show potential digestive troubles.

d. Female gender, female cycles, reproduction and motherhood. Cancer and the Moon rule women, especially mature females, the mother, home and family. They are also closely linked to babies, female organs (ovaries and womb), and functions such as menstruation, conception, pregnancy, gestation and breast-feeding. Hard lunar afflictions in female charts indicate conception, pregnancy and child-raising problems. In all charts, an afflicted Moon represents difficult domestic, family and female relationships.

e. Body fluids, secretions, mucous. Traditionally, the Moon rules white or colourless body fluids such as mucous, lymph and plasma. It also rules pus and phlegm when body fluids become toxic.

f. Lymphatic system, peristalsis. The Sun and Moon are partners, father and mother and both are involved in protecting the physical body from disease. Strong and muscular, he governs the cardiovascular system, using the heart to pump blood around the system. She the Moon, is gentle, co-governs the lymphatic system, using peristaltic waves of contraction to move lymph.

3. Disease

The Moon carries the 4th ray of Harmony through Conflict and in our psychology an afflicted Moon indicates conflict, anxiety, hysteria and stress. These traits debilitate, they wear down the immune system, rendering the body susceptible to epidemics such as influenza. The Moon also carries the 7th ray via Cancer, which is largely responsible for infections and contagious diseases. Consequently, the Moon and Cancer are often implicated in serious disease. An afflicted Moon also shows susceptibility to the indigenous diseases of the planet and of these, cancer is the most dangerous today. Another important point to remember in conjunction with the Moon is that energy circulation through the etheric is governed by the Moon, which means that any hard aspects to the Moon can be read as potential blockages in the etheric, the precursor to disease.

▲ **Psychology**
Alcoholism
Anti-social, dangerous brooders
Anxiety, worry
Bipolar
Borderline personality disorder
Cuts, cutting
Delirium, delusory
Depression
Dreams, troubled
Hallucination
Hysteria
Inner conflict
Manic depression
Mental instability
Mood swings
Neurotics, neuroses
Obsessive compulsive
Panic attacks
Paranoia
Phobias
PTSD
Schizophrenia
Self-harm, self-injury
Sleep-walking
Substance abuse
Trauma, psychological

▲ **Body**
Body fluids
Watery systems in the body

Crown
Brain mass, tissue

Ajna
Eyes

Throat
Lymph, nodes
Lymphatic system
Peristalsis
Sinuses
Thoracic duct

Heart
Stem cells
White blood cells

Solar plexus
Abdomen
Chyle
Digestion
Nutrition
Oesophagus lower
Pancreas
Stomach

Sacral
Babies
Birth
Breasts
Cervix
Conception
Egg ovum
Embryo
Estrogen
Etheric body
Fallopian tubes
Fertility
Gestation
Infancy
Lacteals,
lactation
Maternity
Menstruation
Mothers, mothering
Ovaries
Periods
Placenta
Pregnancy
Procreation
Progesterone
Reproduction
Uterus
Womb

Base
Body containers, sheaths
Body intelligence
Bone marrow
Flesh
Physical body
Secretions
Substance
Tears
Tissue, flesh

▲ **Disease**
Bacterial infection
Contagious infections
Epidemics
Pain and suffering

Crown
Alzheimer's
Brain congenital disorders
Dementia
Huntington's disease
Hydrocephalus
Lewy body dementia
Lunacy
Senile decay

Ajna
Astigmatism
Blindness
Cataracts
Conjunctivitis
Glaucoma
Keratitis
Myopia
Short sighted

Throat
Buboes, plague
Epstein–Barr virus
Glandular fever, swellings
Hodgkin's disease
Lymphoma
Mononucleosis
Sinusitis

Solar plexus
Allergies, digestive
Anorexia
Biliousness
Bulimia
Cancer: all body organs, especially solar plexus organs
Candida
Carcinogenic
Chronic fatigue
Coeliac disease
Cystic fibrosis
Debilitation
Devitalisation
Drug addiction
Dyspepsia
Eating disorders
Fatigue
Flatulence
Food allergies
Food poisoning
Gastric disorders
Immunity low
Indigestion
Lethargy
Metastases
Mucus
Narcolepsy
Nausea
Nightmares
Oedema
Pancreatitis
Peptic ulcer
Peritonitis
Phlegm
Reflux
Sarcoma
Sluggish action of organs
Tissue, insidious changes
Tumours, growths
Vomiting
Water retention
Yeast infection

Sacral
Abortion
Barrenness
Endometriosis
Fibroids in womb
Hereditary diseases
Infertility
Miscarriage
Sterility
Uterine troubles

Base
Athlete's foot
Corpses
Cysts
Dead things
Decay
Fungus, fungi
Melanoma
Ringworm
Thrush
Tinea

- **Ray:** 4.

- **Chakra:**
The Ajna and Throat

- **Sign rulerships:**
Exoteric: Gemini and Virgo.
Esoteric: Aries.
Hierarchy: Scorpio.

Nervous system, arms, hands, fingers

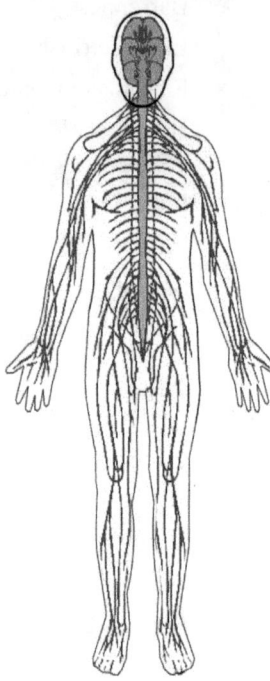

Speech, hearing

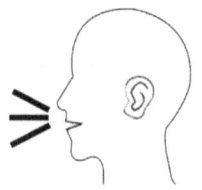

Respiration

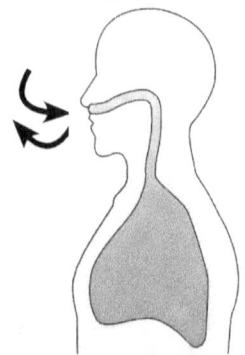

3. Mercury

1. Psychology

Mercury develops our minds and teaches us to think. It gives us curiosity and an urge to know and to understand. Then through formal education and the application of the mind in all manner of life experiences, our mental faculties unfold.

Mercury is the "Messenger of the Gods", shuttling communications back and forth between opposites. This oscillating action is due to its force, ray 4; the force in nature that makes connections between opposite poles. The negative effect of ray 4 causes conflict, mental and emotional. The troubled ray 4 mind is continually at war with itself and projects this disturbance onto others. Such people are always looking for someone to fight with, so they can play out in their external relationships the conflict and drama being experienced within. Constant conflict devitalises the body, opening it up to disease and epidemics. Here are some Mercury negatives that can lead to disease.

Duality	Flightiness, instability
Mind-chatter	Shallowness, being superficial
Trickiness, theft	Worry, agitation, inner suffering

At a higher level Mercury represents the intuitive faculty, pure reason or instant knowing. It is called "the Star of the Intuition". [1]

2. Body

a. Ajna and throat chakras. Mercury governs the ajna with Venus and both planets develop "self-consciousness" which is achieved through these two centres. Mercury rules the antahkarana, [2] also called the consciousness thread. [3] Mercury is also related to the throat chakra, the "speech" centre.

b. Pituitary and thymus glands. As a ruler of the ajna, Mercury is a back-up ruler of the pituitary gland. It is also related to the thymus via Gemini, which rules that gland in disciples and initiates.

c. The nervous system, the brain and spinal cord. Mercury is the messenger and the nervous system is the messaging, signalling and communication system in the body that enables us to become aware and to know. Uranus and Venus are also related to the function of the nervous system.

d. Respiration and airways. Gemini oxygenates the blood and with Mercury governs the bronchial tree and upper lungs.

e. Sound, speech, hearing. Mercury represents the power of speech and governs the organs in the head and throat that are responsible for its production.

f. Intestines. Mercury rules the intestines via Virgo. From the food mass, the intestines discriminate - which nutrients to absorb and which to reject.

g. Tubes in the body. Gemini and Mercury govern transportation and rule tubes in the body that transport substances from one place to another. For example, the alimentary canal that transports food and the fallopian tubes that transport ova.

---

1 Bailey, Alice A; Treatise on Cosmic Fire, 370
2 Bailey, Alice A; Esoteric Astrology, 281
3 Bailey, Alice A; The Rays and the Initiations, 449

h. Shoulders, arms, hands, fingers. These appendages are traditionally ruled by Gemini and Mercury and so is movement. Gemini and its opposite sign of Sagittarius rule movement and mobility.

3. Disease

A good mind/ Mercury is essential for mental and physical health. If the emotional body is more powerful than the mind, if it regularly swamps consciousness with waves of emotional upset and discord this can lead to many of the mental-nervous disorders we see today. Gemini is an air sign and Mercury's diseases primarily affect the airways, the lungs and breathing. Mercury carries the 4th ray, which rules epidemics, and is usually implicated in infectious disease outbreaks such as influenza.

▲ **Psychology**
ADD: attention deficit disorder
ADHD: > hyperactivity disorder
Asperger's
Autism
Bipolar
Conflicted, torn within
Depression
Imbecilities
Insanities
Manic depression, bipolar
Mentally unstable, unpredictable
Mood swings
Negative core beliefs
Past-life soul prison pattern
Psychological troubles
Psychopath
Sociopath
Stalkers
Suicidal thoughts
Trauma, psychological
Worry, agitation, inner suffering

▲ **Body**
Crown
Antahkarana
Cerebral cortex
Consciousness thread
Neocortex
Serotonin

Ajna
Central nervous system
Cerebellum
Cognition
Cornea
Ears
Eye lens
Eyes
Hearing
Hyperactivity
Hypothalamus
Intelligent self-consciousness
Iris
Motor nerves
Nerve fluid
Nerve synapse
Neurons
Pituitary gland
Pupils
Retina
Self-consciousness
Sight
Spinal cord
Spinal fluid
Synapse
Vision

Throat
Airways
Alta-major
Alveoli
Brainstem
Breathing
Bronchial tree
Diaphragm
Ears
Endocrine system
Hearing
Lungs
Medulla oblongata
Pons
Reptilian brain
Respiration
Sinuses
Speech
Thalamus
Trachea
Vocal cords
Windpipe

Heart
Oxygen, oxygenation
Pulmonary circulation
Vagus nerve

Solar plexus
Appendix
Duodenum
Enteric NS
Ileum
Jejunum
Pylorus
Sympathetic NS

Base
Arms, hands, shoulders
Carpal and metacarpal bones
Clavicle
Elbow
Fingers, phalanges
Hands
Humerus
Radius
Scapula
Ulna
Wrist

▲ **Disease**
Contagious infections
Epidemics

Crown
Arrested development
Coma
Insanity, idiocy
Lunacy
Multiple personalities
Possession

Ajna
ALS: amyotrophic lateral sclerosis
Bells Palsy
Cerebral palsy
Deafness
Epilepsy
Guillain-Barre syndrome
Hypo-pituitarism
Labyrinthitis
Lou Gehrig's disease
Meniere's disease
Middle ear balance problems
Motor neurone disease
Multiple sclerosis
Muscle spasms, cramps
Nerve spasms
Neuralgia
Neuro-degenerative diseases
Palsy
Paralysis
Paraplegic, quadriplegic
Parkinson's disease
Polio
Seizures
Shingles
Simmond's disease
Spasms, nerves
Spasticity
Tinnitus
Tourette's syndrome
Tremors
Twitching, tics

Throat
Allergies, breathing
Aphasia
Asthma
Bad breath
Bronchitis
Carpal tunnel syndrome
Chicken pox
Cholera
Colds
Croup
Deafness
Dengue fever
Diphtheria
Dyslexia
Emphysema
Fatigue - thyroid
Influenza
Labyrinthitis
Laryngitis
Learning difficulties
Measles
Meniere's disease
Middle ear balance problems
Nasal congestion
Pleurisy
Pneumonia
Pulmonary tuberculosis
Rubella
Scarlet fever
Sinusitis
Smallpox
Stuttering

Solar plexus
Appendicitis
Chronic fatigue
Colic
Debilitation
Devitalisation
Enteritis
Fatigue
Immunity low
Lethargy
Parasites, intestinal
Tapeworm
Typhoid fever
Worms

Base
Bone fractures: shoulders, arms, hands; hips, thighs

- **Ray:** 5.

- **Chakra:**

The Ajna and Throat; Venus is also related to the Solar Plexus and Sacral chakras

- **Sign rulerships:**

Exoteric: Taurus and Libra.
Esoteric Gemini.
Hierarchy: Capricorn.

Nervous system

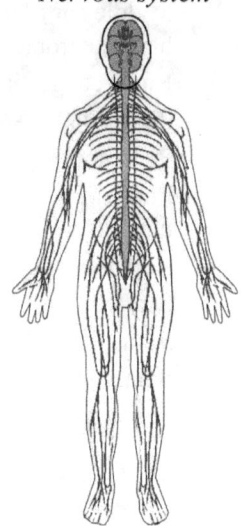

Throat, thyroid

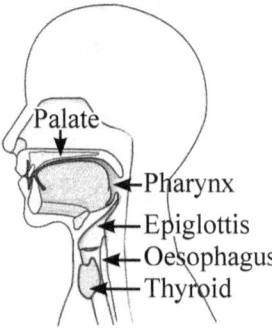

Kidneys, bladder

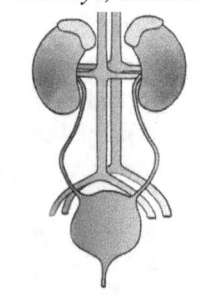

4. Venus

1. Psychology

Venus can be read on several levels, as can all the planets. In average emotional man it works primarily through the sacral chakra where it represents relationship intimacy and sex. It also represents the love of money and material benefit. Venus' force, the 5th Ray of Concrete Mind and Science, working through the ajna, trains us to think accurately and to reason logically. Venus sometimes acts as a substitute for concrete mind. It is involved in the higher mental faculties of comprehension and wise understanding and is a symbol for intelligence. On the highest level, Venus represents the Solar Angel, the guide and mentor of our human soul and of our spiritual development and values.

In the chart, Venus indicates where our thought life needs beautifying, where we should endeavour to think and speak with intelligent love and to radiate soul wisdom. On the negative side, here are some psychological attitudes associated with Venus that can lead to trouble or disease.

Greed	Indolence and laziness
Narcissism, extreme self-love	Pleasure seeking to excess
Unregulated desire	Separativeness (R5)
A clinical and cold mentality (R5)	

2. Body

a. The ajna and throat chakras. Venus rules the ajna chakra and its organs with Mercury. Through Taurus, it governs the throat chakra and its organs.

b. The pituitary and thyroid glands. Venus is the traditional ruler of the thyroid gland, which is the physical anchorage of the throat chakra. Even though Bailey does not give Venus as a ruler of the throat centre, it is obvious there is a direct relationship and Venus should be consulted for thyroid and throat problems.

c. Nervous System. The ajna rules the nervous system, which in turn is ruled by Gemini and Mercury, and by Venus.[1]

d. Venous system. Venus supports the heart chakra in its cardiovascular work, through its rulership of the venous system. This system returns deoxygenated blood to the heart for re-oxygenation.

e. Digestion, glucose and insulin. Venus via Taurus rules the mouth as an organ of digestion and the Limbic System as an organ of desire..

Venus governs the endocrine part of the pancreas - the Islets of Langerhans that secrete insulin to extract glucose from the blood when blood sugar levels are low. Via Libra it represents the balancing of glucose levels. Venus rules sweet foods, sugar and body glucose. People who overload their diet with rich foods and carbohydrates may develop diabetes, a condition, where the insulin function is impaired and the pancreas loses its ability to balance (Libra) blood sugar. Diabetes is the karmic result of wrong inner desire. In this case, desire (Venus in its lowest aspect), is focused on comfort-eating and sweet foods to try to compensate for feelings of emotional emptiness.

f. Female cycles, sex and reproduction. Venus is related to the sex function through its

---

1 Bailey, Alice A; Esoteric Healing, 143.

rulership of Libra and the pituitary and its relation with the sacral chakra. The pituitary stimulates the sex processes in the ovaries and testes. With the Moon, Venus shares rulership over female sex glands, organs and processes that involve reproduction.

g. Kidneys, bladder: Venus rules the elimination of urine and the organs involved via Libra.

3. Disease

A positively placed Venus in the chart has many advantages, not least - if the outer life and actions confirm it, someone who is using the higher faculties of the concrete mind in a visionary and positive way to beautify the world around them. Afflicted, Venus represents the opposite. It represents looseness in character, the misuse of "love" and of the sexual function. Positive Venus has a relaxing, soothing, fertile and nutritive affect. Misused Venus force weakens, loosens and debases. Prolapses for instance, which occur when organs move from their usual positions because of weak muscles, or the leakage of vital fluids because weakened valves or organs start to fail in their tasks. Mars and Venus represent the misuse of sex energy that results in sexually transmitted diseases.

Venus' 5th ray lies behind many of our modern mental troubles today. This is particularly so where feelings of alienation, of being excluded and isolated underlie the trouble.

▲ **Psychology**
Asperger's
Autism
Cleavage, psychological
Imbecilities
Insanities
Psychological troubles

▲ **Body**
Ajna
Amygdala
Balance, equilibrium via pituitary
Central nervous system
Cognition
Dopamine
Hippocampus
Homeostasis via pituitary
Hypothalamus
Intelligent self-consciousness
Limbic system
Nucleus accumben, pleasure centre
Olfactory bulb
Pituitary gland

Regulation, balance

Throat
Adam's apple
Adenoids
Appetite
Carotid gland, arteries
Glottis
Jugular vein
Larynx
Lips
Metabolism
Mouth
Neck
Oesophagus upper
Palate
Parathyroids
Parotid glands
Pharynx
Salivary glands
Submandibular glands
Taste
Throat
Thyroid
Thyroxine
Tongue
Tonsils
Uvula

Heart
Vagus nerve
Veins
Vena Cava
Venous system

Solar plexus
Carbohydrates
Glucose, sugar
Insulin
Islets of Langerhans
Pancreas
Sugar, glucose

Sacral
Clitoris
Estrogen
Fallopian tubes
Labia
Libido
Menstruation
Ovaries
Periods
Puberty
Pubis
Sex hormones, organs
Sex life
Sex relations
Sexual development
Uterus

Vagina
Vulva

Base
Adrenal-cortex
Aldosterone
Atlas axis
Bladder
Cortisol
Gums
Hair
Hyoid bone
Kidneys
Urea
Ureters
Urethra
Uric acid
Urinary tract
Urine

▲ **Disease**
Crown
Brain lesion

Ajna
Achondroplasia
Acromegaly
Balance, all problems of
Dwarfism
Gigantism
Growth stunted
Headaches

Hypo-pituitarism
Migraine
Multiple sclerosis
Simmond's disease
Vertigo

Throat
Goitre
Grave's disease
Hashimoto's disease
Hormonal trouble
Laryngitis
Metabolic disorder caused by emotionalism
Mumps
Postpartum blues
Snoring
Thyroid imbalance
Tonsillitis

Heart
Deep vein thrombosis
Varicose veins
Weight gain or loss, thyroid

Solar plexus
Diabetes
Haemorrhoids
Hyperglycemia, Hypoglycaemia
Pancreatitis
Piles

Sacral
Endometriosis
Frigidity
Immorality
Uterine troubles

Base
Addison's disease
Bright's disease
Cushing's syndrome
Cystitis
Hyper-uricaemia
Kidney infection
Kidney stones
Lumbago
Nephritis
Prolapses
Urinary tract infections

- **Ray: 6.**

- **Chakra:**
The Solar plexus and Sacral: Mars is also related to the Base.

- **Sign rulerships:**
Exoteric: Aries and Scorpio.
Esoteric: Scorpio.
Hierarchy: Sagittarius.

Sex

Blood, red blood cells

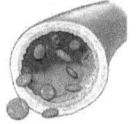

Muscles

Adrenal Medulla

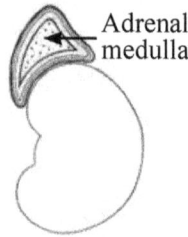

Energy, body warmth

5. Mars

1. Psychology

Mars carries the 6th Ray of Devotion and Idealism, the force that rules the Astral Plane and the majority of human beings who are controlled by their emotions. Mars governs the fiery emotions such as anger, annoyance, irritation, rage, suspicion, hate, avoidance, disgust, loathing, passion, yearning, thirsting, courage and aspiration.

Mars is the primary representative of "desire" which plays out through all the centres. For example, there is sacral chakra desire for sex and tangible rewards. Through the solar plexus, there is desire for love. Then there is higher aspiration, or desire on the Mental Plane associated with the ajna. "Desire" is the fuel we use to drive towards our goals and ideals. This makes Mars a very influential planet. Here are some Mars psychological negatives that can lead to trouble and disease.

Aggression, anger, hate	Defensive, protective
Fanaticism	Glamour
Jealousy, envy, covetousness	One-eyed, blinkered perception
Rampant desire	Reactive emotionally
Self-deceiving, self-deceit	Vindictive, revengeful
Violent, warlike	Warped, narrow ideals

2. Body

a. Solar plexus and sacral chakras. Mars co-rules these centres.

b. The brain, face and skull. Through Aries, Mars is related to the brain and head. Any sudden head or brain problem that creates brain eruptions and explosions or causes physical damage, is associated with Mars.

c. Blood, haemoglobin, vitalisation and purification. Mars' colour is red and it is the primary representative of blood. It governs haemoglobin, the oxygen-carrying protein in red blood cells that gives blood its red colour. Mars vitalises, purifies and stimulates all aspects and organisms in the body, via the blood.

d. Sex and reproduction. Mars governs sex generally and through the sacral chakra is the primary representative of male sexuality, male sex organs and the male hormone testosterone.

e. Adrenals and adrenaline. Mars co-rules the adrenals through Scorpio, especially the adrenal-medulla and adrenaline that is secreted when the fight-flight process is triggered. Mars represents this defensive instinct.

f. The dense physical body and kundalini. Mars rules and controls the physical body - the vital, living, muscled, blood filled, sexual, animal, physical form.

> Mars is definitely the planet which rules and controls the physical vehicle. [1]

Mars also represents kundalini fire that warms the physical body from the base chakra.

g. Excretion. Through Scorpio, Mars is related to the excretory organs.

---

1 Bailey, Alice A; Esoteric Astrology, 210.

3. Disease

Mars brings fever, inflammation and causes eruptions and ulcerated conditions. Toxic Mars emotions poison the blood causing skin eruptions. Nervous system disorders that affect the muscles are related to Mars.

▲ **Psychology**
ADD: attention deficit disorder
ADHD > hyperactivity disorder
Alcoholism
Anti-social, dangerous brooders
Astral maniac
Cuts, cutting
Glamour
Incest
Masochism
Obsessive compulsive
Paedophilia
Self-harm, self-injury
Serial killer
Sex crimes: rape, murder
Sex: license, promiscuity, addiction, rape, perversions, murder, sadism
Stalkers
Substance abuse
Suicidal thoughts

▲ **Body**
Surgery, traditional

Crown
Head

Ajna
Brow
Face
Motor nerves
Nose

Heart
Blood
Constitution
Haemoglobin
Immune system
Iron in the blood
Leukocytes
Prana
Recuperative power
Red blood cells
Vitality (solar fire)

Solar plexus
Anus
Bile
Bowel
Colon
Defecation
Excretion, solid waste
Faeces
Gallbladder
Intestines
Rectum
Sympathetic NS

Sacral
Conception
Cowper's glands
Epididymis
Fertility
Genitals
Libido
Penis
Physical power and strength.
Procreation
Prostate gland
Puberty
Reproduction
Scrotum
Semen
Seminal vesicle
Sex hormones, organs
Sex life
Sex relations
Sexual development
Sexual power
Sigmoid flexure
Sperm
Testes
Testicles
Testosterone
Urethra
Urge to self-perpetuate
Vans deferens

Base
Adrenal-cortex
Adrenaline
Adrenal-medulla
Aldosterone
Biceps
Bladder
Body warmth
Chin
Cortisol
Cranium
Fight or flight
Jaws
Kidneys
Kundalini
Muscles
Physical body
Skull
Survival instinct
Urea
Ureters
Urethra
Uric acid
Urinary tract
Urine
Will to live, to exist

▲ **Disease**
Accidents
Amputation
Plant poisons, drugs

Crown
Ataxia
Blood pressure high, pineal
Brain cells overactive: cancer, tumour, abscess
Brain haemorrhage, inflammation
Cerebral-spinal meningitis
Concussion: head injuries
Convulsions
Encephalitis
Head injuries
Hypertension, pineal cause
Stroke

Ajna
ALS: amyotrophic lateral sclerosis
Lou Gehrig's disease
Motor neurone disease
Multiple sclerosis
Muscle spasms, cramps
Neuralgia
Palsy
Paralysis
Parkinson's disease
Shingles

Throat
Grave's disease
Hashimoto's disease
Strangulation

Heart
AIDS
Allergic reaction from immune
Autoimmune diseases
Blood poisoned
Ebola virus
Fever
High temperature
Immune attack
Inflammation
Lupus
Myasthenia gravis
Sunstroke
Viruses

Solar plexus
Acid reflux
Acidosis
Anal fissure
Colitis
Crohn's disease
Diarrhoea
Diverticulitis
Dysentery
Heartburn
Irritable bowel syndrome
Peptic ulcer
Pus
Reflux
Septicaemia
Ulcers, gastric
Viruses
Vomiting

Sacral
Abortion
Castration
Chlamydia
Frigidity
Genital disorders, warts
Gonorrhea
Herpes, genital
Immorality
Impotency
Infertility
Miscarriage
Premature ejaculation
Prostate trouble
Pubic, crabs
Social diseases
STD: sexually transmitted diseases
Sterility
Syphilis
Venereal disease

Base
Abscesses
Acne
Addison's disease
Alopecia
Baldness
Blister
Boils
Bright's disease
Cramps
Cushing's syndrome
Cystitis
Dermatitis
Eczema
Fatigue: adrenal overload
Fistula
Hernia
Hyper-uricaemia
Impetigo
Kidney infection
Kidney stones
Leprosy
Nephritis
Pimples
Rashes
Rheumatic fever
Rheumatoid arthritis
Scabies
Skin eruptions
Skull: injuries
Sores, weeping
Urinary tract infections

- **Ray:** 2.

- **Chakra:**

The Heart: there is also a relationship to the Solar Plexus chakra

- **Sign rulerships:**

Exoteric: Pisces and Sagittarius.
Esoteric: Aquarius.
Hierarchy Virgo.

Hips and thighs

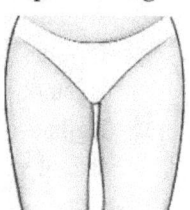

Movement

George G Anatomy Drawings

Liver

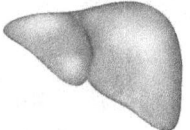

Arteries

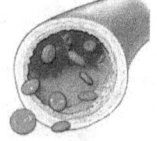

6. Jupiter

1. Psychology

Traditionally, Jupiter, which carries the expanding 2nd ray represents growth, success, rewards and good fortune. It assists the growth of consciousness, expanding it so that it becomes inclusive and group oriented. At its highest, Jupiter symbolises universal love that magnetically attracts to itself that which is desired for the good of the whole. It represents the wisdom of the soul and brings experiences that will expand our vision, broaden our perspective and promote the synthesis of head and heart.

Jupiter also represents those larger than life, exaggerated behaviours such as excess, boastfulness and gambling. This is all due to the expanding and building 2nd ray. Here are some psychological attitudes associated with this side of Jupiter that can lead to disease or irresponsible behaviours.

Amorality (overactive thymus)	Boastfulness
Exaggeration	Gambling addiction
Gluttony	Greed
Irresponsibility	Excessive love of comfort
Materialism	Pleasure seeking
Wastefulness	

2. Body

a. Heart chakra. Jupiter rules the heart centre in spiritually advanced people who have opened the chakra and are radiating inclusive love. In most people its force flows through the solar plexus chakra. Jupiter represents "growth" in the body and along with the Sun, assists the growth and development of our physical bodies.

b. Cardiovascular system. Jupiter, as a co-ruler of the heart chakra, closely supports the work of the Sun in vitalising the body. When Jupiter aspects the Sun by trine, sextile, even by a square or opposition, it represents enhanced and expanded vitality. In the case of hard aspects, if the force is out of balance, if there is too much energy, this can lead to serious health complications.

c. The arteries. Jupiter is the primary ruler of the arteries, the muscular-walled tubes through which oxygenated blood flows from the heart into the body to nourish cell life.

d. Liver: Jupiter supports the work of the solar plexus chakra in its rulership of the liver. This organ performs many functions. For digestion, it separates nutrients needed for the body from waste. It produces bile, routed via the gallbladder into the intestines to digest fatty foods and stores energy from sugar for later release. The liver is also an important participant in metabolism, changing amino acids in foods so that they can be used to produce energy.

The liver also acts as the agent of Pisces, which rules the filtration and drainage systems of the body. After the digestive system has broken down food, the small particles enter the bloodstream and reach the liver. There, waste is filtered from nutrients and toxins are converted into less harmful products before being removed from the body.

e. Hips, thighs, strength, movement and locomotion. Jupiter via Sagittarius rules the hips and thighs. These regions of the body provide the physical power and strength that is required for heavy and stressful tasks. They also (via the sacral chakra) provide the energy required for sexual intercourse.

The hips, thighs and legs when healthy, give us freedom of movement, walking and running. When mobility is impaired, Sagittarius and Jupiter are often implicated in a conflict pattern of some sort.

3. Disease

At all levels, Jupiter force when misused manifests as excess, there is too much energy and the person is not in control. Desire is rampant, and in whichever direction it is being poured, the result is trouble and disease.

In average man, Jupiter's 2nd ray force pours out through the solar plexus chakra. This expands the desire for food, which can lead to over-eating and uncontrolled drinking so that the body gets fat and unhealthy. "Fatness" is particularly related to the misuse of Jupiter's force.

At a cellular level, if Jupiter's building and magnetic force is out of control, cells run amok. Too many cells are attracted and over-building occurs. The result is growths, tumours, cancer, etc.

▲ **Psychology**

All attitudes involving excess, that lead to anti-social, gluttonous or illegal behaviours.

▲ **Body**

Ajna
Sciatic nerve

Heart
Aorta
Arteries
Constitution
Life-force, soul energy
Prana
Recuperative power
Spleen
Vitality (solar fire)

Solar plexus
Liver

Sacral
Locomotion
Movement

Base
Buttocks
Coccyx - tailbone
Femur
Gluteus muscles
Hamstrings
Hips
Ilium
Ischium
Pelvic girdle
Pelvis
Pubis
Quadriceps muscles
Sacroiliac joint
Sacrum
Thighs

▲ **Disease**

Horse riding injuries.

Ajna
Acromegaly
Gigantism

Heart
Aneurism
Arterio-sclerosis
High blood pressure
Hypertension

Solar plexus
Cancer: all body organs
Carcinogenic
Carcinoma
Cellulite, fatness
Cholesterol
Cirrhosis, liver
Diseases caused by excess
Fatness, obesity
Flabbiness
Gluttony
Hepatitis
Hypertrophy
Jaundice
Metastases
Sarcoma
Tumours, growths
Weight gain

Sacral
Locomotive disorders

Base
Body fat
Bone fractures: hips, thighs
Crippled
Dysplasia of the hip
Extra body parts
Gout
Growths, abnormal
Hip disease
Limping
Melanoma
Obesity
Polyps
Swellings
Thigh injuries

The Lord of Love-Wisdom, Who is the embodiment of pure love, is as close to the heart of the Solar Logos as was the beloved disciple close to the heart of the Christ of Galilee. This Life instils into all forms the quality of love, with its more material manifestation of desire, and is the attractive principle in nature and the custodian of the Law of Attraction, which is the life-demonstration of pure Being. This Lord of Love expresses Himself primarily through the planet Jupiter, which is His body of manifestation. [1]

Jupiter gives an inherent tendency to fusion which nothing can arrest. The achievement of ultimate synthesis is inevitable, and this Jupiter promotes. [2]

Leo and Aquarius, through the Sun and Jupiter, are related to Ray 2. Development of the individual consciousness into world consciousness. Thus a man becomes a world server. [3]

---

[1] Bailey, Alice A; Esoteric Psychology I, 23.
[2] Bailey, Alice A; Esoteric Astrology, 139.
[3] Bailey, Alice A; Esoteric Astrology, 67.

- Ray: 3.
- Chakra:
The Throat and Base
- Sign rulerships:
Exoteric: Capricorn.
Esoteric: Capricorn.
Hierarchy: Libra.

Skeleton, bones, vertebrae, joints, knees, teeth

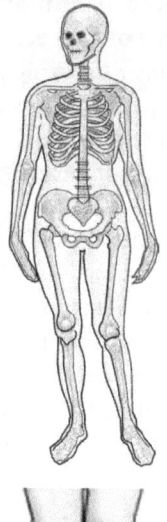
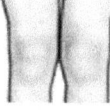

Endocrine system

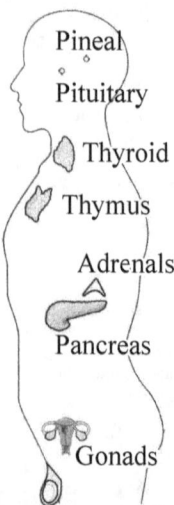

7. Saturn

1. Psychology

Saturn carries the 3rd Ray of Intelligent-Activity and its function is to teach us to act intelligently and responsibly, to make correct decisions and therefore to learn to use the Law of Karma to our advantage. This is the universal law of cause and effect, which teaches us that whatever we give out comes back to us; that evil attracts evil and good attracts good. Capricorn spiritually advances the man or woman who has learnt to kneel in humility and who offers his or her heart and life in service to the greater good.

People with a prominent Saturn are developing inner strength and fortitude. These qualities are required if we are to persevere through challenging karmic times every 7 years when transit Saturn makes hard aspects (conjunctions, squares, oppositions), to its natal position. In these adverse periods, life asks us to correct imbalances of the past and fulfil karmic obligations.

But human beings are disinclined to change so Saturn forces us to evolve through the application of retributive karma. It is the system's head-master who has the thankless task of making us comply with this law. It is a powerful agent of the 1st ray, which is related to karma. Here are some attitudes associated with Saturn that can lead to trouble or disease.

Avarice, greed	Cold and clinical calculation
Hard heartedness	Manipulation, deviousness, dishonesty
Rank materialism	Ruthless ambition

2. Body

a. Throat and base chakras: Saturn governs the intelligent throat chakra and co-rules the base chakra via rays 1 and 3, which it distributes.

b. Thyroid gland, parathyroids. As ruler of the throat chakra, Saturn is related to the health of the thyroid gland and to the parathyroids that regulate calcium in the body. Saturn, the builder of the body structure rules calcium.

c. Endocrine system. The thyroid is the keystone gland of the endocrine system, locking it all together. Saturn's intelligent 3rd ray keeps this system operating efficiently, like clock-work.

d. Dense physical body, skeletal structure and spine. Saturn is a ruler of the base chakra through which the third aspect, [1] the 3rd ray, is powerfully influential. This ray that flows through Saturn, Capricorn and Cancer, rules the dense physical body. Saturn and Capricorn govern the skeletal structure, the bones, spine, muscles, joints, tendons, ligaments and cartilage that tie it together and give it its durability and strength. Saturn is also related to the brain [2] mass.

Saturn/ Capricorn's specific area of rulership is the knee joint, formed by the shinbone, knee cap and lower part of the femur. This joint when healthy, gives the body flexibility in movement. Mental stiffness causes joint stiffness.

---

1 Bailey, Alice A; Esoteric Healing, 209.
2 Bailey, Alice A; Esoteric Astrology, 299.

e. Skin, hair, teeth. The outer structure of the body that Saturn rules includes the integumentary system (skin, hair, nails, exocrine glands), which protects the body from various kinds of external damage, wear and tear.

3. Disease

Saturn afflicted is a warning that we should avoid repressing our emotions and feelings, or use the will to stop the flow of force. Since we know that the free and balanced flow of energy through the body underpins good health, it is easy to see how this sort of trouble represented by Saturn can lead to serious mental and physical health issues. Hardening at a psychological level, leads to hardening in the body.

Saturn carries the 1st ray as well as the 3rd, and is the primary representative of the hardening, crystallising, atrophying and ageing effect of 1st ray in the body. Pluto also carries the 1st ray, and is a back-up ruler for hardening and crystallising 1st ray diseases.

Saturn's sign points to a part of the body that is likely to have a genetic or chronic weakness, which is underdeveloped or impaired in some way. So for instance, Saturn in Cancer points to chronic digestion difficulties, while Saturn in Leo suggests chronic heart problems.

▲ **Psychology**
Con-men
Cyber-bully, stalker, troll
Cyber-criminals
Depression
Frigidity
Hypochondria
Online scammers
Psychopath
Sociopath
Stalkers
Tricksters, con-men

▲ **Body**
Medicine, traditional
Vitamin C

Crown
Brain mass

Throat
Alta-major
Endocrine system
Parathyroids
Thyroid

Solar plexus
Faeces

Base
Birthmark
Body intelligence

Bone marrow
Bones
Calcium
Cartilage, connective tissue
Coccyx - tailbone
Collagen
Dead things
Enamel
Faeces
Flesh
Integumentary system
Joints
Knees
Leg bones
Ligaments
Membranes
Moles, skin
Nails
Old age
Patella
Peritoneum
Physical body
Pleurae
Protein
Ribs
Rigor mortis
Sacroiliac joint
Skeleton
Skin
Spinal column, spine

Substance
Teeth
Tendons
Tissue, flesh
Vertebrae, all

▲ **Disease**
Lead poisoning

Crown
Alzheimer's
Death
Dementia
Huntington's disease
Hydrocephalus
Lewy body dementia
Meningitis
Senile decay

Ajna
Achondroplasia
Dwarfism
Growth stunted

Throat
Bad breath
Fatigue - thyroid
Goitre
Halitosis
Hormonal trouble
Postpartum blues
Sleep apnoea

Thyroid imbalance
Weight gain or loss, thyroid

Solar plexus
Anorexia
Cirrhosis, liver
Gallstones
Hypochondria
Malnutrition
Starvation

Sacral
Barrenness
Fibroids in womb
Impotency
Karmic diseases
Sterility

Base
Aches intense
Ageing unnaturally
Alopecia
Ankylosis spondylosis
Arthritis
Attrition
Back pain
Bone: deformities, crippling
Bursitis
Calcification

Cervical osteoarthritis
Chronic diseases
Constrictions
Corpses
Crippled
Decay
Deformity
Dental problems
Dermatitis
Eczema
Fractures, bones
Geriatric
Gingivitis, pyorrhea
Hardening, stiffening
Hip disease
Impetigo
Joints stiff
Kidney stones
Knee problems
Leprosy
Lesions
Limping
Melanoma
Osteoarthritis
Osteoporosis
Paget's disease
Progeria
Rashes
Rheumatic fever
Rheumatism

Rheumatoid arthritis
Rickets
Scabies
Scleroderma
Sclerosis
Scoliosis
Scurvy
Skin eruptions
Spina bifida
Spinal fractures
Stiffness
Stones
Toothache
Underactive, undeveloped organ
Vertebrae degeneration
Warts
Wrinkles

- **Ray:** 7.

- **Chakra:**
The Sacral; also the ajna and crown

- **Sign rulerships:**
Exoteric: Aquarius
Esoteric: Libra.
Hierarchy: Aries.

Etheric body and Nervous system

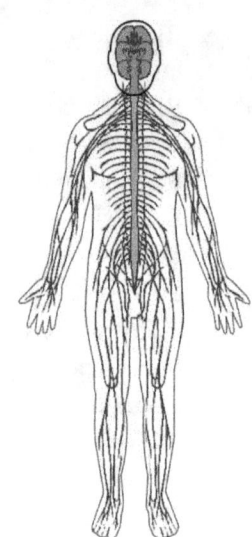

DNA

Calves, ankles

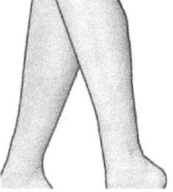

Enzymes

8. Uranus

1. Psychology

Uranus carries the 7th Ray of Ceremony, Order and Magic, the lower pole of the 1st ray. This ray's task is to unite spirit and form such as uniting the etheric body with the dense physical body, and the personality with the soul. On the higher level, Uranus represents the fire of spirit that drives us forward on the path of evolution.

Uranus is also related to the Mental Plane, representing higher powers of the concrete mind such as scientific analysis, experimentation and the abstract mind. It awakens us to new opportunities, urging us to let go of the past, to be free, to rebel, to experiment and generally to explore the new. It is the antithesis of Saturn, which negatively represents stagnation. Very often, insurrections, rebellions and revolutions that are branded by some as terrorism are spiritually inspired uprisings by people fighting for a better way of life. However, when Uranus' force is seriously misused atrocities can occur. Here are some negative Uranus attitudes that may result in disease:

Creating chaos	Destructive wildness
Promiscuity	Repelling all conformity
Selfish individualism	

2. Body

a. Crown and sacral chakras. Uranus governs the sacral chakra and rules the crown chakra in spiritually advanced people who are working through that centre.

b. Etheric body. Uranus rules the sacral chakra and therefore is related to the etheric web that is rooted in this centre.

c. DNA (deoxyribonucleic acid). The basic energy pattern of the physical body is recorded in the physical permanent atom, which is located on the 1st subplane of the Physical Plane. This pattern is replicated in our DNA, which is the carrier of genetic information inherited from our forefathers. Uranus, a ruler of the ethers via the 7th ray, is related to the permanent atom and DNA.

d. Sex and sex attitudes. Uranus represents our mental attitudes to sex. Its task via the incoming 7th ray and the Aquarian Age is to help us bring our sex life into line with universal law by transmuting whatever is aberrant and abnormal, so that the whole field of sex can be moved to a higher level of expression. Consequently, the 7th ray via Uranus is currently bringing sexual behaviour into the spotlight.

e. Germs and bacteria. The 7th ray governs the atomic, cellular level of life and brings together life and matter to create form life on earth. When this process goes awry, aberrant and aborted cells become virulent germs, bacterial infections and contagious diseases. This makes Uranus and the Moon (which also carries ray 7 via Cancer), primary representatives of contagious diseases. The Moon doubly so because it carries the 4th ray which is responsible for epidemics.

f. Blood circulation and blood disorders. Aquarius and the 7th ray govern blood circulation and blood disorders often involve an afflicted Uranus.

g. Calves and ankles: Uranus rules the lower legs through Aquarius.

h. Nervous energy and synapses. The nervous system is the physical manifestation of the fiery etheric web, which Uranus co-rules. Uranus' force is fiery and electrical. It governs nerve synapses, the exchange of nerve information from one nerve cell to the next and electrical signalling in the body generally. Everything we do involves electrical signals running through our bodies. Mercury and Uranus together are the primary rulers of this process. When we refer to the nervous system sending "signals", synapses "firing", or the brain telling the body to take a step forward, what we are talking about is electricity carrying messages from point A to point B. The central powerhouse of the brain thinks and an electrical charge jumps from one cell to the next until it reaches its destination. Any trouble in this process usually involves Uranus or Mercury.

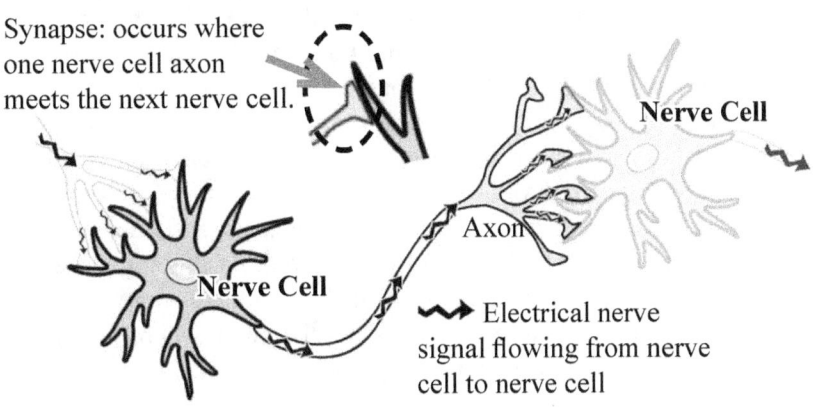

3. Disease

In our psychology, negative Uranus represents chaotic and uncontrolled behaviour, desire gone rampant so that exploration in unhealthy ways occurs. Order breaks down and chaos rules, leading to disease. In the body, Uranus represents conditions and diseases that strike suddenly, which are arrhythmic and that no longer conform to nature's healthy design and pattern. While its task via the 7th ray is to bring balance and coordination into nature's processes, it also represents its aberrations and failures.

▲ **Psychology**
Incest
Masochism
Paedophilia
Serial killer
Sexual: rape,
perversions,
murder, sadism

▲ **Body**
Chemical
medicines, drugs
Chemotherapy
Drugs, medical
Medicine,
modern,
alternative
Minerals
Surgery, modern

Crown
Circadian rhythm
Pineal gland:
initiates
Serotonin

Ajna
Central nervous
system
Cognition
Nerve synapse
Neurons
Retina
Spinal cord
Synapse

Heart
Blood
circulation,
quality
Vagus nerve

Sacral
Chromosome
DNA
Gene, genetics
Physical
permanent atom
Procreation
Reproduction
Sex hormones,
organs
Sex life

Sex relations
Sexual
development

Base
Calves
Catalysts, body
Enzymes
Fibula
Limbs, lower
Tibia

▲ **Disease**
Electrification
Mineral
poisoning
Radiation
poisoning

Crown
Convulsions
Huntington's
disease
Lewy body
dementia

Ajna
Bells Palsy
Cerebral palsy
Epilepsy
Lou Gehrig's
disease
Motor neurone
disease
Muscle spasms,
cramps
Nerve spasms
Neuro-
degenerative
diseases
Palsy
Paralysis
Paraplegic,
quadriplegic
Parkinson's
disease
Polio
Seizures
Spasms, nerves
Spasticity:
Tourette's
syndrome

Tremors
Twitching, tics

Throat
Scarlet fever

Heart
ALS:
amyotrophic
lateral sclerosis
Anaemia
Arrhythmia
Atrial fibrillation
Blood cancer
Blood circulation
problems
Germs
Heart fibrillation
Heart problem,
congenital
Leukaemia:
blood cancer
Palpitations
Pathogens
Reynaud's
disease

Solar plexus
Cholera
Scarlet fever
Typhoid fever

Sacral
Abortion
Congenital
diseases
Frigidity
Gene mutation
Genetic diseases
Immorality
Miscarriage
Premature
ejaculation
Sexual license
Social diseases
STD: sexually
transmitted
diseases
Sterility

Base
Ankle problems
Calf problems
Cramps

- **Ray:** 6.

- **Chakra:**

The Solar Plexus: also the Heart chakra.

- **Sign rulerships:**

Exoteric: Pisces.
Esoteric: Cancer.
Hierarchy: Cancer.

Feet

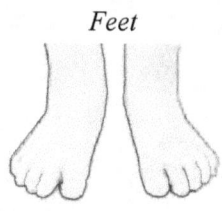

Fluid systems, lymphatic and bloodstream.

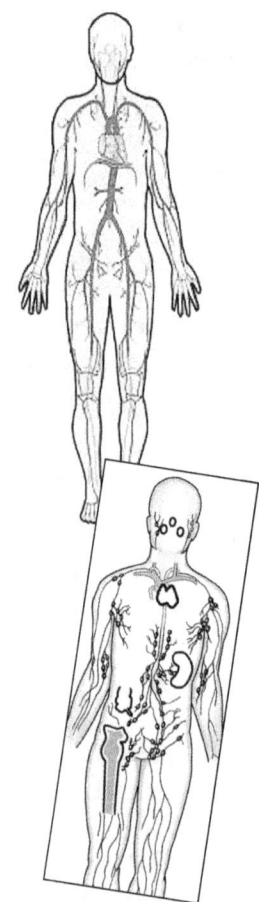

Sleep

9. Neptune

1. Psychology

Neptune carries the 6th Ray of Idealism and Devotion and is the agent of two water signs - Cancer esoterically, and Pisces traditionally. Neptune represents the action of the soul as it refines our emotional expression, softening it up and rendering it more sensitive so that it becomes a fit vessel to express soul love. It rules the higher levels of the Astral Plane and instils in us the finer emotions such as sadness, sorrow, grief, hurt, anguish, anxiety, joy, hope, serenity, ecstasy, bliss and devotion. As this refining process proceeds, consciousness, which was stationed in the solar plexus chakra gradually rises to become heart-centred. At this higher level, Neptune represents a heart connected to the "Heart of the Sun", the source of systemic love and wisdom. Neptune is also a representative of the heart chakra - in spiritually advanced people. Such people love inclusively not conditionally, which is a solar plexus chakra expression.

But Neptune has its dark side, as do all the planets. Here are some negative Neptune attitudes that may result in disease:

A martyr complex	Addictive susceptibility
Astralism	Emotional delusion, glamour
Escapism	Evil perversions
Fanaticism	Fearfulness
Guilt inducing	Subtle hatred
Naivety, guilelessness	No emotional boundaries
Religious eroticism	Self-deceiving
Subtle psychic poisoning	Ungrounded dreaminess
Victim consciousness	Warped, perverted ideals

2. Body

a. Solar plexus chakra. Neptune is related to the function of the solar plexus centre in disciples - those who have refined their emotional expression or are in the process of doing so.

b. Life. Esoterically, Neptune is closely related to the heart organ and its task of vitalising the body. The "heart of the Sun employs Neptune as its agent,"[1] and Neptune represents the life aspect that is carried in the blood.

c. Circular fluid waterways in the body. The water signs Cancer, Scorpio and Pisces are generally related to body secretions and liquids in the physical body. Neptune has general rulership over body fluids with the Moon and may for instance show up in the chart for problems like oedema or excess phlegm. Pisces and Neptune have greater governance over the cyclic "waterways".

- Bloodstream. Neptune governs the bloodstream and is involved if blood flow is restricted through a blockage in the arteries, veins or capillaries.
- Lymphatic system. It is a cleansing, drainage system, keeping our bodies free of garbage by eliminating cellular waste.

d. Feet and toes. Neptune rules the lowest part of the body, the feet and toes via Pisces.

---

1 Bailey, Alice A; Esoteric Astrology, 296.

e. Sleep. We retire to the Astral Plane in the hours of sleep, relating Neptune to sleeping, dreaming, nightmares and all strange things that may occur during sleep including activity on the Astral Plane.

3. Disease

As a ruler of the solar plexus chakra and of the Astral Plane, Neptune in the chart requires close scrutiny as a potential cause of disease. A study of charts from 1920 - 1943, when Neptune was in its detriment in Virgo, shows that it can be virulent. Now we have a new generation who have Neptune falling in Capricorn (1984 - 1998). In our psychology, this combination points to a tendency to repress subtle emotions, or potentially the selling out of higher dreams and ideals for materialistic purposes. Repression is more dangerous for physical health, the latter for our moral health. Generally, people in this group should cultivate ease of emotional expression.

Stagnant and contaminated water is a breeding ground for disease and Neptune afflictions produce mucus and phlegm. Neurodegenerative diseases such as dementia and Alzheimer's that are due to brain fluid atrophy are often indicated by Neptune or Moon afflictions.

Cancer: Neptune is a ruler of the solar plexus chakra, the emotional centre from which much disturbance originates. It carries the 6th ray force in nature that perverts the health of otherwise healthy organisms in subtle and sly ways. In the case of cancer, Neptune can represent carcinogenicity - the ability or tendency to alter the genetic structure of healthy cells so they become cancerous. Alcohol, which Neptune represents, is carcinogenic.

Viruses: Neptune is the primary representative of viruses. The reason why viruses spread so easily is that they are a manifestation of toxic emotions on the physical plane. Viruses are of the nature of negative Neptune - stealthy and subtly poisonous, insidious and debilitating. We become susceptible to them when the immune system (the Sun) becomes debilitated. Viruses try to evade detection by the immune system so they can infect cells. When successful, they rapidly reproduce and spread through the bloodstream like a tidal wave swamping the body. Neptune governs the bloodstream.

▲ **Psychology**
Alcoholism
Astral maniac
Borderline personality disorder
Con-men
Cuts, cutting
Cyber-bully, stalker, troll
Cyber-criminals
Delirium, delusory
Dreams, troubled
Glamour
Hallucination
Hysteria
Neurotics, neuroses
Obscure diseases due to emotionalism
Obsessive compulsive
Online scammers
Panic attacks
Paranoia
Phobias
Psychopath
PTSD
Schizophrenia
Self-harm, self-injury
Sleep-walking
Sociopath
Stalkers
Substance abuse
Tricksters, con-men

▲ **Body**
Anaesthetics
Body fluids
Watery systems in the body

Crown
Sleep

Throat
Lymph, nodes
Lymphatic system
Thoracic duct

Heart
Bloodstream

Base
Feet
Toes

▲ **Disease**
Hidden, obscure disorders
Misdiagnosis
Plant poisons, drugs
Poisonous gas

Crown
Insomnia
Sleep disturbance

Throat
Buboes, plague
Chicken pox
Colds
Dengue fever
Drowns, drowning
Epstein–Barr virus
Glandular fever, swellings
Hodgkin's disease
Influenza
Lymphoma
Measles
Mononucleosis
Rubella
Smallpox

Heart
Blood poisoned
Viruses

Solar plexus
Cancer: all body organs
Carcinogenic
Carcinoma
Cystic fibrosis
Cysts
Diseases caused by excess
Drug addiction
Fatness, obesity
Flabbiness
Gluttony
Hallucinatory, recreational drugs
Metastases
Mucus
Narcolepsy
Nightmares
Obesity
Oedema
Phlegm
Pus
Sarcoma
Septicaemia
Sluggish action of organs
Tissue, insidious changes
Tumours, growths
Typhoid fever
Water retention
Weight gain

Base
Abscesses
Boils
Bunions
Dermatitis
Eczema
Feet problems
Gout
Growths, abnormal
Impetigo
Leprosy
Melanoma
Pimples
Polyps
Rashes
Scabies
Skin eruptions
Sores, weeping
Swellings
Warts

- **Ray:** 1.

- **Chakra:**
The Crown and Base, also the Solar Plexus.

- **Sign rulerships:**
Exoteric: Scorpio.
Esoteric: Pisces.
Hierarchy: Pisces.

Colon, excretory

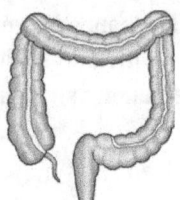

Kidneys, bladder, anus

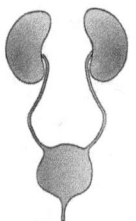

Sleep and Death

Adrenals, the will to live and to survive

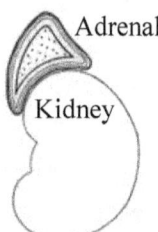

10. Pluto

Pluto is currently the most powerful distributor of 1st ray force on the planet, representing primarily its destructive side. It also represents nature's life and death processes governed by the 1st ray. Most people fear death. But in an evolutionary sense it is a compassionate and vital process that frees the soul from a worn out and often diseased body. In this regard, Pluto is a healer and liberator, assisting our spiritual journey towards enlightenment. This is not necessarily physical death. During the course of life, Pluto's force causes psychological transformation. It may be the death of an old way of life or the letting go of an old and limiting habit. But in either case the drastic change is engineered by Pluto (ray 1) through a life-changing event that forces us to move forward into a healthier future. Here is a powerful quote.

> Through Pluto [man comes] under the destroying power of death—death of desire, death of the personality and of all which holds him between the pairs of opposites, in order to achieve the final liberation. Pluto or death never destroys the consciousness aspect. [1]

The last sentence is a reminder that, even if the physical body dies, the conscious soul lives on and will reincarnate in the future.

1. Psychology

In our psychology, Pluto gives us a powerful and selfish will, a power that comes from the force of the base chakra. Power-hungry dictators, who refuse to move forward in their evolution, stay rooted strongly in the base chakra life after life. Since this is the chakra of matter, this potentially makes them dangerous because they are motivated by very selfish material values. Adolf Hitler had a powerful will and is an example of such a person. Here are some negative Pluto attitudes that may result in trouble or disease:

Arrogance	Controlling
Cruelty, lacking pity	Extremely self-willed
Insensitive, cold, hard	Power hungry
Powerfully destructive	Pure selfishness
Ruthlessly ambitious	Self-aggrandising

As we evolve and integrate as personalities and develop the powers of the mind, our personal power and will increases. As we begin to align with the soul, selfish will transforms into the will-to-good, a force that flows through the crown chakra.

2. Body

a. The crown and base chakras. Pluto governs the base chakra, instilling the will to survive; and the crown chakra in average man. In the brain, its force is more obvious in sleep, death and in disease.

b. Sleep and death: these two aspects are related, because in both, consciousness vacates the physical body and moves onto the Astral Plane. At the end of sleep, the consciousness thread reconnects with the brain via the crown centre.

---

1 Bailey, Alice A; Esoteric Astrology, 127.

In death, consciousness thread does not reconnect. The soul snaps the thread, an act represented by Pluto. It is the Lord of Death and the Arrow of God that delivers death on one level or another. Pluto is related to sleep.

c. Adrenals, the will-to-survive and the fight-or-flight syndrome. Pluto governs the base chakra, which anchors in the adrenals, giving it governance by default over the adrenals and to these survival instincts. The will-to-survive (Pluto) enables the physical elemental - the nature spirit that rules the physical body, to react immediately and instinctively to protect itself. The will-to-survive is also associated with the urge to procreate, driving the animal urge to mate. Pluto's sign Scorpio and fellow ruler Mars, are associated with these instinctive functions.

d. Urinary tract. The base chakra governs the urinary tract, relating the elimination of liquid waste to Scorpio and Pluto.

e. Physical atoms. The atoms in the physical body are energised by the third ray and therefore are related to Saturn, which carries this force. However, the power contained within an atom nucleus is a 1st ray, Plutonic phenomenon. Pluto was discovered in 1930, close to the time that Sir Ernest Rutherford split the atom in 1937. This resulted in the atom bomb. Pluto rules atomic fission, radiation poisoning as well as radiation therapy and chemotherapy used to kill off cancerous cells.

3. Disease

Pluto's 1st ray in our psychology gives us a very powerful will - for good or ill. When misused, people become dogmatic, they refuse to bend or be flexible and can be highly destructive in their words and actions. 1st ray diseases operate the same way. They are relentless and unstoppable unless destiny deems that the time is not yet right for death. Any health issues we get under a hard Pluto aspect is a red-flag warning that a serious disease may be manifesting. In such a case, get a complete medical check-up.

|| *NB. It is important to remember that we all receive hard Pluto aspects regularly and usually they work out as psychological stresses and radical life changes. Resisting healthy change and living in a toxic situation attracts the destructive force of Pluto, which will try to destroy that toxicity. Change is forced upon us, like it or not. If we make the transition, then Pluto ushers us into a totally new situation, filled with new life and promise.*

▲ **Psychology**
Egomania
Megalomania

▲ **Body**
Chemotherapy

Crown
Death
Melatonin
Sleep

Solar plexus
Anus
Bowel
Colon
Defecation
Excretion, solid waste
Faeces

Intestines
Rectum

Base
Adrenaline
Adrenal-medulla
Atoms
Bladder
Catalysts, body
Enzymes
Fight or flight
Kidneys
Survival instinct
Urea
Ureters
Urethra
Uric acid
Urinary tract
Urine

Will to live, to exist

▲ **Disease**
Amputation
Accidents
Bacterial infection
Contagious infections
Electrification
Epidemics
Mineral poisoning
Radiation poisoning

Crown
Alzheimer's
Brain cells

overactive: cancer, tumour, abscess
Death
Dementia
Huntington's disease
Insomnia
Lewy body dementia
SIDS: sudden death infant syndrome

Throat
Asphyxia
Suffocation

Solar plexus
Anal fissure

Colitis
Crohn's disease
Diarrhoea
Diverticulitis
Dysentery
Haemorrhoids
Irritable bowel syndrome
Nephritis: kidney inflammation
Piles

Sacral
Abortion
Castration
STD: sexually transmitted diseases

Base
Bright's disease
Cystitis
Fatigue: adrenal overload
Fistula
Hernia
Hyperuricaemia
Kidney infection
Kidney stones
Murder
Nephritis
Rheumatic fever
Rheumatoid arthritis
Urinary tract infections

- **Ray:** 3.
- **Chakra:** Throat.
- **Sign rulerships:**
The earth does not influence consciousness at the exoteric level.
Esoteric: Gemini.
Hierarchy: Sagittarius.

- **Ray:** 1.
- **Chakra:** Crown
- **Sign rulerships:**
Vulcan does not influence consciousness at the exoteric level.
Esoteric: Taurus.
Hierarchy: Taurus and Virgo.

Vulcan's Hammer, beats common-sense into people

11. The Earth

All people on earth are bathed continuously with nourishing planetary prana, the fluidic emanation of "Mother Nature". When absorbed through the skin and pores, planetary prana (flowing from the Sun to the planet then to us) is therapeutic. We all inherently recognise the wisdom in getting out of cities into nature, into the gentle and green embrace of Mother Earth. The 3rd ray, the green ray, flows through the Earth.

Once we are on the Path, the Earth begins to affect consciousness. It exerts a decentralising effect as a counterbalance to the ego represented by the Sun. The sign it is in - the sign opposite the sun sign, helps us to become more inclusive.

Mother Earth offers us global experience and the opportunity to unfold our faculties, consciousness and group skills. Contact with different continents, races and cultures knocks off our selfish edges and renders us more inclusive and accepting of others.

As far as health goes, the Earth rules the throat chakra and therefore is a ruler of the thyroid gland. Any afflictions to the Sun also afflict the Earth and these indicate difficulty with the absorption of planetary prana and consequent devitalisation.

12. Vulcan

Vulcan only becomes influential when we begin our aspirational journey towards living a higher and finer type of life. At that point, under its influence, we start to apply purification disciplines to improve physical health such as eating the right food and exercising more by doing gym work, yoga, running, etc. We become more discerning in how we use our sexual energy and how we spend our money. When we start changing in this way, it is evidence that Vulcan is becoming influential and that we are on the Path. Vulcan's gift to us is the 1st Ray of Will-Power. It gives us the energy and determination to persist in our efforts to purify the nature and to strive towards greater spiritual understanding and improved life and living.

> || NB. We do not have a credible ephemeris yet for Vulcan but we find it primarily through the Sun and Moon. They veil Vulcan. If the Sun is in Cancer for instance, then Vulcan is in Cancer. If the Moon is in Libra, then so is Vulcan. In the charts of aspirants, this means that the negative Cancer and Libra traits need purifying. When we are at the stage of physical purification, Vulcan can touch many aspects of our nature and life.

Vulcan rules the crown chakra in disciples and initiates. It is related to circulation in the etheric web.

2d. The Etheric Web and Chakras

Esoteric Healing - Law III

Disease is an effect of the basic centralisation of a man's life energy. From the plane whereon those energies are focussed proceed those determining conditions which produce ill health. These therefore work out as disease or as freedom from disease.[1]

---

[1] Bailey, Alice A; Esoteric Healing, 54.

The Etheric Web and the Chakras

The etheric web is the fiery energy field upon which the physical body is constructed. Consequently, it is the media through which the various astrological and psychological energies must travel to reach the physical body. Disturbances of the mind or emotions (represented in the chart as afflictions to planets that rule those bodies), cause trouble in the chakras. If these troubles are brief, then there is no lasting harm. But if enduring habits set in so that thoughts or emotions are routinely troubled or unstable, then congestion and other troubles occur in the etheric. This is the fore-runner to disease.

Artistic impressions of the web and 7 major chakras

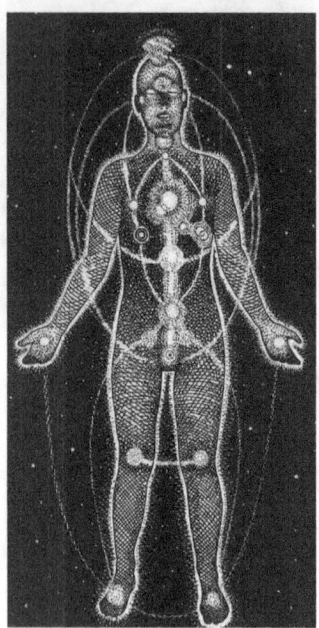

'A Thousand Points of Light', Malvin Artley.

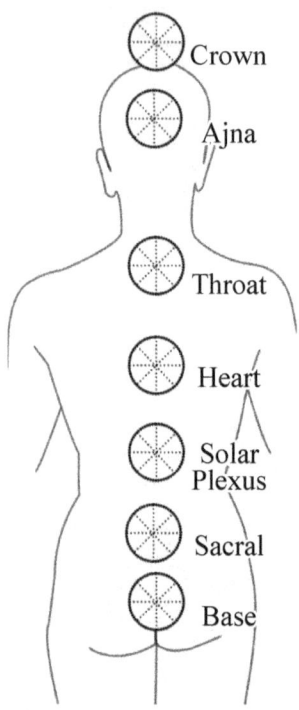

'Radionics and the Subtle Anatomy of Man' David Tansley.

1. The etheric web

The etheric web is a subtle level of the physical universe not normally visible to the naked eye. This golden network of very fine energy lines (nadis) stretches throughout space. All forces that play through the field of space pass through the etheric web to reach the Physical Plane and physical life. This is how astrology works. Far distant systems, stars and signs use the etheric highways to stream their forces to earth and man. Every form in the universe has its own individual etheric web, and each is a tiny link in the overall, universal mother-web. Here is how Bailey describes space in relation to the etheric.

> **The field of space is etheric in nature and its vital body is composed of the totality of etheric bodies of all constellations, solar systems and planets which are found therein. Throughout this cosmic golden web there is a constant circulation of energies and forces and this constitutes the scientific basis of the astrological theories.** [1]

The etheric web is the energy framework and blueprint upon which the dense physical body is constructed and with which it conforms. Underlying and interpenetrating the entire organism, the web gives the physical body quality, energy and life. The sketch top left is from a clairvoyant impression.

Some forces flowing into our web come from higher levels: from the soul, from the mind as mental force and from the astral body as emotional force. On the Physical Plane, we receive solar prana, life-giving energy from the Sun that flows through the web to vitalise the physical body. We also pick up the energies of the particular environment we are in and from the people we mix with and who surround us.

The state of our individual etheric web determines our health. A strong and robust etheric body is an excellent conductor for energy and gives us in return excellent health. A poorly strung together web with obstructions and impediments leaves us impoverished energetically and susceptible to disease and ill health.

Gemini is given by Bailey as related to the etheric body. [2] Aquarius is related [3] through its rulership of the ethers, Uranus because it carries ray 7 that rules the ethers and the Moon is related to etheric circulation. Afflicted planets in Gemini may show potential etheric trouble. For instance, an etheric web that is loosely strung together or is loosely integrated into the physical body causes debilitation and tiredness. Neptune and Venus weaken, and could show this condition if they are afflicted in Gemini or to its ruler Mercury.

If the connection with the dense body is very loose, the soul may have difficulty keeping hold of the physical so that possession occurs; a foreign entity slips in and takes control. Neptune or Pluto afflictions could show this. Another problem that could arise is epilepsy and seizures. Uranus may be a causal factor.

---

1 Bailey, Alice A; Esoteric Astrology, 11.
2 Bailey, Alice A; ibid, 352.
3 Bailey, Alice A; ibid, 303.

2. The chakras

Where many nadis cross in the etheric web, energy vortexes form. These are the etheric reception and distribution centres for energy, the chakras. There are hundreds of chakras, mostly minor. Seven chakras are considered major because they are involved with the development of consciousness. The spleen chakra is not one of these. Five of these seven centres lie up the spine and two are in the head.

Often chakra drawings show the centres in the front of the body. These represent the consciousness of average man - the front of the body carries energy downwards, it is the involutionary route. But once we are on the Spiritual Path of Return, we are told to work and think with the spine and head, to visualise the chakras in the spinal column, which represents the upwards evolutionary route. Here is a chart that gives details of these chakras and their relation to the planets.

Chart 4: The 7 Major Chakras

Centre	Plane, origin	Petals	Gland	Planet rulers
Head	Atma, Monad, jewel in lotus	960	Pineal	Pluto, Vulcan (Uranus)
Ajna	Buddhi, higher mental, egoic lotus	96	Pituitary	Venus (Mercury)
Throat	Mental body, knowledge petals	16	Thyroid	The Earth, Saturn
Heart	Higher mental, egoic lotus, love petals	12	Thymus	Sun, Jupiter (Neptune)
Solar Plexus	Astral Plane, astral centres	10	Pancreas	Mars, Neptune (Moon)
Sacral	Physical Plane, etheric body	6	Gonads	Uranus (Mars)
Base	Physical Plane, Mother Nature	4	Adrenals	Pluto (Saturn)

Planes: Esoteric Healing, 45.   *Planets: Esoteric Astrology 517; brackets - from other sources*

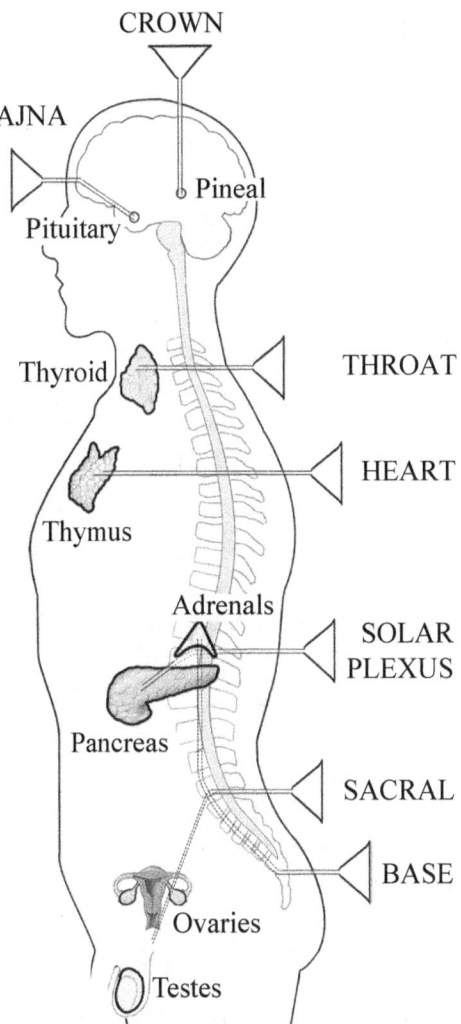

- The *jewel in the lotus* refers to the soul body, also called the causal body/ egoic lotus, located on the higher Mental Plane. It anchors spiritual power. The petals represent knowledge, love and sacrifice qualities.
- The chakras anchor in the seven glands of the endocrine system. The chart shows the chakra - gland relationship.
- Each chakra has a different number of petals. The higher the plane that energises a chakra, the faster are the energy ripples and the more numerous the petals.
- As energy pours through a chakra, it vitalises the associated endocrine gland which in response, releases hormones into the bloodstream.
- Congestion in a chakra occurs when force flowing through a centre is disrupted. If force is blocked as it pours into the centre, then the energy is thrown back upon its originating source - either the astral or mental body, resulting in a psychological disturbance. When the blockage is in the outlet into the physical body, the gland is either overstimulated or undernourished, destabilising its secretion, resulting finally in disease. A major cause of chakra congestion and blockages occurs when we use our wills to repress a natural body impulse, such as sexual desire.

Three etheric spinal channels

Within the etheric spine are three nadis or threads (their Hindu names are *pingala, ida* and *sushumna*) that are related to consciousness and development. Material life pours through Pingala. Soul energy flows via Ida. Sushumna, the central thread, is the path for pure spirit. As consciousness unfolds, energy flow via the nadis increases, until at a very advanced stage spiritual force utilises fully the central thread. The chakras connect into these channels.

1. The Crown or Sahasrara Chakra

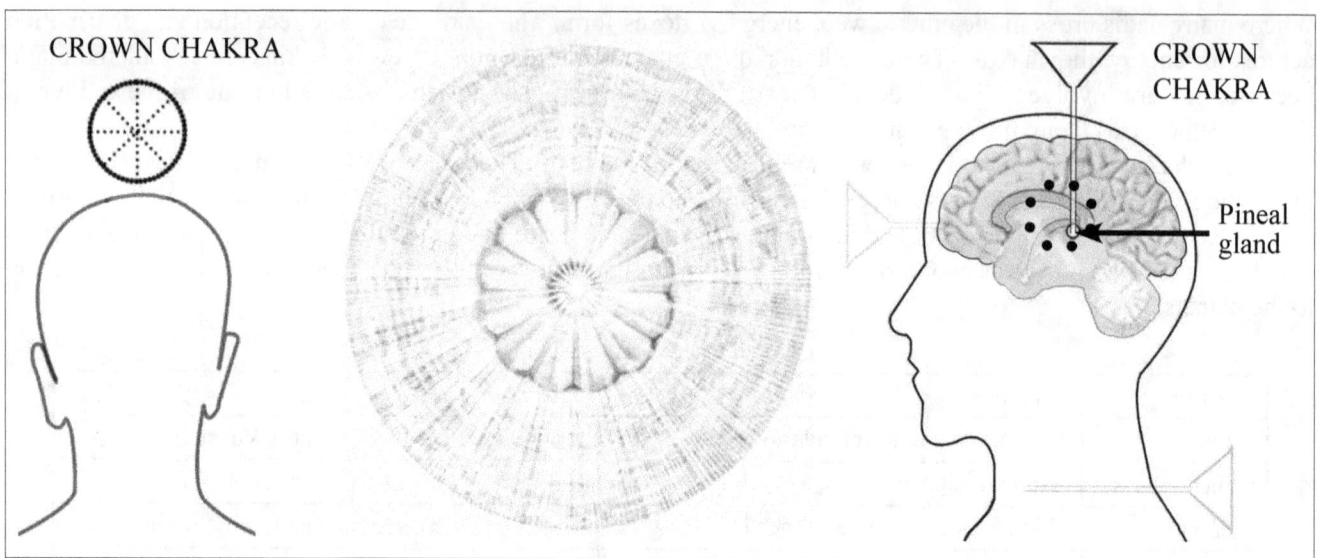

- The crown enters the body through the top of the head. At its centre is a 12-petalled lotus of white and gold. This is the higher correspondence of the heart centre. Around these are 960 secondary petals. [1]
- The crown is vitalised from the Monad, the Atmic Plane, and the egoic lotus on the Mental Plane.
- The crown is an entry portal for Ray 1 of Will and Power.
- The crown chakra enters the body in the Aries ruled region.
- The planet rulers of the crown are Pluto, Vulcan and Uranus.

1. Psychology

The function of the crown chakra and its physical manifestation - the pineal gland, is to provide an anchorage for our spiritual nature. The pineal is called the seat of the soul, and when the soul is in control of the life, it guides affairs and controls the body through that gland. However, the crown chakra is not open in the average person because consciousness is still firmly grounded in the lower self and the lower chakras. At this stage, the crown can be likened to an unoccupied space at the top of a corporate office building, that one day will be the pent-house suite for the Chief Executive Officer.

Ray 1 of Will and Power flows through this centre when it is open, demonstrating as the will-to-good. People who are consciously working at this level are powerful forces for good in the world. Otherwise, before the centre opens, this force pours down and out through the base chakra. There it manifests via Pluto as selfish, personal will, the force that drives dictators.

2. Body

a. The pineal gland. The crown chakra anchors in the pineal gland. This is the only gland that communicates with the outside world. Light activates the pineal to produce *serotonin*, the neurotransmitter responsible for mood levels. Sunlight helps us feel better. Then at night, the absence of light stimulates the production of *melatonin*, which with the light–dark cycle, co-ordinates our internal clock, the 24-hour circadian rhythm. Through melatonin, the pineal maintains and regulates homeostasis during sleep by fine tuning body functions such as sleep, blood pressure and hormone levels.

b. The brain and the upper brain. The crown chakra generally rules the cerebrum and specifically rules a region around the pineal gland. [2] The higher brain is the seat of the intuition [3] and of the soul when intuitive cells around the pineal gland come alive. It is "the entire brain area around the pineal gland, wherein the spiritual man assumes control". [4]

---

1 The chakra drawings in this section are based on clairvoyant investigations by Charles Leadbeater 1854 - 1934.
2 Bailey, Alice A; Esoteric Healing, 45.
3 Bailey, Alice A; From Intellect to Intuition, 211.
4 Bailey, Alice A; Esoteric Psychology II, 581.

Body substance generally is ruled by the 3rd ray of matter via the base chakra. Saturn and the Moon carry the 3rd ray (the latter via its sign Cancer), and they rule brain substance. This means that may be involved in diseases that affect brain tissue such as dementia.

c. The consciousness thread (antahkarana). This stream of lighted energy connects the soul to the brain, in the region of the pineal gland. This region in the head is the seat of consciousness, the seat of the soul. From there, the soul's job is to control human consciousness via the brain and nervous system. But this level of higher soul control takes many, many lives to achieve. Driven by the ego, in average man, consciousness is centred in one of the lower chakras.

d. The right eye of buddhi. The crown chakra governs the right eye, and in those who are conscious on the Buddhic Plane, it distributes love and wisdom from that level.

e. Sleep and death. The crown also governs the sleep-death processes via the consciousness thread. Every night in the hours of sleep, the consciousness thread withdraws from the crown chakra and we die to the Physical Plane and function on the Astral Plane. The process of sleep and death are identical, excepting that in sleep the life thread remains intact so that consciousness can return to the body. In death it snaps.

3. Disease

- Injuries to the head and brain.
- Diseases causing cellular breakdown such - dementia, insanity.
- Brain inflammation - meningitis and tumours, stroke.
- Disturbed sleep rhythm.

a. Trouble via the 1st ray. Sometimes 1st ray force registers in the brain precipitately. If so, it inflames brain cells and may cause the breaking down of the cellular structure of the brain, brain tumours, abscesses and meningitis. This can also happen if a person has a powerful and explosive will and temper, or if kundalini fire rises from the base chakra too soon, caused by unwise spiritual practices. For these conditions, look for afflictions to 1st ray planets Pluto, Saturn or Uranus, or to planets afflicted in Aries.

> **The first aspect when not functioning properly, produces death, insanity and some of the diseases of the brain.** [1]

b. Troubled sleep. Prolonged night use of electronic apparatus that relies on artificial light such as TV, computers and cell-phones damages the eyes and melatonin absorption, degrading sleep quality. Shallow or broken sleep patterns interfere with recuperative processes, which normally take place at night. For instance, blood pressure drops by up to 20 percent, easing stress upon the cardiovascular system. If this cycle is disturbed it increases the risk of high blood pressure and disorders such as anxiety, mood disorders and depression.

c. Trouble with the consciousness thread. Possession or obsession can happen if the life thread is attached to the original owner of the body but the consciousness thread is that of another discarnate person or entity. This may be caused by a loose consciousness thread, a shock or disaster that severs the link of consciousness, or the person just may have great dislike for physical incarnation and withdraws consciousness.

SIDS babies - sudden death infant syndrome, this occurs when both the consciousness thread and the life thread are snapped. Whether this is part of the design of the soul or occurs for some other reason is not clear.

▲ **Psychology**
The powerful and assertive will of the spiritually advanced person.

▲ **Body**
Antahkarana
Brain mass, tissue
Circadian rhythm
Consciousness thread
Head
Melatonin
Pineal gland
Serotonin
Sleep

▲ **Disease**
Alzheimer's
Arrested development
Ataxia
Blood pressure high, pineal
Brain cells overactive: cancer, tumour, abscess
Brain congenital disorders
Brain haemorrhage, inflammation
Brain lesion
Cerebral-spinal meningitis
Coma
Concussion: head injuries
Convulsions
Death
Dementia
Encephalitis
Head injuries
Huntington's disease
Hydrocephalus
Hypertension, pineal cause
Insanity, idiocy
Insomnia
Lewy body dementia
Lunacy
Multiple personalities
Possession
Senile decay
SIDS: sudden death infant syndrome
Sleep disturbance
Stroke

---
1 Bailey, Alice A; Esoteric Healing, 108.

2. The Brow or Ajna Chakra

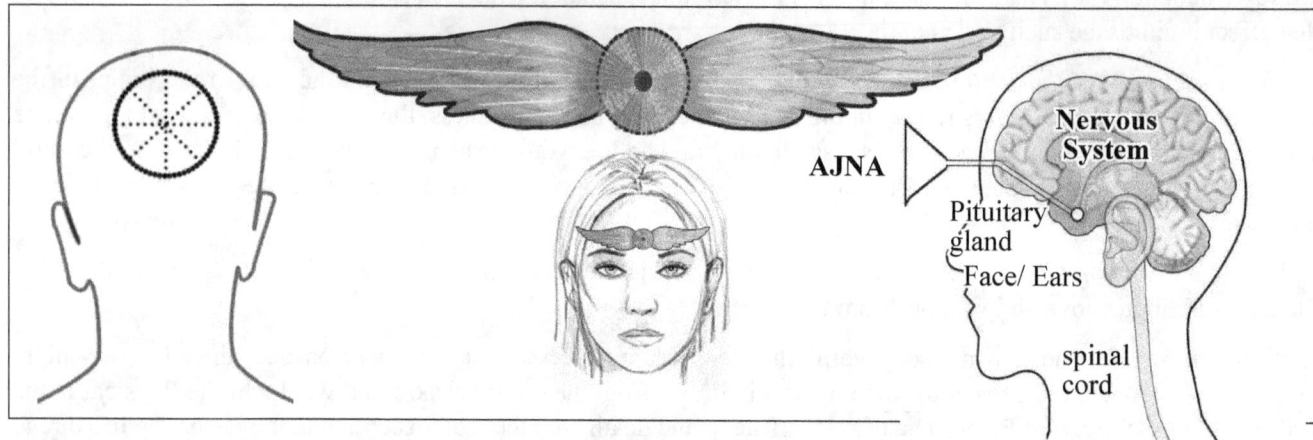

- The ajna enters the body through the front of the head just above the eyebrows, anchoring in the pituitary gland. 96 petals spread out like the two wings of an aeroplane. The diagram above is an artist's impression.
- The ajna is vitalised from the buddhic vehicle, the higher Mental Plane and the egoic lotus.
- The ajna is the main entry portal for Ray 5 of Concrete Mind. Also associated with this centre is ray 4 via Mercury - one of the ajna's rulers, and ray 2 of consciousness [1].
- Aries, Taurus and Gemini all seem to have a link with this centre. It is in the Aries ruled part of the body, but Venus for Taurus and Mercury for Gemini, govern the ajna.

1. Psychology

The ajna focalises the forces of the personality. When developed, the personality is the force of the advanced, intelligent and fully integrated human being who dominates the environment with his dynamic power, intelligent organising skills and visionary imagination. Ray 5 of Concrete Mind and Science flows through the ajna, giving those conscious at this level, their acute and dominant mentality. Before soul wisdom is developed, they are mentally aloof, detached and judgemental. But when the forces of the soul flow through the ajna and therefore through the personality, the higher Venus qualities of intelligent love are expressed.

The ajna rules the face, revealing to the world the character, self-awareness and intelligence of the person that it represents. A large number of human beings are not fully developed at this level. They have the concentration of their force in a lower chakra. However, through widespread education, the ajna is rapidly awakening *en masse*.

2. Body

a. The Pituitary gland. Venus rules the ajna and the pituitary and the influence of its balancing sign - Libra, is seen in the work of the pituitary. Its hormones maintain homeostasis, balance and stability in the body. Scientists say the pituitary body is the master gland, because it appears to direct most endocrine activities. This role is taken over by the pineal when the crown chakra awakens and the spiritual man emerges. Problems in the pituitary can cause inferior moral and intellectual development, excessive growth or dwarfism and abnormal function of ovaries and testes.

b. The lower brain. The ajna rules the "lower brain". The region around the pituitary gland is the temporal lobe, the vicinity in which the Limbic System is located. Here is a definition of lower faculties by Bailey:.

> In the region of the pituitary body, we have the seat of the lower faculties, when co-ordinated in the higher type of human being - here are to be found the emotions and the more concrete aspects of the mind (growing out of racial habits and inherited instincts, and, hence, calling for no exercise of the creative or higher mind). [2]

---

1 Bailey, Alice A; Esoteric Healing, 187-188.
2 Bailey, Alice A; From Intellect to Intuition, 212.

Since, the ajna is the higher intellectual and creative centre, it obviously rules more than this. Perhaps it incorporates parts of the cerebral cortex such as the intellectually advanced frontal lobe that is ruled by the crown chakra. The division between higher and lower brains as envisioned by Bailey is not clear.

c. The central nervous system. The brain can be thought of as a central computer that controls all bodily functions. In comparison, the nervous system is the network that relays messages back and forth from the brain to different parts of the body, all the time gathering information from the senses about what is going on in the world and feeding this information to the brain. Then in response, outward travelling nerve impulses galvanise us into action. These neural pathways are in the spinal cord, which runs from the brain down the back, branching out to every organ and body part. The ajna rules this messaging system.

Although the nervous system is ruled by the ajna chakra, some of its parts can be influenced by other centres. For example, the nerves of the sympathetic nervous system that govern the "fight or flight reaction", emerge from the spinal cord in the solar plexus region and its reactions are largely controlled by the emotions.

d. The Third Eye. This is the etheric correspondence of the pineal gland. It is the eye of the soul and when activated, through right spiritual living and a vegetarian diet, the soul is able to see into the physical world and we will be able to see into higher spiritual realms.

e. Front of the head, eyes, ears and nose. The ajna chakra vitalises all frontal areas of the head including the face, eyes and nose. It shares rulership of the ears with the throat chakra. These sense organs are vital for the development of personality consciousness, which is associated with the ajna.

f. Left eye of manas. Once the personality and soul are aligned, the eyes become distributing channels for higher energies. The crown and the right-eye distribute soul love and wisdom, while the ajna and the left-eye distribute the mental energies of the personality.

3. Disease

- Modern psychological disorders involving dissociation, separativeness, egomania.
- Diseases of the pituitary gland and of of the nervous system.
- Injuries or diseases of the face, eyes, ears and nose.
- Headaches, migraine, epilepsy and seizures.

The nervous system is ruled by Gemini, Mercury, Venus, also Uranus and Aquarius. Nervous disorders will have at least one of these planets involved in a health-triangle, or a planet in one of these signs.

▲ **Psychology**
Asperger's
Autism
Egomania
Imbecilities
Insanities
Megalomania
Psychological troubles

▲ **Body**
Amygdala
Balance, equilibrium
Brow
Central nervous system
Cerebellum
Cerebral cortex
Cognition
Cornea
Dopamine
Ears
Eye lens
Eyes
Face
Hearing
Hippocampus
Homeostasis
Hypothalamus
Intelligent self-consciousness
Iris
Limbic system
Motor nerves
Neocortex
Nerve fluid
Nerve synapse
Neurons
Nose
Nucleus accumben, pleasure centre
Olfactory bulb
Pituitary gland
Pupils
Regulation, balance
Retina
Sclera
Self-consciousness
Sentiency
Sight
Spinal cord
Spinal fluid
Submandibular glands
Synapse
Vision

▲ **Disease**
Achondroplasia
Acromegaly
ALS:
amyotrophic lateral sclerosis
Astigmatism
Balance, all problems of
Bells Palsy
Blindness
Cataracts
Cerebral palsy
Conjunctivitis
Deafness
Dwarfism
Epilepsy
Gigantism
Glaucoma
Growth stunted
Guillain-Barre syndrome
Headaches
Hypo-pituitarism
Keratitis
Labyrinthitis
Lou Gehrig's disease
Meniere's disease
Middle ear problems
Migraine
Motor neurone disease
Multiple sclerosis
Muscle spasms, cramps
Myopia
Nerve spasms
Neuralgia
Neuro-degenerative diseases
Palsy
Paralysis
Parkinson's disease
Seizures
Shingles
Short sighted
Simmond's disease
Spasms, nerves
Spasticity
Tinnitus
Tourette's syndrome
Tremors
Twitching, tics
Vertigo

3. The Throat or Vishudda Chakra

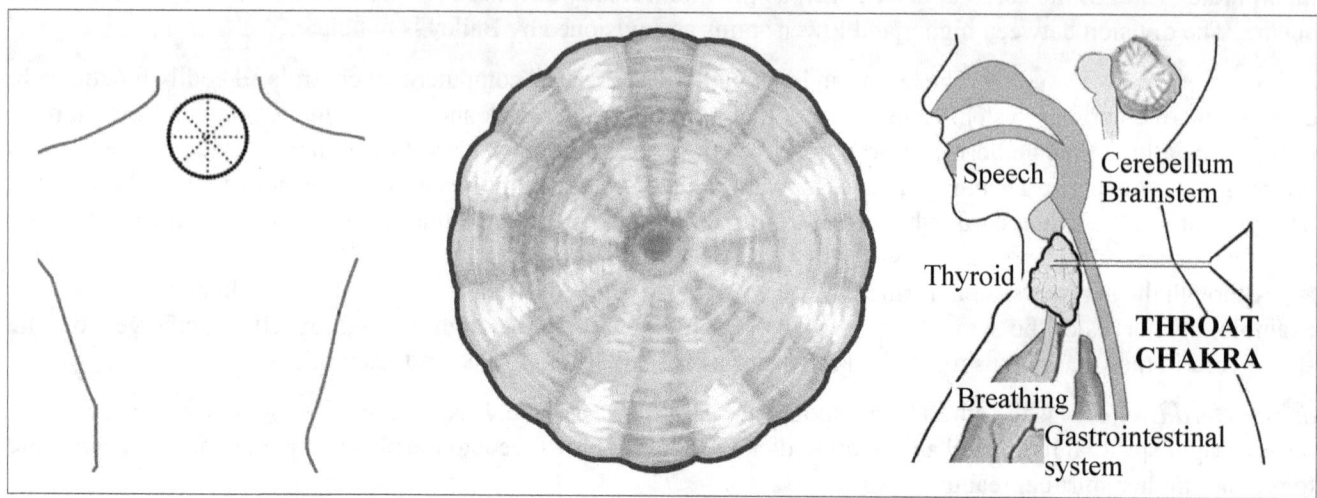

- The throat chakra enters the spine at the base of the neck, between cervical 7 (C7) and thoracic 1 (T1), anchoring in the thyroid gland. Its 16 petals of blue and silver look like moonlight on rippling water.
- The throat is vitalised from the knowledge petals of the egoic lotus and from the mental body.
- The throat is an entry portal for Ray 3 of Intelligent Activity and ray 7 for [1] disciples.
- Taurus and Gemini rule the throat chakra, so do their rulers Venus and Mercury. The Earth and Saturn are the ray 3 rulers of the throat centre.

1. Psychology

The throat chakra represents the powers and faculties of lower mind and only when it is active can we truly identify as a "self", as an "I". Ray 3 of Intelligent Activity flows through the throat and it teaches us to think and speak intelligently. One of this centre's names is "the great organ of creation through sound". [2] When we speak, we create. As we become more confident intellectually, voicing our opinions more coherently and effectively, we start to influence the world around us because of the power of our thoughts and voice. We become true creators, magicians in a sense.

The throat and sacral chakras are partners in that they are the creative centres in the body. But before the throat becomes active, the sacral is the dominant centre and creative power flows straight through the throat down to the sacral to feed the sexual appetites. But once the mind starts to find artistic or scientific subjects attractive, this flow is arrested at the throat and pours into these areas.

Mercury, which rules speech, is a natural ruler of the throat chakra. The Earth rules the throat chakra in average man at a physical health level. But Saturn takes over with disciples, making them karmically responsible for the words they speak. People learn to be more prudent with what they say under Saturn.

2. Body

a. The thyroid gland. The throat chakra anchors in the thyroid gland, which according to Bailey is the "keystone of the endocrine system". [3] A keystone is the central principle that locks all together. When this system is healthy, the glands work together like clock-work, dispensing hormones to maintain homeostasis and keep the body balanced. A disturbed thyroid can cause a whole range of problems

b. Lower brain. The lower brain as defined in the ajna section is also ruled by the throat chakra. [4] The relation of Gemini to this centre, which is involved with upper body movement via the shoulders, arms, hands and fingers, suggests a link to the cerebellum.

---

1 Bailey, Alice A; Telepathy and the Etheric Vehicle, 137.
2 Bailey, Alice A; Initiation, Human and Solar, 98.
3 Bailey, Alice A; The Soul and its Mechanism, 46.
4 Bailey, Alice A; Treatise on White Magic, 284.

c. Respiration and the bronchial tree. The respiratory system supplies the blood with life-giving oxygen. The carotid gland that monitors oxygen content in the blood and controls respiration is part of this system. Oxygen is inhaled into the lungs, clings to red blood cells and is distributed throughout the body by the arteries.

d. Speech. The throat chakra vitalises the organs of speech.

e. Gastrointestinal tract (GI). The throat chakra governs the GI as a whole, but primarily the mouth and oesophagus. The lower part of the GI - the stomach, small intestine, large intestine (including the rectum), and the anus are governed by the solar plexus chakra, which governs digestion.

f. The lymphatic system. This is the sewerage system of the body, relating it to the gastrointestinal tract, which excretes waste from the body. Both are ruled by the 3rd ray via the throat chakra. The lymphatic system is responsible for the removal of interstitial fluid from tissues. When it is sluggish, or when the throat and chest organs are attacked by pathogens, the lymphatic system becomes congested and the tonsils and lymph nodes swell, proof the immune system is doing, or is trying to do its job.

3. Disease

- Problems with the thyroid gland and metabolism.
- Psychological trouble due to mental hyper-activity or manipulative tendencies.
- Infectious diseases especially those that affect breathing, also disorders of the lymphatic system.
- Diseases affecting the mouth and throat, the vocal cords, speech and the ears.

Trouble with breathing, speech impediments or any problems associated with articulating words are related to this centre and the organs it rules. Infectious diseases belong here. They are group diseases (obviously) that are related to the mental nature.[1] This suggests that physical plane infectious diseases are a manifestation or reflection of our collective, irritable, angry, toxic thoughts and words stirring up trouble in astral matter.

▲ **Psychology**
ADD: attention deficit disorder
ADHD: > hyperactivity disorder
Conmen
Cyber: bully, stalker, troll, criminals; online scammers
Psychopath
Sociopath
Stalkers
Suicidal thoughts
Tricksters

▲ **Body**
Adam's apple
Adenoids
Airways
Alimentary canal
Alveoli
Appetite
Brainstem
Breathing
Bronchial tree

Carotid gland, arteries
Cerebellum
Diaphragm
Digestion
Ears
Endocrine system
Gastro-intestinal tract
Glottis
Hearing
Jugular vein
Larynx
Lips
Lungs
Lymph, nodes
Lymphatic system
Medulla oblongata
Metabolism
Mouth
Neck
Oesophagus upper
Palate

Parathyroids
Parotid glands
Peristalsis
Pharynx
Pons
Reptilian brain
Respiration
Salivary glands
Sinuses
Speech
Taste
Thalamus
Thoracic duct
Throat
Thyroid
Thyroxine
Tongue
Tonsils
Trachea
Tubes, body
Uvula
Vocal cords
Windpipe

▲ **Disease**
Allergies, breathing
Aphasia
Asphyxia
Asthma
Bad breath
Bronchitis
Buboes, plague
Carpal tunnel syndrome
Cervical osteoarthritis
Chicken pox
Cholera
Colds
Cystic fibrosis
Croup
Deafness
Dengue fever
Diphtheria
Drowns, drowning
Dyslexia
Emphysema
Epstein–Barr virus
Fatigue - thyroid
Glandular fever, swellings
Goitre
Grave's disease
Halitosis
Hashimoto's disease
Hodgkin's disease
Hormonal trouble
Hyperactivity
Influenza
Labyrinthitis
Laryngitis
Learning difficulties
Lymphoma
Measles
Meniere's disease
Metabolic disorder caused by emotionalism
Middle ear problems
Mononucleosis
Mucus
Mumps
Nasal congestion
Phlegm
Pleurisy
Pneumonia
Postpartum blues
Pulmonary tuberculosis
Rubella
Scarlet fever
Sinusitis
Smallpox
Sleep apnoea
Snoring
Strangulation
Stuttering
Suffocation
Thyroid imbalance
Tinnitus
Tonsillitis
Toothache
Weight gain or loss, thyroid

---
1 Bailey, Alice A; Esoteric Healing, 312.

4. The Heart or Anahata Chakra

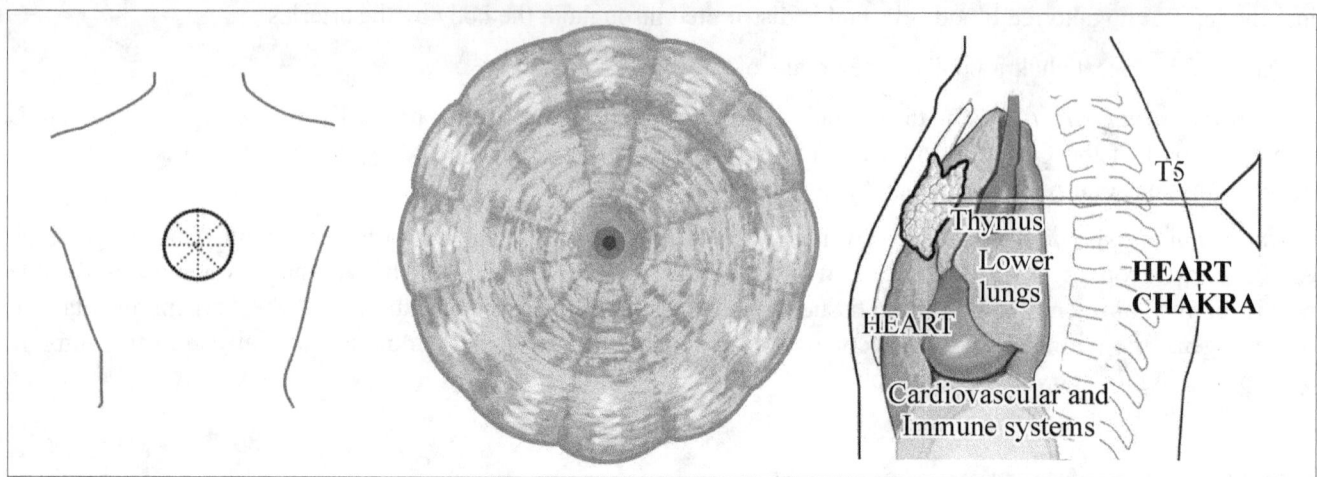

- The heart chakra enters the spine between the shoulder blades, around thoracic 5 (T5), and anchors in the thymus gland. It has 12 petals coloured with a golden hue.
- The heart is vitalised from the higher Mental Plane and from the love petals of the egoic lotus.
- The heart centre is an entry portal for Ray 2 of Love and Wisdom.
- The forces of Leo and the Sun flow through the heart chakra, while Jupiter is influential in disciples.

1. Psychology

The heart chakra is the channel for Ray 2 of Love and Wisdom; it is the organ of spiritual love. The centre comes alive in the higher sense as we purify the astral nature, transmute lower desire into inclusive love and begin to work cooperatively in groups for world good.

Located at the centre of the crown chakra is a higher heart centre - a replica of the 12-petalled lotus found on the spine. As the lower heart centre unfolds due to a growing sense of inclusiveness, group relations and the expression of goodwill, it brings the higher centre alive. When the higher heart portal is functioning, it indicates that divine will-to-good is being expressed.

Unmodified by human emotions, soul love is never personal, selfish and conditional. These are ray 6 emotional and selfish solar plexus traits. St. Paul's verses from the Bible, Corinthians 13:4-7 describe soul love in action.

> Love is patient, love is kind. It does not envy, it does not boast, it is not proud. It does not dishonour others, it is not self-seeking, it is not easily angered, it keeps no record of wrongs. Love does not delight in evil but rejoices with the truth. It always protects, always trusts, always hopes, always perseveres.

The earliest opening of the heart is not necessarily an altruistic affair. Material and selfish leaders at the heart of an organisation open this chakra. The years from 28 to 35 are particularly conducive to heart chakra unfoldment. With the adolescent and youthful years lying behind, with struggles and disappointments softening up the ego, if the heart is not already open the soul will try to bring about its development in this period.

2. Body

a. The thymus gland and the immune system. The heart chakra anchors in the thymus, relating Leo and the Sun to the gland in its connection with the immune system. Killer T-cells of the immune system mature in this gland. In most people around puberty, the thymus starts to shrink. This, however, does not happen in spiritually advanced people who have opened the heart chakra. The gland starts functioning at a new and higher level, which means immune protection is heightened.

b. Life force. A stream or thread of life energy known as the sutratma originates from the Monad, our highest spiritual source, and anchors in the heart centre and physical heart. From there it uses the bloodstream, arteries and veins to give life to the entire organism. The soul utilises the sutratma to hold the body coherently together during life. When death takes place, when the soul snaps the life thread, the atoms disperse and the body falls apart.

c. Cardiovascular system and vitalisation of the body. The heart chakra and heart organ are governed by the Sun. Just as the Sun holds the planets of the solar system together and nourishes them with solar fire, so does the heart chakra operate in the body. Working through the heart organ and channelling inpouring life-force and prana and sending this force out through the cardiovascular system, it maintains the health of the cells of the body, vitalising and nourishing them. The heart chakra rules cell life. [1]

d. The vagus nerve. It allows the brain to monitor and receive information about several of the body's different functions. The heart and base chakras are connected with the vagus nerve. When the soul, functioning through the head brings these two centres under control - when the head, heart and base centre are in a magnetic rapport; the final work of merging the fires of the body, of raising the kundalini fire from the base chakra to merge with the fire of spirit in the crown is undertaken. It is through the stimulation and the control of the vagus nerve that this is accomplished. It swings the entire nervous system into a special form of rhythmic activity and responsiveness, which initiates the process. After this event takes place, the soul is in control of the entire lower nature and its influence - through the purified personality, is profoundly effective for world good.

3. Disease

- Diseases of the heart, the blood and of the cardiovascular system as a whole.
- Problems with cell life.
- Problems with the autonomic nervous system and the vagus nerve.
- Problems with the immune system and autoimmune diseases.

Thousands of people in the world are having their heart chakra's stimulated today as they move from being emotionally and selfishly focused (the solar plexus chakra), up to being inclusive and group conscious. This puts a strain on the heart with subsequent trouble in that organ.

> the transference of all the accumulated energies in the solar plexus centre into the heart centre will cause difficulty, very frequently of a serious nature; this is the reason why today so many advanced people die of heart disease. [2]

The Sun rules cell life and the cardiovascular system nourishes all cells in the body with blood. A very interesting point to note is that germs are living organisms that find their way into the body through the medium of the life-force. As this force flows into the heart and bloodstream and so do the invaders. Once in, if they are not stopped they wreak havoc, attacking cell-life and disrupting the entire organism.

▲ **Psychology**
Group oriented in a greedy material, immoral, selfish way

▲ **Body**
Aorta
Arteries
Blood
Blood circulation, quality
Bloodstream
Capillaries
Cardiovascular system
Cell life
Constitution
Haemoglobin
Heart
Immune system
Iron in the blood
Leukocytes
Life-force, soul energy
Life-thread/stream, sutratma, silver cord
Oxygen, oxygenation
Pericardium
Plasma
Prana
Pulmonary circulation
Recuperative power
Red blood cells
Spleen
Stem cells
Sternum
Thymus
Vagus nerve
Valves - heart
Veins
Vena Cava
Venous system
Vitality (solar fire)
Vitamin D3, sunshine vitamin
White blood cells

▲ **Disease**
AIDS
Allergic reaction
from immune
Anaemia
Aneurism
Angina
Arrhythmia
Arteriosclerosis
Atrial fibrillation
Autoimmune diseases
Blood cancer
Blood circulation problems
Blood poisoned
Bruises
Cardio-myopathy
Deep vein thrombosis
Ebola virus
Fainting
Fever
Gangrene
Germs
Heart fibrillation
Heart attack
Heart disease
Heart problem, congenital
High blood pressure
High temperature
Hypertension
Hypotension
Immune attack
Inflammation
Leukaemia: blood cancer
Lupus
Myasthenia gravis
Myocarditis
Over-growth
Palpitations
Pathogens
Reynaud's disease
Rheumatic fever
Shock
Sunburn
Sunstroke
Varicose veins

---

1 Bailey, Alice A; Treatise on White Magic, 284.
2 Bailey, Alice A; Esoteric Healing, 175.

5. The Solar Plexus or Manipura Chakra

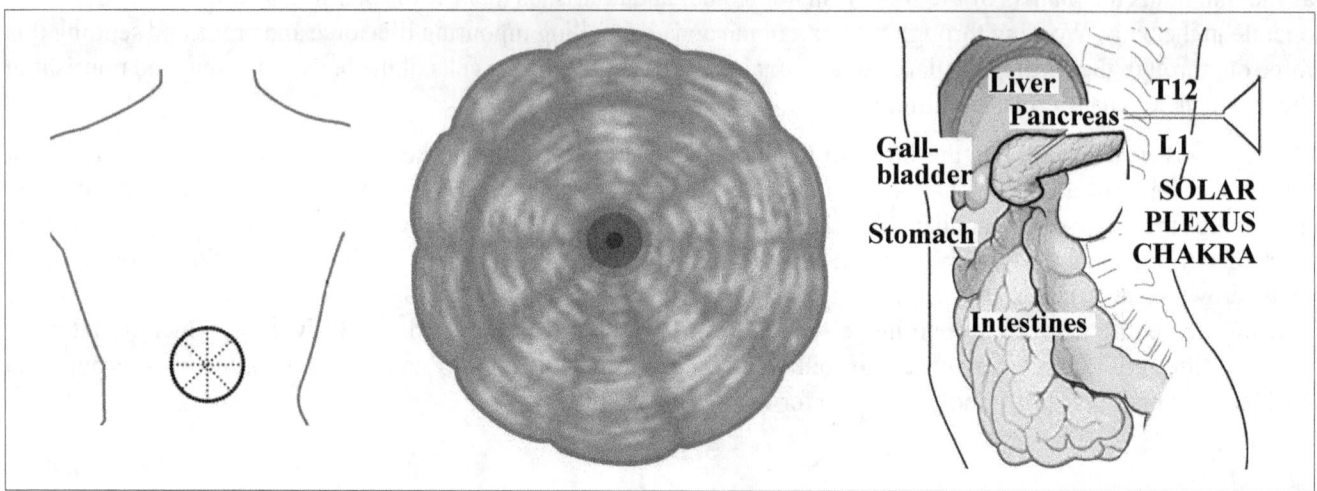

- The solar plexus enters the spine around thoracic 12 (T12) and lumbar 1 (L1), anchoring in the pancreas gland. It has 10 petals. The colour is described as rosy with a mixture of green.
- The solar plexus is vitalised from the astral body and astral centres.
- The solar plexus chakra is the main entry portal for ray 6; ray 2 and the 3rd aspect [1] are also associated.
- Cancer is the traditional ruler of digestion. Its force, ray 3, governs digestion. Planet rulers of the solar plexus chakra are Mars, Neptune and the Moon via Cancer.

1. Psychology

The psychological function of the solar plexus chakra is to give expression to our emotions. It is the doorway to the Astral Plane and the entry portal into the body for the 6th emotional ray. This force dominates the average person, which makes it and the solar plexus chakra very potent.

Our emotions and desires constantly yearn for happiness and pleasure. If they are denied, if we are rejected it registers in the solar plexus. Even if we get what we want, this centre is not satisfied for long. It thirsts for new satisfactions. The forces of emotion and desire keep those under their control swinging between the opposites of pleasure and pain. Getting off this treadmill requires the transmuting of desire into an aspiration for something higher and finer - moving focus from the solar plexus up to the inclusive heart chakra. The reward for those who achieve this is emotional peace and serenity.

From age seven to fourteen, the soul tries to grip the astral body and bring the emotions under its control. Parents can help their children in this period by teaching them to express their emotions in a healthy way.

2. Body

a. The pancreas. The solar plexus chakra anchors in the pancreas, working particularly through the endocrine parts of the gland - the islets of Langerhans. They secrete insulin and glycogen to control blood sugar levels.

b. Digestion. The throat chakra rules the gastrointestinal tract. However, the solar plexus is the primary ruler of digestion and of the digestive organs - the stomach, liver, gallbladder, pancreas, duodenum and intestines.

c. The Sympathetic Nervous System (SNS). It is immediately affected by solar plexus activity. Nerves that signal through the sympathetic system originate from the spinal cord in the solar plexus region.

3. Disease

- The many psychological and nervous disorders caused by unstable emotions.
- Indigestion and diseases of the digestive organs, the pancreas and intestinal disorders.
- Trouble with the bloodstream, sepsis, blood poisoning, skin eruptions.

Troubled 6th ray force causing emotional disturbances and etheric congestion lies behind most health problems. Nervous and gastric disorders are early warning signs that the body is unable to handle the toxicity being produced.

---

1 Bailey, Alice A; Esoteric Healing, 107.

The heart and solar plexus centres are closely allied and problems with blood quality can arise from a solar plexus disturbance. Insidiously, a troubled solar plexus will infect energetically, any other chakra or body organ that has a weakness, causing trouble in their organs.

Cancer: the disease cancer first appeared in the distant past and consequently the seeds of this trouble lie within our DNA. It is caused by overactivity in a centre [1] and a major cause is repression, using the will to stifle a natural expression so that congestion is caused. It is placed in this chakra section because so often, emotions that are repressed or that are wildly out of control cause this congestion and overactivity. This energy infection then can spread to any other part of the body that is debilitated. For instance, cancer may appear in the throat if we are afraid or unable to talk about a serious abuse or tragedy, in our bones if we suppress a fear of life, or in the genitals through forced celibacy. Here is a quote on this latter form of cancer.

> One of the main sources of cancer as related to the sacral centre, and therefore to the sex organs, has been the well-intentioned suppression of the sex life, and of all thought connected with the sex life, by misguided aspirants; they are those who find the teaching—monastic and celibate— of the Middle Ages the line of least resistance. [2]

Cancer is a 2nd ray disease, which causes the overbuilding of cells. 1st ray repression is often a cause. We can help to avoid cancer by keeping our systems free-flowing and happy, by avoiding repressions of any sort and by finding alternative means to express force if a normal outlet is not available. Meditation to achieve inner serenity and the practice of harmlessness and kindness are super-preventatives. But as we age and the soul begins to withdraw, the body breaks down and we can contract any disease - even cancer.

▲ **Psychology**
Alcoholism
Anti-social, dangerous brooders
Anxiety, worry
Astral maniac
Bipolar
Borderline personality disorder
Cuts, cutting
Delirium, delusion
Depression
Dreams, troubled
Glamour
Hallucination
Hypochondria
Hysteria
Inner conflict
Manic depression
Mood swings
Neurotics, neuroses
Obscure diseases due to emotionalism
Obsessive compulsive
Panic attacks
Paranoia
Phobias
PTSD
Schizophrenia
Self-harm, self-injury
Sleep-walking
Substance abuse

▲ **Body**
Abdomen
Anus
Appendix
Bile
Bowel
Carbohydrates
Chyle
Colon
Defecation
Duodenum
Enteric NS
Excretion, solid waste
Faeces
Gallbladder
Glucose, sugar
Ileum
Insulin
Intestines
Islets of Langerhans
Jejunum
Liver
Motor nerves
Nutrition
Oesophagus lower
Pancreas
Pylorus
Rectum
Stomach
Sugar, glucose
Sympathetic NS

▲ **Disease**
Abscesses
Acid reflux
Acidosis
Acne
Allergies, digestive
Alopecia
Anal fissure
Anorexia
Appendicitis
Athlete's foot
Biliousness
Boils
Bulimia
Cancer: major cause of
Candida
Carcinogenic
Carcinoma
Cellulite, fatness
Cholesterol
Chronic fatigue
Cirrhosis, liver
Coeliac disease
Colic
Colitis
Constipation
Crohn's disease
Cysts
Dermatitis
Devitalisation
Diabetes
Diarrhoea
Diseases caused by excess
Diverticulitis
Drug addiction
Dysentery
Dyspepsia
Eating disorders
Eczema
Emotionalism: all diseases caused by
Enteritis
Fatigue
Fatness, obesity
Flabbiness
Flatulence
Food allergies
Food poisoning
Fungus, fungi
Gallstones
Gastric disorders
Gluttony
Gout
Growths, abnormal
Haemorrhoids
Hallucinatory, recreational drugs
Heartburn
Hepatitis
Hyper-glycemia, hypo-glycaemia
Hypertrophy
Impetigo
Immunity low
Indigestion
Irritable bowel syndrome
Jaundice
Leprosy
Lethargy
Malnutrition
Metastases
Narcolepsy
Nausea
Nightmares
Obesity
Oedema
Pancreatitis
Parasites, intestinal
Peptic ulcer
Peritonitis
Piles
Pimples
Pus
Rashes
Reflux
Rheumatic fever
Ringworm
Sarcoma
Scabies
Scleroderma
Scurvy
Septicaemia
Sluggish action of organs
Sores, weeping
Starvation
Swellings
Tapeworm
Thrush
Tinea
Tissue, insidious changes
Tumours, growths
Typhoid fever
Ulcers, gastric
Viruses
Vomiting
Water retention
Weight gain
Wind
Worms
Yeast infection

---

1 Bailey, Alice A; Esoteric Healing, 239.
2 Ibid, 239.

6. The Sacral or Svadhisthana Chakra

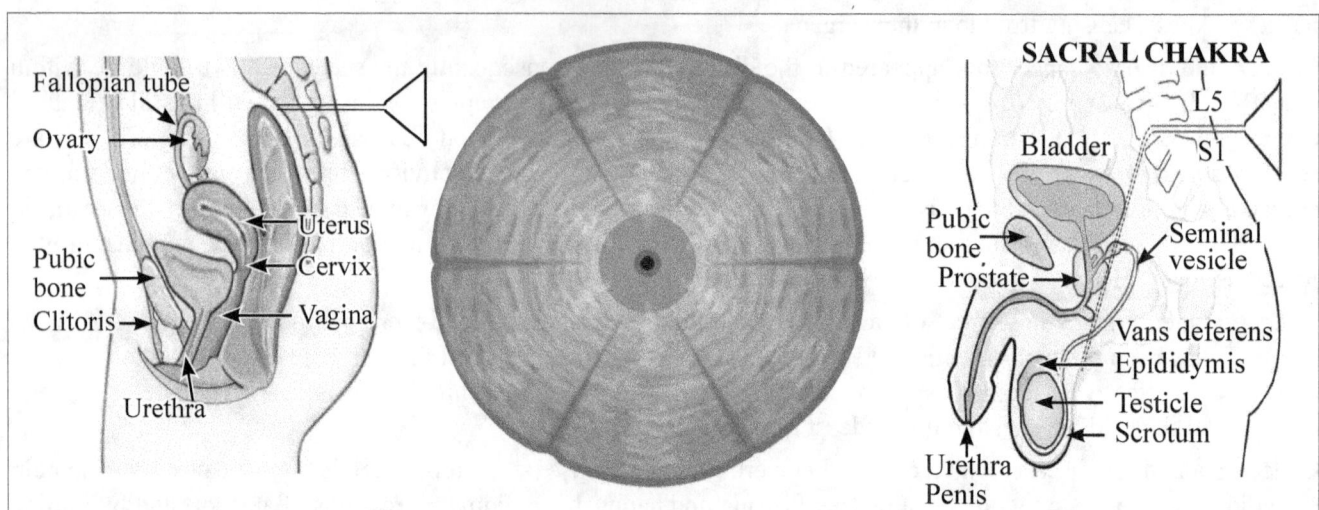

- The sacral enters the spine around lumbar 5 (L5) and sacral 1 (S1), anchoring in the reproductive organs – the testes in males and the ovaries in women. It has six petals and the colour is described as being vermilion.
- The sacral is vitalised from the etheric body and the Physical Plane.
- The sacral is the main entry portal for Ray 7 of Ceremony, Order and Magic. But other rays play through it as well. Another important ray that plays through the sacral centre is ray 6. [1] This is the ray of desire and the sacral chakra houses or harbours lower desire.
- Scorpio and Mars are the traditional rulers of sex and reproduction. However, Cancer is also a prime ruler of reproduction, especially in women. Uranus that carries the 7th ray governs sexual attitudes and the building of forms for reproduction. Sagittarius governs the sacral chakra which provides the energy for the use of the creative powers of the physical life. [2]

1. Psychology

The sacral chakra gives expression to our sexual and material desires. The desire to be rich and have a luxurious life or a desire for comfort or security (economic, social or religious), these are sacral chakra expressions. The 6th ray of desire influences this centre. Although most people on earth are focused in a higher centre, the sacral remains powerful because the lower appetites still drive most people. If the sacral is overemphasised, people can become obsessed and unstoppable in their urge to satisfy their sexual cravings. We see this in sexual criminals and deviants.

The sacral and throat centres are opposite poles. A great evolutionary change occurs when the focus of desire rises to the throat. This occurs as sexual-desire transforms into an aspiration for higher intellectual, artistic or spiritual pursuits. Desire does not disappear, it simply mutates into a higher form. The 7th ray that flows through the sacral assists this process. It transforms our attitudes to sex.

2. Body

a. Etheric web. The vitalising energy body, the etheric web on which the dense physical body is constructed, anchors in the sacral chakra. [3]

b. Sex and reproduction. The sacral chakra governs sex, right from the sexual act to its intended final result - reproduction. It rules the male and female reproductive systems in their entirety. [4] The female reproductive system consisting of the uterus or womb, fallopian tubes and the ovaries are ruled primarily by Cancer and the Moon. Cancer carries two rays that rule sex and reproduction, rays 3 and 7. They also rule pregnancy, birth, babies, nursing and motherhood. The vagina, clitoris, pubis, vulva and labia - these sexual reproductive organs are primarily ruled by Venus and Mars.

---

1 Bailey, Alice A; Esoteric Psychology I, 420.
2 Bailey, Alice A; Esoteric Astrology, 191.
3 Bailey, Alice A; Esoteric Healing, 45.
4 Ibid, 202.

The male reproduction system consists of the penis, testicles, scrotum, epididymis, vas deferens, prostate, Cowper and seminal glands. Scorpio and Mars rule these organs and male sexuality.

c. Reproduction: DNA, foetal development, congenital and genetic disorders. The basic energy pattern of the physical body is recorded in the physical permanent atom, which is etheric in nature, and in our DNA. In early foetal development, genes give out the instructions that tell the body how to build and grow. This work takes place in the sacral chakra. The 7th ray via the sacral centre, builds all forms of expression.[1]

When the soul is ready to reincarnate, it sounds its note and the vibration attracts to the physical permanent atom, appropriate substance from which the foetus develops. The same occurs on astral and mental levels.

Ray 7 and the sacral are involved when things go wrong during conception and pregnancy. This is shown in the chart by afflictions to 7th ray Uranus or to the Moon that carries the 7th ray via Cancer, or to planets in Cancer. The Moon is the mother of form and is linked again to the sacral chakra by the "lunar lords" (nature's builders) which work through this centre.

3. Disease

- Genetic or congenital diseases.
- Problems or diseases concerning sex or reproduction.
- Perverted attitudes towards sex or marriage.

Trouble in this region is often due to suppressed desire or through the misuse of sexual force. On a higher level, another cause is due to the transfer of desire from the sacral to the throat, an important evolutionary development. In such a case, disease may arise in the organs ruled by either centre until energy flux evens out.

A congenital defect occurs when the foetus develops an abnormality in the womb. This may be due to a genetic disorder that is caused by an abnormality in DNA, passed on by parents who have the condition or who are healthy carriers of the mutated gene. Or, the abnormality may occur due to an aberration in the womb, for instance as cells divide.

▲ **Psychology**
Divorce
Gambling addiction
Incest
Marriage problems
Masochism
Paedophilia
Predatory behaviour
Serial killer
Sexual promiscuity, addiction
Sexual: rape, perversions, murder, sadism
Wasteful

▲ **Body**
Babies
Birth
Breasts
Cervix
Chromosome
Clitoris
Conception
Cowper's glands
DNA
Egg ovum
Embryo
Epididymis
Estrogen
Etheric body
Fallopian tubes
Fertility
Gene, genetics
Genitals
Gestation
Infancy
Labia
Lacteals, lactation
Libido
Locomotion
Maternity
Menstruation
Mothers, mothering
Ovaries
Penis
Periods
Physical permanent atom
Physical power and strength.
Placenta
Pregnancy
Procreation
Progesterone
Prostate gland
Protective power
Puberty
Pubis
Reproduction
Sciatic nerve
Scrotum
Semen
Seminal vesicle
Sex hormones, organs
Sex life
Sex relations
Sexual development
Sexual power
Sigmoid flexure
Sperm
Testes
Testicles
Testosterone
Urethra, for semen
Urge to self-perpetuate
Uterus
Vagina
Vans deferens
Vulva
Womb

▲ **Disease**
Abortion
Barrenness
Castration
Chlamydia
Congenital diseases
Endometriosis
Extra body parts
Fibroids in womb
Frigidity
Gene mutation
Genetic diseases
Genital disorders, warts
Gonorrhea
Hereditary diseases
Herpes, genital
Immorality
Impotency
Infertility
Karmic diseases
Locomotive disorders
Miscarriage
Premature ejaculation
Prostate trouble
Pubic, crabs
Sciatica
Sexual license
Social diseases
STD: sexually transmitted diseases
Sterility
Syphilis
Underactive, undeveloped organs
Uterine troubles
Venereal disease

---
1 Bailey, Alice A; Esoteric Psychology I, 261.

7. The Base or Muladhara Chakra

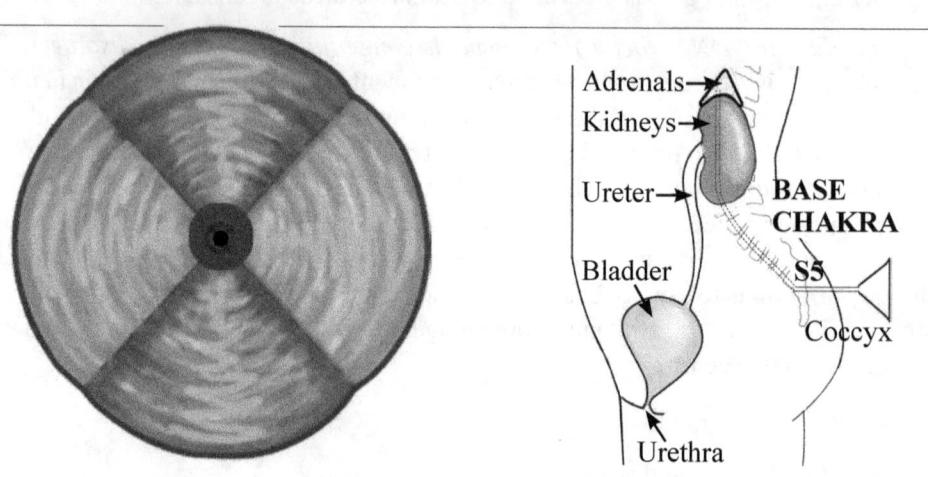

- The basic chakra enters the spine at the base of the spine around sacrum 5 (S5) and the top of the coccyx, anchoring in the adrenal glands. It has 4 petals, arranged in the shape of a cross that radiates orange fire.
- The base is vitalised by the Mother of the World, Mother Nature.
- The base is an entry portal for ray 1, and ray 3, [1] Other associated rays are 4 and 7.
- The base chakra rules the body mainframe structure and so do Capricorn and Saturn, confirming that they are the prime rulers on the physical level. All the signs from Sagittarius to Pisces, rule the body from the hips to the feet and are related to the base. Pluto invests the base chakra and adrenals with the 1st ray will to live.

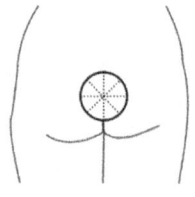

1. Psychology

Dictators who have very strong and selfish personal wills use the 1st ray power of the base chakra. The physical body will to live and to survive is anchored in this centre and dictators draw on this force. For example, Adolf Hitler - he was a highly intelligent and evil man, with an extraordinary will. The tone he set in the world was base and materialistic, indicating that he drew upon the power of the basic material centre. Such people try to rule the world through war, fear, cruelty and materialism.

2. Body

a. The adrenal glands. The base chakra anchors in these glands, which are located at the top of each kidney. The inner part of the gland, the adrenal-medulla, produces adrenaline, a hormone involved in the fight or flight syndrome. This is a 1st ray via Pluto and Scorpio instinct, which when playing through the base gives the animal nature the "will to survive". Libra and Venus rule the outer part of the gland, the adrenal-cortex. It helps regulate metabolism and salt-water balance in the blood.

b. Kidneys and elimination. Food travelling through the digestive system is broken down and sent through to the kidneys via the blood to filter out impurities. The kidneys are the major organs of the urinary tract. Other components are the ureters, bladder and urethra. The kidneys filter out liquid waste, which then passes to the ureters and bladder to be disposed of through urine. Ray 1, Libra, Scorpio, Mars and Pluto rule the kidneys.

c. The dense physical body, vertebral column and kundalini. This chakra vitalises tissue throughout the entire body, excepting for those main organs governed by the six higher chakras. This rulership also covers the skeleton and the entire "spinal column". [2] Located at the bottom of the spine, this centre functions like a basement boiler in an apartment block, whose job is to keep all higher levels of the building warm and pleasant for residents. This heat is provided by kundalini, the fire of matter, which is housed in this centre.

---

1 Bailey, Alice A; The Destiny of the Nations, 117-8.
2 Bailey, Alice A; Esoteric Healing, 202.

For the first four years in life, the base is the dominant chakra, vitalising rapid body growth. In these early years, the soul hovers over its physical form. Then from age four to seven (earlier in souls who are advanced), the soul tries to grip the body and get it under its control via the nervous system. If this process is disrupted because of accident or abuse, soul-body control may not be completed or be inadequate. The result would be an under-functioning base chakra and an inadequately earthed or grounded physical body, physical weakness, disease and illness.

3. Disease

- Problems and diseases of the spine and nerves branching out of the spine.
- Problems with the body structure, including the skeleton, bones, tissue, muscles and skin.
- Diseases of the adrenals, of the urinary tract - the kidneys and bladder.

The base chakra in most people is only partially open, just enough to do its job of vitalising the physical form. It is the last centre to open fully. This occurs when spiritual union with the soul takes place in consciousness. Then kundalini rises up the spine to merge with spiritual force in the crown. If kundalini rises prematurely through unwise spiritual practices, tissue is burnt which can result in insanity, even death.

▲ **Psychology**
Combativeness
Egomania
Megalomania

▲ **Body**
Adrenal-cortex
Adrenaline
Adrenal-medulla
Aldosterone
Ankles
Arms, hands, shoulders
Atlas axis
Biceps
Bladder
Body containers, sheaths
Body fat
Body intelligence
Body warmth
Bone marrow
Bones
Buttocks
Calcium
Calves
Carpal and metacarpal bones
Cartilage, connective tissue
Catalysts, body
Chin
Clavicle
Coccyx - tailbone
Collagen
Corpses
Cortisol
Cranium
Elbow
Enamel
Enzymes
Feet
Femur
Fibula
Fight or flight
Fingers, phalanges
Flesh
Gluteus muscles
Gums
Hair
Hamstrings
Hands
Hips
Humerus
Hyoid bone
Ilium
Integumentary system
Ischium
Jaws
Joints
Kidneys
Knees
Kundalini
Leg bones
Ligaments
Limbs, lower
Membranes
Minerals
Moles, skin
Muscles
Nails
Old age
Patella
Pelvic girdle
Pelvis
Peritoneum
Physical body
Pleurae
Protein
Pubic bone
Pubis
Quadriceps muscles
Radius
Ribs
Rigor mortis
Sacroiliac joint
Sacrum
Scapula
Secretions
Skeleton
Skin
Skull
Spinal column, spine
Substance
Survival instinct
Tears
Teeth
Tendons
Thighs
Tibia
Tissue, flesh
Toes
Ulna
Urea
Ureters
Urethra
Uric acid
Urinary tract
Urine
Vertebrae, all
Will to live, to exist
Wrist

▲ **Disease**
Aches intense
Addison's disease
Ageing unnaturally
Ankle problems
Ankylosis spondylosis
Arthritis
Athlete's foot
Attrition
Back pain
Baldness
Birthmark
Bone fractures: shoulders, arms, hands; hips, thighs
Bone: deformities, crippling
Bright's disease
Bunions
Bursitis
Calcification
Calf problems
Cervical osteoarthritis
Chronic diseases
Constrictions
Cramps
Crippled
Cushing's syndrome
Cystitis
Dead things
Decay
Deformity
Dental problems
Dysplasia of the hip
Fatigue: adrenal overload
Feet problems
Fistula
Fractures, bones
Geriatric
Gingivitis, pyorrhea
Hardening, stiffening
Hernia
Hip disease
Hyper-uricaemia
Joints stiff
Karmic diseases
Kidney infection
Kidney stones
Knee problems
Lesions
Limping
Lumbago
Melanoma
Meningitis
Murder
Nephritis
Osteoarthritis
Osteoporosis
Paget's disease
Polyps
Progeria
Prolapses
Rheumatism
Rheumatoid arthritis
Rickets
Scleroderma
Sclerosis
Scoliosis
Skull: injuries
Spina bifida
Spinal fractures
Stiffness
Stones
Urinary tract infections
Vertebrae degeneration
Warts
Wrinkles

ASTROLOGY - CHAKRA DIVISIONS

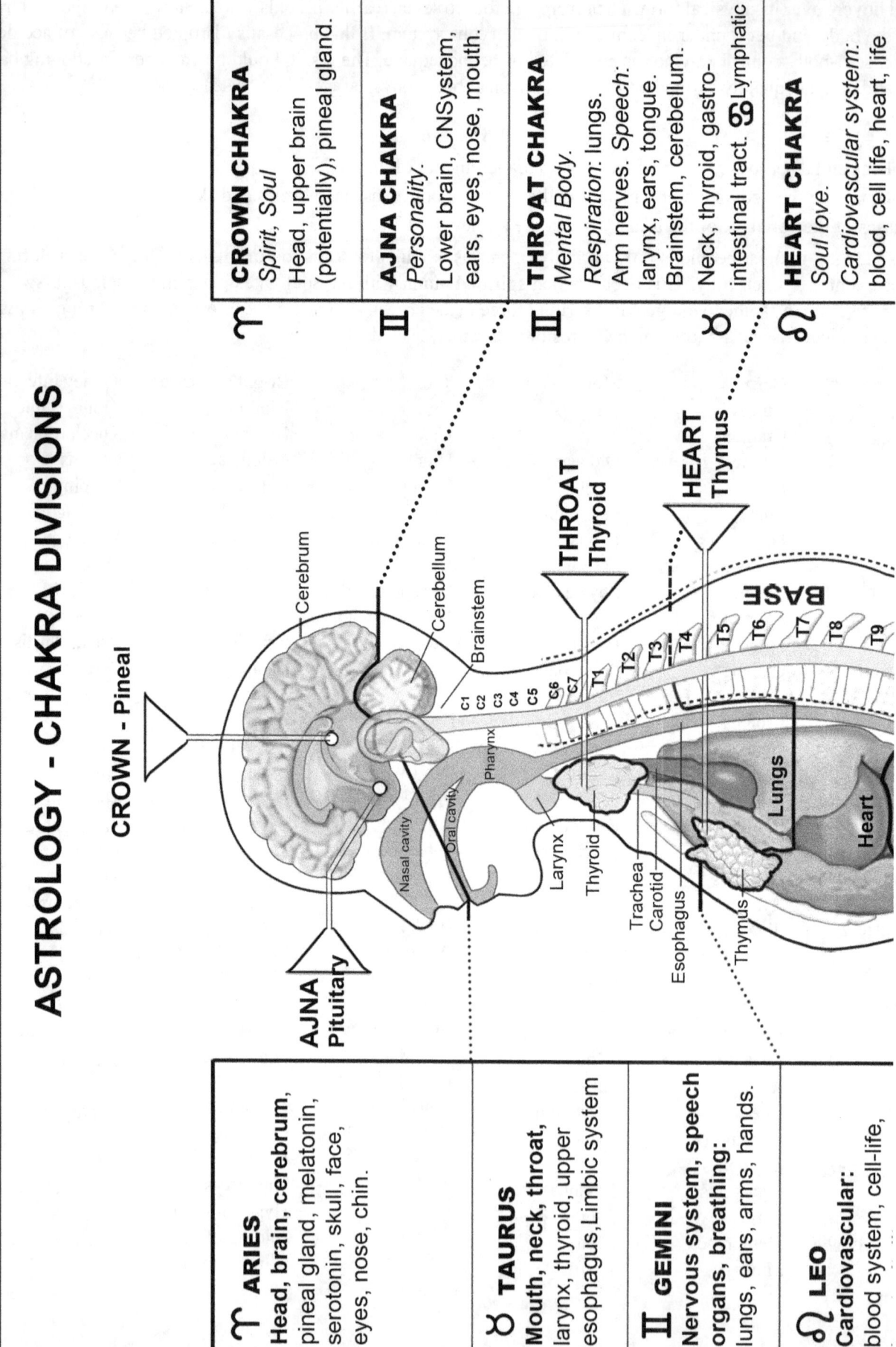

CROWN - Pineal

AJNA - Pituitary

THROAT - Thyroid

HEART - Thymus

BASE

♈ **ARIES**
Head, brain, cerebrum, pineal gland, melatonin, serotonin, skull, face, eyes, nose, chin.

♉ **TAURUS**
Mouth, neck, throat, larynx, thyroid, upper esophagus, Limbic system

♊ **GEMINI**
Nervous system, speech organs, breathing: lungs, ears, arms, hands.

♌ **LEO**
Cardiovascular: blood system, cell-life,

♈ **CROWN CHAKRA**
Spirit, Soul
Head, upper brain (potentially), pineal gland.

♊ **AJNA CHAKRA**
Personality.
Lower brain, CNSystem, ears, eyes, nose, mouth.

♊ **THROAT CHAKRA**
Mental Body.
Respiration: lungs. Arm nerves. *Speech:* larynx, ears, tongue. Brainstem, cerebellum. Neck, thyroid, gastro-intestinal tract. ♋ Lymphatic

♌ **HEART CHAKRA**
Soul love.
Cardiovascular system: blood, cell life, heart, life

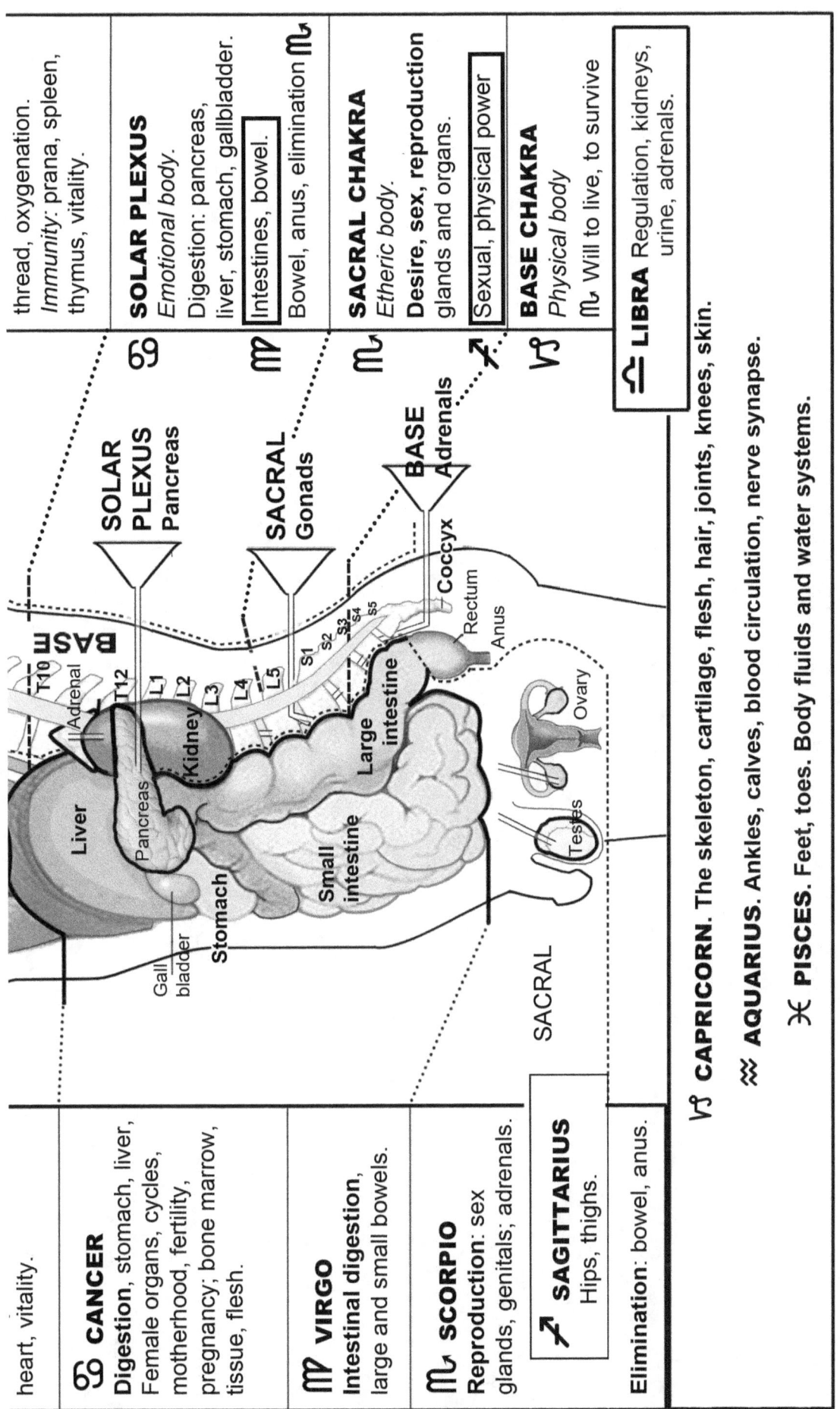

© Leoni Hodgson 2018.

3. DISEASE AND ITS DIAGNOSIS

"The TRIANGLE is... the basic geometric form of all manifestation .. underlying the entire fabric of manifestation, whether it is the manifestation of a solar system, a man", or in this case disease.

1. Disease and its cause - it is simply misuse of energy

In a general sense the cause of disease is simple - disharmony with life. Clashing energies and conflicts cause disease. In man, the immediate problem is disharmony with his soul.

> **All disease is the result of inhibited soul life, and that is true of all forms in all kingdoms.** [1]

This means that prior to enlightenment, which is that advanced state when soul-personality illumination occurs and the flow of soul energy through the form is full and free; illness is inevitable. Most people cannot do anything about this because their bodies and the forces which play through them are inherited from past lives and are programmed with wrong rhythms and misused forces. The average person is stuck with what he has and is unable generally to improve matters apart from living a clean and healthy life.

The body may not break down until life's end through the degradation of the form that ageing causes; but the rule holds good. Disease is simply nature's way of letting us know that its flow is blocked and that an adjustment or easing of that blockage is required. Consequently, its effect is purificatory and the final act of adjustment, release and purification that we go through on earth, is the death of the physical body.

1. The emotional body is the primary cause of disease

> Disease is simply the misuse of the forces of the etheric, the astral and of the dense physical levels.

The physical body is an animal form and when it has no inherited weaknesses and vitality flows freely, it is resistant to germs and infection. Primitive man had this type of body and excellent physical health, but when the emotional nature and later the mind started to unfold, trouble started. Their misuse distorts energy flow as these steps show:

a. The mind thinks, it plans, it idealises and has ambitions.
b. The thoughts it creates descend to the Astral Plane where they blend with astral force. When disappointments and frustrations set in because things don't go the way we would like them to or because we cannot get what we want, bitterness sets in. Then disease follows according to the weaknesses we have inherited in the physical body.

Ninety per cent of the causes of disease are to be found originating in the astral and etheric bodies; [2] wrong use of mental energy and misapplied desire are major contributing factors. This is because most people are still emotional or Atlantean in consciousness.

The mind is not usually a causal factor of disease. Bailey said that only 5 percent of all modern disease originates in the mental body. Even then, the accompanying emotional reaction causes the problem. For instance, a person may think that he is a superior person, but it is only when that thought is taken over by negative emotions such as hatred or dislike that trouble arises. Unstable and erratic emotions generate toxic chemical reactions in the physical body and if left unresolved they manifest as a physical illness.

Trouble can also arise from the mental body when we are mentally aloof and live in a world of our own. In such a case our thoughts are not put into action in our physical life, but remain on the Mental Plane and in the mind body, building a wall between its owner and others. This is a problem of cleavage covered in the Ray 5 section.

From an esoteric perspective, disease is the working out into manifestation of undesirable, subjective conditions - mental, emotional and etheric. In the future, as the race becomes more intellectual, the percentages given above will change.

> **In summary, if our thoughts and emotions are violent, disturbed or repressed, this causes disruption in the etheric body and the glandular release of toxic chemicals in the physical that eventually lead to disease. The drawing on the following page - "Disrupted Energy Flow resulting in Disease" depicts this process.**
>
> **If our thoughts and emotions are positive and filled with joy, then energy flow will be smoother and the result will be more wholesome and health benefiting. So the good news is we can do something to improve the body we are stuck with, by improving energy flow through the mind, emotions and through the physical body.**

---

1 Bailey, Alice A; Esoteric Healing, 5.
2 Bailey, Alice A; Esoteric Healing, 112.

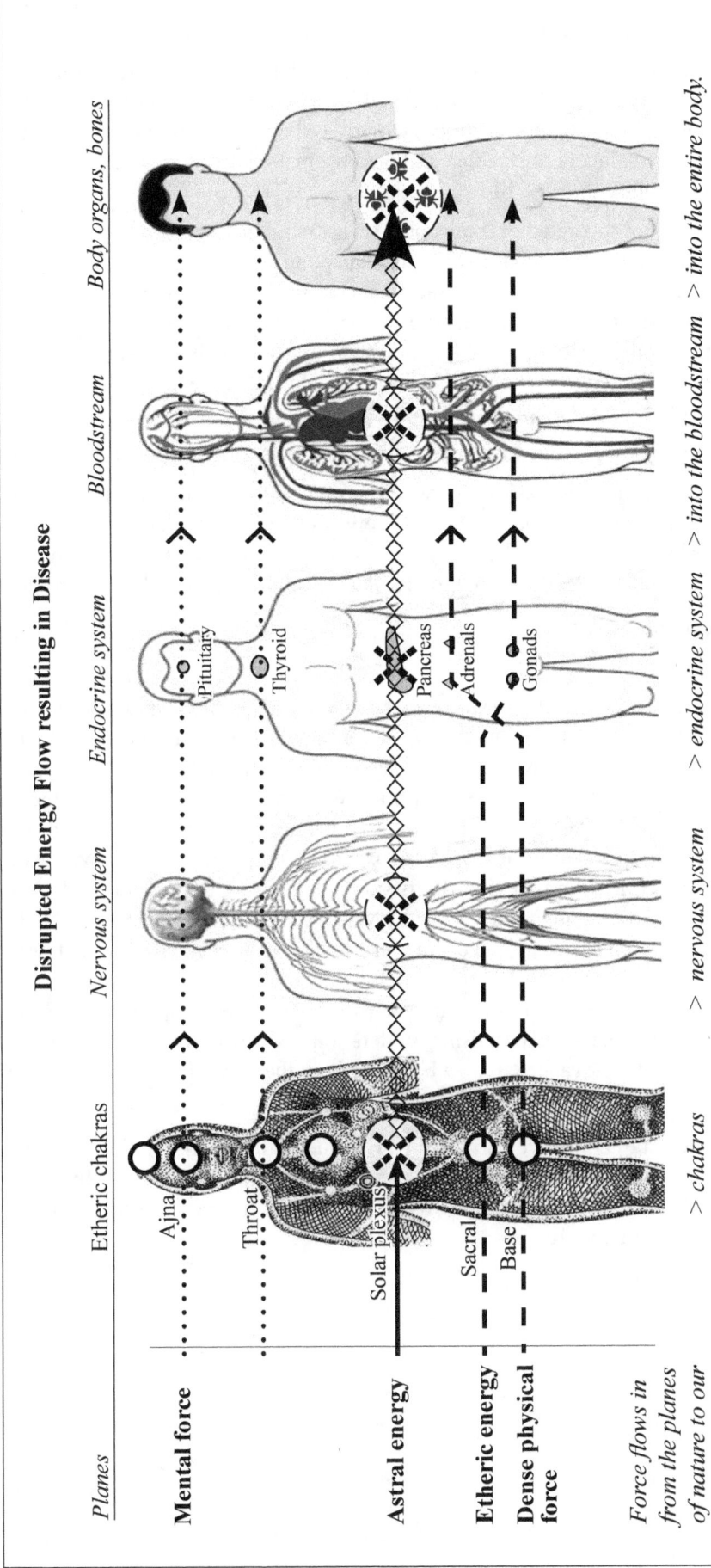

2. Clear thoughts and clear emotions are the key to good health

When we are able to carry our thoughts - undamaged or unchanged to the physical brain and from there use them to direct our life-actions; it usually results in good health. Here is how the Tibetan puts it:

> When the thought can be carried through to the physical brain and there becomes a directing agent of the life force, you will usually have a condition of good health.. whether the individual thought has been good or bad, rightly motivated or wrongly oriented. It is simply the effect of integration, because saints and sinners, the selfish and the unselfish and all kinds of people, can achieve integration and a thought-directed life. [1]

If the thoughts behind our actions are not corrupted or interrupted by an astral disturbance it benefits health. This is because good health is a consequence of good energy flow. The Tibetan points out that both good and bad people can do this. However, wrong intention and bad thoughts will attract karmic retribution at some point in time.

Ultimately though, good health occurs when we are able to express the harmonious, holistic and inclusive rhythms of the soul. These energies straighten out any kinks in our energy streams, benefiting health. Taking this a step further, if we are able to carry soul energy on the wings of our thought life and express these with good intent, we become natural healers, of ourselves and of others.

Soul energy, expressed through right thinking, can cure diseases to which man is prone. [2]

This happens whether we are in the healing professions or not. Many of us have had the experience when in the presence of a really good and compassionate person, we find ourselves feeling uplifted, energised and inspired by the contact. This is evidence of the healing power of the love and wisdom of the soul. Many of us who are practising spiritual disciplines such as meditation and are expressing goodwill are becoming natural healers or already are.

3. The primary cause of personal disease is karmic

a. Personal karma.

During the life span of the physical body, just as a motor car wears out and starts to break down, so does the physical body. But some people have better bodies than others and enjoy better health. The reason for this is karmic. Karma is the universal law of cause and effect, whatever we do has consequences. Karma determines the type of body we are born with and the type of diseases to which we are susceptible. We carry karma from life to life. All that we are at the end of one life is recorded in "memory cells" called permanent atoms, which are located on the mental, emotional and physical levels. This is replicated in our DNA (deoxyribonucleic acid) in the next incarnation. The karmic pay-off is that, if we abuse our bodies through vice, drugs, alcohol, laziness, etc., then we inherit a weakened physical body in the next. Similarly, on emotional and mental levels; if we are still driven by abusive thoughts and uncontrolled emotionalism when we die, we are fated to inherit that type of psychological pattern in our next incarnation.

The good news is, it is possible to reverse or minimise many karmic and physical impairments. By harmonising thoughts, acting with compassion and kindness and practising moderation in the way we live, we can build healthier bodies. Or, if a disease's progression is too advanced, reap a better body in the next life.

b. Collective karma and disease.

We also inherit diseases that are a result of collective karma, that arise due to the racial, religious, cultural or family group into which we are born. Additionally, all physical bodies carry the seeds of three ancient illness passed down from our forefathers through our DNA - these indigenous diseases are syphilis, cancer and tuberculosis. Bailey divides the diseases we inherit into five major groups:

1. Tuberculosis.
2. Syphilitic or sexually transmitted diseases.
3. Cancer.
4. Heart difficulties.
5. Nervous diseases. [3]

---

[1] Bailey, Alice A; Esoteric Healing, 96.
[2] Ibid, 94.
[3] Ibid, 55.

Heart and nervous difficulties are afflictions that are more recent. This is due to the mass opening of the heart and ajna chakras in modern man. Heart difficulties are due to group work, the bonding together of individuals towards a common goal that may be spiritual or material. Heart disease is a consequence of giving our heart life-blood metaphorically, to the group or to the organisation in which we carry heavy responsibilities. Brain and nervous difficulties are a consequence of wide-spread modern education, which is stimulating the latent mental faculties of the masses into life. If soul and mental force pouring in is too much for the existing equipment to handle, the brain and nerve cells will be overstimulated.

4. Other causes of disease

a. Accidents: those that are true accidents and those due to our own karma.

Surprisingly, personal karma causes most so–called accidents. They are generated by the unkind thoughts and critical words of those involved in the accident. Hatred, jealousy or vindictiveness generates explosions of force that rebound on their owners like a boomerang.

Apart from this, it is possible to be accidentally in the wrong place at the wrong time and to be the victim of a catastrophe or catch a disease to which we have no karmic link. True accidents do happen. A car crash or succumbing to an epidemic or contagious complaint could just be an accident.

b. Problems of Mystics and Disciples.

People who are transforming spiritually through meditation and other spiritual disciplines get the same diseases as everyone else. But the cause may differ. For instance, in average man disease in the solar plexus region is caused by emotional trouble. In aspirants and disciples, it is caused as the solar plexus refines and energies start moving upwards to the selfless heart. But generally, more advanced people tend to get diseases in the upper part of the body while those still focused in the lower chakras have trouble there.

There are other problems that belong peculiarly to this group of people as a consequence of being impressed with soul illumination. When the door to this inner force opens and soul light pours through, those who have not yet stabilised their mental and emotional equipment will have trouble. The incoming force of a higher and finer vibration than the person has been accustomed to is more than they can handle. Lower psychic powers we share with animals are brought to life again. Visions are seen of holy ones and beloved teachers that are astral distortions stemming from the wish life. The doorway to the Astral Plane may open leading to paranoia, glamour and delusion. The powerful yearning to be one with God can become so compelling, the physical body is starved of energy. These are primarily problems that occur when the intellect has not yet stabilised, discrimination has not yet been developed and the astral nature is over-stimulated.

5. Death is a natural process

We have died many times before. More correctly, the physical body has repeatedly died, not consciousness, which continues to evolve and grow through the bodies it picks up and then discards until enlightenment is reached.

Death releases the soul from a body that can no longer serve its need to evolve.

In the normal course of events in our final years, the soul prepares to release the physical form and the consequent lowering of vitality means that the body may succumb to any germ or illness. The actual death process is initiated by the soul who withdraws the etheric and subtle bodies from the dense form, the consciousness thread from the brain and the life thread from the heart. This completely disrupts the body, reducing it to its essential elements - chemical, mineral and inorganic substances which can be absorbed into the soil of the planet. The atoms disperse, to be regenerated and refreshed until called upon again by the soul to form a new body in the next incarnation.

The fear of death, which has ridden mankind for aeons is beginning to lose its power. This is because many more men and women every day are realising that their true Self is the soul, not the body. As part of this, the belief in a devil and the horror of going to hell is also fading.

> It is interesting to note that the work of the Devil, the imprisoner of souls, is beginning to lose its power, for the race is on the verge of understanding that true death is immersion in form, and that matter is but a part of the divine whole. [1]

---

[1] Bailey, Alice A; A Treatise on White Magic, 240.

2. Diagnosing Disease via Chakras and Psychology

The first step in diagnosing disease, even before looking at the astrology chart, is to determine whether a person is primarily emotional or mental in focus and is spiritually oriented or not. Conversation with a client will usually determine this. A query about how crises are dealt with will reveal whether the mind is used to problem solve or if the emotions determine the course of events. Most people in the west use an aspect of mind even if at a very basic level. But if the thought life is primarily coloured and shaped by the emotions, people fit into the emotional group. A query about higher ideals helps to determine spiritual orientation. If there is an aspiration to something higher and finer, a desire to see the greater good come about, the person is on the Path. Obtaining this information helps the astrologer to find the rays that are more likely to be troublesome, the etheric chakras the person is primarily expressing through and therefore the organs in the body that are more susceptible to disease. Here are some broad generalisations covering four groups, remembering that people cannot be so easily stereotyped and that there are always exceptions.

a. *Average emotional man is stationed in the solar plexus chakra*

Emotional and desirous people are stationed primarily in the solar plexus and sacral chakras. Ray 6 emotionalism and ray 4 of conflict are the problem forces. This means that the Astral Plane rulers - the Moon, Mars and Neptune should be carefully consulted, because they are quite likely at the root of any serious disorder. Such people will manifest trouble in the lower part of the body, in the vicinity of the solar plexus, sacral and base chakras.

Even if a person is clearly a mind person and is not emotionally ruled, these planets and ray should be considered carefully, because we all have emotions and troubled emotions cause most diseases.

b. *Intelligent, non-spiritual man focuses in the ajna and/ or the throat chakra*

Mind people, work primarily through the ajna, throat and solar plexus chakras. R5 mind types are more careful with facts, are more reserved and inclined to be separative. For this group, consult Venus, Aquarius and perhaps Uranus. Their problems will likely be in the ajna region, in the brain and psychological, dissociative disorders. R3 types are tricksters, opportunists, are more charming and have the gift of the gab. For this ray 3 group consult Mercury and perhaps Saturn. Their problems will likely be in the throat, the thyroid, airways and digestive.

c. *Strong wilful people carrying the power ray 1, focus in the crown or base*

Strong-willed and highly assertive or aggressive people are drawing on the power of the 1st ray and from either the crown or base chakras. If they are generally good and kind, it is the crown chakra; otherwise it is the base. Both types may have brain and head trouble; the latter group will also have trouble in the vicinity of the base chakra. For them, consult Pluto, Saturn and sometimes, Uranus.

d. *People on the Path of Spiritual Development focus in the heart, ajna and crown chakras*

People on the Path have the same health problems as the former groups, but as previously pointed out, in their case the cause is usually different because they are raising their forces to a higher chakra. This creates an energy imbalance and trouble in the organs ruled by both chakras.

- *Aspirants*. They are still largely selfish and tend to oscillate between the higher, altruistic values and goals and the material life. They are purifying their physical appetites and are raising their focus from the sexual sacral centre into creative work through the throat centre. They are also beginning to open up the heart chakra. They are subject primarily to throat and chest problems and diseases in the sacral chakra region.
- *Disciples*. They are lifting their focus from the solar plexus emotional life into the heart chakra and group life. They are subject primarily to heart disease and problems in the solar plexus chakra region.
- *Advanced disciples and initiates*. They are working fully or partially from the crown centre and are starting to bring all the lower chakras under the control of the higher will. They are subject to brain troubles, nervous disorders and heart disease. Because the base chakra is transferring its force to the crown, trouble may also arise in that part of the body.

These points will help astrologers familiarise themselves with the different types of diseases that arise in relation to the psychology of a person - because of the forces habitually used and the parts of the body normally vitalised with the thought and emotional life. If any of the signature planets for each group appear in a health-triangle, you can immediately link the problem to the person's psychology.

This chart will help readers identify these different levels of consciousness and associated psychological problems. Use it in conjunction with the charts given in the 'Find a Health-Triangle' section.

Chart 5: Chakras and Psychology

Chakras	*Consciousness and the Body*	*Psychology negatives by Ray*	*Astrology*
Crown	**Spiritual man, higher will.** Brain (upper), brain mass, cerebrum, circadian rhythm, consciousness thread, death, head, melatonin, right eye. serotonin, sleep.	Ray 1 (R1): The spiritually advanced person awake at this level could demonstrate stubbornness.	*Chakra rulers:* Pluto, then Vulcan, Uranus. *Traditional:* Aries, Mars. Brain mass: Moon, Saturn.
Ajna	**Mind. Higher intelligence.** Brain (lower), eyes, ears, face, left eye, nervous system, nose.	R5: Anti-social, aloof, cleavages, disassociates, divisiveness, cold and clinical analysis without heart or feeling, sectarianism, separativeness, Psychological troubles such as asperger's, autism, egomania, imbecilities, insanities, megalomania.	*Chakra rulers:* Venus, Mercury, Gemini. *Traditional:* also Aquarius, Uranus.
Throat	**Mind. Intelligent man.** Airways, alimentary canal, breathing apparatus, bronchial tract, ears. endocrine system, lungs (upper), mouth, lymphatic system, neck, oesophagus, speech, trachea.	R3: ADD, ADHD. Cyber: bully, stalker, troll, online criminals and scamming; con-men, dishonesty, fraud, lying, manipulation, psychopathic, trickery, sociopath, trickster, theft, white collar crime.	*Chakra rulers:* the Earth, Saturn. (Also) Mercury, Gemini. *Traditional:* Venus and Taurus for the throat.
Heart	**Higher feelings.** Blood, cardiovascular system, cell life, heart, immune system, lungs (lower). prana, spleen, vitality.	(In its lowest expression) R2: group oriented in a greedy material, immoral, selfish way.	*Chakra rulers:* Sun, Jupiter. *Traditional:* also Leo.
Solar plexus	**Emotions. Average man.** Digestion organs: stomach, liver, gallbladder, intestines, colon, bowel, excretion, faeces. Nervous system (sympathetic).	R2: Amoral, excessive, gluttonous, greedy, no emotional boundaries. R4: Inner conflict, mood swings, mental-emotional instability. R6: Emotionally reactive: anger fear, hurt, frustration.	*Chakra rulers:* Mars, Neptune. *Traditional. Digestion:* Moon, Cancer, water signs; Mercury, Virgo intestines. *Bowel, excretion:* Scorpio, Mars, Pluto.
Sacral	**Etheric body, sex life.** Animal life, desire, DNA, genetics. life force, physical plane force, reproduction, sex organs, vital energy.	Rays 6 and 7: Misuse of sex, perversions, sadism. Ray 7 governs moral problems regarding sex and in the marriage relationship.	*Chakra rulers:* Uranus, Mars, Sagittarius. *Traditional:* also Scorpio, Pluto, Moon, Venus.
Base	**Dense physical body, the will to live and to survive.** Adrenals, bladder, body substance, fight or flight, kidneys, kundalini, skeleton, spinal column, urinary tract.	R1: Controlling, despotic, destructive, egomania, megalomania, wilful. R7: Crystallised attitudes.	Chakra rulers: Pluto, Saturn-Capricorn via R3. Traditional: Libra: kidneys. Sagittarius: hips, thighs. Capricorn: knees, joints, skeleton. Aquarius: ankles. Pisces: feet.

3. Diagnosing Disease via Astrology

The planets represent man on all levels - spiritual, psychological, and physical. They also represent the universal forces that pour through the signs and planets to us. The planets are receivers, conductors and distributors of energy on all levels. The signs govern different parts of the body and the planets that govern each sign, also govern those same body parts. Every body organ, every process, every function is represented by at least one planet, sometimes more. Ill health is found in the natal chart by examining the planets, the patterns they make and their location in the signs and houses.

One of the first steps in medical astrology is to assess the strength of each planet, especially the strength of the personal planets, Sun, Moon, Mercury, Venus and Mars. This is because they are the primary rulers of our mental, emotional and physical states. This will reveal the health or otherwise of the organs and parts that each planet rules. A well aspected planet is conducive to good health; a poorly aspected or afflicted planet points to the potential for malfunction and disease. A planet is considered "afflicted" if it is in a sign hostile to its force, if it has many hard aspects, is unaspected or retrograde. Healthwise, a planet is also considered potentially afflicted if it is located in the 12th house of hospitals or in the 6th house of health.

All planets can represent a disease, but the outer planets more so. In traditional, pre-psychological astrology, these planets were called "malefic" - Mars, Saturn, Uranus, Neptune and Pluto; because it was thought they had an evil effect. This concept remains valid today where health is concerned for the simple reason that they each represent ways the body breaks down in serious ways and succumbs to disease. Mars inflames, Saturn blocks, Uranus causes aberrations, Neptune perverts and Pluto destroys. Of the others: the Sun inflames, the Moon and Mercury debilitate, Venus weakens and Jupiter represents cell over-growth.

An afflicted planet in the chart does not necessarily mean that disease will follow. Everyone has them. An examination of the charts of highly successful people shows planet afflictions everywhere. What makes the difference is how we deal with stress. If we learn from our disappointments and challenges to be wiser and make better choices in the future, if we go forward with positivity rather than succumb to bitterness; metaphorically, we transmute our "squares" into "trines". For instance, Saturn square Mercury can manifest as a fear of speaking out and if this eventuates, can lead to throat problems. Overcoming the fear and speaking courageously transmutes the negative force into a positive character attribute, easing throat trouble.

a. Is the planet strengthened or weakened by sign?

Chart 6: Planetary Strengths and Weaknesses in the Signs

Planets	Dignified *strengthened*	Exalted *strengthened*	Detriment *energy distorted*	Falls *energy distorted*
☉ Sun	Leo	Aries	Aquarius	Libra
☽ Moon	Cancer	Taurus	Capricorn	Scorpio
☿ Mercury	Gemini-Virgo	Aquarius	Sagittarius-Pisces	Leo
♀ Venus	Taurus-Libra	Pisces	Scorpio-Aries	Virgo
♂ Mars	Aries-Scorpio	Capricorn	Libra-Taurus	Cancer
♃ Jupiter	Sagittarius-Pisces	Cancer	Gemini-Virgo	Capricorn
♄ Saturn	Capricorn	Libra	Cancer-Leo	Aries
♅ Uranus	Aquarius	Scorpio	Leo	Taurus
♆ Neptune	Pisces	Cancer	Virgo	Capricorn
♇ Pluto	Scorpio	Aries	Taurus	Libra

The chart shows which signs strengthen a planet and which signs weaken them through energy distortion.

b. Is the planet strengthened or weakened by aspects, or by being retrograde?

Planet aspects reveal the quirks in our psychology and where we hold stress. The most problematic "hard" aspects are the *square, opposition* and *conjunctions*. They show where we tend to block our force. Examine these aspects carefully, especially if malefics are involved. Trouble will arise according to the nature of the planets. Other minor hard aspects such as the *semi-square, quincunx, sesquiquadrate, septile, decile* and *quindecile*; these all indicate energy disruption and potential weakening of organs.

The *trine* and *sextile* are considered fortunate. Energy flows, but this does not always indicate good health. The easy flow of energy may be toxic. Keep this in mind and use a trine or sextile to build a health-triangle if it seems appropriate to do so. Personal planets that are unaspected should also be carefully noted. They indicate a serious problem with energy flow.

c. Is there a planetary pattern?
Planet patterns occur when 3 or more planets are locked together by aspect. With the exception of the grand-trine (3 planets in an equilateral triangle), they are often at the heart of any serious disease, especially if they touch the 12th or 6th houses. The most stress-filled patterns are the t-square and grand-cross.

- *T-square:* 2 planets opposite each other and both square a third planet. It represents hard attitudes that if not eased over time, will cause health problems.
- *Grand-cross:* 4 planets in all four quadrants of the chart square and opposing each other. It shows the most serious hardening of attitudes and of potential disease.
- *Easy-opposition:* 2 planets oppose each other, trine and sextile a third planet. In practice, this pattern seems to appear most often. The easy aspects promise an easing of the condition but this is not always the case.
- *Yod:* 2 planets sextile to each other, both inconjunct to a third, which is called "the Finger of God". This is another trouble making pattern. The owner is continually trying to resolve conflicting issues.

Planets appear to be *retrograde*, moving backwards, due to a visual phenomena that occurs when the planet is being passed by a faster moving one. They indicate a weakening of energy, an introversion or subversion of a planet's force, especially when the personal planets Mercury, Venus and Mars are retrograde. The outer slow moving planets are always being passed by the inner planets so their being retrograde is less important.

d. Exercise: assess planets for Scott Hamilton, world and Olympic Gold Medal Champion.
In the 90's, Hamilton had testicular cancer, which was successfully treated. But now (2017) he is fighting pituitary tumours, which keep re-growing after treatment. The chakras and planets that rule the pituitary are the ajna, Venus and Mercury. The sacral chakra, Mars and Uranus govern the testes. Step by step, let us assess Hamilton's planets to see what we find.

a. Are any planets strengthened or weakened by sign? Yes. Mars is in detriment in Taurus and Uranus is in detriment in Leo. These two planets rule the sacral chakra and the reproductive organs. It shows he inherited a weakness in that region. In adulthood he developed testicular cancer.

b. Are any personal planets retrograde? Yes, Mercury. This shows an inherited problem in the ajna chakra region, which Mercury co-rules. Trouble manifested as pituitary tumours, which Hamilton is currently fighting.

c. Where is the focus of stress in the chart? The five planet group represents a cocktail of forces that do not sit well with each other. This is the central point of stress in the chart. The signs involved are Leo and Virgo. Leo rules cell life via the Sun. Mercury afflicted in Leo points to trouble with pituitary cells.

d. What are the planet aspects telling us? The Moon and Mars, which are both representatives of the emotions - and also of sex in Mars' case, are afflicted. We know that emotional repression causes cancer and the chart shows Hamilton would clamp down on his. The clamping is being done by two 1st ray planets (Saturn inconjunct Mars, Pluto opposing the Moon). The involvement of the Moon points to exhaustion (ray 4) that can render the body susceptible to cancer, to unhealthy tissue changes.

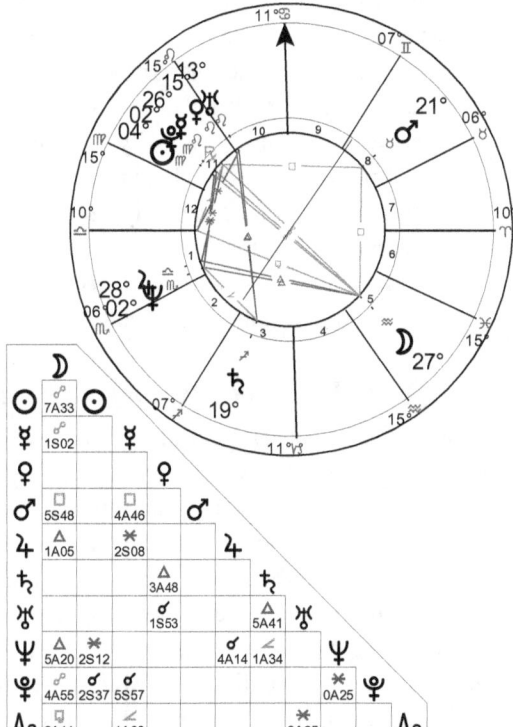
Scott Hamilton, American figure skater (28 August 1958, 9 am, Toledo OH)

There is a t-square, Mars, Moon, Mercury-Pluto. In this stress-pattern we have representatives of the pituitary (Mercury) and the testes (Mars and Pluto). There is more to be uncovered, and Hamilton's chart is analysed in greater detail later. But in these four steps, we found the cancer and tumour trouble and the underlying cause, major repressions in Hamilton's emotional and sexual force.

a. Examine the Sun - how strong is this person's will, heart and vitality?

A well placed and well aspected Sun in the natal chart indicates a cardiovascular system that absorbs prana (solar energy) easily, vitalising cell life and boosting the immune system. It gives the power and the will to throw off disease and to recover quickly from illness. Solar power increases in Aries and Leo, signs in which the Sun is most compatible; and in Sagittarius, another fire sign. Easy aspects from Mars and Jupiter to the Sun boost vitality. These planets when located in Leo, the Sun's sign, will have a similar vitalising effect. Even hard aspects from these two planets are better than none. In this case, energy is available, though if misused will lead to burn-out and inflammation. An afflicted Sun shows potential trouble in the heart chakra, the heart organ, cardiovascular system and the immune system. Vitality and immune health can be improved by sunbathing with the naked back to the Sun for a few minutes daily. Taking the Sun's vitamin B3, will also help.

John Howard (26 July 1939, 02:21 Earlwood Australia).

Howard was the Australian PM from 1996-2007. The Sun in its dignity in Leo conjunct 1st ray Pluto, gives Howard a very strong personality and will. It also gives a strong heart action and potentially good vitality. This is accentuated with the trine to expansive Jupiter in Aries, opposing fiery Mars in exaltation in Capricorn. The Sun-Mars opposition does indicate potential heart trouble at some time; but Howard's excellent health and vitality served him well. He was in politics for 40 years, the longest serving PM whose 'heart' held his party and the country together for many years. He retired when he lost the support of the people and his seat in the 2007 elections.

Henry Fonda (16 May 1905, 14:00, Grand Island NE).

Fonda died of heart disease on 12 August 1982. His Sun is weak when compared with Howard's. Taurus can give a strong, "bullish" constitution and there is a trine to the ascendant, which is helpful. But that is as good as it gets. The Sun is located in the cadent 9th house (9H), which is not physically energising. Its inconjunct to the Moon in Libra indicates a troubled connection with the etheric body causing debilitation. Psychologically, Sun square Saturn in the 6H of health represents difficulty in giving from the heart. This manifested physically as poor circulation and heart disease. Readers who remember Fonda may recall he moved languidly, as if he was conserving energy.

b. Examine Mercury and Venus - how stable is the mind, the nervous system?

Mercury rules the intelligent ajna chakra along with Venus. When Mercury in particular is well placed and well aspected, it promotes a positive mental attitude and healthy nervous system. This is extremely helpful when there are health challenges because a positive mind alone is like a tonic to an ailing body. It also helps to keep energy flowing through the etheric body, because Mercury's sign Gemini rules the etheric.

Owners of a balanced Mercury will communicate symptoms to their healer intelligently and honestly and follow a course of treatment as prescribed. Aspects to Mercury from 1st ray planets Saturn and Pluto strengthen the mind for good or ill. Hard aspects show rigidity in thought and extreme stubbornness, which is detrimental to healing unless directed into a positive direction. Mercury-Saturn people tend to pessimism and can slip into depression unless there are other compensating factors in the chart. Mercury-Uranus contacts also strengthen the will, but there is greater flexibility (if erratic) in thought and such people will often seek out alternative healers or treatments.

Hard aspects from 6th ray planets Mars and Neptune or from the Moon, or when Mercury is located in water signs, indicates that the emotions can swamp rational thought. Consequently, when ill, such people can be assailed by fears that hamper recovery. They may also entertain the thought of escaping their emotional pain through alcohol, drugs or some other destructive way.

*All that has been said for Mercury applies to Venus as well. Sometimes, in charts,
Venus is the signifying factor instead of Mercury, for nervous system trouble.*

Friedrich Hegel (27 August 1770, 04:50, Stuttgart Germany).

German philosopher who had an excellent mind and it shows in his chart. Mercury is in dignity in Virgo, in the 1H of personal affairs, in a grand-trine with scientific Uranus and delving Pluto. He was argumentative (Mercury square Mars), and philosophically inclined (square Jupiter). With the conjunction to Neptune, he was also potentially intuitive. Hegel had an acute mind (due to a robust nervous system and good oxygenation of the blood - Mercury rules oxygenation) until he died from an intestinal bacterial disease at age 61. Aquarius on the 6H of health - ruler Uranus governs bacterial infections.

Heath Ledger (4 April 1979 06:30, Perth Australia).

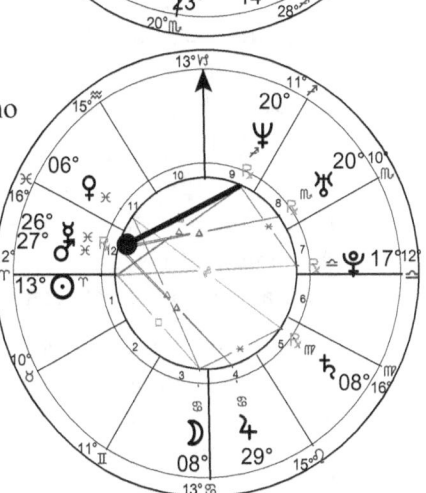

Australian actor who had a dynamic personality via his Aries Sun, but who also had a secretive and dark side with Mercury in the 12H of hidden things. He died from an over-dose of prescription drugs. Ledger had a strategic mind (Mercury conjunct Mars, trine Uranus), and was Australia's junior chess champion at age 10. But with Mercury's location in Pisces, in aspect to the two rulers of the Astral Plane - square Neptune, conjunct Mars; we can tell that his mind could be swamped by negative emotions. Spiralling down into a well of despair (Mercury in the 12H of self-undoing), he used drugs to try to escape from his imaginative demons (Mars-Neptune). This was the cause of his death. Mars rules the 8H of death.

c. Examine the Moon, Mars and Neptune - how is emotional expression?

The Moon and Mars are the primary representatives of emotions in most people and Neptune in the more advanced. Since disturbed emotions cause most diseases, their influence in the chart should be carefully studied. The Moon in particular is potentially a contagious point. Its force indicates that which is past, the baggage we hold on to and the habits we fall back on when we are in fear or confusion. Esoterically, it shows where the "prison of the soul is to be found". [1]

> The Moon carries Ray 4 of Harmony through Conflict, which debilitates and exhausts if we are besieged with inner conflict. This then can make us susceptible to the indigenous diseases of the planet, which are cancer, tuberculosis and sexual diseases.

The following brief statements have been drawn up specifically for the Moon and Mars in the twelve signs. For each, they link psychological - emotional reactions to diseases. Included also are lower and higher keynotes for each sign.

- *Aries*: emotions are hot, powerful and volatile. Fiery upsets affect the brain and head. There could be inflammatory brain explosions such as a stroke or accidents because of angry and impulsive actions. The lower note is "Let form again be sought", meaning, powerful desires rule the mind. The higher note is "I come forth and from the plane of mind - I rule". The intelligent mind should rule all actions.

- *Taurus*: emotions and desires are powerful and intense. The Moon is exalted so its effect on health is more benign than with Mars, which falls in this sign. However, they both cause emotional instability and conflict, trouble in the throat, thyroid and reproductive area via Mars. The lower note is, "Let struggle be undismayed", meaning, inner conflict is a real problem. The higher note, "I see and when the eye is opened, all is light", refers to self-observation and self-understanding; which when adopted will bring emotional stability.

---

[1] Bailey, Alice A; Esoteric Astrology, 19.

- *Gemini*: emotions are rationalised (Moon), or there is mental irritation (Mars). In both, there is a tendency to split the mind off from the emotions so that emotional trouble or trauma may not be recognised until nervous disorders arise or inflammation or phlegm affects the airways and lungs. The lower note is "Let instability do its work", meaning, mental - emotional instability is a problem. Balance and insight will bring forth wisdom and better health - "I see my other self, and in the waning of that self, I grow and glow".

- *Cancer:* the lower note is "Let isolation be the rule and yet the crowd exists"; emotions are highly defensive, conflicted, warlike and tend to be repressed. Mars falls in this sign. This upsets digestion and body fluids, creating phlegm and trouble in digestion and reproduction. Emotional refinement will strengthen the body and improve intimate relationships - "I build a lighted house and therein dwell".

- *Leo*: the lower note "Let other forms exist, I rule", tells us that pride and arrogance is this sign's downfall. Fiery, volcanic emotions and explosions lead to inflammatory conditions of the heart, its valves, walls and sepsis of the blood. An orientation towards a higher life demonstration represented by the higher note, "I am That, and That am I", will strengthen the heart and life.

- *Virgo*: emotions are tight and desire for perfection can lead to their repression by the fussy and critical mind. If so, trouble will seep out unhealthily in the intestinal and bowel region. The lower note is "Let matter reign"; meaning, materialism is fine in its place but can entrap the soul. The aspirational goal is to reach for something finer, represented by the phrase, "I am the mother and the child, I God, I matter am".

- *Libra*: the lower note is "Let choice be made", referring to the oscillating mind of the Libran who is stuck in indecision. If upset emotions are flicked aside to avoid facing the truth or from hurting people; "pissed off" feelings that affect the kidneys will be left behind. This is especially true of Mars, which is in detriment in this sign. The development goal is to be decisive and to move straight forwards with confidence - "I choose the way which lies between the two great lines of force".

- *Scorpio*: the lower note is "Let maya flourish and let deception rule". Holding on to grievances, dark and poisonous emotions, harbouring revenge and thoughts of attack, all this gives rise to strokes, blood disorders and festering infections in the gut and reproduction organs. Scorpio's have to fight to free their minds from delusion and emotionalism. The war-cry, which will help them reach victory, is "Warrior I am, and from the battle I emerge triumphant".

- *Sagittarius*: Over-indulgence is a problem, the lower note is "Let food again be sought". Sometimes this refers to a dark, predatory side and criminal activities. Loss of faith stiffens hips, thighs and mobility generally. Aspiring to the heights is the goal for Sagittarian's - "I see the goal, I reach that goal, and then I see another". This will help them move forwards in the right direction.

- *Capricorn*: "Let ambition rule and let the door stand wide"; selfish, greedy ambition (Mars) and emotional repression (Moon in detriment), leads to crystallisation and stiffness, particularly the knee joints. Using all one's power and resources for the greater good is the goal - "Lost am I in light supernal, yet on that light I turn my back". Having seen the "light", one carries it to those who suffer.

- *Aquarius*: powerful and selfish desires (the lower note is, "Let desire in form be ruler"), coupled with mental separativeness disrupts energy flow between the mind and emotions. A psychic barrier is erected that impairs blood circulation and the quality of blood. Stiffness and crystallisation in the lower leg region and ankles especially, affects mobility. The higher note, "Water of life am I, poured forth for thirsty men" reminds Aquarius people that their life destiny is to assist those who are in need.

- *Pisces*: the lower note of Pisces, "Go forth into matter", is an instruction to the Piscean person who is still focused in the solar plexus chakra, to continue swimming in the waters of emotional life. This leads to devitalisation, eventually upsets the watery systems of the body and causes swelling and various other problems with the feet that affect mobility. The aspirational goal that will help to improve health and well being is to pour energy into service - the higher note of Pisces is, "I leave my Father's house, and turning back, I save".

Liza Minnelli (12 March 1946, 07:58, LA, CA).

American singer and actress, the daughter of fabulous Judy Garland. Both mother and daughter had great difficulty with emotional expression and problems with alcohol and drug abuse. Of Minnelli, a writer said, "Her life has been a Big Dipper ride in which manifestations of her talent alternate with displays of self-destruction"; which is a creative but accurate description.

It is not surprising with her inhibited emotional life. Mars and the Moon are in Cancer, conjunct the great "repressor", Saturn. The lower note for Cancer gives us insight into her emotions - "Let isolation be the rule and yet the crowd exists". Amongst fame and glory she feels alone and unloved. The problem lies within her - she is afraid to open up and trust at a deep and intimate level because she fears she cannot handle rejection.

Queen Elizabeth II (21 April 1926, 02:40 London UK).

The Queen's expression and smile shows us that she is happy. Her whole life demonstration, how she has attended to her royal and public duties, is one of remarkable graciousness and inclusive kindness. This indicates that she is spiritually advanced and that Neptune is the primary indicator of her emotional expression.

Neptune is in Leo, in a t-square with Saturn at the hub and Mars-Jupiter. From one angle, this tells us that the Queen burns with zeal to meet her royal duties (Neptune in Leo), steadfastly (Saturn), energetically and wisely (Mars-Jupiter). She has given up her personal life for duty (Saturn, ruler of the 1H conjunct the MC, square Neptune and planets in the 1H, Neptune retrograde). But this is not a hardship for the Queen because she in on the Path and service is the spontaneous reaction to soul contact.

The three rulers of the solar plexus chakra are all connected - Neptune opposes Mars and is in a wide conjunction with the Moon. Neptune is the supreme "refiner" and its contact with these planets is indicative of the Queen's refined emotional vehicle. She has never demonstrated the arrogance of lower Leo, rather, she has been poised and serene in all her public interactions. Her steady, dedicated service to her country is reflective of the higher note of Leo - "I am That, and That am I". It instructs Leo people to identify with the very highest which is in them and to radiate that sunny inner warmth and spiritual power into the world. The fact that the Queen has had robust health all her life is evidence her emotional field is balanced and quite likely is being used by her soul to help harmonise the world.

|| *NB. The Queen's chart was interpreted positively and at a higher level, than it would have been if her life and character demonstration was not so exemplary.*

d. Examine the 6th and 12 "health" houses

If a healthy person enquires about future potential health problems, examination of the 6th and 12th houses and their rulers would be the first thing to do.

The 6th house traditionally rules health. If a challenging planetary pattern has points in the 6th - especially if the pattern contains malefics, it is a red flag warning for health. The sign on the house cusp, the planet ruler and the sign it is in, and planets in the 6th; all of these could represent organs that potentially could become diseased.

Apply the same rule to the 12th house that traditionally rules hospitals. We only end up in hospital if we have a serious health condition, so it can be considered as representing major illnesses.

|| *NB. Throughout the book "H" has been used as an abbreviation for "house".*

4. Find a Health-Triangle

The health-triangle is a triangular pattern formed by a minimum of three planets in any aspect. Esotericists consider the triangle to be the basic geometric form that underlies the entire fabric of manifestation,[1] whether this be a solar system, a man, *or in this case disease*. The triangle represents a disease and its cause:

  1. **A psychological or/ and a karmic disturbance.**
  2. **... which causes congestion in a chakra and an organ.**
  3. **.. which in turn manifests as a physical disease.**

The astrologer searches the chart to find planets to represent these three factors in the formation of disease.

  ▲ **Triangle point 1, the CAUSE (C).** Find the core planet that represents the psychological disturbance or karmic-genetic factor that gives birth to the physical disease.

  ▲ **Triangle point 2, the Organ (O).** Find a planet to represent the affected organ / chakra, which the disease targets or lodges in.

  ▲ **Triangle point 3, the EFFECT (E).** Find a planet or planets to represent the physical disease and the noticeable impairments that occur in the body and life as a consequence of the disease.

Two charts will assist readers in this task. Chart 7 assembles information by the seven rays, Chart 8 via the chakras.

Chart 7: The 7 Rays, Psychology and Disease

Ray	Disease pathology	Psychological keywords	Disease examples	Astrology
1	Ages, atrophies, contracts, cripples, crystallises, hardens, scars, stiffens.	Aggressive, controlling, egomania, hard, inflexible, inhibited, megalomania, obsessive, repressive, wilful.	Arthritis, atherosclerosis, blindness, cancer through repression, dementia, meningitis, multiple sclerosis, paralysis, scleroderma, stroke.	Pluto, Saturn, Uranus; Aries (and Mars), Leo, Capricorn.
2	Excessive growth and vitality, overdevelops, suffocates, too many atoms.	Amoral, excessive, gluttonous, greedy, impressionable, no emotional boundaries.	Blood disorders, cancer, heart disease, extra body parts, gluttony, tumours.	Sun, Jupiter; Gemini, Virgo, Pisces.
3	Diseases that are highly energetic, unstable, quick moving, subtly invasive, that trick the body.	Avarice, dishonesty, hyperactive, lying, manipulative, trickery, stealing, white collar crime, sociopathic.	Breathing troubles, certain brain disorders; gastric, stomach, intestinal disorders; sexually transmitted diseases.	Saturn, Earth, also Mercury; Cancer, Libra, Capricorn.
4	Constant conflict that devitalises and debilitates, opening the body up to disease.	Agonising, inner conflict, mental-emotional instability. mood swings.	Chronic fatigue, debilitation, epidemics such as influenza, susceptibility to indigenous diseases - cancer, tuberculosis, syphilis.	Moon, Mercury; Taurus, Scorpio, Sagittarius.
5	Builds barriers, separates, hardens, cleaves, splits apart.	Aloof, anti-social, cleavages, disassociates, divisive, many modern psychological disorders, separative.	Brain lesions, consciousness thread trouble, imbecilities. migraine.	Venus; Leo, Sagittarius, Aquarius.
6	Emotional or desire force out of control; violently expressed or repressed.	Emotional disorders: anger, delusion, fear, frustration, hurt, jealousy, reactive, sectarian, warped ideals.	Carcinogenicity, digestion problems, sexual diseases and perversions, viruses.	Mars, Neptune; Virgo, Sagittarius, Pisces.
7	Promiscuity at a cellular level leading to genetic mutations, germs and bacterial infections.	Perfectionism, regimenting, perverting, promiscuity.	Blood circulation problems, epidemics, sexually transmitted diseases, reproductive problems.	Uranus; Aries, Cancer, Capricorn.

Esoteric Healing 106-109, 298-304; plus other sources

---
1 Bailey, Alice A; Esoteric Astrology, 429.

3. Disease and its Diagnosis ▲ 109

|| *Notes*
- Usually it is best to find the affected organ first (O), then either the cause (C) or disease (E) planets.
- When looking for the cause, remember that disease is primarily caused by an emotional disturbance, so look for a connection from the organ or disease planet to one of the emotional representatives - the Moon, Mars or Neptune or to a planet or the ascendant in a water/ emotional sign - Cancer, Scorpio or Pisces. A psychological pattern may involve several planets and that same pattern may also represent the manifested disease. But usually one planet in particular will be more representative of the core psychological problem. In practice, it has proven to usually be the Moon. Sometimes, if the cause is karmic or genetic, Saturn or Uranus may represent the cause.
- Another point to remember is that all the planets represent aspects of our psychology as well as the body, so one planet could represent more that one point of a health-triangle. For instance, Mars could represent anger, the brain and a stroke; the psychological cause (C), the organ (O) and the disease (E).

Chart 8: Chakras and the Body

Chakra	*Gland*	*Consciousness and the Body*	*Disease suggestions*	*Astrology*
Crown Ray 1	Pineal	**Spiritual man, higher will.** Brain (upper), brain mass, cerebrum, circadian rhythm, consciousness thread, death, head, melatonin, right eye. serotonin, sleep.	Brain disease, cerebral palsy, coma, concussion, dementia, haemorrhages, high blood pressure, insanity, meningitis, pineal trouble, sleep disorders, stroke.	*Chakra rulers*: Pluto, Vulcan, Uranus. *Traditional*: Aries, Mars. Brain mass: Moon, Saturn.
Ajna Ray 5	Pituitary	**Mind. Higher intelligence.** Brain (lower), eyes, ears, face, left eye, nervous system, nose.	Epilepsy, eye-ear trouble, headache, mental and nervous disorders, migraine, paralysis, pituitary trouble, seizures.	*Chakra rulers*: Venus, Mercury, Gemini. *Traditional*: also Aquarius, Uranus.
Throat Ray 3 (7)	Thyroid	**Mind. Intelligent man.** Airways, alimentary canal, breathing apparatus, bronchial tract, ears. endocrine system, lungs (upper), mouth, lymphatic system, neck, oesophagus, speech, trachea.	Asthma, breathing problems, colds, goitre, group diseases, influenza, laryngitis, lymphatic trouble, phlegm, sinusitis, thyroid trouble, tonsillitis, speech and hearing problems.	*Chakra rulers*: the earth, Saturn. (Also) Mercury, Gemini. *Traditional*: Venus and Taurus for the throat.
Heart Ray 2	Thymus	**Higher feelings.** Blood, cardiovascular system, cell life, heart, immune system, lungs (lower). prana, spleen, vitality.	AIDS, autoimmune disease; blood disorders, circulation/ cardiovascular trouble, heart disease, tuberculosis.	*Chakra rulers*: Sun, Jupiter. *Traditional*: also Leo. [Base chakra: Sun, Saturn for spine].
Solar plexus Ray 6, 2 (4)	Pancreas	**Emotions. Average man.** Digestion organs: stomach, liver, gallbladder, intestines, colon, bowel, excretion, faeces. Nervous system (sympathetic).	Digestive-intestinal disorders, fatigue, obesity, oedema, nervous-emotional troubles, skin eruptions.	*Chakra rulers*: Mars, Neptune. *Traditional. Digestion*: Moon, Cancer, water signs; Mercury, Virgo intestines. *Bowel, excretion*: Scorpio, Mars, Pluto
Sacral Ray 7 (6)	Gonads	**Etheric body, sex life.** Animal life, desire, DNA, genetics. life force, physical plane force, reproduction, sex organs, vital energy.	Congenital and foetal abnormalities, hereditary - genetic disorders, reproductive problems, sexually transmitted diseases.	*Chakra rulers*: Uranus, Mars, Sagittarius. *Traditional*: also Scorpio, Pluto, Moon, Venus.
Base Ray 1 (3)	Adrenals	**Dense physical body, the will to live and to survive.** Adrenals, bladder, body substance, fight or flight, kidneys, kundalini, skeleton, spinal column, urinary tract.	Adrenal trouble, hardening of tissue, spine and structural problems, stiffening of the body, urinary tract trouble.	*Chakra rulers*: Pluto, Saturn-Capricorn via R3. *Traditional*: Libra: kidneys. Sagittarius: hips, thighs. Capricorn: knees, joints, skeleton. Aquarius: ankles. Pisces: feet.

Exercise 1: Joseph Stalin (18 December 1878, time unknown, chart set up at 12 noon, 0 degrees Aries rising) Stalin died from a stroke in March 1953.

We will search for a health-triangle to represent the stroke, the affected organ and the psychological cause. Use the charts provided to assist you: "Chart 7: The 7 Rays, Psychology and Disease" and "Chart 8: Chakras and the Body". The information is condensed and does not cover every situation. But it is a place to start. Although the Moon's location in Stalin's chart's is approximate, for the exercise we will work with it as being exact.

a. The organ (O) and disease (E) points.

We start by searching for the organ, the brain in this case. Consulting chart 8, we see that the brain mass is ruled by the crown chakra, by ray 1, Aries, Mars and Pluto. Saturn and the Moon are associated.

In Stalin's chart there are no planets in Aries and we see that Mars opposes Pluto, which is sesquiquadrate the Moon, which in turn is semi-square Mars. We have a triangular pattern and these three planets have the ingredients to form the health-triangle. A quick interpretation could be:

> a blockage (Pluto carrying ray 1 that blocks), stopped blood flow (Mars) to the brain (Moon), causing a stroke (Mars), that killed him (Pluto).

In this case, the Moon represents the brain mass (O) point and Pluto and Mars represent aspects of the disease, the (E) point.

The black dot always represents the organ

b. The psychological (C) cause.

Now our search turns to the emotional, psychological cause behind the stroke. The Moon and Mars, two planets that rule the emotions are in the pattern we are working with. The negotiating and procrastinating energies of the Moon in Libra do not fit a stroke. But Mars does.

> *To find the planet that represents the psychological cause of a disease - (1) identify the ray energy of the disease then (2), match that energy to a planet of the same energy, or that is in a sign of the same energy.*

By consulting Chart 1 on the Rays, we see that (1) a stroke is a 1st ray disease and (2), Mars carries the 1st ray via Aries. It is our candidate as the cause (C) point. Mars is in Scorpio and by consulting the "emotional expression" list in the previous section we can determine that:

> "Stalin would hold on to grievances, he had dark and poisonous emotions, harboured revenge and thoughts of attack" and this is the psychological cause behind the stroke. We could elaborate further by saying "he had explosive rages" (Mars opposite Pluto), "that would adversely affect brain tissue" (the Moon).

Mars represents both the psychological (C) cause behind the stroke and the stroke itself. Consequently, the health-triangle could be written like this.

▲ (C) Mars, Pluto. (O) Moon. (E) Mars, Pluto.

Mars appears twice and to simplify the triangle could be dropped from the (E) point. Other planets could be linked into the disease effects by following aspects from Mars and Pluto. For instance, Pluto is sesquiquadrate Mercury - the stroke paralysed his nervous system.

Exercise 2: Scott Hamilton (28 August 1958, 09:00, Toledo OH)
Cancer and Tumours.

Find a health-triangle for testicular cancer (late 1990's)

Scott Hamilton is a retired American figure skater and 1984 Olympic gold medalist. In the chart, there are two t-squares, so we begin our search in those patterns.

a. The organ (O) and causal (C) points.

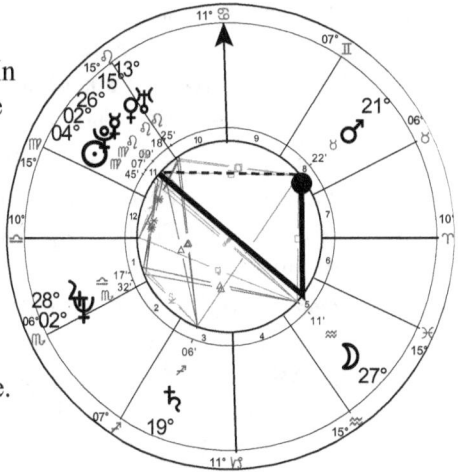

The sacral chakra rules the sex organs and Mars is a ruler of the testes. In Hamilton's chart, Mars stands out. It is the dominant point of a T-square and falls in Taurus. *Mars is our (O) candidate.*

Then we see that Mars squares the Moon, the latter being one point of a t-square that Mars is in. Both these planets rule the emotions. Since Mars is occupying the organ spot, it leaves the Moon as the natural choice for the emotions, the *(C) point*.

Hamilton was a Virgo Sun perfectionist who rationalised his emotions (opposite Moon in Aquarius) and clamped down on sexual desire (Mercury square Mars), to maintain control of his world and life. The suppression of force lies always at the root of cancer.

b. The disease (E) point.

We are left with two planets at the third point of the t-square (Pluto and Mercury), as our candidates for cancer. 1st ray Pluto is first choice, since its force oppresses. Pluto opposes the Moon so this fits like a glove. Pluto also causes cell malignancies and it is in Virgo, which carries the 2nd cell over-building ray. *Pluto is our candidate for the disease (E) effect of the triangle.*

We could include Mercury as part of the disease effect message. For instance we could speculate that his mobility and flexibility was impaired, most devastating for a champion athlete. The health-triangle is:

▲ (C) Moon. (O) Mars. (E) Pluto, Mercury.

Find a health-triangle for pituitary tumours (2004, 2010, 2017)

The triangle we chose for testicular cancer could also represent the pituitary condition, by nominating Mercury for the pituitary (O) point. It is a substitute ruler. Pluto would remain a representative for Cancer and the Moon for the cause. This would leave Mars as an additional (E) point. But rather than go with Mercury, we will work with Venus, the other ruler of the pituitary.

Formulating the health-triangle.

Venus is our organ (O) candidate, which means that Mars now represents an aspect of the disease (E) . It could represent surgery, or sexual problems since Mars afflicted in Taurus rules the thyroid, which when troubled can lower the libido. The Moon remains the candidate for the emotional cause (C). Although there is no direct aspect between the Moon and Venus, there are three indirect connections and these are explored as an exercise:

- Moon-Venus are related via their respective squares to Mars.
- Uranus conjunct Venus, disposits the Moon and this forms another link between the Moon and Venus.
- Mars is exactly midpoint Venus and the Moon and this is the most powerful energy connection.

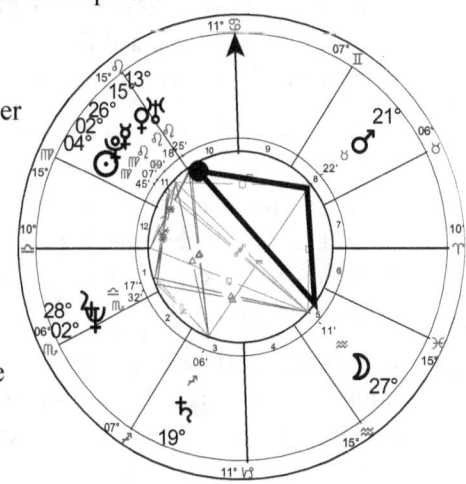

This leaves Uranus. It carries ray 1 and disposits the Moon in Aquarius and from this angle represents emotional repression. Uranus' force also causes cellular aberrations. From this second angle it can represent the pituitary cancer (E) point, especially since it conjuncts Venus. The health-triangle for the pituitary cancer in its simplest form can be drawn like this:

▲ (C) Moon. (O) Venus. (E) Mars, Uranus

Hamilton's Solar-arc Directions (SA) June 2016

The chart is advanced by solar-arc to 1 June 2016. A solar-arc chart gives better results when searching for disease because the dangerous outer planets are included. The tumours appeared in 2004, 2010 and 2016.

- 2004. The Moon by solar-arc was on the decendant, opposing the ascendant, and all were squared by transit Saturn in Cancer, which formed a t-square. The tumours appeared.

- 2010. Solar-arc Venus was in the 12H at 6 Libra applying to the ascendant; and transit Uranus was in the 6H representing aberrant pituitary growths.

- 2016: (the chart). Solar-arc Uranus and Venus were at 10-11 Libra, sitting on the ascendant. solar-arc Mars at 18 Cancer was being opposed by transit Pluto from 17-18 Capricorn. Both solar-arc Moon and transit Uranus were conjunct at 23 Aries. The whole health-triangle, that is the disease, was active.

Hamilton has a successful marriage and says he is blessed beyond his wildest imagination. It shows that he is harmonising his stress triangles and the trouble should not recur next life.

Tips to help find links between planets

a. Widen the traditional orbs or rules.
   - Widen aspect orbs, especially with the Sun or Moon. Eminent astrologer from early last century, Alan Leo, used orbs up to 15 degrees for the Sun and Moon.
   - If you have two favoured planets who are a few degrees beyond an aspect and there are no other suitable candidates, and you are sure that you have not overlooked another more suitable pattern, then extend the orbs. If the disease exists, so does the pattern.
   - Planets in opposite signs, even if not in a traditional orb, are related and can be considered hostile to each other. Taking this a step further, consider planets in the same mode (cardinal, fixed or mutable), as being hostile to each other.

b. Accept that you have a triangle, even if two of the three planets are not aspecting each other. For example, planet A squares planets B and C, but B and C are not in aspect to each other. Even so, you have three planets to form a triangle and if this is your best option, go with it.

c. Consider dispositorship. A planet disposits all planets located in its sign. For instance, Saturn disposits Mercury in Capricorn and this creates a link between Mercury and Saturn. Mercury disposits any planet in Gemini and Virgo and is thereby connected to any planets located in these signs.

d. Consider the decanates. Each sign has three decanates, which are ruled by the signs and ruling planets of the same element.
   - Taurus for instance: Taurus and Venus rule the first decanate, Virgo and Mercury the second, and Capricorn and Saturn govern the third decanate. If you are looking for a link between Saturn and Mercury, and Mercury is located in the third decanate of Taurus, ruled by Capricorn, this creates a link between Saturn and Mercury.

e. Consider the midpoints. They are a very valuable means of finding non-obvious links between planets. The midpoint degree is a dynamic point where the forces of two planets meet. If for instance, Mercury lies at the midpoint between Saturn and say the Moon, a triangle is formed between the three planets.

Exercise 3: find a health-triangle for Jacqueline Du Pre
(26 Jan 1945, 11:30, Oxford, UK) who died from Multiple Sclerosis (MS)

Du Pre was a musical prodigy, a cellist with a brilliant talent. A passionate person (Moon opposite Mars), she released her inner tension through her music and the fiery intensity of her virtuosity brought her fame. MS brought this all to a crashing halt in the early 1970's.

In Chart 7 on the Rays, we see that paralysis is a ray 1 disease. In MS, the immune system attacks the brain and spinal cord relentlessly, never letting up. It causes damage to the myelin sheath, the protective covering that surrounds nerve cells. Control of the body is consequently lost as nerve signals slow down then stop. There is a scarring, general atrophying of the body and restriction of movement.

Find a health-triangle for Du Pre.

In this exercise, Mercury and Venus that both represent the nervous system will be investigated. This is because they are both in separate triangles, and both could represent the condition. This is being done to show readers that if there is more than one cause of the disease, it may show up twice in the chart.

Triangle 1: Mercury is first choice for the nervous system (O); and it is conjunct Mars representing the attacking immune system, MS (E). The Moon is our choice for the psychological cause (C).

> *The Moon is often the first choice for the psychological cause of a problem, especially if it forms part of a strong triangular pattern. This is because it represents the emotions and the "prison of the soul" pattern. This pattern consists of any negative core beliefs and other unresolved issues we bring through from past lives that contribute to the breakdown of our health.*

Although Saturn's conjunction to the Moon is wide, it will be read as conjunct and opposing Mars-Mercury. This is because the Moon disposits Saturn and the IC/ MC axis draws the four planets involved together energetically.

Du Pre was emotionally inhibited (Moon-Saturn), a consequence of her own karma and due to overprotective and repressive parents. The opposition from Saturn-Moon to Mars-Mercury showed she expected biting criticism from her parents and later from her managers and handlers; criticisms she later replayed to herself, as she castigated herself for her shortcomings. These four planets are at the core of the self-attack pattern and health-triangle.

Because Mars-Mercury are conjunct and so are Moon-Saturn, it gives us the opportunity to include another planet in the triangle. Saturn squares Neptune and Jupiter in the 6H of health. Together these three planets represent the weakening, crippling and paralysing effects of MS. Jupiter also co-rules the 12H of hospitals and the 8H of death. MS eventually killed Du Pre and Jupiter is included in the triangle as a second (E) point. Here is the simplest triangle.

▲ (C) Moon, Saturn. (O) Mercury (E) Mars, Saturn, Jupiter.

Triangle 2: Venus represents the nervous system (O) in the second triangle. It is sesquiquadrate Pluto in Leo, that represents the attacking immune system (E). Leo rules the immune system and Pluto carries the 1st ray that governs atrophying and hardening diseases like MS.

Venus is in emotional Pisces and represents the cause (C). It shows she harboured deep seated emotional issues about love. Venus is in the 12H, which rules the unconscious. In this hidden part of the mind, negative core beliefs are stored and from there they emerge when triggered. Venus > Pluto in the 5H of romance, shows a belief that love will always die, or that love will destroy you.

For the third point of the triangle we also include Jupiter. Pluto is semi-square Jupiter and Venus opposes it. Here is the triangle that contains Venus for the pituitary.

▲ (C) Venus in Pisces. (O) Venus (E) Pluto in Leo, Jupiter.

The first triangle shows that the causal factor behind the disease is due to emotional inhibition; the second triangle shows that there is a negative core belief associated with the trouble. Both triangles are valid. But when the disease first struck, the first triangle with Mercury was more potent when compared to solar-arc planets. It is wise to test a hypothetical health-triangle against the astrology existent when the disease appeared. If your planets are correct, they will make dynamic connections to the natal or progressed planets.

Experiment with the triangles. They can be drawn different ways. All the planets may contribute to a disease and its cause, but try to find at least three to represent the core factors involved in the appearance of a disease.

-----

4. Disease appearance

The disease began to affect Du Pre in 1971 when she started to lose control of her fingers. Diagnosed in 1973, she stopped playing when she could no longer judge the weight of the bow in her hands. Diseases such as MS are active before symptoms show and Triangle 1 shows the likely activation date is 1968

Solar-arc Directions April 1968

- 1968-1970: the Moon by solar-arc was at 7 Leo, moving towards natal Pluto; and solar-arc Mars-Mercury at 8 Aquarius opposed it. The disease was seeded. It must have been accompanied by devastating emotional distress - Pluto co-rules the 7H of marriage. Although Mars-Mercury-Moon had cleared Pluto by 1971, the solar-arc Saturn point was still moving towards Pluto, marking the relentless progression of the disease.

- During this period, the solar-arc Jupiter point progressed through the 6th and was at 20 Libra, inconjunct Venus, linking the two triangles and marking the onset of the loss of feeling in her hands.

- With Mars-Mercury travelling by solar-arc with the midheaven, her physical devastation was played out in public adding extra stress.

Du Pre lived for another 17 years, dying on 19 October 1987. Benevolent Jupiter was moving over her ascendant. It is a blessing for the soul to be freed from a seriously impaired body.

This completes this section on finding health-triangles. Study the three steps involved then work with charts to familiarise yourself with how it works. Often when you look at a chart a triangle stands out and each point simply slots into place. Other times, a little more effort is required to put the three points together.

As long as you think in terms of energy and consider the problem as being due to the misuse of energy, you cannot go wrong. Identifying the ray energy that lies behind a disease, then making a connection from the disease to a psychological disturbance of the same energetic nature, is the essential part of the triangle technique.

-----

4. CASE STUDIES

Esoteric Healing - Rule Three

Let the healer train himself to know the inner stage of thought or of desire of the one who seeks his help. He can thereby know the source from whence the trouble comes. Let him relate the cause and the effect, and know the point exact through which the help must come.

Bailey, Alice A; Esoteric Healing, page 134-135.

4a. Crown Chakra Diseases

The crown chakra rules the pineal gland, the brain, sleep and death. It receives energy from Ray 1, Aries, Pluto, Vulcan, Uranus.

4a.1. The Brain

Aneurysm in the brain

An aneurysm is a weak spot in the wall of a blood vessel that balloons out and fills with blood. Life is under threat if the aneurysm bursts. The weakness can be present at birth or be the result of other health conditions. A violent temper that may be coupled with emotional repression so that tension builds until there is a psychological or physiological explosion underlies an aneurysm.

Cacilda Becker (6 April 1921 09:25, Pirassununga Brazil)

Latino stage and film actress who achieved success in her natal Brazil. She was volatile and passionate, marrying three times. During a performance on stage on May 6 1969, she collapsed - she had suffered a brain aneurysm that resulted in a stroke. Although she was immediately rushed to the hospital she died a few weeks later on 14th June 1969.

Cause: emotional. Becker found it difficult to express her emotions, to release anger. She would brood on her hurts, hide them away and hold them in. This built up tension and stress and is linked to her brain trouble. (Mars is in detriment in the 12H of hidden things).

Organ: crown. Mars for the brain, head and blood; the arteries Jupiter.

Effect: aneurysm. Becker developed high blood pressure (Mars). Artery walls weakened and an aneurysm developed (trine Jupiter afflicted in Virgo, conjunct retrograde Venus). It ruptured suddenly, killing her (easy-opposition pattern; Mars, Uranus and Jupiter that rules the 8H of death).

▲ (C) Mars. (O) Mars, Jupiter. (E) Mars, Venus, Uranus.

Joe Biden (20 November 1942 08:30, Scranton PA)

American politician, the 47th Vice President of the United States serving with the first black President of the US, Barack Obama. He survived a brain aneurysm at age 45, which required two operations to correct.

Cause: emotional. Biden has a volcanic temper (Pluto in Leo square Mars), is exceedingly stubborn and suppresses his emotions until he is like a pressure-cooker about to explode (Moon in Taurus square Jupiter in Cancer). These patterns are related to his aneurysm.

Organ: crown - brain mass the Moon; the arteries Jupiter.

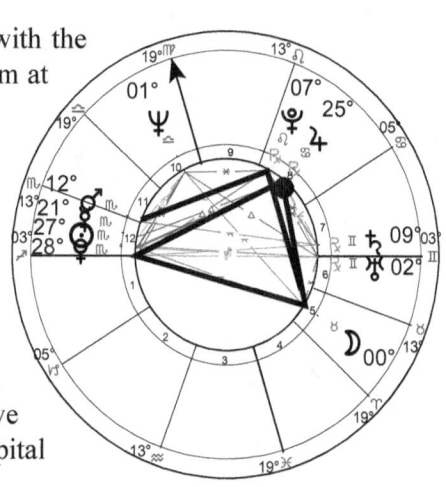

Effect: aneurysm. Repression of force caused high blood pressure (Pluto > Mars). Artery walls weakened and he developed a cerebral aneurysm (Jupiter trine Venus that weakens, inconjunct the Moon). He was lucky to have beneficial Jupiter on his side (trine the Sun, Venus and ascendant). His hospital treatment was successful and he evaded death.

▲ (C) Mars, Pluto, Moon. (O) Moon, Jupiter. (E) Pluto, Mars, Venus.

Biden's line-up of planets in the 12H of hospitals is a warning that potentially, his own actions (the 12th is the house of self-undoing), could undermine his health and bring him down. But he has thrived in the cut and thrust world of modern politics (Uranus opposite the Sun and Venus, trine Neptune in the 10th house of government). He is helped by his Sun trine Jupiter, which gives him great vitality and a lot of luck.

a. Brain cancer, tumours

Ray 2 that over-builds governs cancer. But the 1st ray when used to stifle force is a major cause. It causes congestion in the chakras, affecting related body tissue. Then if cells start to multiply (ray 2) cancer will appear and grow.

George Gershwin (26 September 1898 11:09, Brooklyn NY).

American composer famous for works such as 'Rhapsody in Blue'. A fast growing tumour in his temporal lobe killed him, 11 July 1937.

Cause: emotional. Gershwin was stubborn and strong willed (Saturn-Uranus on the ascendant). He would stifle his feelings of hurt and anger rather than deal with them directly and this caused congestion in the brain region (sesquiquadrate Mars, which falls in Cancer).

Organ: crown - brain mass, Mars in Cancer.

Effect: tumour. Cells began to multiply rapidly and a fast growing tumour suddenly emerged (Jupiter square Mars > Uranus).

▲ (C) Mars, Saturn, Uranus. (O) Mars. (E) Mars, Uranus, Jupiter.

• In December 1936, ten months before his death, the progressed Moon moved into the 8H of death and crossed natal Mars. In that month, there was also an eclipse on Mars, showing an acceleration of trouble in the brain.

[There is a second pattern: cancerous cells (the Sun carrying the second ray, falls in Libra), in the temporal region (semi-square Venus ruling the pituitary gland), of the brain (Venus trine Mars in Cancer; square Moon)].

Yves Saint-Laurent (1 August 1936 19:45, Oran Algeria)

Famous French fashion designer Saint-Laurent was diagnosed with a brain tumour just 2 weeks before he died on June 1 2008.

Cause: emotional. A friend said of Yves said "he was an unhappy person, depression ran deep". We see this with the Moon, the emotions, in detriment in chilly and arid Capricorn. He also had a volatile and angry side that he repressed and that simmered away underneath (Moon opposing Mars in Cancer, conjunct Pluto). The seeds of his brain trouble are rooted here.

Organ: crown - brain Mars in Cancer, brain mass the Moon.

Effect: tumour. Consequently, carcinogenic changes (Neptune) occurred in brain tissue (trine the Moon on the cusp of the 12H of hospitals; septile Mars in the 6H of health). The tumour developed and grew (Neptune square Jupiter).

▲ (C) Moon, Mars, Pluto. (O) Mars, Moon. (E) Neptune, Jupiter.

b. Brain trauma - killed

Sonny Bono (16 February 1935, 21:21, Detroit, MI)

American entertainer who was killed on 5 January 1998, in a skiing accident. He hit a tree, dying instantly from brain trauma.

Cause: emotional. Most accidents are self-inflicted, caused by chronic anger. Bono had such a pattern: a t-square with three volatile planets fighting each other (Pluto, Uranus and Mars). This bred emotional toxicity that rebounded on him like a boomerang.

Organ: crown - brain and head, Mars in the 1H.

Effect: brain trauma. While skiing (Uranus rules the 5H of recreation), he suffered a massive blow to the head and died (Pluto-Mars > Uranus in Aries, which is located on the cusp of the 8H of death).

▲ (C) Mars, Pluto, Uranus. (O) Mars. (E) Mars, Pluto, Uranus.

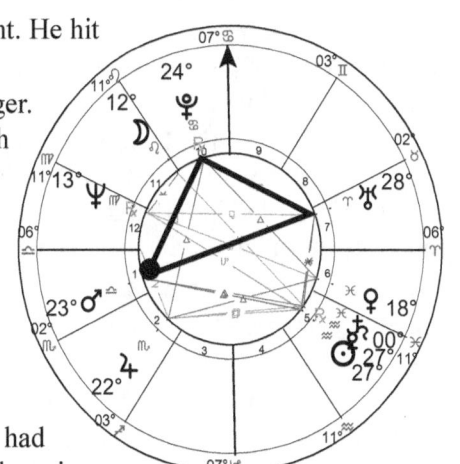

• On the day Bono died, the Mars wing of the t-square by solar-arc, had progressed to 26 Sagittarius, the midpoint of Mars-Saturn. The event was karmic.

Ennis Cosby (15 April 1969, 00:28 Los Angeles CA)

Son of Bill and Camille Cosby. On 16 January 1997, while repairing his car tire, he was shot in the head during a robbery.

Cause: emotional. Cosby was hot-headed with a temper that could rapidly erupt (Moon in Aries - trine Mars, opposite Uranus). This type of force attracts "accidents".

Organ: crown - brain mass, the Moon in Aries.

Effect: brain trauma. Cosby was shot (Mars), in the brain (Moon in Aries), and died (Uranus in the 8th house of death).

▲ (C) Mars, Moon. (O) Moon. (E) Mars, Uranus.

- On the day Cosby was shot, solar-arc Mars (guns and violence), had progressed to 13 Capricorn and was on the ascendant, which is related to the head.

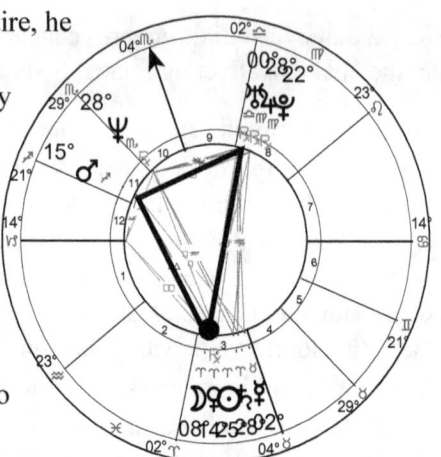

Abraham Lincoln (12 February 1809, 06:54 Hodgenville KY)

Lincoln, the 16th President of the United States was a disciple. People at this level are able to release tension positively through service activities. This means that the cause of death that occurred on April 14 1865 was not caused by his anger or negativity. His goodness attracted fanatics.

Cause: karmic. Lincoln was stalked and attacked by a fanatic who opposed him ideologically and the core values he stood for (Mars, ruler of the 2H of values, semi-square Neptune). The fanatic belonged to a secret organisation (Neptune septile Moon in Capricorn in the 12H of hidden things). With Saturn conjunct Neptune, karma was involved.

Organ: crown - head, Mars, brain mass the Moon.

Effect: brain trauma. The fanatic shot Lincoln in the brain (Mars square Moon), and he died (Mars in the 8H of death).

▲ (C) Saturn, Neptune. (O) Mars, Moon. (E) Mars.

- On the fatal day, transit Mars was at 7 Cancer, square natal Venus at 7 Aries, the ruler of the 8H of death. Additionally, transit Saturn, ruler of the 12H of hidden enemies, was moving over natal Mars. The killer was an agent of his political and ideological foes.

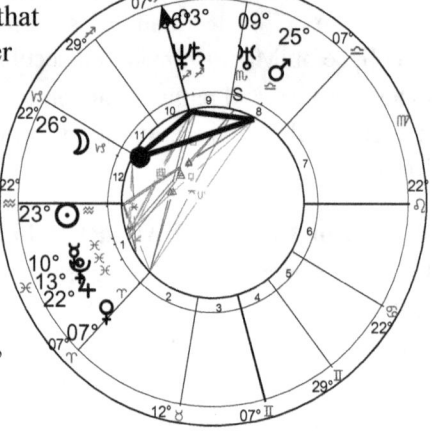

c. Hydrocephalus

Congenital hydrocephalus is caused by a brain malformation, a structural defect in the brain present at birth, which causes excessive cerebrospinal fluid to accumulate in brain cavities. The brain mass and structure are ruled by the 3rd ray, carried by Cancer, Capricorn and their rulers Saturn and the Moon.

Linda Martel (21 August 1956, 03.30 BST, Guernsey UK)

British child born with spina bifida and hydrocephalus. A prodigy, Martel healed some 2000 people before she died at age 5. An advanced soul, she may have returned briefly to work off personal karma to do with parenting and children (Saturn is in the 5H of children).

Cause: karmic-genetic. Defective DNA, a karmic implication from a past life (Moon in Aquarius, in the 8H of inheritances, square Saturn), caused a deformity in the brain structure and serious abnormalities in the spine (opposite Sun-Pluto in Leo; a t-square).

Organ: crown - brain mass the Moon, the spine Leo.

Effect: hydrocephalus. Brain malformations let fluid to leak into brain cavities (Moon > Saturn).

▲ (C) Saturn, Moon. (O) Moon, Leo. (E) Saturn, Pluto.

- Martel died at 5. The Moon by solar-arc had moved to 28 Aquarius, exactly opposite the natal Sun and Pluto that rules death.

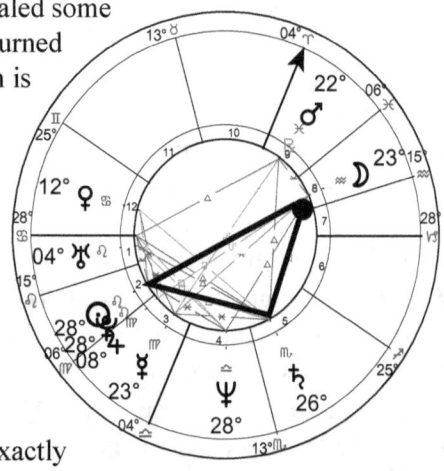

d. Meningitis

The meninges membranes (Moon or Saturn), that cover the central nervous system become inflamed due to an infection caused by a bacteria (Uranus), a fungus (Moon), or virus (Neptune). It is life-threatening, especially if Pluto is involved in the health-triangle.

Alexander Eben (11 December 1953, 02.42 am, Charlotte NC)

Eben is an American neurosurgeon and author of 'Proof of Heaven' in which he describes his 2008 near-death experience while in a meningitis-induced coma. He has a 'Kite' planetary pattern with Pluto as the focal point. Pluto is a ruler of the crown chakra and brain, and Eben is a neurosurgeon, which fits Eben's profession.

Cause: emotional. A volatile and explosive temper is behind the trouble. His fiery displays invited inflammatory attacks like meningitis (Mars, co-ruler of the 6H of health with Aries sharing the cusp, square Uranus).

Organ: crown - brain mass and meninges, Cancer and the Moon.

Effect: meningitis. Reports say Eben had a bacterial infection. This is helpful, because from the chart it is hard to tell whether a virus (Neptune) or bacteria (Uranus), caused his attack. Both these planets aspect Mars. The brain infection caused seizures (Uranus square Mars, the Moon disposits Uranus).

▲ (C) Mars, Uranus. (O) Cancer, Moon. (E) Uranus, Mars.

- In 2008, the Kite pattern had rotated by solar-arc, so that the Pluto wing was at 20 Libra and stationed on the ascendant. Eben contracted meningitis and nearly died. The ascendant represents soul purpose. Eben changed. Now he uses his experience to help others.

Oscar Wilde (16 October 1854, 03:00, Dublin Ireland)

Irish playwright and poet, Wilde died lonely, broke and disease-ravaged from acute meningitis on 30 November 1900. The Moon represents the "prison of the soul". It is in luxury loving Leo, in close proximity to the 12H cusp. He lived an extravagant lifestyle, which contributed to his self-undoing.

Cause: misuse of sexual force. The cause of the disease is reported as being syphilis related (Uranus). Though married, he was promiscuous and had affairs (Uranus, the ruler of the sexual sacral chakra falls in Taurus, the sign of desire).

Organ: crown - brain meninges the Moon, nervous system Mercury.

Effect: meningitis. The trouble is shown by a t-square. Wilde picked up a bacterial infection (Uranus), which attacked the meninges (Moon) of the nervous system (Mercury). There were seizures and he died (Uranus - Mercury in Scorpio, the natural ruler of the 8H of death).

▲ (C) Uranus. (O) Moon, Mercury. (E) Uranus.

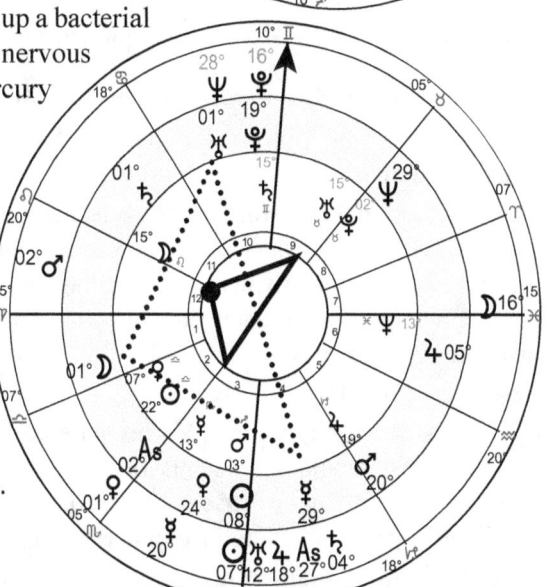

Chart for 30 November 1900: inner chart natal, middle chart solar-arc directions, outer chart transits.

- When Wilde died, the progressed Moon was in the 8H, moving towards Pluto.
- At the same time, the t-square had rotated by solar-arc, so that all three planets aspected natal Pluto. Solar-arc Moon was in the 1st house, inconjunct Pluto; solar-arc Uranus was at 1 Cancer sextile Pluto; solar-arc Saturn was at 1 Leo square Pluto. The dying process for Wilde was not easy.

e. Sleep disorders

Sleep is governed by the 1st ray and the crown chakra. Melatonin produced by the pineal gland affects the circadian rhythm, which keeps us in harmony with the 24-hour day.

Astro.com 12077 (29 January 1952, 15:30) - narcolepsy

American male with narcolepsy, a disorder where there is excessive daytime sleepiness and uncontrollable, sudden, falling asleep. He was the grandson and son of two narcoleptic women.

Cause: emotional. This condition can occur with people whose physical plane grounding is very weak, who are astral in consciousness and are focused in the solar plexus. This enables them to slip away easily to the Astral Plane.

Organ: crown - sleep, represented by 1st ray Pluto, Neptune governs the sleep state.

Effect: narcolepsy. The Moon in Pisces represents the trouble. It is the "finger" of God point in a Yod planetary pattern, with the two planets associated with sleep - Neptune and Pluto, the prongs. Developmentally, our subject was being asked to ground himself securely in his physical body (earth-sign Virgo is opposite the "finger point"). This would close the easy-access door to the Astral Plane, restoring balance to his sleep patterns (Moon in Pisces inconjunct Neptune in Libra sextile Pluto).

▲ (C) Moon, Neptune. (O) Pluto, Neptune. (E) Pisces, Neptune.

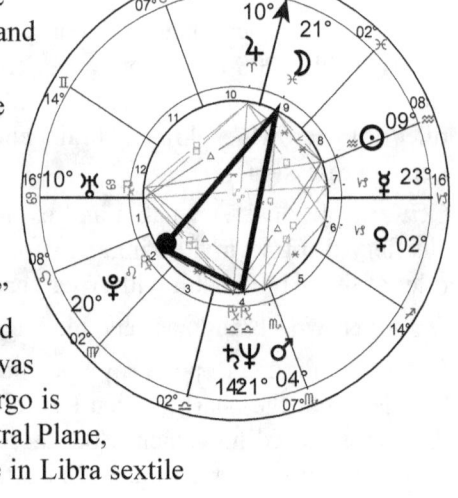

Linda Ronstadt (15 July 1946, 17:39, Tucson AZ) - sleep apnoea

American singer of country, folk, ballads and rock who had obstructive sleep apnoea, a problem associated with obesity.

Cause: emotional. Disturbed emotions dominated Ronstadt's life (Moon, the handle of a "bucket" pattern, standing alone on one side of the chart). To offset anxiety she would mentally detach from her feelings (Mercury opposite the Moon in Aquarius), and comfort-eat fatty and sugary foods (Mercury in Leo, ruler of 6H of diet; Moon trine Jupiter in Libra).

Organ: throat - airways, Mercury.

Effect: sleep apnoea. As a consequence of diet, a fatty-tissue blockage formed in the airways (Jupiter sextile Mercury). This interrupted breathing during sleep (Pluto conjunct Mercury). It is a dangerous condition that can result in death.

▲ (C) Moon. (O) Mercury. (E) Jupiter, Pluto.

Billy Martin (16 May 1928 15:43, Berkeley CA) - insomnia

American baseball player who had treatment for insomnia and acute melancholia following a divorce in 1955.

Cause: emotional. Martin was very intense emotionally and was powerfully invested in his marriage (Pluto in Cancer square the Moon in the 7H of marriage). Consequently, when his marriage broke apart he was so distressed he had a temporary mental break-down. Pluto in Cancer is the primary instigator of the trouble.

Organ: crown - sleep, 1st ray Pluto.

Effect: insomnia, depression. Martin suffered from insomnia his disturbed emotions just would not let his brain rest (Pluto square Moon in Aries conjunct Jupiter; ruler of Aries - Mars, conjunct Uranus). Exhausted, he went into deep depression (Pluto inconjunct Saturn, trine the Moon).

▲ (C) Moon, Pluto. (O) Pluto. (E) Moon in Aries, Saturn.

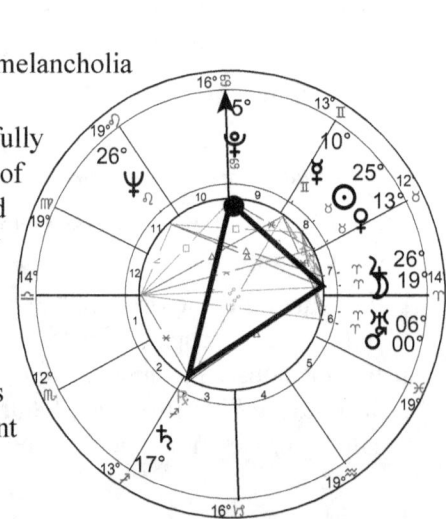

f. Stroke

A stroke occurs when the arteries block or rupture so that life-giving blood does not reach the brain and cells die from lack of oxygen. Stroke is a 1st ray disease, carried by Pluto, Mars via Aries, Uranus and Saturn. Jupiter rules arteries and Saturn is the major "blocker".

John Quincy Adams (11 July 1767, 11:00, Quincy Neck MA)

Adams was an American statesman and the 6th President of the United States. He had a paralytic stroke in Boston in 1847, and died 23 February 1848.

Cause: emotional. Adams was a sensitive and emotional Cancer Sun person and being President of the US placed great strain upon him. There was tremendous frustration and pressure in both his professional and family life (Cancer-Capricorn opposition across the 10th - 4th houses). Matters were not helped by his volatile temper, which caused pressure to build (Mars in Leo square Uranus, which is sesquiquadrate Jupiter in the 12H of self-undoing. Jupiter rules the 6H of health with Pisces on the cusp). This latter pattern is related to his eventual stroke.

Organ: crown - brain, Mars.

Effect: stroke. Quincy was 81 when he had his stroke so his body was ageing and stiffening. Finally it was all too much. High blood pressure caused a paralysing stroke and he died (Mars > Jupiter and Uranus that is in the 8H of death).

▲ (C) Mars, Uranus. (O) Mars. (E) Mars, Uranus, Jupiter.

- When Adams died, the Sun > Pluto-Moon aspect, had rotated by solar-arc so that it straddled the decendant - ascendant axis, rendering the head and brain (the ascendant) vulnerable to trouble.

Hilda Doolittle (10 September 1886, 12:35, Bethlehem PA)

Doolittle was an American poet and novelist who become known for her association with early 20th century avant-garde poets. She was very independent for her time and an individualist (Moon in Aquarius, handle of a "bucket" planet pattern). She suffered a stroke in July 1961 and died two months later.

Cause: emotional. Saturn in Cancer is emotionally debilitating. People like Doolittle who have it, wall off their emotions because they are unable to deal with hurt feelings that follow rejection. This was easy for Doolittle, because with the Moon in cerebral Aquarius, she rationalised how she felt. But she also harboured revengeful anger, which she vented on friends or those in her group (Mars in Scorpio in the 11H of friends, square the Moon). This anger and repression of emotions, built up stress.

Additionally, a love of rich, sweet foods (Venus in Leo is the ruler of the 6H of diet with greedy Taurus on the cusp), and alcohol (square Neptune in the 6H of health); contributed to fatty build up in the arteries (Venus semi-square Jupiter).

Organ: crown - brain mass the Moon.

Effect: stroke. Eventually, a blockage (Saturn), to blood flow (inconjunct Moon in Aquarius), brought on a stroke (Moon square Mars), which eventually killed her (Saturn in the 8H of death).

▲ (C) Saturn in Cancer, Moon, Mars. (O) Moon. (E) Saturn, Mars.

- In the month Doolittle had her stroke (July 1961), Mars by solar-arc was at 27 Capricorn, with transit Saturn sitting on top of it, representing loss of blood supply and the stroke.

- Venus represents the nervous system and also the cardiovascular system because of its natal location in Leo. By solar-arc it had rotated to natal Mars. The stroke occurred, and these systems were damaged.

- Progressed Moon, the ruler of the 8H of death was at 16 Scorpio, still 2 degrees out from the exact square to the natal Moon at 18 Aquarius. She withstood death for 2 more months before the soul freed itself.

4a. 2. Dementia

Dementia is the breakdown of the cellular structure of the brain so that consciousness is unable to work through the nervous system. The result is fading cognition. The brain mass is governed by ray 3, carried by the Moon via Cancer, and Saturn. Sometimes Mars via Aries represents the brain. Damage causing brain shrinkage is a 1st ray effect, brought on primarily by Saturn and Pluto. Nervous system rulers (Mercury, Venus, Uranus and planets in Gemini), represent cognition. There are three main types of dementia.

- The most common is *Alzheimer's* (50-70% of dementia cases). Nerve cells die, forming plaques and tangles that impair brain function. There is tissue loss, the cortex shrinks and atrophies. Pluto and Saturn are the danger planets.
- In *vascular dementia* (VCD - 25%), a part of the brain dies because it does not get enough blood due to damaged brain blood-vessels, typically caused through small strokes. Look particularly at Mars for strokes and alternatively, Uranus.
- *Lewy body dementia* (LBD - 15%). There are visual hallucinations and Parkinson-like movements. Abnormal protein deposits in the brain cause problems with thinking, movement and mood. Uranus may be involved.

a. Alzheimer's

Harold Wilson (11 March 1916, 10:45, Huddersfield UK)

Ex-British Prime Minister renowned for his razor like intellect. In April 1976, when he resigned, commentators say he was showing the symptoms of intellectual decline. He died in May 1995.

Cause: emotional. Wilson used his formidable will to suppress his emotions and this served him well in his career where he demonstrated powerful self-resolve (Saturn-Pluto in Cancer on the ascendant, Pluto trine MC).

Organ: crown - brain mass, the Moon.

Effect: Alzheimer's. But Wilson's habit of blocking force caused congestion in the crown chakra (Pluto), wreaking havoc with brain tissue (Moon), causing the disease. Pluto and Saturn are midpoint the Moon and Neptune, representing brain tissue destruction and descent into oblivion (Neptune).

▲ (C) Pluto and Saturn in Cancer. (O) Moon. (E) Pluto, Saturn, Neptune.

- In 1974-75, two years before he retired, Wilson went through his second Saturn return and at the same time, the Sun progressed into the 12H, symbolising consciousness going into obscuration. Astrologically, this could pinpoint the start of his mental decline.

Ronald Reagan (6 February 1911, 04:16, Tampico, IL)

American movie star and US President. Publicly, he was diagnosed in 1994, though symptoms were already showing in 1984.

Cause: emotional. Reagan was an intelligent Aquarian Sun person with a stubborn Taurus Moon, which he hid this under a benevolent Sagittarius appearance (ascendant). The combination - with good looks, brought him popularity in film and politics. But stubbornness and a tendency to fester over slights is related to the disease (Moon semi-square Pluto in Gemini that rules the 7H of "others"; Pluto inconjunct Uranus-Mercury).

Organ: crown - brain mass the Moon, cognition Mercury.

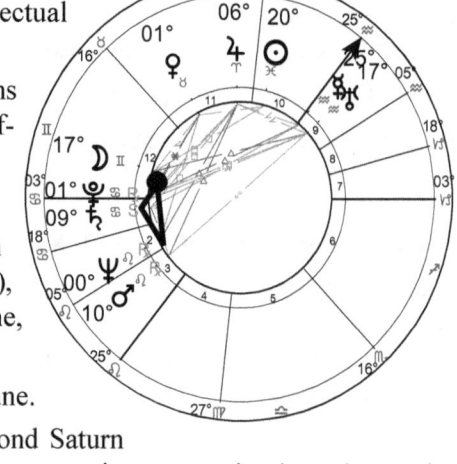

Effect: Alzheimer's. By the time he reached 70, his habit of blocking force plus the deteriorating effects of age caused damage to brain cells (Pluto in the 6H of health > Moon). Cognition was gradually destroyed (Pluto in Gemini > Uranus-Mercury in ageing Capricorn). Side-effects of the disease eventually killed him (Mercury co-rules the 8H of death with Virgo sharing the cusp).

▲ (C) Moon, Pluto. (O) Moon, Mercury. (E) Pluto, Uranus.

b. Alzheimer's caused by a syphilitic gene

A cause of dementia is the syphilitic gene which most of us have inherited from our fore-fathers. The sacral chakra rulers - Mars and Uranus may be implicated.

> [Dementia] due to the breaking down of the brain tissue. Far more of these are definitely syphilitic in origin.. for the physical sex organs are a lower correspondence of the negative-positive relation existing in the brain between the two head centres and the pituitary and pineal glands. [1]

Glen Campbell (22 April 1936, 20:14, Delight, AR)

American country music singer, known for a series of hit songs in the 1960's and 70's. He had many tumultuous affairs and married four times.

Cause: sexual misuse. With the influence of sensuous Taurus powerfully embedded in his nature and romantic Venus afflicted in aggressive and lusty Aries, we see that Campbell had a powerful sex drive and was inclined to promiscuity. It is likely with this line up on planets and their influence in the 6H of health that he caught STD's.

Organ: crown - brain Mars, consciousness Uranus.

Effect: Alzheimer's. Campbell inherited the syphilitic gene (Mars wide conjunction to Uranus). Brain tissue was damaged as brain fluid atrophied (Mars in an easy-opposition pattern with Saturn in Pisces and Neptune afflicted in Virgo). Consequently, consciousness disappeared into oblivion.

▲ (C) Taurus, Mars. (O) Mars, Uranus. (E) Mars, Saturn, Neptune.

- Loss of memory probably started as early as 2001 when the Taurus stellium by solar-arc started to move over natal Pluto. Serious trouble started in 2009-2010 when Mercury crossed, then Mars in 2009-2010. Campbell went public in June 2011 with the news that he had Alzheimer's. He became a patient at an Alzheimer's long-term care and treatment facility in 2014 and died of the disease on August 8 2017.

c. Huntington's Disease

Huntington's that leads to dementia is genetic (Uranus). Accompanying symptoms are mood swings (Moon) and jerky movements (Uranus). Because it is inherited, examine the Moon or Uranus from a psychological angle to try to uncover toxic attitudes being passed down the family line.

Sophie Daumier (24 November 1934, 05:30; Boulongne sur Mer, France)

French film actress who inherited and died from Huntington's. So did her son.

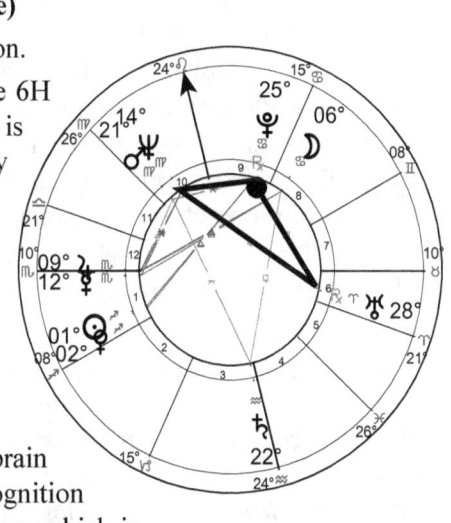

Cause: genetic. The defective gene is shown by Uranus, retrograde in the 6H of health. Uranus rules the 4H of family, so its location tells us that there is a history of chronic ill health in the family arising from this DNA legacy (Uranus square destructive Pluto in Cancer, and dispositing Saturn).

Daumier's family life was not easy, with disciplinarian Saturn standing guard over the family on the 4H cusp, ready to deal out biting criticism and public shaming for any mistakes she made (Saturn inconjunct Mars-Neptune in the 10th house of status). The passing on of this horrendous disease is due to family karma.

Organ: crown - brain mass Pluto in Cancer, cognition Uranus.

Effect: Huntington's. The gene caused the destruction of brain tissue and brain neurons (Uranus in Aries square Pluto in Cancer), resulting in the loss of cognition so that consciousness slipped into oblivion (Uranus sesquiquadrate Neptune, which in turn is semi-square Pluto).

▲ (C) Uranus. (O) Pluto in Cancer, Uranus. (E) Pluto, Neptune.

---

[1] Bailey, Alice A; Esoteric Healing, 316.

Woody Guthrie (14 July 1912, Okemah, OK).

Unknown time, 12 PM midday used and the 0 degrees Aries House System.
American singer-songwriter who died from complications of Huntington's disease
on 19 November 2015.

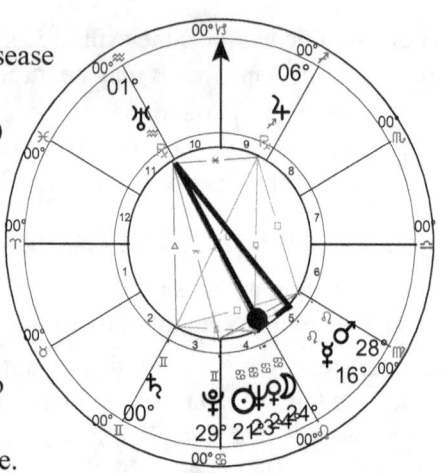

Cause: genetic. Potential trouble is quickly seen - the defective gene (Uranus)
opposes a Cancer stellium that includes the Moon, which rules the brain mass.
The unhealthy family pattern being passed down the family line points to
hidden abuse (Uranus opposite Neptune, the natural ruler of the 12H).

Organ: crown - brain mass the Moon, cognition Uranus and Mercury.

Effect: Huntington's. The gene (Uranus) caused aberrations in brain tissue
that resulted in mood swings (Cancer planets and the Moon). As damage
proceeded, there was a loss of cognition as consciousness disappeared into
oblivion (Uranus quindecile Mercury, opposite Neptune).

▲ (C) Uranus, Cancer. (O) Moon, Uranus, Mercury. (E) Uranus, Neptune.

d. Lewy Body Dementia (LBD)

LBD differs from Alzheimer's because it incorporates a form of Parkinsonism, resulting in tremors (Uranus), visual hallucinations (Moon-Neptune), mood swings and depression (Saturn).

Robin Williams (21 July 1951, 13:34, Chicago IL)

American actor who became famous in the TV series Mork and Mindy. He hung himself on 11 August 2014. Afterwards it was revealed he had LBD.

Cause: genetic-emotional. Behind his funny, joke-quipping facade, Williams was deeply troubled. He was very sensitive emotionally (Moon in Pisces), but also explosively angry (Mars conjunct Uranus), and would brood over slights. He released tension through his film work, but there was a manic, unstable aspect (Mars-Uranus in Cancer). This was the root cause of the trouble, since Mars rules the 6H of health.

Organ: crown - brain mass, Mars in Cancer and Jupiter in Aries.

Effect: LBD. Damage to brain cells manifested rapidly in 2013. There was inflammation (Mars and Jupiter in Aries), chemical disturbances and mutations in brain neurons (Uranus). As his cognitive function dissolved, he hallucinated (Uranus square Neptune on the cusp of the 12H of the mysterious and unknown).

▲ (C) Mars, Uranus. (O) Mars in Cancer, Aries. (E) Mars, Uranus, Neptune.

- Trouble started around November 2013, when there was an eclipse on the ascendant, a warning of the serious brain and nervous system trouble that was unfolding.
- At the same time, transit Pluto was in Capricorn, moving opposite natal Uranus-Mars at the hub of the t-square. 1st ray fire attacked, triggering the neurological trouble. Williams was lucid one minute then a minute later was lost in confusion - classic symptoms of LBD.
- When Williams hung himself on 11 August 2014, Pluto was still in this position, opposing Mars in the 8th house of death. Additionally, transit Mars was on his Scorpio ascendant, a sign that rules suffocation.

|| NB. SUICIDE. No one is expected to suffer the rigours of a broken or diseased body. The sage Djwhal Khul said: *"Lives are preserved in form (frequently an unconscious invalid, an old person whose response apparatus of contact and response is imperfect, or a baby who is not normal) that could be well permitted liberation. They serve no useful purpose and cause much pain and suffering to forms which nature (left to herself) would extinguish.* ***Through our overemphasis on the value of form life and through the universal fear of death.. we arrest the natural processes and hold the life, which is struggling to be free****."* [1]

Suicide is not sanctioned, but the releasing of the soul from a seriously damaged body is within the "law" if there is no quality of life and the body is being unnaturally preserved by modern medicine and technology.

---

[1] Bailey, Alice A; Esoteric Healing, 350-1.

e. Vascular Dementia (VCD)

In VCD, look for evidence of strokes (Aries, Mars, Uranus), and deprivation (Saturn, Pluto) of blood (Mars, Uranus, Neptune, perhaps the Sun and Leo) to the brain. Brain explosions such as strokes are manifestations of emotional explosions caused by unresolved anger and hatred.

Margaret Thatcher (13 October 1925, 09:00, Grantham UK)

Thatcher was a long serving Prime Minister of the United Kingdom from 1979 to 1990. She made some hard economic decisions that earned her the approval of some and hatred from others. A neurologist said that Thatcher had a series of small strokes over many years that went unnoticed until her legendary memory started to slip. The public was informed she had dementia in 2005.

Cause: emotional. Thatcher had dreams of greatness (Moon-Neptune in Leo conjunct the MC), which she realised. She was called the Iron Lady because of the toughness she displayed in pushing through her conservative economic reforms and policies. We see this force coming from the grand-trine of 1st ray planets (Saturn on the Scorpio ascendant, trine Pluto and Uranus) and it brought her political success.

Thatcher was fine when things were going her way (the grand-trine, but she could be explosive when she was crossed (Pluto in a t-square with Mars and Jupiter). This latter pattern underlies her trouble, since Mars rules the 6H of health.

Organ: crown - brain mass Pluto in Cancer, cognition Uranus.

Effect: dementia. Arteries hardened (Jupiter in Capricorn), and she had a series of small strokes that destroyed brain tissue (Mars). The consequence was loss of cognition and disengagement from reality at the end of life (Uranus in Pisces in the 4H of life endings).

▲ (C) Mars, Pluto. (O) Pluto in Cancer, Uranus. (E) Jupiter, Mars, Uranus.

Andrew Sachs (7 April 1930, 09:00, Berlin Germany)

British actor born in Berlin, his family immigrated to London in 1938 to escape Nazi persecution. Diagnosed with VCD in 2012, it eventually left him unable to speak and move without a wheelchair. He died on 23 November 2016, aged 86.

Cause: emotional. Sachs was tough and hard (t-square with three 1st ray planets - Uranus, Pluto, Saturn), and had difficulty processing his emotions in a healthy way. Defensive and protective he would repress injured feelings (Pluto in the 1H in Cancer opposite Saturn; Moon in Cancer quindecile Saturn); then would explode in a volcanic rage when he could no longer hold this force in (the t-square forces).

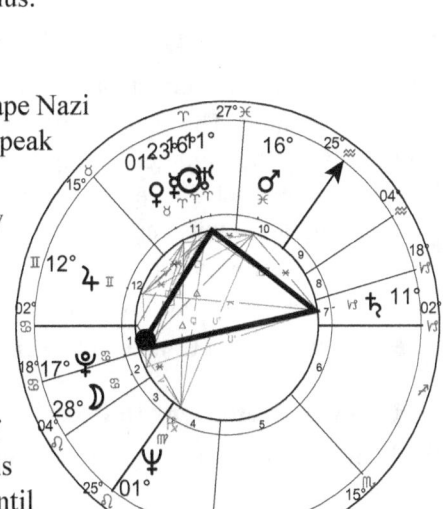

Although this pattern is related to his disease (Pluto rules the 6H of health), it did not manifest until he was in his 80's. This tells us that Sachs managed to achieve a state of relative harmony and balance in his life until common ageing took its toll.

Organ: crown - brain mass Pluto in Cancer; nervous system and cognition Uranus in Aries.

Effect: dementia. In later life as blood vessels hardened and stress built (the t-square), Sachs had a series of small strokes, which restricted blood flow to the brain (Uranus in Aries > Pluto in Cancer), so that brain tissue and cognition were gradually destroyed. Sachs lived on several years after the disease began to incapacitate him, destroying his quality of life and mobility so that he was wheelchair bound (Saturn inconjunct Jupiter in the 12H of major illnesses and hospitals).

▲ (C) Pluto in Cancer in the 1H. (O) Cancer, Uranus (E) Saturn, Uranus, Pluto.

• The condition struck him as the Uranus point of the health-triangle by solar-arc, approached and moved over the ascendant.

4b. Ajna Chakra Diseases

The ajna rules the pituitary gland, the nervous system, the senses and the eyes, ears, nose and face. It receives energy from Rays 5 and 4, Aries and Gemini, Venus and Mercury.

4b.1. Ears

When hearing is impaired, sound waves or nerve electrical impulses are not passed to the brain. The most common cause is disease or damage to the auditory nerves through injuries or noise explosions. Defective genes that affect hearing can be passed down to children. A foetus may incur damage if mother has a disease such as rubella, or again if a child itself has rubella or other virulent infection. The ears are ruled by the ajna (Mercury, Venus and Gemini) and also the throat chakra (Mercury). The psychology underlying deafness is related to an unwillingness to hear bad news. Saturn, which blocks, is the primary indicator of deafness.

a. Congenital deafness

Astro.com 13842 (13 January 1963, 10:05, London)
A British man, deaf from birth.
Cause: genetic-karmic. Hypothetically, there is a karmic backlash for misusing speech in a previous life (Saturn conjunct Mercury in the 12H).
Organ: ajna - ear nerves Mercury and Venus.
Effect: deafness. A bacterial infection (Uranus), which the mother contracted while pregnant (conjunct Moon in the 6H of health), damaged nerve cells (square Venus, inconjunct Mercury), resulting in shrivelled auditory nerves and deafness (Mercury conjunct Saturn).
▲ (C) Uranus, Saturn. (O) Mercury, Venus. (E) Uranus, Saturn.

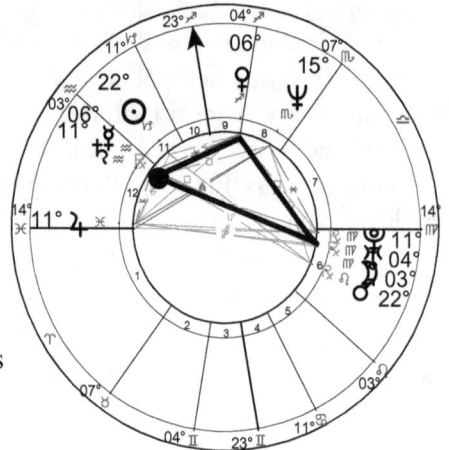

Astro.com 12561 (14 January 1954 06:58, Berwyn Il).
American male with congenital deafness, unknown cause.
Cause: congenital. The cause of his deafness was probably a virus (Neptune), contracted by the mother during pregnancy (square Uranus in Cancer, Neptune inconjunct the Moon). The virus targeted the organs of hearing (Neptune square Venus and Mercury, a t-square).
Organ: ajna - ear nerves Mercury and Venus.
Effect: deafness. He was left deaf (Venus-Mercury in Capricorn).
▲ (C) Uranus in Cancer. (O) Mercury, Venus. (E) Neptune, Capricorn.

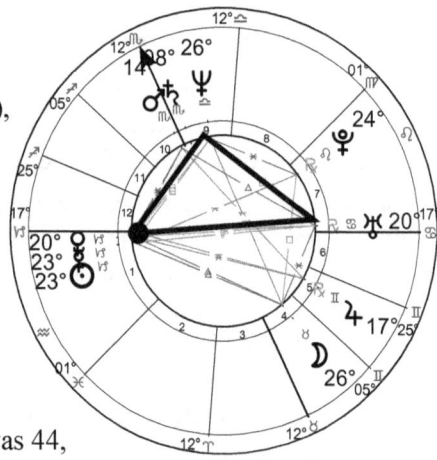

Ludwig van Beethoven (16 December 1770, 03:40, Bonn Germany).
Brilliant musician, who began to lose his hearing at age 26. By the time he was 44, he was almost completely deaf.
Cause: congenital. Beethoven was born with a susceptibility to ear infections (Mercury in detriment in Sagittarius, conjunct the Moon, square Neptune, opposite Mars in Gemini. Mars rules the 6H of health).
Organ: ajna - ear nerves, Mercury.
Effect: deafness. By the time he reached his middle twenties, his ear nerves were damaged to the point he had difficulty hearing.
▲ (C) Moon. (O) Mercury. (E) Mars, Neptune.
- In 1796 when he was 26, Neptune was transiting backwards and forwards over the natal ascendant, exacerbating his trouble.
- Additionally, solar-arc Mercury (ear nerves) had progressed to malevolent Pluto in Capricorn, indicating nerve damage.

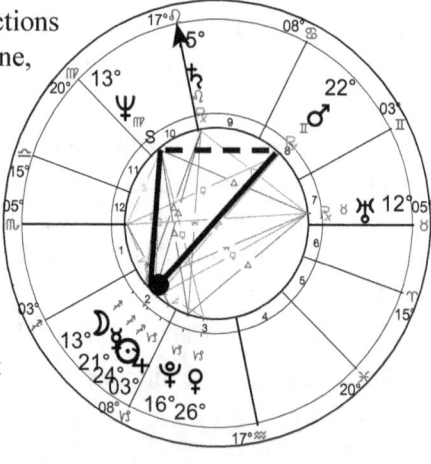

b. Deafness caused by Measles/ Rubella

Charles Eyck (24 March 1897, 11:00, Meerssen, Holland).

Dutch visual artist who had several gallery and museum exhibitions. At age 11, he became deaf after contracting rubella.

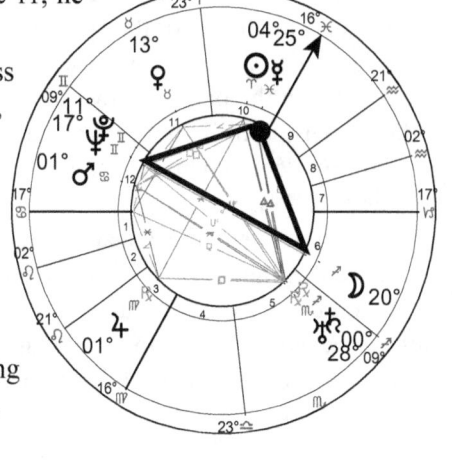

Cause: emotional. Eyck was born with a pattern that shows an unwillingness to hear bad news (Mercury square Neptune in the 12H of hidden things), which would explain why he was born with a congenital weakness in his ear nerves (Moon in the 6H of health square Mercury in detriment in Pisces). He was also susceptible to ear damage from viral infections. Mercury and Neptune are in a hostile mutual reception, are in each other's signs, which in this case is detrimental to auditory health.

Organ: ajna - ear nerves, Mercury and Gemini.

Effect: deafness. A viral attack (Neptune), destroyed ear nerves causing deafness (Mercury square Neptune that is in turn conjunct Pluto in Gemini).

▲ (C) Moon. (O) Mercury, Gemini. (E) Neptune, Pluto.

• In 1908, transit Neptune moved over his ascendant, indicating the viral attack.

Astro.com 14115 (20 November 1965, 16:47, Chester PA).

This American child was given a measles vaccine at age one. Two days later he had terrible pain in his ears. a high fever and he lost his hearing.

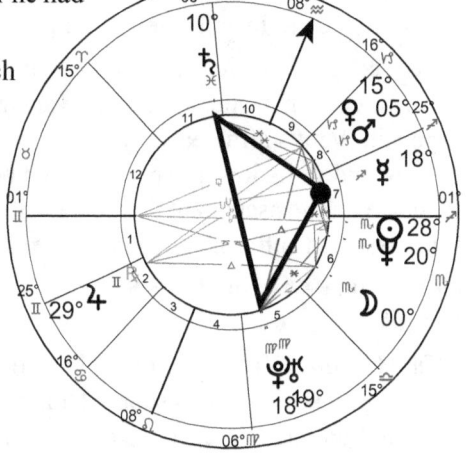

Cause: karmic. Our subject had lessons to learn about the misuse of speech (Saturn square Mercury). It seems this karma came via a vaccine (opposite Uranus) that may have been contaminated (Uranus conjunct Pluto). Pluto co-rules the 6H of health with Scorpio sharing the cusp.

Organ: ajna - ear nerves, Mercury.

Effect: deafness. A violent reaction to the vaccine left the child deaf (Mercury in detriment in Sagittarius in a t-square with Uranus, Pluto and Saturn). If the child's astrology chart had been consulted the parent's would have been alerted to the dangers of "modern" (Uranus) medicine.

▲ (C) Saturn. (O) Mercury. (E) Uranus, Pluto, Saturn.

c. Deafness caused by Otosclerosis

Dame Kathleen Ollerenshaw (1 October 1912, 07:00, Manchester UK)

British mathematician and politician who was Lord Mayor of Manchester from 1975 to 1976 and an advisor on educational matters to Margaret Thatcher's government in the 1980s.

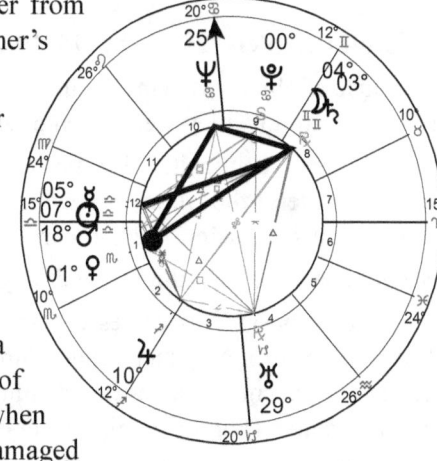

Cause: karmic-emotional. Ollerenshaw inherited a hearing problem from her father's side (the Moon co-rules the 10H of the father with Cancer sharing the cusp, in Gemini; conjunct Saturn, in the 8H of inheritances). Mercury is buried in the 12H of hidden matters, a classic placement for a person who does not want to hear bad news, a psychological pattern related to deafness.

Organ: ajna - ear nerves, Mercury, Venus and Gemini.

Effect: deafness. Ollerenshaw was born partially deaf due to otosclerosis, a condition where middle ear bones fuse, preventing normal transmission of sound from the eardrum into the inner ear (Moon-Saturn in Gemini). Then when she was 8, a viral infection (Neptune ruling the 6H of health) further damaged ear nerves, leaving her almost completely deaf (septile Gemini planets, square Venus afflicted in Scorpio; Saturn inconjunct Venus).

▲ (C) Saturn, Moon. (O) Mercury, Venus, Gemini. (E) Saturn, Neptune.

4b.2. Eyes

Vision depends upon the ability of the eye to receive and focus light rays and transfer this information to the occipital lobe of the brain for processing. The key element is *light*. The physical eye came into being in response to the light of the Sun. The Sun rules the eyes, particularly the right eye. The Moon reflects the light of the Sun and co-rules the eyes, particularly the left eye. Light rays enter the eye through the cornea, which bends the light rays so they pass freely through the pupil and eye lens, which in turn focuses the light ray onto the retina. The bringing in, carrying and transporting of light messages through the eye is a Mercury function. The cells in the retina absorb and convert the light to electrochemical impulses, which are transferred along the optic nerve to the brain. This is a Mercury-Uranus function.

Certain points in the zodiac have a detrimental effect on sight, especially when the Sun or Moon is located here. These are the Pleiades at 29 Taurus, the Ascelli at Leo 6 and Antares at Sagittarius 8.

When vision is lost through disease, it suggests on a psychological level, that what is seen is not liked and that by closing the eyes we can block out reality. Babies with a vision handicap at birth or in early childhood, have a karmic carry-over from a previous life that may belong to them personally or to the family.

a. Congenital Blindness

Stevie Wonder (13 May 1950, 16:15, Saginaw MI).
Wonder is a blind African-American musician and singer. Neptune on the ascendant was both a blessing and a curse - he inherited magical music talent, but strange events related to his birth left him blind.

Cause: congenital. Wonder was born with a pattern of obscuring reality (Neptune on the ascendant) when he did not want to face the truth or see unpleasantness (opposite Venus afflicted in Aries, conjunct the Moon). Neptune carries the 6th ray and in its lower aspect is a symbol for racial bigotry and fanaticism. Its place on the ascendant that represents life perception, suggests Wonder's blindness and suffering is connected to racial abuse in a past life.

Organ: ajna - eyesight the Sun and Moon, eye nerves Mercury, Venus and Uranus.

Effect: blindness. Born prematurely (Moon in Aries), eye nerves were undeveloped (Moon > Neptune, Venus square Uranus); causing the retinas (Uranus) to detach.

The Sun and Mercury are conjunct the "dangerous to sight degree" of 29 Taurus. When oxygen was inappropriately pumped into the incubator, eye nerves were destroyed causing permanent blindness. Sun-Mercury (oxygen) are midpoint Uranus (incubator) and Venus (eye nerves).

▲ (C) Neptune. (O) Sun, Moon, Mercury, Venus, Uranus. (E) Neptune, Uranus.

The Roles Triplets (25 May 1975, 10:20, Sydney Australia).
The cause of blindness in these Australian triplets was the same as for Stevie Wonder. Born prematurely, they were given oxygen that damaged their eyes.

Cause: karmic-congenital. The birth was premature and foetal development was incomplete (the Moon is sesquiquadrate Saturn and Venus in Cancer). With Saturn's inclusion, we know the trouble is karmic.

Organ: ajna - eyesight the Sun and Moon, eye nerves Venus.

Effect: blindness. Blood vessels in the eyes were undeveloped and shrivelled (Saturn conjunct Venus; Sun opposite Neptune, which rules the bloodstream). The babies were left blind when they were given oxygen in their incubators (Sun in Gemini > Neptune, which is conjunct the Sagittarius 8th degree that is dangerous for eyesight).

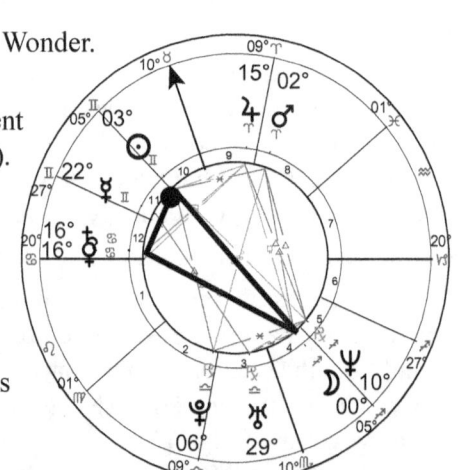

▲ (C) Saturn, Moon. (O) Sun, Moon, Venus. (E) Saturn, Neptune.

b. Blinded by Injuries

Georgie Borkowski (13 January 1950, 19:25, Medford Oregon).
American astrologer and student of religious philosophy, Borkowski's sight was destroyed in a bungled caesarean birth.

Cause: emotional. The Moon (eyes) is afflicted. It falls in Scorpio and opposes the 29 Taurus "dangerous to sight" degree. The injury may be karmically linked to serious past life family transgressions, with Pluto on the ascendant, the doorway into life, square the Moon in the 4H of family.

Organ: ajna - eye nerves Venus, sight the Moon.

Effect: blindness. Instruments (Uranus), used with roughness and lack of care at birth (semi-square Pluto on the ascendant), destroyed eye nerves (Pluto opposes Venus that is retrograde in Aquarius. Venus is sesquiquadrate Uranus). The result was blindness.

▲ (C) Moon. (O) Venus, Moon. (E) Uranus, Pluto

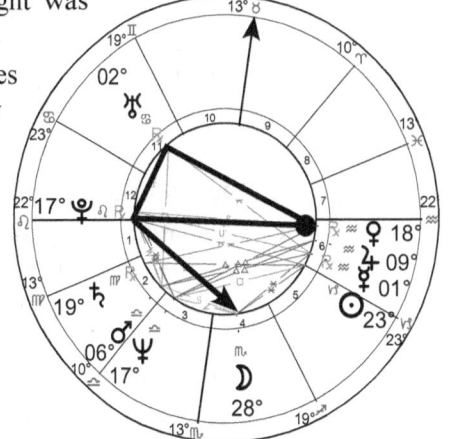

Vincent Humbert (3 February 1981, 10:32, Evreux France).
A car accident on 24 September 2000, left this youth blind, mute and quadriplegic.

Cause: emotional. Humbert was an explosively angry youth (Mars square Uranus), a pattern that lies behind many so-called accidents. It is a dangerous pattern because Uranus is in the 8H of death. Although the accident did not kill him, he was left in a condition where he wanted to die. He could only move his fingers.

Organ: ajna - eye nerves Mercury and Uranus.

Effect: blindness. The accident severed spinal nerves (Mars in Aquarius sesquiquadrate Saturn in the 6H of health. Uranus is septile Saturn), and damaged eye nerves (Mars conjunct Mercury, square Uranus). Uranus opposes the "dangerous to sight degree" of 29 Taurus.

▲ (C) Mars, Uranus. (O) Mercury, Uranus. (E) Mars, Uranus, Saturn.

- On the day of the accident, solar-arc Pluto at 14 Scorpio was exactly square the natal Sun, and transit Mars at 4 Virgo opposed the progressed Sun at 4 Pisces.
- Unhappy with his situation, Humbert begged to die, but euthanasia was not available in France. Eventually his mother, with the assistance of a doctor, helped him die on 26 September 2003. The progressed Moon was in Scorpio, in the 8H of death conjunct Uranus.

Mel B, Melanie Brown (29 May 1975, 17:59, Leeds UK).
English singer who was a member of the Spice Girls pop group. She was left blind in her left eye after botched laser eye surgery sometime around 1999.

Cause: emotional. When she is afraid, Mel B has great difficulty facing and dealing with life without a huge emotional reaction (Uranus on the ascendant, square the Moon and Venus in Cancer). There is an unconscious fear that something shocking (Uranus) will happen and this underlies the trouble.

Organ: ajna - eye nerves Venus, left eye the Moon.

Effect: blindness. Laser surgery (Uranus) damaged nerves in the left eye (the Moon), causing blindness (Moon quindecile Saturn). With this pattern and Uranus in the 12H of major illnesses, Brown should be very careful in the future of ultra-modern medicine, especially of an experimental nature. She should also deal with her anger (Uranus inconjunct Mars) to avoid any "accidents" in the future.

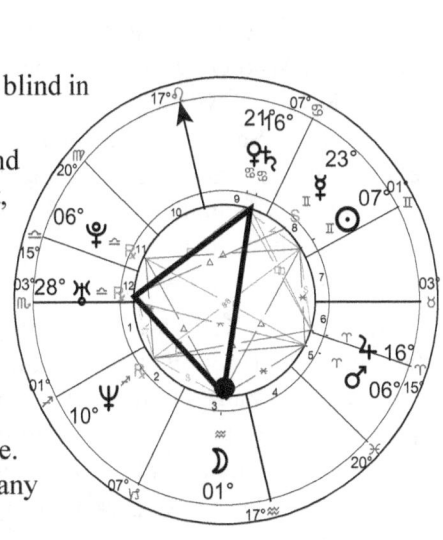

▲ (C) Moon. (O) Moon, Venus. (E) Uranus, Saturn.

- In 1999, transit Mars moved over Uranus and ascendant from January to July. It is very likely the botched operation took part during that period.

Timothy Knatchbull (18 November 1964, 16:00, London UK).

Knatchbull was blinded by an IRA terrorist bombing while on holiday.

Cause: karmic. The attack targeted the aristocracy to which Knatchbull belonged, indicating family or group karma (Saturn rules 10H of royalty, with Capricorn on the cusp). Terrorists planted the bomb (the malefic planet group in Virgo, which carries the fanatical 6th ray). The attack occurred while Knatchbull was on holiday (malefics in the 5H of recreation). It killed his grandfather, Lord Louis Mountbatten and his identical twin.

Organ: ajna - eyesight the Sun, eye nerves Mercury, Uranus.

Effect: blindness. An ominous sign for eye health, is Knatchbull's ascendant which conjuncts the Pleiades at the "dangerous to sight" 29 Taurus degree - opposed by the Sun at 26 Scorpio. The bomb damaged eye nerves (Mars conjunct Uranus square Mercury), destroying vision (Mars disposits the Sun; Saturn square the Sun; Mercury square Pluto). Mercury rules the 6H of health.

▲ (C) Saturn. (O) Sun, Mercury, Uranus. (E) Mars, Saturn.

Chart set for 27 August 1979: inner chart - natal, middle chart - secondary progressions, outer chart - transits.

- The bomb exploded on 27 August 1979. The Sun had progressed to 11 Sagittarius, conjunct Antares at 8 Sagittarius, a "dangerous for sight" region.
- Mars (the bomb), by progression, it was within 1 degree of the conjunction to Uranus. By transit, it was at 12 Cancer, inconjunct the progressed Sun (the eyes) and Antares.
- Saturn was transiting over Mars-Uranus-Pluto, highlighting the karmic factor.

Later, Knatchbull forgave Martin McGuinness, the man who most likely sanctioned the attack. When the Queen met McGuinness as her deputy First Minister of Northern Ireland in 2012, Knatchbull reportedly said, "We should be grateful to him for having changed".

c. Blinded through a Virus

Helen Keller (27 June 1880, 16:02, Tuscumbia Alabama)

American Keller contracted an illness when she was a child, which left her deaf and blind. The story of how she learned to communicate was made into a film called 'The Miracle Worker'. Keller blossomed and was the first deaf-blind person to earn a Bachelor of Arts degree.

Cause: karmic. Serious childhood diseases will usually be due to karma and Keller's chart shows potential damage to vision. Malefic Pluto is conjunct the "dangerous to sight" point - 29 Taurus, opposing the ascendant that is related to birth, the head and eyes.

Organ: ajna - eyesight the Sun, eye nerves Venus.

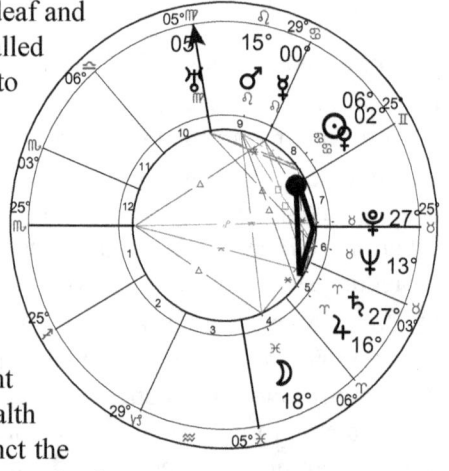

Effect: blindness. Keller was fine at birth, and then at 19 months in December 1881 she caught a virus, which damaged the eye nerves. Pluto is midpoint Venus (nerves) and Saturn in Aries (blindness). Neptune in the 6H of health represents the virus and its attack on eye nerves (semi-square Venus conjunct the Sun. Neptune is midpoint Pluto and Saturn, indicating a virulent and dangerous virus).

▲ (C) Saturn. (O) Sun, Venus. (E) Neptune, Saturn, Pluto

- Advancing the natal chart by 1 and a half to 2 degrees (for 19 months of age), solar-arc Pluto is now exactly on the fatal 29 Taurus degree. Solar-arc Neptune (the virus) is exactly square natal Mars, and the ascendant (the body and eyes) is almost within 1 degree exactly opposite Pluto. Keller was left blind and deaf.

Eye disease

a. Cataracts

Most cataracts develop through ageing or injury. Tissue that makes up the eye's lens become less flexible, less transparent and thicker. Psychologically, being unable to see any hope in the future is related to the problem.

James Cheek (4 December 1932, 14:30, Roanoke Rapids, NC).

Cheek is an African American academic who has received many honours. He was born with a severe congenital, cataract condition.

Cause: congenital. Cheek inherited his condition (Sun and Mercury retrograde in the 8H of inheritances, square the Moon that rules "the past"). It is possible the problem arose because of a family history of racial abuse, bigotry and violence (Moon opposite Mars and Neptune that carry the fanatical 6th ray). Closing one's eyes to what is occurring and blotting out the sight of lynching's etc. either way, is a means to cope emotionally.

Organ: ajna - eyesight the Sun and Moon, eye nerves Mercury.

Effect: cataracts. Both the Sun and Moon are afflicted in a t-square with Neptune - cataracts developed, clouding and distorting vision.

▲ (C) Moon. (O) Sun, Moon, Mercury (E) Neptune.

Larry King (19 November 1933, 10:38, Brooklyn NY)

American TV personality Larry King, developed cataracts in his 70's.

Cause: ageing. King's eyes had a weakness and he wore glasses (Mercury retrograde), but the main problem was due to ageing.

Organ: ajna - eyesight the Sun, eye nerves Mercury.

Effect: cataracts. King developed age-related cataracts. The Sun and Mercury that represent vision and eye nerves are midpoint the malefics that most commonly represent age-related clouding of vision - Saturn and Neptune. Mercury rules the 6H of health.

▲ (C) Saturn. (O) Sun, Mercury. (E) Saturn, Neptune.

• In 2006-7 just before the trouble, solar-arc Neptune moved over the Mercury-Sun point, while solar-arc Saturn made an inconjunct aspect. This accelerated the damage and clouding of vision. He had cataract surgery in 2009.

b. Glaucoma

Glaucoma is caused by an imbalance in eye fluid that puts pressure on the eye, destroying the optic nerve. Emotional stress and pressure so that life is hard to look at, seems related to this disorder.

Andrea Bocelli (22 September 1958, 05:15, Pisa Italy).

Popular Italian singer of opera and romantic ballads who is blind.

Cause: karmic, emotional. Bocelli was born with hereditary glaucoma, which suggests his family has a history of emotional suppression (Saturn is in the 4H of family, semi-square Neptune; and the Moon in Capricorn).

Organ: ajna - eye nerves, Mercury and Venus.

Effect: glaucoma. An imbalance in eye fluid (Mercury-Venus semi-square Neptune), put pressure on the eye (square Saturn), resulting in glaucoma, damage and loss of vision.

▲ (C) Saturn, Neptune. (O) Mercury, Venus. (E) Neptune, Saturn.

• Bocelli went completely blind at 12 when he was hit by a ball. Solar-arc Pluto was conjunct Venus and transit Pluto was on the natal Sun.

Jose Feliciano (10 September 1945, 10:00, Lares Puerto Rica)

Puerto Rican singer known for hit songs such as 'Feliz Navidad', who has been blind from birth because of congenital glaucoma.

Cause: congenital. Feliciano has great difficulty with emotional expression (the Moon is in detriment in Scorpio and Saturn is in detriment in Cancer). The Moon is related to eye problems, so there is a link between these afflictions and his trouble. Further, mother (the Moon) may have caught a bacterial infection that caused the trouble (sesquiquadrate Uranus).

Organ: ajna - eyesight the Sun and Moon.

Effect: glaucoma. Fluid imbalance and consequent pressure in the eye (Moon), caused damage to the optic nerve (Uranus), destroying sight (Uranus squares the Sun, while the Moon is semi-square to the Sun).

▲ (C) Moon, Saturn in Cancer. (O) Sun, Moon. (E) Scorpio, Uranus.

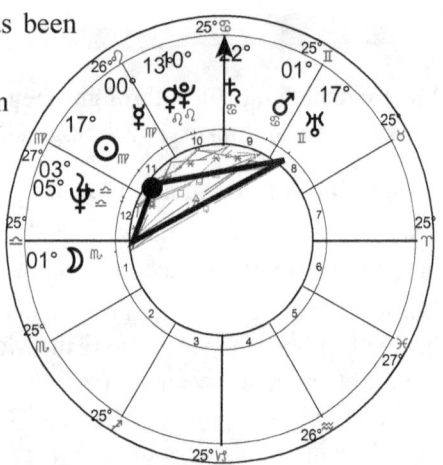

c. Macular degeneration

The macula is a small area at the centre of the retina responsible for seeing straight ahead and fine details. When diseased there is blindness at the centre of vision. 'Dry' macular degeneration is age-related; 'wet' degeneration occurs when blood vessels under the retina haemorrhage. The disease is related to a combination of heredity and environmental factors such as smoking and diet.

Colleen McCullough (1 June 1937, 19:30, Wellington Australia).

Australian author, famous for her novel 'The Thorn Birds'.

Cause: genetic, emotional. McCullough inherited the eye disorder from her mother (Mars that rules the 4H of mother opposes Mercury. Mercury in turn is conjunct Uranus and semi-square Saturn in the 4H in Aries, a sign related to the eyes. Uranus is afflicted in Taurus).

Organ: ajna - eyesight the Moon, eye nerves Mercury and Uranus.

Effect: macular degeneration. In 2003, McCullough suddenly lost sight in the left eye (Moon) due to a haemorrhage (Mars and Uranus). The macular was destroyed (Mercury conjunct Uranus, and Uranus semi-square Saturn).

▲ (C) Uranus, Moon. (O) Moon, Mercury, Uranus. (E) Mars.

- The Moon-Mars aspect was triggered in June 2003, when transit Uranus and Mars came together at 0 degrees Pisces, and crossed the natal Moon simultaneously.

Stephen King (21 September 1947, 01:30, Portland Maine).

American writer of supernatural stories, King was diagnosed with macular degeneration at 49 and is gradually going blind.

Cause: genetic. King inherited an eye weakness (the Sun is square Uranus in Gemini, ruler of the 8H of inheritances with Aquarius on the cusp), and a pattern that showed premature ageing of his vision (the Sun is semi-square Pluto conjunct Saturn - two 1st ray ageing planets).

Organ: ajna - eyesight the Sun, eye nerves Venus and Uranus.

Effect: macular degeneration. Deterioration of the macular began relatively early for King, at 49 in 1996. He is now legally blind.

▲ (C) Uranus. (O) Sun, Venus, Uranus. (E) Saturn, Pluto.

- Timing for the trouble in his 49th year is shown by Uranus. By solar-arc it had rotated to 14 Leo, conjunct natal Pluto, triggering the age-related damage.

- Simultaneously solar-arc Pluto and Saturn were at 2-6 Libra, sitting on natal Venus and Neptune representing vision being gradually destroyed.

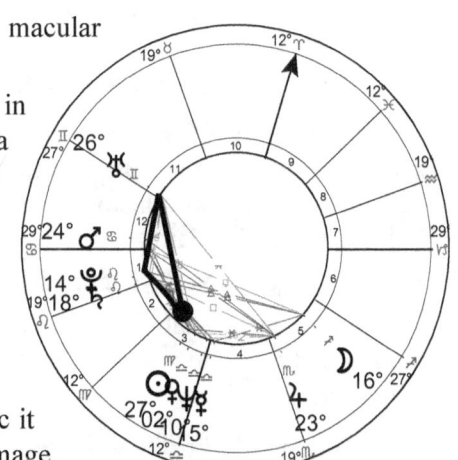

4b.3. Nose

The ajna - and therefore Venus and Mercury, govern the senses and organs for smelling. Aries and Mars govern the nose, especially if trouble is caused by an accident.

a. Sinusitis

Sinusitis is inflammation or swelling of the tissue lining the sinuses (the Moon), causing blockages that allow bacteria (Uranus) to breed, resulting in swelling and pain. Psychologically, something has "got up one's nose".

Stephen Fry (24 August 1957, 06:00, Hampstead UK).

English comedian, actor and TV presenter, suffered painful bouts of sinusitis. He wrote, "Awoke with satanically painful sinusitis, wanted to wrench my left eye out. Work, pseudoephedrine!"

Cause: emotional. What "gets up Fry's nose"? Hidden family hypocrisy (Mars, the nose, squares Saturn in the 4H of family). However, it is Fry's own tendency to criticise himself (Mercury semi-square the Moon), that is behind his sinus trouble and pain.

Organ: ajna - sinuses the Moon, nerves Mercury.

Effect: sinusitis. The linings (Moon) of his breathing passages became inflamed (conjunct Uranus in Leo), and congested (Saturn). Bacteria bred (Uranus), causing excruciating nerve pain (Uranus semi-square Mercury). He would take medicine (Uranus trine Saturn) and retire to bed.

▲ (C) Moon. (O) Moon, Mercury. (E) Uranus, Saturn.

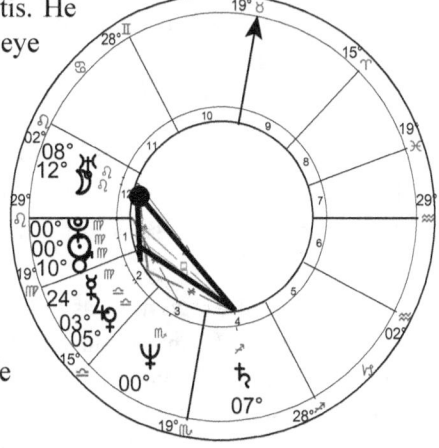

b. Broken nose

Silvio Berlusconi (29 September 1936, 05:40 Milan Italy)

Italy's 54th Prime Minister was attacked and his nose broken when he was addressing a public rally on 13 December 2009.

Cause: karmic. Berlusconi liked bizarre sex (Mars trine Uranus afflicted in Taurus in the 8H of sex), and partied with prostitutes (sextile Venus in Scorpio, in the 2H of money). Karma (Saturn), due to the misuse of sexual force triggered the attack. His improprieties (Mars-Uranus) raised the ire of the conservative public (Mars quindecile Saturn, which is conjunct the Moon in the 6H of health), attracting anger towards him and health issues.

Organ: ajna - nose Mars, teeth and bones Saturn.

Effect: sinusitis. Someone from the public (Moon) attacked him (Mars, Uranus), fracturing his nose and breaking his teeth (Saturn).

▲ (C) Saturn. (O) Mars, Saturn. (E) Moon, Mars, Uranus.

• When he was attacked, solar-arc Saturn was at 1 Gemini, squaring natal Mars. It was karmic.

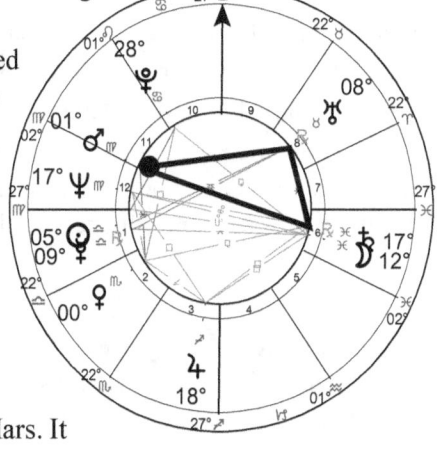

c. Cocaine damage to the septum

Stevie Nicks (26 May 1948, 03:02, Phoenix Arizona).

Singing star of Fleetwood Mac, a popular 70's group. Nick's has been called the Queen of Rock and Roll. For 10 years she sniffed cocaine, burning a hole through the cartilage of her nose.

Cause: emotional. Nicks had a yearning for love (Neptune square Venus) that manifested as a drug addiction. This is seen in a t-square: a habit (Moon), of loving (Venus), drugs (Neptune).

Organ: ajna - nose cartilage, Moon in Capricorn.

Effect: cartilage. Nicks self-indulged (Venus) in a cocaine habit (Neptune) that dissolved the cartilage in her nose (square Moon).

▲ (C) Moon, Neptune. (O) Moon. (E) Venus, Neptune.

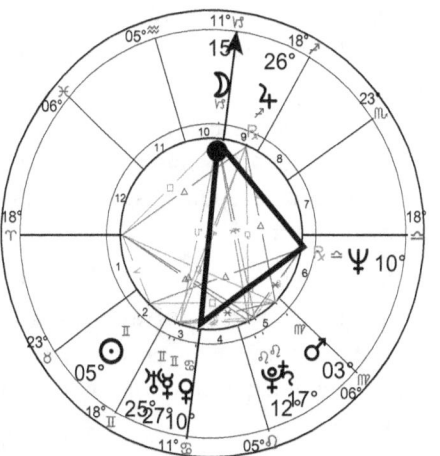

4b.4. Nervous System

The ajna chakra rules the nervous system, the means through which consciousness interacts with the environment. Impressions flow along the millions of nerve pathways to the brain. Here they transform into information and in response, outward travelling nerve impulses galvanise us into action. In emotional man, the solar plexus chakra dominates consciousness via the sympathetic nervous system.

a. Amyotrophic lateral sclerosis, Motor Neurone Disease (ALS)

ALS is a fatal and progressive neurological disease, which is characterized by progressive muscle weakness. Researchers believe it is an autoimmune disease. Sufferers become gradually immobile, developing a "locked-in" state. The nature of the disease suggests the inner child is angry but feels inadequate and powerless to deal with whatever is happening and curls inwards to avoid further punishment or pain.

Stephen Hawking (8 Jan 1942, Oxford, UK).
Unknown time, 12 PM midday used and the 0 degrees Aries House System.
One of the most famous scientists of the 20th Century, Hawking was diagnosed with ALS in 1963 when he was 21.

Cause: emotional. Hawking was easy-going (grand-trines: Sun-Moon-Saturn; Mercury-Neptune-Uranus), but he had an explosive, angry side (t-square: Mars-Mercury-Pluto), which he would vent with cutting thoughts and words. Because the disease manifested, we know he turned this toxic force relentlessly upon himself, triggering an autoimmune attack.

Organ: ajna - the nervous system Mercury.

Effect: nervous system. While a first year doctoral student at Cambridge University, Hawking was assigned a supervisor beneath his talents. He must have felt deeply enraged as well as helpless, because the immune-system (Mars) attacked the motor nerves (Mercury), and gradually muscles compressed (Pluto). He has become locked-in physically.

▲ (C) Mars, Pluto. (O) Mercury. (E) Mars, Pluto.

- In 1963 by solar-arc, the Mars point of the health-triangle had reached Saturn, showing that lesions on nerve cells had reached the point that muscles were affected. Simultaneously, the Pluto point was square natal Uranus showing serious damage to nerve cells.

b. Cerebral Palsy

Cerebral palsy is caused by damage to the developing brain either during pregnancy or shortly after birth. Most people are born with it. Nerves fire but muscles spasm (Uranus), causing jerky movements. The fundamental psychological pattern is great fear and hesitation in moving forward in life, in taking action.

Fred Berry (20 December 1949, 23:36, Salem Massachusetts)
American politician born with cerebral palsy. In spite of his infirmity, he became a Massachusetts State Senator, serving for 30 years.

Cause: congenital. Measles can cause cerebral palsy and it is possible that Berry's mother caught the virus and this caused his infirmity (Moon in the 4H of mother, square Neptune, the ruler of the 6H of health). The same Moon in Capricorn - Neptune aspect shows Berry's fear and hesitancy in moving forward in life.

Organ: ajna - the nervous system, Mercury.

Effect: cerebral palsy. He was born with palsy (Moon conjunct Mercury square Neptune) that caused muscle spasms (Mercury disposits Mars that squares Uranus; Mercury is conjunct the Moon that disposits Uranus).

▲ (C) Moon. (O) Mercury. (E) Neptune, Mars, Uranus.

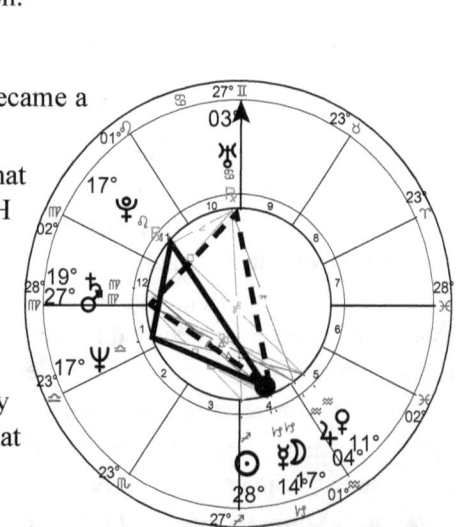

c. Epilepsy

An epileptic seizure occurs when large numbers of brain cells fire uncontrollably. One cause of epilepsy is due to a loose consciousness thread,[1] an attack occurs when the thread temporarily withdraws. Other causes are head injuries and strokes. Uranus governs electrical signalling and is often central to the disorder.

Dionne Quintuplets (28 May 1934, 03:56, Corbeil Canada).
Canadian quintuplets born two months premature. The government displayed the babies in a theme park called Quintland. But when the public lost interest (they were 14), they were given back to the parents.
Cause: karmic, congenital. The experience was due to family karma and misuse of power in a previous life (Saturn ruler of the 10H square the Moon).
Organ: ajna - the consciousness thread, Venus.
Effect: epilepsy. Born prematurely (the Moon is inconjunct Uranus in 12H of hospitals), building work on the nervous system was incomplete (Uranus is conjunct Venus and the Moon squares Saturn in Aquarius). The consciousness thread (Venus) was not securely grounded (inconjunct the Moon), resulting in epilepsy (Uranus) whenever it loosened. Venus co-rules the 6H of health with Libra sharing the cusp.
▲ (C) Saturn, Moon. (O) Venus. (E) Uranus, Saturn.

Afonso Pedro (23 February 1845 13:35, Rio de Janiero Brazil)
The 2 year old child of Emperor Dom Pedro II of Brazil died on 11 June 1847, from an epilepsy seizure.
Cause: genetic. Afonso was born sickly and with low vitality (Sun in Pisces in the cadent 9H, inconjunct the Moon); a genetic condition related to inbreeding (Mars square the Moon in fussy Virgo and dispositing Uranus).
Organ: ajna - the consciousness thread, Mercury.
Effect: epilepsy. An epileptic attack occurred whenever the consciousness thread in the brain loosened (Mercury is midpoint Mars ruler of the 6H of health and Uranus in Aries).
▲ (C) Uranus. (O) Mercury. (E) Uranus, Mars.

d. Guillain-Barre Syndrome (GBS)

An autoimmune disorder, where the peripheral nerves are attacked by the immune system (Sun, Leo, Mars).

Anita Cortesi (1 October 1955, 17:45, Zurich Switzerland)
Swiss professional astrologer. In 2010, she caught GBS and was from then on confined to a wheelchair.
Cause: emotional. Cortesi is an easy going Libra personality who is dominated by a fiery emotional body (the Moon is in Aries in the 1H of self, opposite the Sun). This showy anger is the outer display of hurt and frustration hidden within; Mars, the dispositor of the Moon is in hypercritical Virgo. This is the root cause of the trouble because Mars is in the 6H of health. The fact that Cortesi developed an autoimmune disease tells us that she turned the force of stinging criticism on herself (Mars is opposite the ascendant).
Organ: ajna - the nervous system Mercury and Uranus.
Effect: GBS. Continual self-criticism provoked a reaction from the immune system (Mars) and it attacked the peripheral nerves (Mars is conjunct the midpoint between Mercury and Uranus). The damage caused paralysis (Mercury is conjunct Neptune, and 1st ray Pluto afflicts Jupiter (movement) in the 6H of health.
▲ (C) Mars. (O) Mercury, Uranus. (E) Mars, Neptune, Pluto.

---
1 Bailey, Alice A; Esoteric Psychology II, 418.

e. Multiple Sclerosis (MS)

An example of multiple sclerosis was given previously in the coverage of Jacqueline du Pre. The immune system attacks nerve cells, damaging the myelin sheath covering so that nerve signals are not passed on.

At the root of autoimmune diseases is a self-hatred pattern arising from persistent negative thoughts such as being "stupid, dumb, naive" etc. In time, the immune system responds and attacks the body. Connect nervous system rulers (Mercury, Venus and Uranus) with immune system rulers (Mars, the Sun or planets in Leo).

L1001. (30 August 1959, 19:55, St. Louis, Missouri)

An intelligent American lady with a modest Virgo personality, who studies trans-Himalayan and other esoteric modalities. This point is important because contact with soul energy through meditation keeps ill health at bay. She was relatively healthy prior to the onset of MS. After twenty years and three children, in 1999 her marriage dissolved. Becoming re-established over the coming years took its toll. Symptoms started in 2003; she was diagnosed in 2004 and unable to work since 2010.

Cause: emotional. Our subject had a habit of criticising herself (Virgo planets with Venus in Virgo opposite the ascendant); and finding herself coming up short when she measured herself against her important values and principles. The disease cause lies here. The 6th house has a five planet stellium within it, showing a lot of energy being poured into work and duty. But since the disease developed this focus has turned to the care and management of her condition.

Organ: ajna - the nervous system, Venus, Mercury and Uranus.

Effect: MS. In response to her negative thoughts, the immune system attacked the nervous system (the Sun and Pluto conjunct Venus; the Sun is midpoint Mars and Mercury). The disease causes scarring of nerve cells (Mars square Saturn), so that nerve signalling is gradually inhibited (Saturn is sesquiquadrate Uranus, which in turn is conjunct Mercury).

▲ (C) Mars in Virgo. (O) Venus, Mercury, Uranus.
   (E) Sun, Mars, Saturn.

- Trouble always starts before symptoms appear. In 1999, Mars, a representative of the immune system, had rotated by solar-arc to conjunct natal Neptune at 4 Scorpio. The marriage dissolved.
- Simultaneously, solar-arc Uranus was conjunct natal Mars at 26 Virgo, triggering self-recrimination and beginning the manifestation of the disease.

From 2014, there have been exacerbations (flare-up of symptoms). The client notices that these occur when planets transit through Virgo and her 6th house. Severely weakened during those times, she still walks,

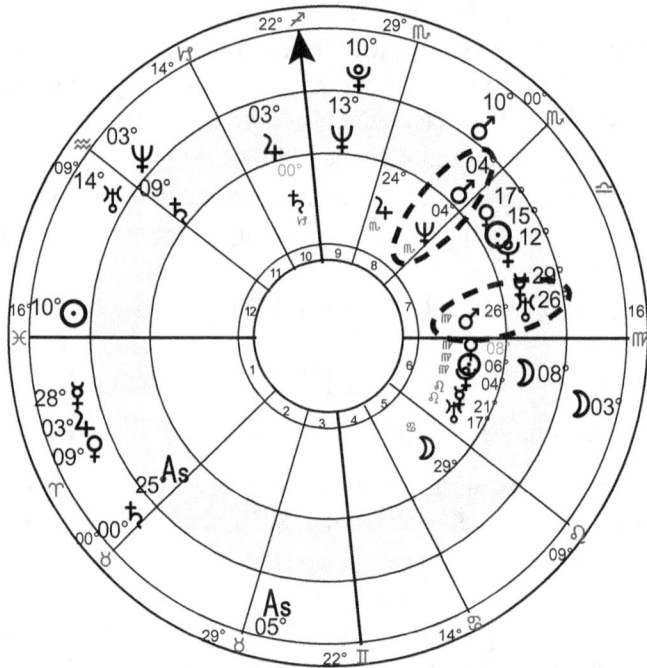

Chart set for May 1999. Inner chart Natal, middle chart solar-arc, outer chart transits

even if just for short distances. By 2017, lesions had spread to her brain and spinal cord.

This student of the Wisdom Teachings understands the effect our psychology has upon our health and combines allopathic medicine with alternative and complementary healing modalities, including meditation and her spiritual studies, to try to alleviate symptoms. She does not take MS medications that help slow the disease, or go on a special diet, finding these do not work for her. She believes that her practice of "gratitude" has positive effects on her health.

She does not "look sick" (in 2017) and is grateful she has retained her independence, is able to live by herself and take care of things with the appropriate modifications. She maintains hope that her condition will improve, at least to where she does not have exacerbations all the time.

f. Quadriplegia

Christopher Reeves (25 September 1952, 03:12, Manhattan NY).
American actor who became quadriplegic after being thrown from a horse.
Cause: emotional. Reeves' anger erupted would arise suddenly in temper ((Uranus in Cancer inconjunct Mars). This pattern is related to the accident.
Organ: ajna - the spine Saturn; nerves Uranus.
Effect: quadriplegia. Through a horse-riding accident (Mars in Sagittarius), he suffered terrible injuries. Spinal nerves (Uranus sitting on the 12H of hospitals) were severed (inconjunct Mars), and he was paralysed (Mars sextile Saturn that squares Uranus).

▲ (C) Mars, Uranus. (O) Saturn, Uranus. (E) Mars, Uranus, Saturn.
The accident happened on May 27 1995.
- Transit Mars was at 0 Virgo, exactly conjunct solar-arc Uranus at the same degree. Spinal nerves were severed.
- Transit Uranus was at 0 Aquarius, conjunct solar-arc Mars in the 6H of health, indicating the accident.
- Solar-arc Jupiter was at 2 Cancer, square natal Sun and Mercury - the spinal injuries inhibiting movement.

g. Polio

The polio virus multiplies in the intestines then enters the bloodstream to paralyse the central nervous system.

Franklin D. Roosevelt (30 January 1882, 20:45, Hyde Park, NY)
FDR served as the 32nd President of the US. In 1921, he contracted polio and was left with permanent paralysis from the waist down.
Cause: emotional. FDR prized freedom (Uranus on the ascendant). Married in 1905, within years he wanted to leave the marriage for a mistress but was forced to remain for political reasons. He felt trapped (Saturn, the jailer, conjunct Neptune that rules the 7H of marriage with Pisces on the cusp; square the Sun and Venus in the 5H of romance). When wife Eleanor discovered his infidelity in 1918, he was beset with guilt. This sapped his vitality, opening his system up to disease.
Organ: ajna - the nervous system, Venus and Uranus.
Effect: polio. In 1921 the polio virus (Neptune) invaded the intestines (trine Uranus in Virgo), perverting cell life it spread through the body via blood circulation (the Sun in Aquarius). It attacked the nervous system (Venus, Uranus), paralysing him (Saturn > Venus-Sun; also Pluto square Mercury in the 6H of health).

▲ (C) Neptune, Saturn. (O) Venus, Uranus. (E) Neptune, Saturn.
- In 1921, transit Neptune was in Leo moving opposite the natal Sun-Venus conjunction and forming a t-square with its natal position in Taurus. At that time he was susceptible to viral attacks.
- Solar-arc Neptune was moving towards natal Mars at 27 Gemini, representing the viral attack.

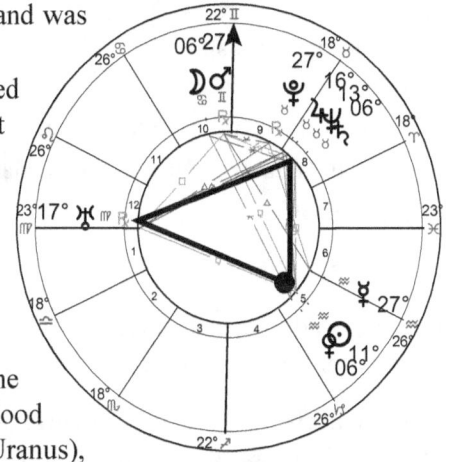

h. Parkinson's disease

Parkinson's affects nerve cells. They fire but muscles can't respond properly, resulting in tremors.

Muhammad Ali (17 January 1942, 18:35, Louisville, Kentucky).
American champion boxer. Parkinson's symptoms began in 1978 as vocal stutters and trembling hands. He died on June 3 2016.
Cause: emotional. Growing up in racist Kentucky, Ali learned to hide his rage (Mars square Pluto in the 12H of hidden things), because open defiance would bring dangerous repercussions. This contributed to his health disorder.

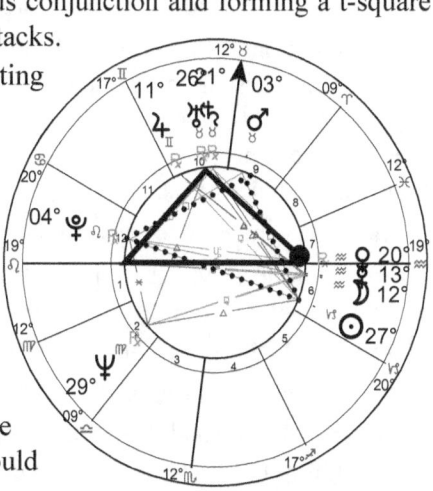

Organ: ajna - the nervous system, Mercury, Venus, Uranus; the body, the ascendant.

Effect: Parkinson's. The battering to Ali's head eventually affected the nervous system (Mars is in detriment in Taurus and is disposited by Venus in Aquarius). Scarring and damage to neurons occurred (Saturn-Uranus). Parkinson's developed - the misfiring of synapses and jerky, rigid, movements (t-square: Venus, Saturn-Uranus and the ascendant).

▲ (C) Mars, Pluto. (O) Mercury, Venus, Uranus; the ascendant. (E) Mars, Saturn, Uranus.

- Trouble started in 1975 when progressed Mars began moving over natal Saturn-Uranus (a nine year period) triggering the health-triangle. Ali fought 14 times in this period and any of these matches potentially started and contributed to the trouble.

i. Nerves - Shingles

Shingles is caused by the same virus that causes chickenpox. It can strike nerves and skin anywhere in the body, causing intense nerve pain.

David Letterman (12 April 1947 06:00, Indianapolis IN)

American talk show host in late night TV. In February 2003, he suffered a painful bout of shingles.

Cause: emotional. Letterman has a busy active mind, which is sharp and witty and can be biting and caustic (Mars in Aries conjunct Mercury). It helped to make him famous, but it also affected his health - Mercury rules the 6H of health.

Organ: ajna - the nervous system Mercury and Uranus; the skin Saturn.

Effect: shingles. Letterman's nerves are susceptible to a viral attack (Mercury in detriment in Pisces), and an attack of shingles struck in February 2003, raising a painful rash on his skin (Mars conjunct Mercury and trine Saturn; Mercury square Uranus that is in turn semi-square Saturn).

▲ (C) Mars. (O) Mercury, Uranus, Saturn. (E) Pisces, Mars, Saturn.

- When the attack occurred, transit Mars was around 25 Sagittarius, square natal Mars and Mercury.

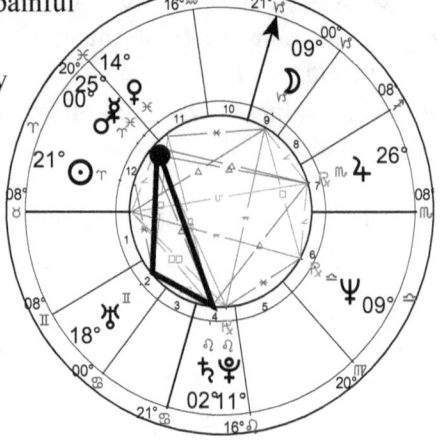

j. Tourette's syndrome

Tourette syndrome causes repeated, involuntary physical movements and vocal outbursts. It is the most severe kind of tic syndrome, a reaction to serious, unresolved trauma buried in the unconscious.

Jim Eisenreich (18 April 1959 16:19, St. Cloud Minnesota)

Eisenreich played American major league baseball. Since age 6 he had tics, jerks and his eyes would blink uncontrollably. Sometimes he had to come off the field because he could not control muscle spasms. In 1984, he retired to seek a cure. Later, he returned and had a few more years of success.

Cause: emotional. People with Tourette's have experienced serious trauma in childhood. Eisenreich's home life was especially harsh with mental and physical abuse (t-square, Mars and Mercury with Saturn located in the 4H of family). The appearance of Tourette's testifies to the fact he was emotionally traumatised and scarred.

Organ: ajna - the nervous system, Mercury.

Effect: Tourette's. Mercury in the t-square represents the trembling nervous system and its reaction to trauma buried in the unconscious (Mercury rules the 12H of the unconscious), and the flinching, eye blinking and muscular contractions.

▲ (C) Mars, Saturn. (O) Mercury. (E) Mars.

- In 1984 when he had treatment, solar-arc Mercury was moving over the natal Sun, bringing the buried trauma into the light of the conscious mind so he could see his trauma and deal with it.

4b.5. Pituitary Gland

a. Acromegaly (gigantism)

Anthony Robbins (29 February 1960, 20:10, Los Angeles CA)

Successful American life-coach, Robbins grew almost 10 inches in his junior year. When he was 31, he was told he had a pituitary tumour and acromegaly. Since his growth had stabilised, he refused surgery.

Cause: emotional. The pattern representing the disease is a t-square with Neptune at the hub and Venus and Uranus. The psychological cause hypothetically, is confusion and anxiety over being abandoned in some way when young (Uranus opposite Venus in the 4H of family).

Organ: ajna - pituitary Venus; muscles Mars.

Effect: acromegaly. In his teen years, aberrations in cells (Uranus in Leo) in the pituitary (Venus) occurred and a tumour grew (Neptune carries the 2nd ray via Pisces). Body-muscular over-growth occurred (Mars conjunct Venus).

▲ (C) Neptune. (O) Venus, Mars. (E) Uranus, Neptune.

- Venus in Robbins' chart governs the 8H of transformation. The same triangle that represented the disease also represents his ability to change the way he thinks. He demonstrates how a latent disease, even if it should be triggered, may not progress to a morbid stage. Robbins teaches a form of positive thinking, which is a modern off-shoot of Raja Yoga, the kingly science of mind. This science teaches us how to transform negative thoughts and forces we inherit into positive thoughts and life expressions.

b. Dwarfism: Proportionate, Growth Hormone Deficiency (GHD)

Charles Stratton (4 January 1838, Bridgeport CT).

Unknown time, 12 PM used and the 0 degrees Aries House System for both charts.

Stratton achieved great fame as "General Tom Thumb", in P. T. Barnum's Circus. Normal at birth, he reached 25 inches tall at six months and then suddenly stopped growing in height. He was perfectly proportioned.

Cause: genetic. Uranus the ruler of genetics is conjunct the pituitary, Venus in the 12H of major illnesses.

Organ: ajna - pituitary Venus, cells the Sun.

Effect: dwarfism. An abnormality (Uranus) in pituitary cells (conjunct Venus semi-square the Sun), resulted in GHD, a diminished body size (Venus square Saturn).

▲ (C) Uranus. (O) Venus, Sun. (E) Saturn.

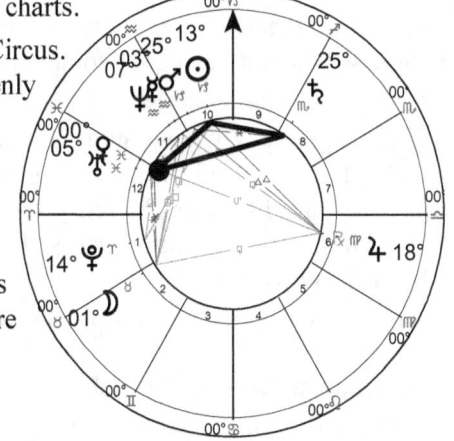

Lavinia Warren (31 October 1842, Middleboro MA).

Lavinia Warren came from a genteel New England family. Normal at birth, healthy and well-proportioned, she reached 2.6 feet. She joined show business where she met and married Charles Stratton. They were reality celebrities of their day, becoming famous and wealthy.

Cause: genetic. Family (Moon), karma (square Saturn), was responsible for the genetic abnormality (Venus, the pituitary, disposits the Moon).

Organ: ajna - pituitary, Venus.

Effect: dwarfism. Warren inherited a genetic (Uranus) form of GHD (square Venus), a consequence of in-breeding, because sexual partners (Venus) were drawn from a too narrow breeding pool (square Mars in fussy Virgo in the 6H of health). Growth was stunted (Jupiter conjunct Saturn).

▲ (C) Uranus. (O) Venus. (E) Mars, Jupiter, Saturn.

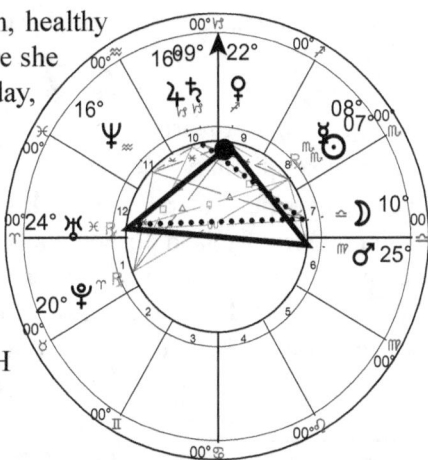

c. Migraine

A migraine is a severe headache, often accompanied by nausea, vomiting and sensitivity to light and sound. It can last for days. Researchers say migraines are linked to heightened neurovascular reactivity in response to stress caused by something not liked in the environment. This fits with two causes given by Bailey: firstly that migraines are related to heightened activity in the ajna; secondly, being separative in attitude (a ray 5 trait) causes a lack of relation between the pituitary and pineal glands [1] that can lead to migraine. The charts on this page have inhibiting Saturn in 5th ray Aquarius.

Charlotte Bronte (21 April 1816, 14:41, Thornton, UK).
The oldest of three talented sisters, Bronte became famous for her novel Jane Eyre. She suffered from migraines.
Cause: emotional. Bronte is reported as being bossy and controlling. She was also exceedingly cool, reserved and isolative emotionally (Moon and Saturn in Aquarius, semi-square Venus in detriment in Aries). This latter pattern is linked to her migraine trouble.
Organ: ajna - pituitary, Venus.
Effect: migraine. Stress and the tendency to distance herself from others emotionally (Saturn-Moon), disturbed neurovascular balance, increasing activity around the pituitary that resulted in migraines (Venus square Mars, Mars trine Moon-Saturn).

▲ (C) Moon in Aquarius. (O) Venus. (E) Saturn, Mars.

Loretta Lynn (14 April 1932, 16:00, Van Lear Kentucky).
American Country and Western singer Lynn said her father suffered from migraines and so had she since age 17. They were so severe sometimes she lost consciousness when she had an attack.
Cause: emotional. Lynn was fiery (Aries Sun) and dismissed and walled out people she did not like (Leo Moon opposite Saturn in Aquarius).
Organ: ajna - pituitary, Mercury.
Effect: migraine. Divisive attitudes can cause brain trouble. When Lynn was tired and stressed (Moon > Saturn that squares Mars in Aries), severe migraines would occur (Mercury the pituitary, square Pluto the pineal). Sometimes she lost consciousness (Uranus sesquiquadrate Neptune in the 12H of the unconscious).

▲ (C) Moon, Saturn in Aquarius. (O) Mercury. (E) Mars, Pluto.

Lisa Kudrow (30 July 1963, 04:37, Encino Ca).
American actress, star of the popular TV show, Friends. Kudrow inherited migraines from her father and had excruciating attacks as a child.
Cause: emotional. Kudrow adored her father. She inherited his susceptibility to migraines, which means she inherited his attitudes - compartmentalising her feelings and building walls between her and people she dislikes (the Moon square Saturn in Aquarius).
Organ: ajna - pituitary, Mercury.
Effect: migraine. Mental walls cause trouble, a dissonance between the pituitary (Mercury) and pineal glands (opposite 1st ray Saturn representing the pineal). This tendency plus stress and tiredness (t-square: Saturn-Moon-Mercury) resulted in migraines. Kudrow must be developing more inclusive attitudes because her attacks have diminished over the years.

▲ (C) Moon in Aquarius, Saturn. (O) Mercury. (E) Saturn.

---
[1] Bailey, Alice A; Esoteric Healing, 302.

4b.6. 5th Ray Psychological Disorders

The activity of the 5th ray flowing through the ajna, is responsible for many dissociative / cleavage type mental disorders. A cleavage is best described as being torn in two directions. When it occurs within the personality, causing one part of the nature to be out of touch with another, serious mental health issues arise.

a. Autism Spectrum Disorder (ASD): Autism and Asperger's

ASD is defined as a serious developmental problem characterized by great difficulty in communicating and forming relationships because of avoidance and dissociation tendencies. These are 5th ray "cleavage" traits - one part of the nature is out of touch with another, bringing ASD under its auspices. Here is a quote.

> In the activity of [the 5th ray] will be found eventually the source of many psychological disorders and mental trouble. Cleavage is the outstanding characteristic—within the individual or between the individual and his group, rendering him anti-social. Other results are certain forms of insanities, brain lesions and *those gaps in the relation of the physical body to the subtle bodies which show as imbecilities and psychological troubles.* [1]

In ASD, brain and nervous system function is impaired. Scientists who have studied autism say there are fewer alpha and beta waves, which points to under-connectivity especially in important strategic areas that have to do with the emotions and relating. They now believe autism is a genetic disorder. This also fits with the esoteric understanding that individual disease is mostly karmic and therefore comes through an inherited gene. It is also possible we are dealing with souls who greatly dislike physical incarnation and who try to avoid it and this creates the cleavage. Look for communication problems that translate into brainwave and nervous system under-connectivity - afflictions to Mercury and Venus, or to planets in Gemini and Aquarius.

Autism

Tagtrug Mukpo (9 March 1971, 18:50, Boulder Colorado)

Tibetan-American, [1] the son of Chogyam Trungpa Rinpoche and his wife, Lady Diana Mukpo. Severely autistic, Mukpo requires 24-hour supervision. Over the years and with ongoing care and attention, his condition is reported as having improved.

Cause: ray 5 cleavage. Tagtrug's case is intriguing. He was born to spiritually advanced parents and it is possible the karma is theirs. Lord of Karma, Saturn, is in the 8H of inheritances and co-rules the 4H of the mother with Capricorn sharing the cusp. Saturn is in Taurus, the sign of desire.

Organ: ajna - the mind and nervous system Mercury; senses Mars.

Effect: psychological. The serious communication difficulty is shown by the condition of Mercury, the mind. It is afflicted in Pisces, which suggests a mind that resides primarily on the Astral Plane because its access through the brain is seriously impeded. This impediment is a cleavage between the mind and the brain, shown by 5th ray Venus in Aquarius, which is midpoint Mercury square Mars. This also suggests an atrophying of the sense perceptions or *vrittis* (as the father of Raja Yoga, Patanjali called them), since Mars rules the five senses.

The serious obstruction is shown by Pluto, which rules the crown chakra that vitalises the brain. It sits on the ascendant, which is a representative of the head and the brain. Its opposition to Mercury suggests serious damage or limitation in connectivity with the nervous system and strategic parts of the brain.

Mukpo's case is severe, indicating also a possible disruption with the consciousness thread, which is governed by Mercury. In any event, the mind is unable to work through the brain in any intelligent way, hence the trouble.

▲ (C) Venus in Aquarius. (O) Mercury, Mars. (E) Pluto.

---

1 Bailey, Alice A; Esoteric Healing, 302.

Jett Travolta (13 April 1992, 00:33, Daytona Beach Florida)

Son of American actor John Travolta, was a high-functioning autistic. He died 2 January 2009, from a head injury sustained during a seizure.

Cause: ray 5 cleavage. Saturn in 5th ray Aquarius is central to Travolta's trouble. It suggests a history of living exclusively in his thought life, to the detriment of the physical body.

Organ: ajna - the mind Mercury, Venus; brain the ascendant.

Effect: psychological. Trouble with the mind and its ability to communicate effectively via the nervous system is immediately seen with both its rulers afflicted - Venus in Aries and Mercury in Pisces. The gap in the relation between the mind and the brain that is causing the trouble is represented by Saturn in Aquarius. It is midpoint the ascendant, the brain; and Mercury, the mind. Travolta also suffered from seizures, which suggests that he may have had a loose consciousness thread (Mercury) connection which is a cause of that malady.

▲ (C) Saturn in Aquarius. (O) Mercury, Venus; ascendant. (E) Saturn.

Asperger's

Asperger's people are less introverted emotionally than those with autism. There are more left brain connections and a higher IQ, but they still have communication difficulties. Autistic savants seem to fit in this group. An evolutionary advancement that nature has not perfected yet, may account for talented savants like Negro.

Andrea Negro (25 August 2001, 17:00, Nice, Fr)

A prodigy with Asperger's, he got a Bachelor in Science for maths at age 13.

Cause: ray 5 cleavage. Though lacking social skills, Negro has mathematical brilliance. Perhaps he lived too exclusively on the Mental Plane in his last life and his condition is a karmic consequence (Saturn in Gemini, in the 6H of health, semi-square Venus).

Organ: ajna - the mind, Mercury.

Effect: psychological. The mind/ Mercury is strong in Virgo, but its ability to communicate through the brain and nervous system is impaired by a cleavage, represented by Uranus in Aquarius, which is inconjunct Mercury. Negro struggles to communicate with the world generally (Mercury square Saturn in Gemini, ruler of the ascendant).

Negro's mathematical genius suggests he was using the higher abstract mind. Mercury represents both the concrete and abstract minds. [1]

▲ (C) Uranus in Aquarius. (O) Mercury. (E) Saturn.

Susan Boyle (1 April 1961, 09:50, Blackburn Scotland)

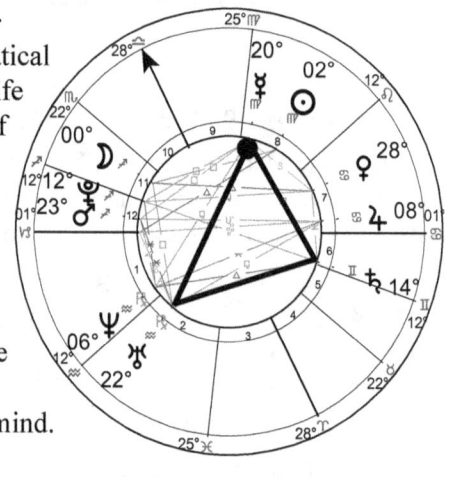

Scottish singer who became famous for her beautiful voice after she appeared on the TV programme Britain's Got Talent in 2009.

Cause: ray 5 cleavage. Boyle's Asperger's was diagnosed as being caused by brain damage as a child. If so, it was karmic (Venus square Saturn).

Organ: ajna - the mind and nervous system, Mercury, Venus.

Effect: psychological. Communication difficulties are highlighted (the rulers of the nervous system are afflicted - Venus in Aries, Mercury in Pisces). The cleavage related to brainwave under-connectivity is represented by 5th ray and retrograde Venus, which squares Saturn; and Mercury semi-square to Saturn. Mercury rules the ascendant, highlighting her social and communication difficulties.

▲ (C) Venus. (O) Mercury, Venus. (E) Saturn.

---

1 Bailey, Alice A; Esoteric Astrology 281.

b. Insanity as a consequence of narrow crystallised thinking and partisan devotion

Anders Breivik (13 February 1979, 12:50, Oslo Norway).

Far-right, racist Norwegian who killed over 70 people on 22 July 2011. He is diagnosed with a narcissistic personality disorder (Venus opposite the ascendant) but is quite insane. His trouble arises from intense mental activity and devotion to his narrow belief that he is part of a white master race that needs to kill to maintain superiority in the world. These thoughtforms now control him. Here is an esoteric description of the malady.

> A thought form of such potency is built, it holds the man mentally and emotionally. There is no sense of balance, no sense of proportion and no sense of humour. He has become a victim of the thought form, it holds him and controls him. "Such people are the violent partisans in any group, in any church, order or government. They are frequently sadistic.. and willing to sacrifice or to damage anyone who seems to them inimical to their fixed idea of what is right and true. The men who engineered the Spanish Inquisition.. are samples of the worst forms of this line of thought and development... People tainted with this psychological trouble of blind adherence to ideas and of personality devotions are found [everywhere].. the trouble from which they suffer is contagious. They are a menace..¹

Cause: desire and lower-will. Breivik is a cold, critical, humourless fanatic and bigot (the Moon conjunct Saturn in Virgo). The thoughtforms that drive him are represented by the Mercury, Sun and Mars group in separative Aquarius, clustered on the MC. He has delusions of White Supremacy greatness, to be achieved through mass murder (Mars trine Pluto), and revolution (square Uranus). Killing people for his political goals was a sport to him, they were fair game (Uranus in the 5H of pleasure and sport).

Organ: ajna - the mind, Mercury.

Effect: mental. Driven forth by the delusory thought life which controlled him, he committed mass murder.

- ▲ (C) Mars, Saturn, Uranus. (O) Mercury. (E) Mars, Pluto.
- On the day of the slaughter, solar-arc Mars had reached 21 Pisces, trine his natal Uranus in the sign of death, Scorpio. Simultaneously, solar-arc Pluto was conjunct natal Uranus. We all get patterns like this during life but most of us use the experience as a stepping stone to improve psychological health and quality of life.

Charles Manson (12 November 1934, 16:40, Cincinnati Ohio).

American leader of the 'Manson Family', a cult that committed a series of murders in 1969, notably that of pregnant actress Sharon Tate.

Cause: desire and lower-will. Manson was born with past-life delusional fantasies of greatness (Moon in separative Aquarius in the 10th house of status). He had a powerful will (Uranus in Aries) and was an intelligent personality working through the ajna. He was also insane, being controlled by thoughts and desires of world domination and control - a grand-cross pattern anchored by destructive Pluto on Cancer. It showed he was torn by internal conflicts and tried to control the world around him in an attempt to bring order to his inner life.

Organ: ajna - mind, Mercury.

Effect: mental. Manson was a murderous and sadistic thug (Mars conjunct Neptune) who manipulated his group of followers to commit mayhem (Uranus sesquiquadrate Mars). The grand-cross pattern seems to represent the burning cross of warped fanatics like Manson and the Ku Klux Klan.

- ▲ (C) Uranus, Pluto. (O) Mercury. (E) Pluto, Uranus.

1 Bailey, Alice A; Esoteric Psychology II, 455-456..

4c. Throat Chakra Diseases

The throat chakra rules the thyroid gland, respiration, speech, hearing, digestion and the lower brain. It receives energy from rays 3 and 7, Taurus and Gemini, Saturn and Mercury

Throat and chest disorders arise from congestion in the throat chakra, a consequence of emotionalism. Phlegm is a manifestation of emotional congestion. Aspirants who are transmuting sexual sacral force, raising and expressing it through the throat chakra can also have throat trouble.

4c.1. Breathing Problems

a. Asthma

Asthma is a respiratory condition marked by attacks or spasms in the bronchi that causes difficulty breathing. The underlying psychological pattern is emotional shock, being in terror for one's life.

Theodore Roosevelt (27 October 1858 19:4 5, New York NY)

American statesman, soldier, reformer who served as the 26th President of the United States. His asthma problems began in early childhood.

Cause: emotional. Roosevelt was sensitive emotionally (Moon in Cancer). But he harboured anger (Moon opposite Mars), perhaps as a consequence of hidden physical and verbal abuse that would strike suddenly and unexpectedly (Mars sesquiquadrate Uranus in Gemini in the 12H of hidden things). This pattern is related to his breathing difficulties.

Organ: throat - airways, Uranus in Gemini.

Effect: asthma. Anxiety that he might be hurt caused the spasms (Moon > Mars > Uranus in the 12H. Mars rules the 6H of health).

▲ (C) Moon, Mars. (O) Gemini. (E) Mars, Uranus.

b. Bronchitis

Bronchitis is inflammation of the lining of the bronchial tubes. Heavy phlegm (Moon, Mars, Neptune) is coughed up. It can be caused by a virus (Neptune), a bacterial infection (Uranus) or air-borne contaminants.

Dixie Lee Ray (3 September 1914, 01:00, Tacoma WA).

Marine biologist who served as a governor of Washington State. She died in 1994, having suffered from a severe bronchial condition for several months.

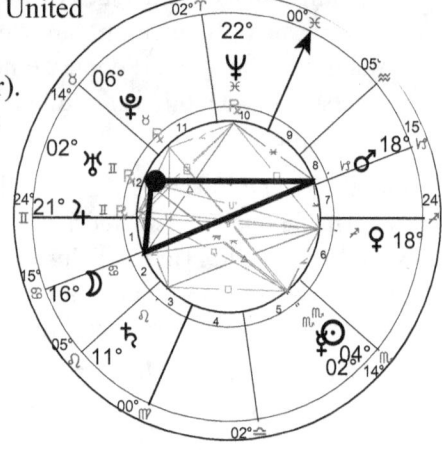

Cause: ageing. Immediately we see the dangerous 1st ray planets Pluto and Saturn in emotional Cancer, in the 12H of major illnesses. It indicates emotional repression, phlegm and bronchial trouble that could migrate into a serious health condition if not appropriately dealt with. This was not easy for Ray, a scientist who felt more comfortable mentally disconnecting from her feelings (Moon in Aquarius). However, she had reasonable health most of her life, dying at 80, which tells us that she found emotional balance (Saturn-Pluto are in a grand-trine with Venus and the Moon).

Organ: throat - airways, Mercury.

Effect: bronchitis. Towards the end of her life a virulent bacterial infection invaded Rays' airways and lungs (Uranus-Jupiter inconjunct Mercury). There was a rapid build-up of phlegm (Jupiter sesquiquadrate Pluto-Saturn in Cancer in the 12H of hospitals). Ray could not shake off the infection and she died (Aquarius planets in the 8H of death).

▲ (C) Saturn. (O) Mercury. (E) Pluto, Jupiter-Uranus.

• When Ray died on 2 January 1994, transit Pluto was on her progressed Sun at 28 Scorpio. Pluto carries the 1st ray and rules death.

c. Croup

A viral infection of the throat and windpipe that causes noisy breathing, a hoarse voice and a barking cough.

Amy Rodden (23 November 1949, 00:45, Palo Alto CA)

American musician who at age 2, contracted croup which ended up as pneumonia.

Cause: emotional. A lung-phlegm related disease signifies that emotionally we are drowning in emotional tides. In Rodden's case, her Moon in Capricorn shows a paucity of nurturing (real or imagined), resulting in grief and sorrow (the Moon square Neptune). It is very interesting because mother was famed astrologer Lois Rodden. From the chart we see that Amy felt abandoned, thought that her mother's professional life was more important to her mother than she (Moon opposing Uranus - the astrologer, in the 10H).

Organ: throat - airways, Mercury.

Effect: croup. There is susceptibility to chestiness and phlegm, spasms and coughing (Mercury afflicted in Sagittarius, inconjunct Uranus in Cancer, ruler of the 6H of health). She developed croup that migrated into pneumonia (Mercury > Uranus in Cancer; Jupiter disposits Mercury).

▲ (C) Moon, Neptune. (O) Mercury. (E) Uranus.

• Solar-arc Mercury was exactly inconjunct Uranus when Rodden caught croup.

d. Diphtheria (various body parts)

A serious bacterial infection that causes fever and a thick coating in the nose and airways.

Princess Alice (25 April 1843, 04:05, London UK).

Queen Victoria's third child. She married Prince Louis of Hesse in 1862 and died of diphtheria on 14 December 1878. She was aged 35.

Cause: emotional. Alice would hide her feelings, her pain and disappointments (the Moon is in the 12H of hidden things, square Mars). Emotionally congested, she was susceptible to chest complaints.

Organ: throat - airways, Mercury.

Effect: diphtheria. Alice caught diphtheria (Uranus) and the infection (Mars) invaded her airways and lungs (Mars sesquiquadrate the Sun and Mercury, the planets that rule the 6H of health).

▲ (C) Moon. (O) Mercury, (E) Mars, Uranus.

• When she died, solar-arc Uranus (the bacterial infection), was conjunct the natal Sun-Mercury point in Taurus and so was transit Neptune.

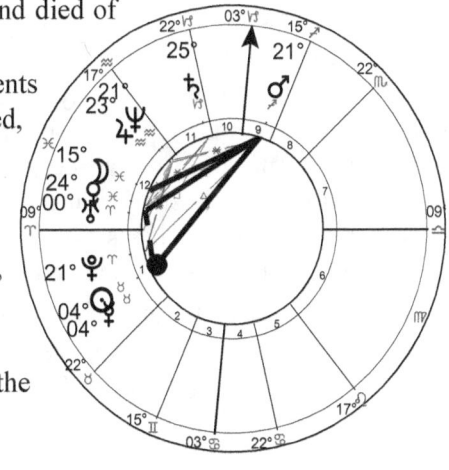

e. Emphysema

Damage to air sacs results in shortness of breath. 85% of the time emphysema is caused by smoking.

Dean Martin (7 June 1917 23:55, Steubenville OH).

Italian-American singer and actor who smoked and died of emphysema.

Cause: emotional. Martin had difficulty expressing his emotions in a healthy way. He repressed them (Saturn in Cancer, Moon in Capricorn), and self-medicated with alcohol and smoking (Neptune conjunct Saturn that is semi-square the Sun, the ruler of the 6H of health).

Organ: throat - airways, Mercury, Sun (for lower lungs).

Effect: emphysema. Smoking damaged the air sacs in the lungs (semi-square the Sun in Gemini, sextile Mercury), causing shortness of breath (Uranus in Aquarius square Mercury). It was made worse by chronic bronchitis (Mercury conjunct Jupiter and Mars, sextile Saturn in Cancer). Mars rules the 8H of death - he died from the effects of emphysema on 25 December 1995.

▲ (C) Saturn, Moon. (O) Mercury, Sun. (E) Neptune, Saturn, Uranus.

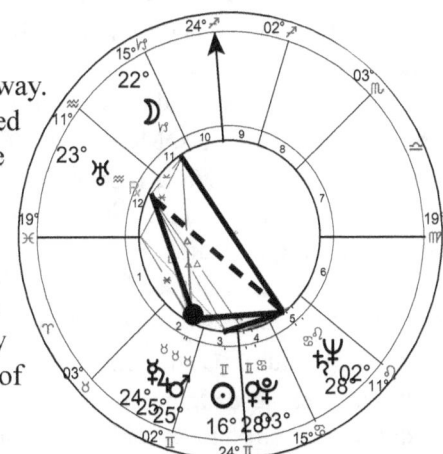

f. Hay fever

Air-borne contaminants cause hay fever, resulting in itchy, watery eyes and sneezing.

Astro.com 3118 (13 March, 1884, 03:34, New Orleans, LA)

American hay fever victim who suffered for many years from seasonal attacks. She moved often in an effort to find a congenial environment

Cause: emotional. As a child she suffered abuse (malefics in the 4H of family). As an adult, fear and constant vigilance that bad things would continue to happen manifested as hay fever (Saturn square Mercury). Our subject constantly moved house, but when emotional damage from abuse is not dealt with the consequences follow us no matter where we go.

Organ: throat - airways, Mercury.

Effect: hay fever. Air-borne contaminants (Saturn in Gemini) caused an exaggerated reaction from the immune system (sextile Mars in Leo conjunct Jupiter). It caused watery eyes and sneezing (Mercury afflicted in Pisces, sesquiquadrate retrograde Jupiter in Cancer in the 6H of health, conjunct Mars).

▲ (C) Mars, Saturn. (O) Mercury. (E) Saturn, Mars.

g. Influenza

A highly contagious viral infection of the respiratory tract causing fever, pain and phlegm.

Inayat Khan (5 July 1882, 23:28, Baroda India)

Khan came to the West as an Indian classical musician and founded the Sufi Order in 1914. He died from influenza on 5 February 1927, aged 44.

Cause: discipleship work. Khan was a spiritual teacher whose mission took him amongst the masses (Moon in Pisces in the 12H of universal sacrifice).

Organ: throat - airways, Gemini, Mercury.

Effect: influenza. Khan's airways were susceptible to viral infections (Mercury is retrograde in phlegm-producing Cancer, semi-square Neptune that disposits the Moon in Pisces). He was caught up in an influenza epidemic (Moon opposite Uranus that carries the 4th and 7th epidemic producing forces). His lungs flooded with cell debris (Jupiter in Gemini square the Moon in Pisces), and he literally drowned.

▲ (C) Pisces. (O) Gemini, Mercury. (E) Neptune, Jupiter, Uranus.

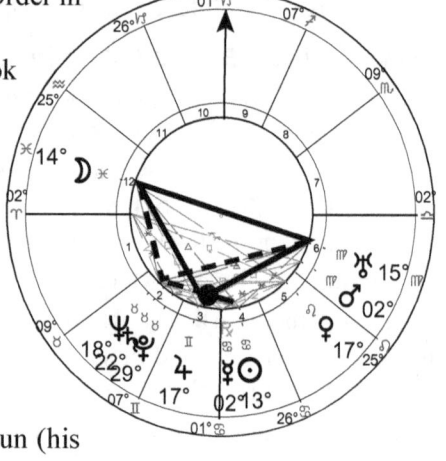

- When Khan died, transit Neptune (the flu virus) was on the progressed Sun (his life and vitality), on the cusp of the 6H of health, at 26 Leo.

h. Pneumonia

In pneumonia, lungs become inflamed, the air sacs fill with pus and other liquid, making breathing impossible.

Lorne Greene (12 February 1915 20:30, Ottawa Canada)

Canadian actor who starred as Ben Cartwright in the TV show Bonanza. He caught pneumonia in hospital, dying 11 September 1987, at age 72.

Cause: ageing. Greene's death was age related (Saturn), which means he lived a relatively moderate and balanced life.

Organ: throat - airways, Mercury and Gemini.

Effect: pneumonia. While recovering in hospital from ulcer surgery Greene caught a bacterial infection that migrated into pneumonia (Uranus conjunct the Moon, sesquiquadrate Saturn in Gemini; Saturn conjunct Pluto in Cancer; Pluto trine Mercury in Pisces in the 6H of health). There was a rapid build-up of fluid in the lungs (Mercury conjunct Jupiter in Pisces).

▲ (C) Saturn. (O) Mercury, Gemini. (E) Uranus, Pluto, Saturn, Jupiter.

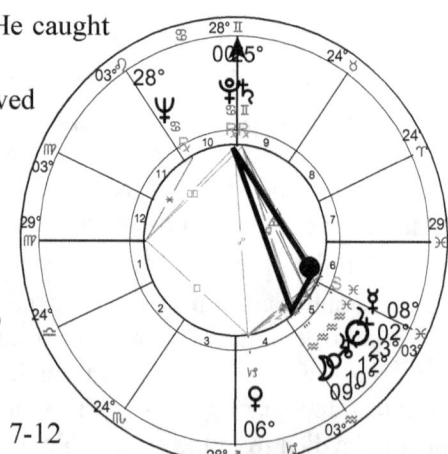

- When Greene caught pneumonia, solar-arc Saturn and Pluto were at 7-12 degrees of Virgo in the 12H of major illnesses, inconjunct natal Mars and Uranus.

i. Pulmonary Tuberculosis (TB)

An infectious bacterial disease characterised by the growth of nodules (tubercles) in lung tissue.

Princess Mathilde (17 August 1877 21:00, Munich Germany)
Bavarian princess, who died of tuberculosis on 6 August 1906, aged 29.
Cause: emotional. Mathilde yearned to be free but felt imprisoned by her royal status (Moon in Sagittarius, conjunct Jupiter, square Saturn ruling the 10H of royalty, in the obscure 12H). Her unhappiness manifested as constant illnesses (t-square the 6th-12th health houses).
Organ: throat - airways, Mercury.
Effect: TB. Mathilde was prone to infections in the airways (Mars in Pisces, opposite Mercury in the 6H of health), and she developed pulmonary tuberculosis (square Jupiter).

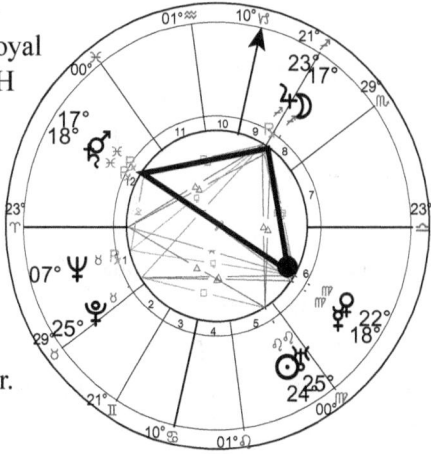

- ▲ (C) Moon, Saturn. (O) Mercury. (E) Mars, Jupiter.
- When Mathilde died, solar-arc Pluto was at 23 Gemini opposite Jupiter. Both Pluto via Scorpio, and Jupiter via Sagittarius, rule the 8H of death.

j. Smallpox

Smallpox spreads mainly through the air and launches its attack on the entire body from the respiratory organs. It cripples the immune system, breeds its toxicity in the body, shown by a skin rash with small blisters.

Abraham Lincoln (12 February 1809 06:54, Hodgenville KY)
President of the United States, he caught and recovered from smallpox.
Cause: epidemic. Although his vitality is good with the Sun on the ascendant trine Mars, these planets are in their detriment. His responsibilities could quickly debilitate his energies, rendering him susceptible to illnesses (Saturn conjunct Neptune on the MC, and Neptune semi-square Mars). He was also prone to depression (the Moon is afflicted in the 12H, rules the 6H of health).
Organ: throat - airways, Mercury.
Effect: smallpox. Just after the Gettysburg Address in November 1863, he was caught up in a smallpox epidemic (the Moon carrying the 4th ray). The virus (Neptune), invaded his airways (square Mercury). He recovered. It was not his destiny to die at that time.

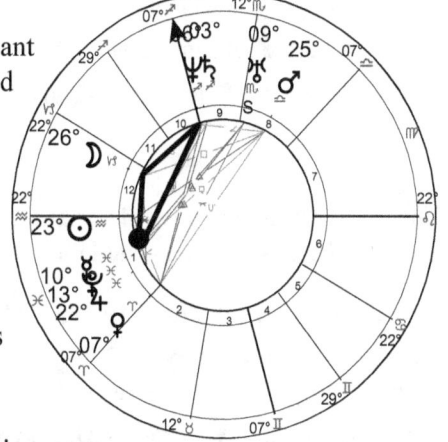

- ▲ (C) Moon. (O) Mercury. (E) Neptune.
- When Lincoln caught smallpox, solar-arc Moon was at 22 Pisces moving over progressed Mercury and natal Jupiter.

Mary Stuart (14 November 1631 04:00, London UK)
Eldest daughter of King Charles I of England-Scotland-Ireland. She died from smallpox on 24 December 1660, aged 29.
Cause: emotional. Stuart was an emotionally intense (4 planets in Scorpio), a pattern that made her susceptible to breathing and chest infections because Mercury and Neptune in Scorpio rule the 12th and 6th health houses.
Organ: throat - airways, Mercury.
Effect: smallpox. Stuart was caught in a smallpox (Neptune) epidemic (semi-square Uranus) that quickly spread through the masses (trine Pluto). The virus was lethal. It attacked her airways (Neptune conjunct retrograde Mercury) and she died (Mercury quindecile Pluto in the 8H of death).

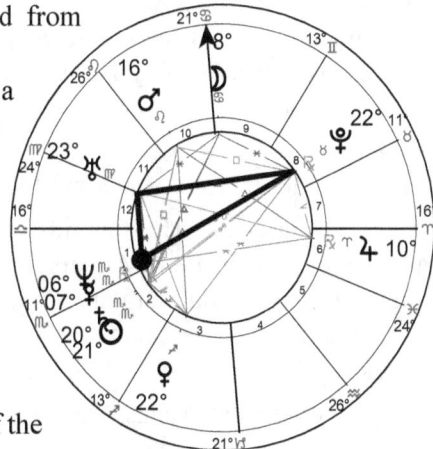

- ▲ (C) Neptune. (O) Mercury. (E) Neptune, Uranus, Pluto.
- When Mary Stuart died, solar-arc Sun had reached natal Venus, the ruler of the 8H of death; and solar-arc Pluto was opposing Venus from 22 Gemini.

4c.2. Thyroid Disorders

The thyroid gland is the physical anchorage of the throat chakra. Its hormonal functions include the regulation of metabolism, breathing and heart rate, etc. Thyroid disorders are often caused by emotional hyper-activity.

> [an over-developed and over-stimulated] astral body, leading to over-sensitivity of the solar plexus centre or of the throat centre. Much of the thyroid instability of the present time is based upon this. [1]

a. Graves' Disease (GD)

Graves' disease is an autoimmune disorder that causes the thyroid to over-produce hormones. It disturbs moods, behaviour and judgement. Racing anxiety is a psychological cause.

President George H. W. Bush (12 June 1924, 10:30, Milton MA)

Bush was the 41st President of the United States from 1989 to 1993 and father of the 43rd President George W. Bush. In 1991, he was diagnosed with GD.

Cause: emotional. Bush represses his emotions and moderates what he says (Saturn conjunct Moon in Libra in the 3H of communications). This is to present himself in the best possible light (Sun in the 10H of status, Leo on the ascendant). If he fails, if he does the wrong thing, he may mentally or even physically attack himself (Saturn trine Mars in Aquarius opposite the ascendant).

Organ: throat - thyroid, Venus.

Effect: GD. In response to his negative impulses, the immune system (Mars) attacked the thyroid causing over-activity in hormone production (sesquiquadrate retrograde Venus); dangerously so if not treated (Pluto-Venus).

▲ (C) Moon, Saturn. (O) Venus, Mercury. (E) Mars, Pluto.

b. Hashimoto's Disease

The thyroid is underactive. The autoimmune system attacks the gland causing chronic inflammation and its eventual failure. There is tiredness and lethargy.

Oprah Winfrey (29 January 1954 04:30, Kosciusko MS)

Talk-show host Winfrey, in 2007, exhausted and gaining weight she was diagnosed with a thyroid disease. There are two patterns that link into 1st ray Pluto.

Cause: emotional. Winfrey was born with low self-esteem (Sun conjunct Venus square Saturn), quite likely a consequence of growing up as an impoverished black girl in the racist Southern States. She felt devalued and attacked (Aquarius planet group in the 2H of values, Mercury square Mars). Negative self-talk and self-attack when she failed to meet her own high expectations is behind the thyroid trouble (Mercury rules the 6H of health). The positive side of this is that Winfrey felt motivated to succeed in life in spite of the obstacles placed in her way (Sun square Saturn in the 10H of professional success).

Organ: throat - thyroid, Venus and Mercury.

Effect: Hashimoto's. The thyroid was attacked by the immune system (Venus quindecile Pluto in Leo, Mercury in a t-square with Mars and Pluto), impairing and inhibiting (Saturn and Pluto) hormone production.

Depression and verbal attacks were followed by comfort eating (Venus trine Jupiter in the 6H of food habits). Coupled with a slow metabolism, she gained weight.

▲ (C) Mars. (O) Venus, Mercury. (E) Mars, Pluto, Saturn.

---

1 Bailey, Alice A; Esoteric Psychology II, 315.

4c.3. Cancer in Throat Chakra Organs

a. Lymphatic cancer

Lymphatic cancer or lymphoma strikes the lymphocytes, disease infection-fighting white cells that cycle within the lymphatic system. The most common type of lymphoma is non-Hodgkin. In Hodgkin's disease, different white cells are affected.

Richard Harris (1 October 1930 11:20, Limerick Ireland)

Irish actor and singer described as a "hell-raiser", "half man, half maniac", with a love of booze. He was diagnosed with Hodgkin's disease in August 2002 and died on the 25th of October of that year.

Cause: emotional. Harris' chart shows he suffered enormous emotional conflict and pain in his childhood and family life (Moon in Capricorn opposite Mars and Pluto in Cancer). To cope, he repressed his emotions, a dangerous habit where health is concerned. He also drank excessively (Mars conjunct Jupiter in Cancer, semi-square Neptune), and had a wild, partying lifestyle (square Uranus in the 5H of recreation), which brought its own set of health problems (Mars rules the 6H of health).

Organ: throat - lymphatic system, the Moon, Neptune.

Effect: cancer. The Moon and Cancer are rulers of the lymphatic system, and the health-triangle is based on this polarity. Due to stress and congestion in the body, lymphocytes (the Moon), became perverted (6th ray Mars), malignant (Pluto) and cancerous (Jupiter). The square from the Cancer planets to Uranus indicates that his wild and undisciplined life-style contributed to the onset of the disease and to the aberrant behaviour of cells (Uranus opposite the Sun).

▲ (C) Cancer planets, Moon. (O) Moon, Neptune. (E) Mars, Pluto, Jupiter, Uranus.

- When Harris was diagnosed in 2002, the solar-arc ascendant had reached 27 Capricorn and was passing over the natal Moon, representing the trouble occurring in body tissue. Simultaneously, the other ruler of the lymphatic system - Neptune, by solar-arc it had reached 16 Scorpio and was conjunct the ascendant. The cancer grew and spread via the bloodstream, which Neptune rules.
- On the day he died, the transit Moon entered the 8H of death.

Charles Harvey (22 June 1940 09:16, Little Bookham UK)

British astrologer. In 1999, Harvey contracted a form of lymphatic cancer. After a heavy treatment of chemotherapy, he died on 22 February 2000.

Cause: emotional. Serious trouble affecting the fluids of the body can be seen with Cancer dominating the 12H of hospitals. Cancer the disease becomes a candidate when we see that Harvey had a habit of repressing his thoughts and feelings (Pluto conjunct Mercury and Mars in Cancer). This caused congestion in the throat chakra, the ruler of the lymphatic system.

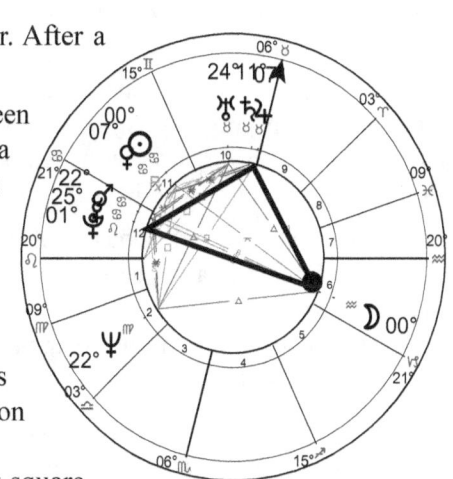

Organ: throat - lymphatic system, the Moon and Cancer.

Effect: cancer. White blood cells (the Moon opposite Mars in Cancer) became malignant (Pluto) and cancerous (square Jupiter). Blood quality was seriously degraded (the Moon in Aquarius > Mars), inhibiting oxygenation (Mercury) and the nourishing of blood cells.

Chemotherapy (Pluto) could not stop the march of the disease (Pluto in a t-square with Jupiter and the Moon), and the cancer eventually killed him. Jupiter rules the 8H of death with Pisces on the cusp.

▲ (C) Moon, Mars. (O) Moon, Cancer. (E) Pluto, Jupiter.

- When Harvey was diagnosed in 1999, the progressed Moon was moving through the 8H of death and was still there when he died in 2000.

b. Mouth and Jaw Cancer

Gordon MacRae (12 March 1921, 07:15, East Orange NJ)

American actor and singer, who was best known from his Rodgers and Hammerstein musical films, Oklahoma (1955) and Carousel (1956). On January 24 1986 at the age of 64, he died of pneumonia, the result of complications from cancer of the mouth and jaw.

Cause: emotional. MacRae was emotionally reactive and fiery (Moon-Mars in Aries), which clashed with his down-to-earth perfectionist tendencies where his craft was concerned (inconjunct Saturn in Virgo in the 6H of work). He worked exceedingly hard and was hyper-critical of his and other people's performances if he thought they fell below par. He could not let go of disappointments and frustrations and would worry about them, undermining his health (Saturn quindecile Mercury in detriment in Pisces, opposite the Sun in the 12H of self-undoing).

Organ: throat - mouth, jaw Mars in Aries, Venus in Taurus.

Effect: cancer. Congestion and trouble in the throat chakra (Saturn retrograde in the 6H of health), caused carcinogenic changes (quindecile Uranus in Pisces in the 12H of major illnesses), in tissue in the mouth and jaw (inconjunct Mars-Moon in Aries in the 1H; sesquiquadrate Venus). Cancer grew (Saturn conjunct Jupiter).

▲ (C) Moon, Mars, Saturn. (O) Mars, Venus. (E) Uranus, Jupiter.

- When he died in 1986, solar-arc Venus was at 7 Cancer, conjunct malignant Pluto in Cancer. This represented the final onslaught of the disease in his throat that caused his death - Pluto rules the 8H of death.

- He died of pneumonia due to a build-up of phlegm and cell debris in his lungs (Pluto in Cancer trine afflicted Mercury in Pisces in the 12H).

c. Throat Cancer

Medical experts tell us the human papilloma virus (HPV) is a leading cause of throat cancer and may spread from person to person via oral sex. Astrologically, it fits. Venus, which rules the throat, also rules sex.

Michael Douglas (25 September 1944 10:30, New Brunswick NJ).

American actor and son of actor Kirk Douglas. In mid-August 2010, he announced he had stage four throat cancer and that oral sex was a cause. Though he later retracted this, it probably is the truth - many sexually active people have the HPV virus and his chart shows he was susceptible. After successful treatment, Douglas returned to his acting career.

Cause: karmic - sexual. Douglas is a Libran who inhibits his emotions (Saturn in Cancer in a t-square with the Moon in Capricorn, and Neptune), in order to try to create peace and equilibrium around him. But this creates congestion and trouble in the solar plexus chakra, which in the long term leads to overall debilitation and susceptibility to viruses and disease generally.

Organ: throat, Venus.

Effect: cancer. Oral sex (Venus conjunct Mars), although it is generally accepted as being a normal part of sexual expression, health-wise it is a misuse of the sexual function because it spreads the HPV virus. In Douglas' case, the virus (Mars, ruler of the 6H of health with Aries on the cusp), attacked the throat and mouth (Venus). Tissue became carcinogenic (square Saturn in Cancer) and cancer eventually developed (semi-square Jupiter afflicted in Virgo).

▲ (C) Saturn, Mars. (O) Venus. (E) Mars, Saturn, Jupiter.

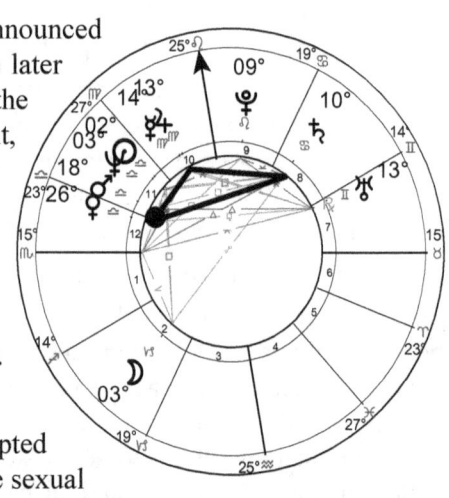

4d. Heart Chakra Diseases

The heart rules the thymus gland, vitality and the cardiovascular, immune and lymphatic systems. It receives energy from ray 2, from Leo, the Sun and Jupiter.

4d.1. Blood Disorders

The cardiovascular system overall is ruled by the Sun and Leo. Blood is ruled primarily by Mars, arterial blood by Jupiter, and venous blood by Venus. Blood circulation is governed by Aquarius and the bloodstream by Neptune. The 7th ray is usually involved when there are problems with the blood, primarily through Uranus.

a. Anaemia - Aplastic

Bone marrow fails to produce enough blood cells.

Marie Curie (7 November 1867 12:00, Warsaw Poland)

French physicist and chemist, who pioneered research on radioactivity, but years of exposure resulted in aplastic anaemia. She died on 4 July 1934.

Cause: discipleship. Curie was a disciple who focused in the higher chakras, quite likely the crown chakra since it is ruled by Pluto, a planet that rules radiation. The Sun on the MC opposing Pluto, suggests that the 12-petalled heart lotus at the centre of the crown chakra was coming alive and in response, kundalini (Pluto) was rising. The cause of the disease was due to radiation poisoning, an accidental by-product of her discipleship work.

Organ: heart - cell life and health, the Sun.

Effect: anaemia. Radiation poisoning (Pluto afflicted in Taurus), impairs the body's ability to produce healthy cells from bone marrow (sextile Uranus retrograde in Cancer), and destroys the health of cell life and blood (opposite the Sun). Life was leached from blood cells (Uranus in Cancer), draining away the life-force (Sun).

▲ (C) Pluto. (O) The Sun. (E) Pluto, Uranus.

b. Anaemia - Pernicious (PA)

Vitamin B12, which is needed to make healthy red blood cells, is destroyed by the immune system.

Robert Peary (6 May 1856 12:04, Cresson PA)

American explorer who died of pernicious anaemia on 20 February 1920.

Cause: emotional. Because an autoimmune disease arose, we know Peary attacked himself psychologically. He had an authoritative "parent voice" playing in his head chastising him for his unworthiness (Saturn in Gemini square Mars in the 2H of self-worth). It was quite likely imprinted on his consciousness by a bullying patriarchal figure in whose presence he felt helpless (Mars afflicted in Libra and retrograde). This is at the root of the disorder.

Organ: heart - red blood cells and B12, Mars.

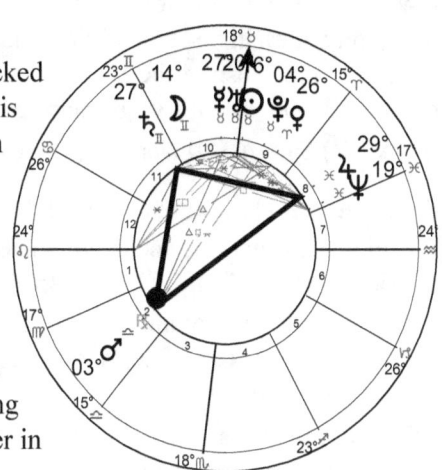

Effect: anaemia. The immune system attacked and destroyed B12 preventing the production of healthy red blood cells so that the blood was leached of its vitalising life (t-square: Mars > Saturn, opposite Jupiter in Pisces representing the impaired blood quality). Peary became anaemic (Saturn) and died (Jupiter in the 8H of death).

▲ (C) Mars. (O) Mars. (E) Mars, Saturn, Jupiter.

• When Peary died, solar-arc Saturn was in the 1st house at 29 Leo, inconjunct natal Jupiter at 29 Pisces, representing the devitalisation taking place in the blood. Solar-arc Mars was at 4 Sagittarius, inconjunct natal Pluto at 4 Taurus, representing the destruction of the body's ability to produce healthy red blood cells.

c. Anaemia - Sickle Cell

Red blood cells take a sickle shape and die early, leaving a shortage of healthy red blood cells. Diseased cells block blood flow, causing pain.

Tionne Watkins (26 April 1970, 18:55, Des Moines IA)
American singer of hip hop girl-group TLC. As a child, Watkins was diagnosed with sickle-cell anaemia and since the age of seven has been in and out of hospital. Many African-Americans have the disease.

Cause: genetic, emotional. Although this is a genetic (Uranus) disorder, Watkins' emotional disturbances are connected. This is because Mars, which rules red blood cells is also a ruler of the solar plexus and Watkins' emotions are powerful. They swamp her (Neptune opposite Mars), and she tries to repress them (Moon in Capricorn). This caused trouble.

Organ: heart - red blood cells, Mars.

Effect: anaemia. Watkins inherited a gene (Uranus) that perverts (sextile Neptune) red blood cells (Neptune opposite Mars), so that oxygenation and vitalisation of the body is severely impaired (Mars in Gemini).

▲ (C) Uranus, Mars. (O) Mars. (E) Neptune.

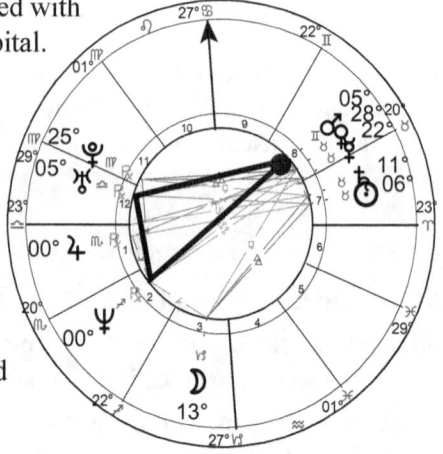

d. Haemophilia

An inherited genetic disease, where blood does not clot leading to prolonged bleeding. Queen Victoria was a carrier and passed it on to several royal houses.

Queen Victoria (24 May 1819, 04:15, London UK)
Queen Victoria did not inherit the gene haemophilia. The mutation was spontaneous and her passing on the "royal disease" cursed many royal houses in Europe. Females only have mild symptoms if any at all while male children inherit the full disease.

Cause: karmic. We are entering into the Aquarian Age of universal brotherhood and the time for autocratic royal houses is over. Perhaps the Lord of Karma was making this point with the gene mutation.

Organ: heart - bloodstream Neptune and Pisces; gene Uranus.

Effect: haemophilia. The gene (Uranus) that clots blood (square Saturn), was corrupted (Pluto conjunct Saturn, Neptune conjunct Uranus). This meant blood flow would not clot (Jupiter in Aquarius that rules blood circulation, is midpoint Saturn in Pisces, and Neptune). The gene was passed to her descendants (Uranus on the cusp of the 8H of inheritances, sesquiquadrate Mercury, co-ruler of the 5H of children with Virgo sharing the cusp).

▲ (C) Saturn. (O) Neptune, Pisces, Uranus. (E) Pluto, Neptune, Jupiter.

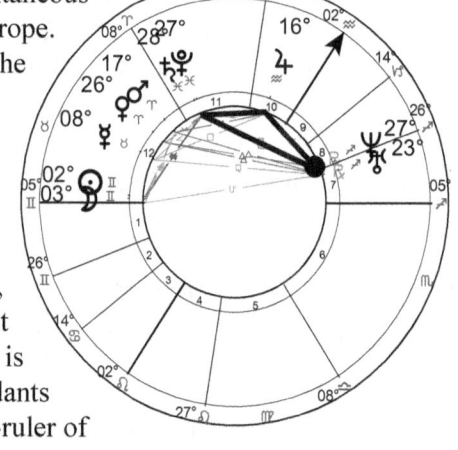

Prince Alexei (12 August 1904 01:15 pm, Petrodvorec Russia).
Alexei was the great-grandson of Victoria and heir to the Russian throne. He was murdered with his family by the Bolsheviks.

Cause: genetic. Alexei inherited the defective gene (Uranus) from his mother and the royal line (trine the Moon conjunct the MC).

Organ: heart - blood, Mars.

Effect: haemophilia. The gene prevented the blood from clotting (Uranus inconjunct Mars square Jupiter in the 6H of health; Jupiter trines Uranus).

▲ (C) Uranus. (O) Mars. (E) Jupiter.

- Alexei was murdered with his family by the Bolsheviks around the 16th or 17th July 1918. Solar-arc Mars was at 12 Leo symbolising the dominant "Red" Army that took his life (square the ascendant).

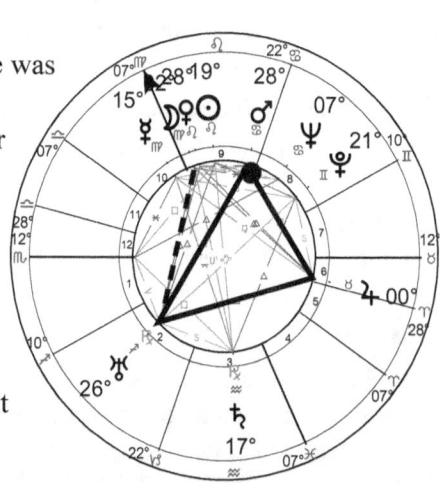

4d.2. Cardiovascular Diseases

a. Angina

Inadequate blood supply to the heart results in severe chest pain that may spread to the shoulders, arms and neck.

Sir Ernest Shackleton (15 February 1874, 05:00, Kilkea Ireland)
British explorer who examined sections of Antarctica.
Cause: emotional. Shackleton was emotionally detached and could repress his feelings, a habit that affects circulation (the Moon-Saturn conjunction in Aquarius).
Organ: heart - blood circulation Uranus in Leo, arteries Jupiter.
Effect: angina. Consequently, circulation became restricted as arteries hardened (Saturn in Aquarius opposite Uranus in Leo, trine retrograde Jupiter). He developed painful angina and eventually the disease killed him (Jupiter in the 8H of death).

▲ (C) Moon, Saturn. (O) Uranus, Jupiter. (E) Saturn, Uranus.
• When Shackleton died on January 5 1922, solar-arc Jupiter (the arteries) had progressed to 18 Scorpio, moving opposite natal Pluto at 19 Taurus.

b. Aortic Aneurysms

An aneurysm is a weak spot in the wall of a blood vessel that balloons out and fills with blood. Life is under threat if the aneurysm bursts. High blood pressure is often a cause.

Joe Louis (13 May 1914, 08:00, Lafayette, AL)
African-American professional boxer, world heavyweight champion from 1937 to 1949. In October 1977, he had an aortic aneurysm.
Cause: emotional. Louis's body took a battering, which contributed to his health issues. Psychologically, he had hidden and unexpressed anger (Mars semi-square Saturn in the 12H), which builds up stress in the cardiovascular system so that problems like aneurysms arise.
Organ: heart - arteries, Jupiter.
Effect: aneurysm. Stress (Saturn) caused high blood pressure (semi-square Mars in Leo), and an aneurysm (Venus trine Jupiter symbolises the weakening and the swelling aneurysm), developed in an aortic artery.

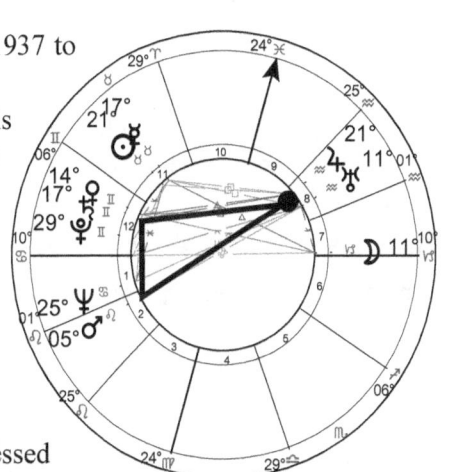

▲ (C) Mars, Saturn. (O) Jupiter. (E) Saturn, Mars, Venus.
• Louis died of a heart attack on 12 April 1981. Solar-arc Saturn had progressed to 21 Leo, exactly opposite natal Jupiter, which rules the 6H, completing the final blockage that finally knocked out the champ.

c. Arteriosclerosis - Artherosclerosis

Artery walls harden and thicken, restricting blood flow to organs.

Evangeline Booth (25 December 1865, 15:00, London UK)
British theologian and 4th General of The Salvation Army from 1934 to 1939. She died 17 July 1950, from the effects of arteriosclerosis.
Cause: emotional. There was a hard-hearted side to Booth (Sun conjunct Jupiter afflicted in Capricorn), a lack of compassion (square Neptune conjunct the Moon in bossy Aries), which is related to the trouble.
Organ: heart - arteries, Jupiter.

Effect: arteriosclerosis. The walls of the arteries thickened and hardened (Uranus in Cancer opposite Jupiter conjunct the Sun), restricting blood flow (Uranus and Neptune are connected with circulation).

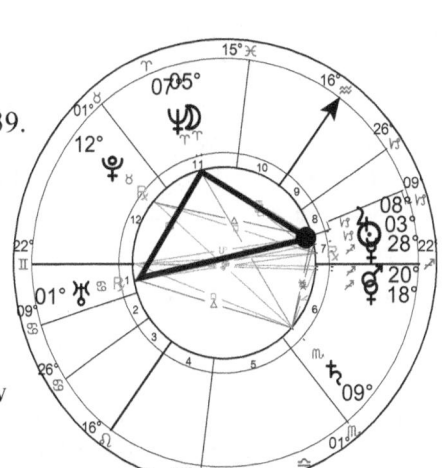

▲ (C) Moon. (O) Jupiter. (E) Uranus.

c. Deep Vein Thrombosis (DVT)

DVT is a blood clot that forms in the veins of the leg, that then breaks loose and travels through the blood until it lodges in an organ - for instance in the lungs. It causes serious damage, even death.

Charles Chaplin Jr. (5 May 1925 06:10, Los Angeles CA)

Son of legendary actor-comic Charles Chaplin and Lita Gray. He died of a pulmonary embolism on 20 March 1968, aged 42. In the previous week he broke his leg and it seems this trouble contributed to the formation of the dangerous blood clot.

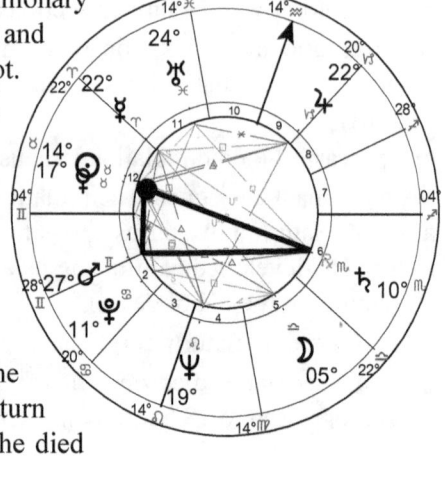

Cause: karmic. Psychologically, a blood clot suggests that there is interference to the flow of life, a loss of joy and being cut off from an important love. With Venus in the 12H of hidden things opposite Saturn, Chaplin was inclined to be fearful and guarded about love and relationships. These two planets, Venus and Saturn, are included in the health-triangle. Saturn in the 6H of health indicates karma.

Organ: heart - the veins Venus, blood Mars, lungs the Sun.

Effect: heart - blood clot. The clot (Saturn) formed. It travelled through the blood (Mars) and veins (Venus), lodging in the lungs (Mars in Gemini, Saturn opposes the Sun in the 12H of major illnesses). Blood flow blocked and he died (Saturn co-rules the 8H of death).

▲ (C) Saturn in Scorpio. (O) Venus, Mars, Sun. (E) Saturn.

• When Chaplin died, solar-arc Sun and Venus were at 25-28 Gemini, straddling natal Mars; simultaneously, solar-arc Saturn was at 22 Sagittarius opposing natal Mars. The blockage occurred.

d. Fibrillation, arrhythmia,

Heart arrhythmia or atrial fibrillation is an irregular and often rapid heart rate that occurs when the two upper chambers of the heart experience chaotic electrical signals. Caffeine, cigarettes, and other stimulant drugs can set off an attack.

Elton John (25 March 1947 15:28, Pinner UK)

Popular English singer, pianist and composer, John collapsed on a plane as he flew to sing at the wedding of Posh Spice and David Beckham who were married on 4 July 1999. He had an irregular heart-beat and was fitted with a heart pacemaker.

Cause: emotional. The heart is a muscle, so Mars, which rules all muscles in the body is of interested psychologically when heart trouble occurs. Mars squares Uranus in Gemini, pointing to emotional verbal tirades. Mars is also in Pisces, which is related to drug use via Neptune. John has confessed to being a drug addict for a great period of his life, and this would have contributed to the fibrillation trouble.

Organ: heart - heart muscle, Mars.

Effect: heart fibrillation. Drug use (Mars in Pisces), contributed to John's fibrillation trouble (square Uranus), but it was not the only cause. The chart shows he was born with a latent weakness in the heart (Saturn and Pluto are in Leo that rules the heart, in the 12H of hidden things. Uranus is semi-square Saturn in Leo; and Saturn is sesquiquadrate Mars).

▲ (C) Mars in Pisces. (O) Mars. (E) Uranus, Saturn, Pluto.

• At the time of the attack - about 3 July 1999, transit Neptune was in the 6H of health at 3 Aquarius, opposing natal Saturn. If John was taking drugs at the time - as Neptune suggests, it triggered the latent heart weakness and he collapsed.

• When the pace-maker was fitted on 9 July, transit Uranus was in Aquarius in the 6H of health, trine its natal position. The irregularity was fixed through modern, medical science.

e. Heart Disease - Congenital

Congenital heart problems are structural defects that are present at birth. For example, holes in the heart, leaking valves, problems with the heart muscle or walls and bad connections between blood vessels. Such defects can lead to heart failure because the heart pumps inefficiently. In practice, look for afflictions to the Sun or to a planet in Leo and build on that; Saturn and/ or the Moon for congenital conditions. A third planet gives further information - for instance, Uranus when, due to a premature birth and organ building is not finished, Mars for a hole and Neptune for a leak.

L1002 (14 November 1956 07:56, Philadelphia PA)

American male, a lawyer who represented individuals with disabilities and toddlers who had been sexually and physically abused. Retiring after 20 years, he is now a licensed Acupuncturist.

He was born with a block in the intestines - pyloric stenosis and almost died during corrective surgery. Virgo rules the intestines and the life-threatening problem is shown by Pluto in Virgo square to Mercury (tubes), and Saturn (a blockage), and the Sun (life threatening).

Dangerous conditions like these in babies are a karmic carry-over from a previous life. Great difficulty in digesting life is at the root of this condition because of hidden abuse, likely in a religious setting (Pluto in the 9H of religion). He had a speech impediment that was corrected, but was bullied for this by a nun teacher (Pluto > Saturn representing the hard, religious disciplinarian).

Cause: discipleship. Physical heart problems are related to hard-heartedness in the average person, or to the development of an inclusive spirit in the more advanced. This latter involves the transference of energy from the selfish, emotional solar plexus chakra (Mars), up to the inclusive heart centre (opposing Jupiter). Our subject has dedicated his life to helping others, so is in the latter category. Consequently, his heart should be stronger and healthier in his next incarnation. It is interesting to note however that Jupiter, the higher ruler of the heart chakra, is afflicted in Virgo and opposes Mars pointing to a deep heart wounding being incurred in a previous life. This is related to the trouble.

Organ: heart - heart organ, the Sun; the arteries Jupiter.

Effect: congenital heart problem. From the teens onwards, he had heart pain but was told all was well. Then in 2009 at age 53, the pain became serious and he had a mild heart attack. Cardiologists discovered that the main coronary artery (left anterior descending) "goes up instead of down, eventually became buried in the heart muscle and winding up between the main vessels at the top of the heart".

The Sun in the 12H of hospitalisation can point to an inherited heart defect, because the prognosis is that one day an inherent heart condition will require hospitalisation and therefore serious treatment. The 12th house also represents 'hidden things' and consequently, the condition was not discovered until he was in his 50's, most likely due to his living a healthy lifestyle. His heart was very strong, with no plaque. The positive aspects between the Sun (heart and vitality), Jupiter (expansive) and Mars (energy), show an otherwise healthy body with good energy flow, which helped the heart do its job in spite of the physical defect.

The congenital condition was inherited (Sun sesquiquadrate Moon in the 4H of family, Moon trine Uranus in Leo in the 8H of inheritances). The defect lies buried in the family DNA (Uranus). A perversion occurred to the construction of the foetal heart within the 1st month (Neptune in the first degree of Scorpio, square Uranus). The result was an aberration in artery placement (Jupiter, the arteries, is midpoint the Sun and Uranus). Jupiter rules the arteries and the problem of the artery going in the wrong direction is shown by Jupiter being afflicted in Virgo, opposite Mars in Pisces representing trouble with the plumbing configuration.

He had heart bypass surgery but reports that the fix was worse than the problem. "I go through periods of vagus nerve issues, like the congestive heart failure and other annoying symptoms. I self-medicate".

▲ (C) Jupiter. (O) Sun, Jupiter. (E) Uranus.

- In 2009, transit Saturn was moving back and forth over natal Jupiter, crystallising the arterial defect so he had physical pain and discomfort. Additionally, transit Uranus was in Pisces, moving opposite Jupiter, representing modern science's attempt to fix the problem.

f. Heart Attack

A heart attack occurs when the heart is suddenly deprived of blood due to an artery blockage.

Peter Sellers (8 September 1925 06:00, Southsea UK)

English film actor and comedian who suffered his first heart attack in 1964 and died following a third heart attack on 24 July 1980.

Cause: emotional. Sellers was born with a healthy heart, but there were latent problems that were exacerbated by his attitudes. He was known for being "flawed, spiteful and selfish" (Sun conjunct Mars in Virgo, opposing Uranus). Hard-heartedness causes the heart muscle to harden (the Sun-Mars conjunction is midpoint Saturn and Pluto).

Organ: heart - heart organ, the Sun.

Effect: heart attack. Sellers died from heart disease.

▲ (C) Mars, Uranus. (O) Sun. (E) Pluto, Saturn.

- At 39, he suffered his first attack; solar-arc Pluto had reached the Sun in Virgo and was moving over it. On his final attack in 1980, the solar-arc Sun-Mars point had reached natal Saturn at 10 Scorpio.

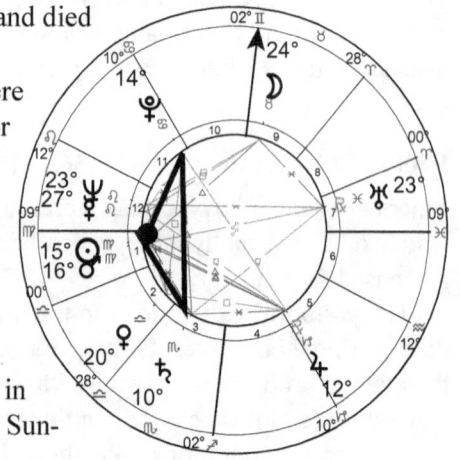

g. Heart Failure

Heart failure occurs when the heart fails to pump blood around the system. The cause may be due to a birth defect, a heart attack, high blood pressure or just from ageing. Mars represents the pumping action.

Elizabeth Taylor (27 February 1932 02:30, London UK)

British-American actress, renowned for her great beauty. She suffered from congestive heart failure in her later years, dying from it on March 23 2011.

Cause: emotional. Taylor was 79 when she died, pointing to ageing and lifestyle as contributing to heart failure. She had a good appetite (Taurus on the 6H of food habits), loved rich food and lots of it (Venus trine Jupiter in Leo), and alcohol (the Sun in Pisces opposite Neptune).

Organ: heart - heart organ the Sun.

Effect: heart failure. Due to her age, diet and sedentary lifestyle the heart muscle gradually, weakened and failed to do its work (the Sun conjunct Mars in Pisces, and Mars semi-square Venus).

▲ (C) Venus, Jupiter. (O) Sun. (E) Venus, Mars in Pisces.

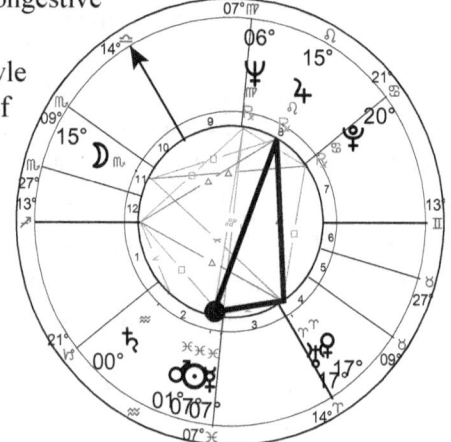

h. High Blood Pressure, Hypertension (HBP)

HBP causes the heart to work harder and can lead to complications such as a heart attack and stroke.

Barry White (12 September 1944, 16:42, Galveston TX)

American R&B singer, who had HBP for years, contributing to kidney failure in 1995. He died 4 July 2003, from his problems and a low-grade infection.

Cause: emotional. White grew up feeling emotionally deprived (Saturn in Cancer). He ate and drank rich foods and alcohol to fill an emotional void, because he felt unloved (Saturn in the 6H of diet square Venus).

Organ: heart - blood pressure, Mars.

Effect: heart failure. Cholesterol build-up in the arteries (Saturn in Cancer in the 6H of health, sextile Jupiter afflicted in Virgo), obstructed blood flow (Saturn square Mars).

▲ (C) Saturn in Cancer. (O) Mars. (E) Jupiter, Saturn.

- When White died, solar-arc Venus had reached 9 Sagittarius, inconjunct natal Saturn at 9 Cancer, square Jupiter in the 8H of death.

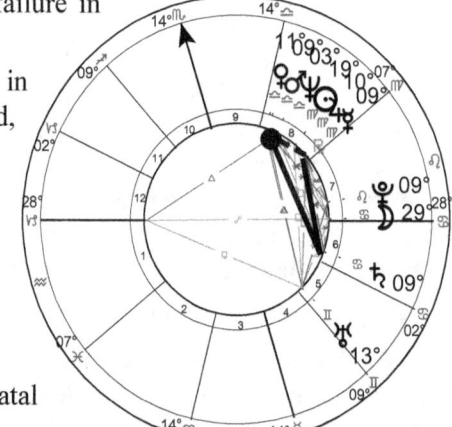

4d.3. Immune System

a. Acquired immune deficiency syndrome (AIDS)

The HIV (human immunodeficiency virus), attacks the immune system, so that gradually the body's resistance to disease is destroyed. In the final stages when immune cell count is very low and viral cells predominate, the disease has progressed to AIDS.

Rudolph Nureyev (17 March 1938 13:00, Irkutsk Russia)

Nureyev was a Soviet ballet dancer and choreographer who defected from the Soviet Union to the West in 1961. Regarded as one of ballet's most gifted male dancers, he died from AIDS on 6 January 1993, age 54.

Cause: emotional. Emotionally very intense (Sun in Pisces trine Pluto in Cancer), Nureyev tried to find relief, happiness and self-understanding through deep and serious sexual encounters (Pluto in the 1H square Mars).

Organ: heart - immune system, the Sun and Mars.

Effect: AIDS. He caught the virus (Neptune septile Pluto in Cancer), which attacked the immune system and gradually but persistently destroyed it (Neptune opposite Sun, sesquiquadrate Mars; Pluto trine the Sun and square Mars). We do not know what psychological changes Nureyev went through as the disease progressed. But with Pluto in the personal 1st house, changes would have been deep and profound.

▲ (C) Pisces. (O) The Sun, Mars. (E) Neptune, Pluto.

- Two years before he died, in 1991, solar-arc Neptune had reached 11 Scorpio and was opposing natal Uranus at 11 Taurus; and solar-arc Pluto had reached 19 Virgo and was passing over natal Neptune. In this period he either contracted the deadly virus, or if he already had it, its progress accelerated.

b. Chronic Fatigue Syndrome (CFS), Myalgic Encephalomyelitis (ME)

Chronic fatigue syndrome is extreme fatigue that cannot be explained by any underlying medical condition. A primary cause is incessant anxiety and worry, 4th ray negatives carried by the Moon and Mercury. This wears down and debilitates the system.

Michael Crawford (19 January 1942, 06:00, Salisbury UK).

British actor and singing star of 'The Phantom of the Opera'. In 2004, he was working in a show when he began to feel unwell. His tiredness became so extreme he had to pull out. He was diagnosed with CFS.

Cause: emotional. Prior to his illness, living a conflict-filled life was normal for Crawford. Aggressive and sexual Mars was strong in his nature (t-square: Mars in detriment in Taurus, square the Sun and Pluto). The source of stress came from his home and family life (Mars in the 4H of family). There were reports of his affairs and infidelity.

Organ: heart - vitality, the Sun.

Effect: CFS. Continuous conflict (Mars in 4th ray Taurus), grinds down (Pluto) vitality (the Sun). It triggers the fight-flight system (Mars), depleting adrenal reserves, adding to the trouble. Debilitated and exhausted, in 2004 he developed CFS. He may also have had an underactive thyroid; Saturn is in Taurus that rules the thyroid and the 6H of health.

▲ (C) Mars. (O) The Sun. (E) Pluto.

- In 2003-4, the progressed Sun, representing the immune system, reached 29 Pisces, opposite natal Neptune. His energy levels melted away, he had no reserves left.

- By getting in touch with his feelings and harmonising his inner conflict, Crawford restored his vitality levels to normal within 4 years.

c. Immune deficient - Leukaemia

Leukaemia is cancer of the immune system, a malignant progressive disease in which the bone marrow and other blood-forming organs produce increased numbers of immature or abnormal leucocytes (white blood cells). These suppress the production of normal blood cells, leading to anaemia and other symptoms. It is thought to be a genetic disease but not inherited. The psychology associated with it is a sense of being smothered by a myriad of events that one has no control over.

L1003 (3 July 1963, 12:50, Melbourne Australia.

Australian female scientist who worked in a fulfilling job and led an active and healthy lifestyle. The year before diagnosis, at age 50, there were a series of events that were upsetting to her. She lost her job, broke her left foot, had an unpleasant confrontation with a close friend and suffered deeply with a friend who had a miscarriage.

Cause: emotional. Our subject is a kind and easy-going Cancerian. But underneath, she has a heightened sense of survival (the Moon is afflicted in Scorpio), a sense that she has to continually fight to maintain order in her life if she is going to survive (square Saturn and Uranus-Pluto). This operated at a subliminal level and it exhausted her health reserves.

Organ: heart - immune system, Mars.

Effect: leukaemia. All the incidents previously mentioned tapped into fears connected with the Scorpio Moon - anxiety she has about friendships (Moon square Uranus) and her career (Cancer on the 10th house cusp).

Within 6 months she developed a chest infection that would not go away and heavy sweating. Diagnosed in February 2014, her leukaemia is of the type where a "genetic switch" occurs. It happened around November 2013. A gene went aberrant (Uranus) and when it "switched", abnormal leucocytes (lymphoblast) cells began to be produced from bone marrow (square the Moon afflicted in Scorpio), in large numbers (conjunct Pluto). Gradually the fighting power of the immune system was destroyed (Pluto conjunct Mars) and blood quality corrupted (Moon square Saturn in Aquarius; Pluto quindecile Saturn).

▲ (C) Moon, Saturn, Pluto. (O) Mars. (E) Uranus-Pluto, Saturn.

The chart is set for November 2013, the date when the specialist told our subject the genetic-switch occurred.

- By solar-arc (SA), the health-triangle had rotated so that Pluto, the Lord of Death, was on the ascendant, the point in the chart that represents "birth", with Uranus following behind. Together they represent the astounding radical change and transformational set of circumstances that cause a genetic switch or mutation.

- SA Moon (the form), is at the bottom of the chart. The 4th house governs life's ending, so in a way, the Moon crossing the IC represents a mini-death and rebirth. The Moon rules bone marrow, and the subject received new DNA with a bone marrow transplant on 1 August 2014.

- SA Saturn, another ruler of bone marrow, is in the 6H of health. Uranus, which rules DNA and brings radical change, is transiting over Saturn; symbolising the genetic switch.

Three years later in 2017, our subject is off medication and immunosuppression and "the donor cells are making blood and marrow beautifully".

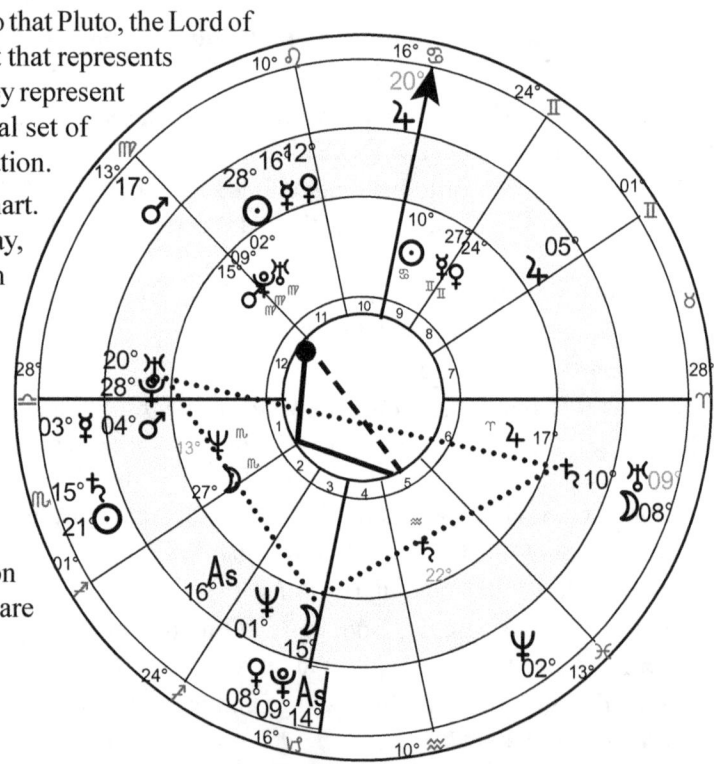

Inner chart - natal; middle chart - solar-arc directions; outer chart - transits.

d. Immune deficiency

David Vetter (21 September 1971, 07:00, Houston TX)
American child known as "Boy in the Bubble." His body could not produce T and B lymphocytes due to defective DNA - a fatal disease without treatment. To keep alive, he lived in a germ-free bubble for 12 years. His last 15 days were spent out of the bubble, in hospital undergoing corrective surgery. It failed and he died 22 February 1984, aged 13.
Cause: Karmic. Saturn dominates the chart from the 9H of moral judgements. This was a karmic, teaching/ learning experience.
Organ: heart - immune system the Sun, Mars; white cells the Moon.
Effect: immune deficiency. The body's ability to produce immune-fighting cells (Moon) was subverted (conjunct Uranus that rules the 6H of health). This destroyed the fighting power of the immune system (Pluto conjunct the Sun, and sesquiquadrate Mars), leaving the body defenceless against invading pathogens (Saturn). Vetter was kept isolated from the world to save his life, in an oxygen bubble (Mercury, ruler of the ascendant is in the 12H of isolation). Mercury and Gemini rule oxygenation.

▲ (C) Saturn. (O) Sun, Mars, Moon. (E) Uranus, Pluto, Saturn.

Astro.com 7221 (20 March 1933, 05:50, Tacoma WA)
American child, immune deficient, requiring constant hospital treatment.
Cause: karmic. The Moon in Capricorn represents a karmic cause.
Organ: heart - immune system, the Sun and Mars.
Effect: immune deficiency. The body was unable to produce white immune blood cells from bone marrow (the Moon is afflicted in Capricorn, and opposes Pluto in Cancer). The result was an immune system (the Sun and Mars) that was rendered useless (Neptune that is afflicted in Virgo is conjunct Mars and disposits the Sun; it is sesquiquadrate the Moon and semi-square Pluto). The body was left defenceless against invading pathogens.

▲ (C) Moon in Capricorn. (O) Sun, Mars. (E) Pluto, Neptune.

e. Ebola virus

Ebola is a deadly virus, placed in this chakra section because its primary attack is on the heart chakra organs. It is caught by contact with body fluids of an infected person, including sweat, blood etc. It damages the immune system and organs and inhibits blood-clotting so that uncontrollable bleeding occurs.

Ameyo Adadevoh (27 October 1956, Lagos Nigeria)
Unknown time, 12 PM midday used and the 0 degrees Aries House System.
Female Nigerian physician who died of ebola on 19 August 2014.
Cause: epidemic. Adadevoh harboured emotional tension and conflict that was debilitating (the Sun square Uranus-Moon), rendering her susceptible to viral attacks (the Sun conjunct Neptune) and epidemics (Uranus-Moon).
Organ: heart - cardiovascular organs, the Sun, Leo.
Effect: ebola. The virus attacked blood cells and spread through the body via the bloodstream (the Neptune-Sun point is sesquiquadrate Mars), damaging cardiovascular organs (square Uranus in Leo). There was massive haemorrhaging (Mars inconjunct the Moon, which is conjunct Uranus).

▲ (C) Moon, Uranus. (O) Sun. (E) Neptune, Mars, Uranus.

- The attack of the virus on the body in August 2014 is shown by solar-arc Mars that had reached 13 Taurus, square the Moon at 13 Leo. When she died, transit Mars had joined them to form a t-square from 14 Scorpio.

4d.4. Lung Cancer

Although the lungs are part of the respiratory system governed by the throat chakra, the heart chakra shares rulership of the lungs, particularly the lower lobes. The following quote helps to clarify the differences.

> If the patient should be suffering from difficulty in the heart or the lungs the healer will use the heart centre, employing the throat centre for diseases of the bronchial tract... [1]

To ascertain which centre a lung disease belongs to, examine whether the Sun (heart) or Mercury (throat) is most afflicted by planets that represent the disease. Smoking (Neptune) is the primary cause of lung cancer. In these two examples, Neptune squares the Sun, which is why they are in the heart section.

Brian Keith (14 November 1921 02:00, Bayonne NJ)

American film and television actor who worked successfully in the industry for 60 years. During the latter part of his life, Keith suffered from emphysema and lung cancer, despite having quit smoking ten years earlier. Ironically, he had appeared in an endorsement campaign for Camel cigarettes in 1955. On June 24 1997, he shot himself to avoid suffering a cancer death.

Cause: emotional. Keith was highly disciplined (Scorpio Sun semi-square Saturn rising), and repressed his emotions (Saturn conjunct Mars in Libra) to maintain a semblance of balance in his life. He smoked (Neptune square the Sun) to help relieve tension and obviously did not know at that time, that smoking was carcinogenic and was going to affect his health (Neptune co-rules the 6H of health with Pisces sharing the cusp).

Organ: heart - the lungs, the Sun.

Effect: lung cancer. A combination of emotional repression and smoking caused carcinogenic cell changes in the lungs (Neptune > Sun), which led to lung cancer (the Sun semi-square Jupiter). Not wanting to face the suffering of a slow death that cancer brings, he shot himself (Mars rules guns, and the 8H of death with Aries on the cusp).

▲ (C) Mars, Saturn, Neptune. (O) The Sun. (E) Jupiter.

- When Keith shot himself, transit Mars was in the 1st house that rules the head, and was beginning to move over natal Saturn and Mars. He took action to avoid having to go through the prolonged pain and suffering that accompanies cancer.

Rosemary Clooney (23 May 1928 02:30, Maysville KY).

American singer who came to prominence in the early 1950's with songs such as 'Come On-a My House'. A long-time smoker, Clooney was diagnosed with lung cancer at the end of 2001. Despite surgery, she died six months later on June 29 2002. Her nephew, George Clooney was a pallbearer at her funeral, which was attended by numerous stars.

Cause: emotional. A bubbling Gemini Sun person, underneath Clooney was very sensitive and suffered anxiety attacks (the Sun square Neptune in Leo). Smoking helped relieve the tension, but exacerbated health problems.

Organ: heart - the lungs, the Sun.

Effect: lung cancer. Smoking was dangerous for Clooney's health because Neptune, which rules smoking, is located in the 6H of health. It also co-rules the 12H of hospitals with Pisces sharing rulership of the cusp. Smoking had a malignant effect on the lungs, causing carcinogenic changes in cells (Neptune > Sun in Gemini) that resulted in malignant cancerous growth (Pluto and the Moon in Cancer, midpoint the Sun and Neptune). It killed her (Pluto rules the 8H of death).

▲ (C) Neptune. (O) Sun. (E) Neptune, Moon-Pluto in Cancer.

1 Bailey, Alice A; Esoteric Healing, 602.

4e. Solar Plexus Chakra Diseases

The solar plexus chakra rules the pancreas glands, mid-region digestion and the emotions. It causes trouble in all other chakras and many examples of this have been included in this section. The solar plexus receives energy from ray 6 primarily, and also from Cancer, Virgo, Mars, Neptune and the Moon.

4e.1. Allergies

An allergy is a hypersensitive response to a substance that is normally harmless. The immune system over-reacts, producing antibodies that cause cells to release too many chemicals, causing the reaction. The condition is related to the fight or flight syndrome, governed by the sympathetic nervous system, which is in turn governed by the solar plexus chakra. Fear, fright and frustration are emotions associated with allergies.

a. Allergic to anaesthetics

Jean-Pierre Chevenement (9 March 1939 23:00, Belfort FR)

A French politician in the 80's and 90's. On 2 September 1998, he suffered a heart attack after an allergic reaction to an anaesthetic administered for gall bladder surgery. It left him in a coma for eight days.

Cause: emotional. Chevenement was intensely sensitive and emotionally reactive to things he disliked. This affected his immune system response, making it also super-sensitive (Sun in Pisces opposite Neptune).

Organ: heart - the immune system, the Sun.

Effect: allergic reaction. Chevenement's immune system (the Sun) reacted suddenly and violently and his body went into shock (sextile Uranus afflicted in Taurus), when given an anaesthetic. He went into a coma (Neptune).

▲ (C) Pisces, Neptune. (O) Sun. (E) Uranus, Neptune.

- In September 1998, when he had his violent reaction, solar-arc Neptune was stationed on the ascendant at 20 Scorpio, rendering his whole organism super-sensitive generally and to drugs in particular.
- The progressed Sun was in the 6H of health at 17 Taurus, conjunct progressed Uranus at 17 Taurus. The shock of his body's reaction caused the heart attack.
- Jupiter, the "lucky" planet, was transiting back and forth over 20 Pisces during 1998, conjunct his natal Sun and trine solar-arc Neptune and ascendant. While this contributed to the over-reaction, it also helped him to survive.

b. Anaphylaxis - allergic to bee stings

A severe, potentially life-threatening allergic reaction.

Karen, Astro.com (16 July 1945, 01:35, Cleveland OH)

American female seriously allergic to bee stings so that she must treat herself immediately or she could die.

Cause: emotional. Extreme emotional sensitivity and reactivity (Moon conjunct Neptune and sesquiquadrate Mars), due to a fear of being hurt (Moon squares Saturn and is septile Mars); underlies Karen's reaction to bee stings (Mars).

Organ: heart - the immune system, the Sun.

Effect: allergic reaction. Mars, a ruler of the solar plexus chakra, the immune system and of insect attacks, is in the 1st house that rules the physical organism as a whole. It is in detriment in Taurus indicating that her physical and emotional reactions can be extreme (Mars > Saturn, which is conjunct the Sun). Her violent reaction to bee stings is a physical equivalent to how she felt emotionally when she was traumatised as a child (Saturn conjunct the Sun on the 4H of family cusp).

▲ (C) Moon, Neptune, Mars, Saturn. (O) Sun. (E) Mars.

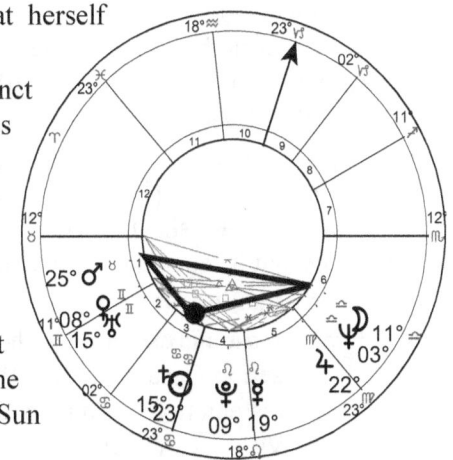

c. Allergic to gluten - celiac/ coelic disease

Celiac disease is an autoimmune condition triggered by consuming gluten. Some symptoms are diarrhoea and bloating. An inability to digest life at some level is related to allergic reactions to food.

Jane Swift (24 February 1965, 07:48, North Adams MA)

First female Governor of Massachusetts had many medical examinations before being diagnosed with celiac disease.

Cause: emotional. Any autoimmune attack is triggered by a self-attack at some level. Swift had high ideals (Moon in Sagittarius in the 9H of morals), and criticised herself when she fell short of her idea of perfection (square Mars in Virgo). This had health repercussions in the gut (Virgo in the 6H of health).

Organ: solar plexus - intestines, Virgo.

Effect: allergic reaction. Self-criticism caused the immune system to attack the intestines causing diarrhoea (Mars in Virgo), and bloating (Moon inconjunct Jupiter).

▲ (C) Moon, Mars. (O) Virgo planets. (E) Mars, Jupiter.

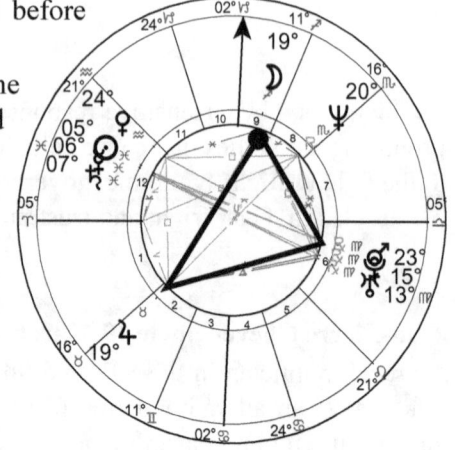

d. Allergic to milk

Astro.com 6814 (18 October 1930 10:00; 41n27, 79w40)

American infant, normal at birth, who died suddenly at six weeks of age on 28 November 1930, of milk poisoning.

Cause: karmic. There are 3 planets in Cancer, which rules digestion, in the 8H of inheritances, opposed by karmic Saturn (by sign). Psychologically, the pattern points to difficulty giving and receiving emotional nourishment. This occurred in a previous life, the Moon rules the past. In the current life, it manifested as repudiation by the body for the most basic source of nourishment for babies - mother's milk (Moon).

Organ: solar plexus - digestion the Moon, intestines Virgo.

Effect: allergic reaction. Milk was toxic to this child (Moon conjunct Neptune in detriment in Virgo, semi-square Mars and Pluto in Cancer), and the intestines would not absorb it (Virgo).

▲ (C) Moon, Neptune, Saturn. (O) Moon, Virgo. (E) Saturn, Pluto, Neptune.

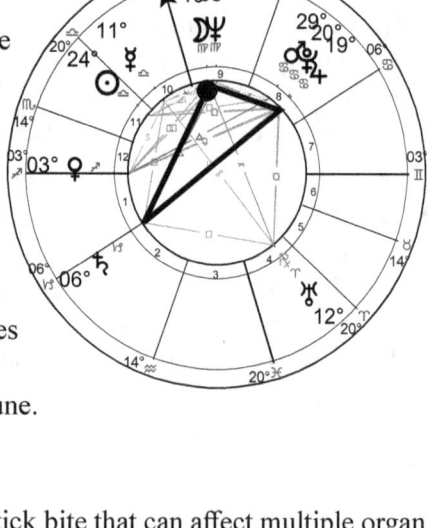

e. Lyme Disease

Lyme disease (borreliosis) is an inflammatory bacterial infection caused by a tick bite that can affect multiple organ systems. It is placed in this section because Mars, which rules insect bites, rules the solar plexus chakra.

Yolanda Hadid (11 January 1964, Papendrecht, Netherlands)

Unknown time, 12 PM midday used and the 0 degrees Aries House System.

US "reality" star in the TV show the 'The Real Housewives of Beverly Hills'. Hadid was diagnosed with lyme disease in 2012 and suffers debilitating exhaustion.

Cause: emotional. Deep exhaustion is a 4th ray problem, the result of chronic inner conflict. Hadid's inner child is constantly trying to flee and be free of (Moon in Sagittarius), a critical, menacing presence (square Pluto-Uranus in Virgo). This is an after-shock of a childhood trauma. The Moon's location is approximate, but it squared the 2 malefics throughout the day.

Organ: heart - vitality, Mars.

Effect: lyme disease and exhaustion. She was bitten by a tick (Mars), causing a bacterial infection (sesquiquadrate Pluto-Uranus). But the true cause of her exhaustion is emotional. Hadid's unresolved issues keep gnawing away at her "guts" (Virgo), cannibalising her energies.

▲ (C) Moon, Pluto, Uranus, (O) Mars. (E) Pluto.

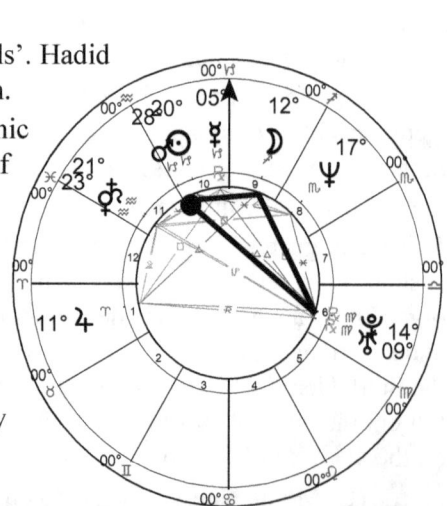

4e.2. Gallbladder and Stomach

a. Acid Reflux

Mark Spitz (10 February 1950, 17:45, Modesta CA)

Cause: emotional. Olympic swimming champion Spitz had acid reflux. Competition (Moon in Sagittarius, the sign ruling the 5H), caused nervousness that affected his digestive system (semi-square Mercury).

Organ: solar plexus - digestion, the Moon and Mercury.

Effect: digestive. The muscles (Mars) that should keep acid in the stomach (Moon) were weak (Mars in detriment in Libra, trine retrograde Venus) and were not doing their job. A liking for alcohol (Neptune conjunct Mars), sweet, fatty and fast-foods (trine Jupiter and Venus in the 6H of diet) contributed to his acid reflux problem (Mars > Jupiter).

▲ (C) Moon. (O) Moon, Mercury. (E) Mars, Jupiter.

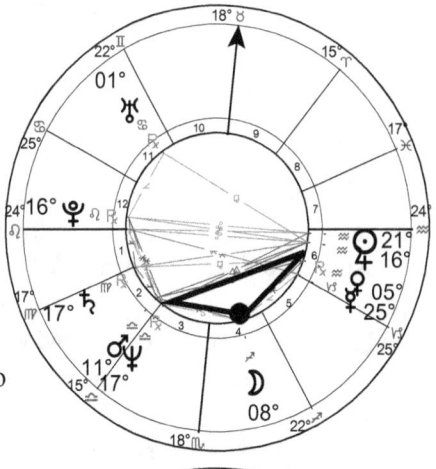

b. Food poisoning

Harry Shaw (7 May 1916 03:00, Port Bannatyne Scotland)

80 year old Scottish pensioner, who died from food poisoning (E-coli).

Cause: emotional. Shaw had violent emotional reactions (Mars) to things he did not like (opposite Uranus) and this disturbed his digestive system (Mars, ruler of the solar plexus chakra in the 6H of health).

Organ: solar plexus - digestion, Cancer.

Effect: digestive. At a social lunch (Venus in Cancer), virulent bacteria lurked in the food (conjunct Pluto sesquiquadrate Uranus). It attacked the bowel (Pluto semi-square Mars), putting Shaw into hospital (Mars > Uranus 12H), where he died.

▲ (C) Mars, Uranus. (O) Cancer. (E) Uranus, Pluto

- On 26 November 1996 when Shaw died, the natal pattern was triggered by transit Uranus. It was in the 12H at 1 Aquarius, inconjunct Pluto at 1 Cancer.

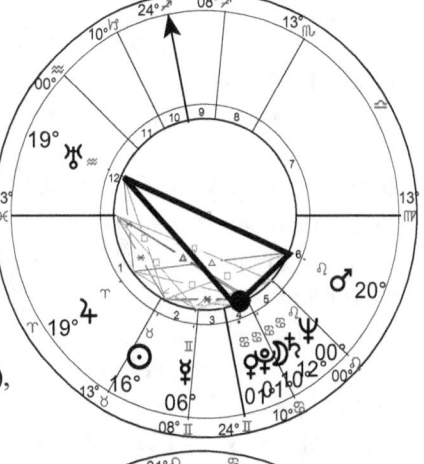

c. Gallstones

Eric Clapton (30 March 1945, 20:45, Ripley UK)

English rock and blues guitarist, singer, and songwriter had surgery in October 2009 to remove gallstones.

Cause: emotional. Trouble is shown in a t-square: he repressed his emotions (Saturn in Cancer) to avoid grief (Neptune) and pain (the Sun in Aries in the 6H of health).

Organ: solar plexus - gallbladder, Saturn in Cancer.

Effect: gallstones. His repression caused gallstones.

▲ (C) Saturn in Cancer, Neptune. (O) Saturn in Cancer. (E) Saturn, Sun.

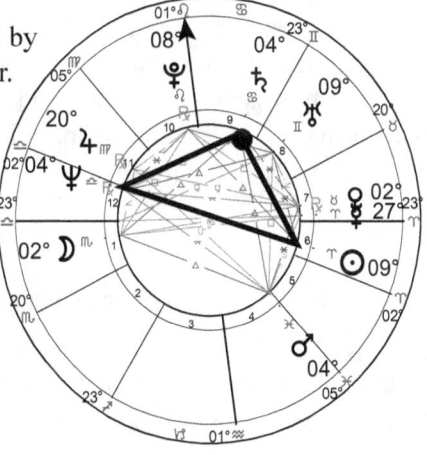

d. Stomach Ulcers

Nat King Cole (17 March 1919 03:00, Montgomery AL)

Cole collapsed from stomach ulcers in 1953.

Cause: emotional. In confrontations, Cole's natural instinct was to keep the peace (Moon in Libra). To do so he repressed his anger (t-square: Moon, Mars, Pluto), backing up emotional toxicity that caused trouble later.

Organ: solar plexus - stomach, the Moon.

Effect: ulcer. Repressed anger manifested as corrosive acid that burnt its way through the stomach lining (Mars > Pluto in Cancer in the 6H of health).

▲ (C) Moon, Mars, Pluto. (O) Moon. (E) Pluto in Cancer

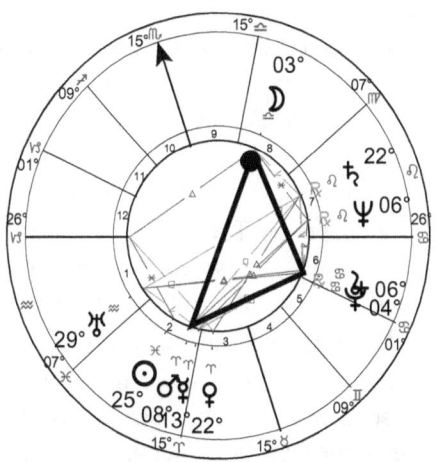

4e.3. Liver

a. Cirrhosis

In cirrhosis of the liver, healthy cells are replaced by scar tissue, impairing liver function. Excessive alcohol consumption is a primary cause of liver cirrhosis, but it can also occur through hepatitis or fatty liver disease.

Billie Holiday (7 April 1915, 02:30, Philadelphia PA)
American jazz singer. She suffered from long term drug and alcohol abuse, developing cirrhosis of the liver and dying of the disease on July 17 1959.
Cause: emotional. Holiday was an insecure and emotional Negro woman growing up in racist America (Moon in detriment in Capricorn, opposite Neptune in Cancer, the sign ruling the USA). She self-medicated with alcohol to alleviate anxiety (Neptune 6H of health).
Organ: solar plexus - liver, Jupiter.
Effect: cirrhosis. Alcohol and drug abuse (Neptune), damaged Holiday's liver beyond repair (sesquiquadrate Jupiter; the Moon is in the 12H of serious illnesses septile Jupiter), and she died of liver disease.
▲ (C) Moon, Neptune. (O) Jupiter. (E) Neptune.

Florence Aadland (20 September 1914 23:50, Salt Lake City UT)
American mother of teenage ingénue Beverly Aadland, who had an affair with ageing actor Errol Flynn. An alcoholic, she started bleeding internally from cirrhosis of the liver and died 10 May 1965.
Cause: emotional. With a Libran Moon and ruler Venus in the 5H of pleasure, partying and drinking helped Aadland overcome her emotional insecurities (Saturn and Pluto in Cancer in the 12H of hidden things).
Organ: solar plexus - liver, Jupiter.
Effect: cirrhosis. Excessive alcohol consumption damaged the liver (Jupiter that rules the 6H of health squares Venus, and is inconjunct the ascendant, which in turn is conjunct Pluto and Saturn). Cirrhosis developed, the liver haemorrhaged and she died (Jupiter is conjunct Uranus in the 8H of death).
▲ (C) Moon, Saturn-Pluto in Cancer. (O) Jupiter. (E) Neptune, Uranus.

b. Hepatitis A

The Hepatitis A virus is spread when traces of faeces containing the virus is ingested through food or water. The liver becomes inflamed, there may be nausea, vomiting and fatigue, but its effect is usually short lived.

L1004 (30 June 1944, 14:04, Gisborne NZ)
New Zealand woman from a large family that lived in a rural, farm setting, caught hepatitis-A as a child.
Cause: emotional. An emotional Cancer stellium person who preferred to hide away from the world (Moon in the 12H of hidden things). She was hypersensitive, defensive and susceptible to viruses (Cancer planets square Neptune).
Organ: solar plexus - liver, Jupiter.
Effect: hepatitis. The Hep-A virus was picked up through eating contaminated food (Neptune square the Cancer planets). The liver was infected (the Cancer planets semi-square Jupiter) and she was sick for a few months.
▲ (C) Cancer planets. (O) Jupiter. (E) Neptune.

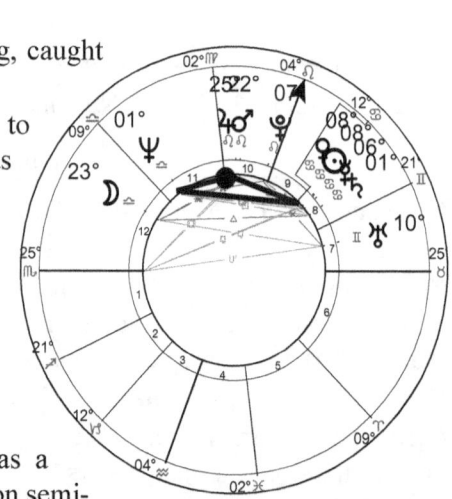

In later life, the subject developed a fatty-liver condition most likely as a consequence of eating dairy foods - especially milk, in large quantities (Moon semi-square the Cancer planets).

c. Hepatitis C

The Hepatitis C virus is most commonly spread through contact with infected blood. It is dangerous. About 85% of hepatitis C infections lead to chronic liver disease, cirrhosis of the liver or liver cancer.

L1005 (7 October 1953, 1:28)

Australian male who contracted the Hep-C virus through intravenous drug use in the late 1970's and early 80's, before he finally broke the habit in 1984. In 2013, he had chemotherapy to kill the virus.

Cause: emotional. Jupiter is in detriment in Gemini, which indicates the liver is not as robust as it could be. Psychologically, the negative force generated by self-criticism (Moon in Virgo, square Jupiter), and unresolved emotional issues (the Moon rules the 12H of self-undoing), will lodge in the organ.

The addictive pattern is Moon square Jupiter (a habit of excess). The Moon is in the third, Taurus decanate, the sign related to the desire pleasure centres in the brain.

Organ: solar plexus - liver, Jupiter.

Effect: hepatitis. The Hep-C virus (Neptune), entered the body through contact with contaminated blood (sextile Pluto in Leo), lodging in the liver (trine Jupiter).

▲ (C) Moon. (O) Jupiter. (E) Neptune, Pluto.

- 1979-1983. The drug addiction phase began in 1979. Solar-arc Jupiter (excess), conjunct Uranus at 22 Cancer (excessive experimentation), and squared natal Neptune at 23 Libra (with drugs). Simultaneously, solar-arc Moon moved over Neptune (becoming addicted).

    During 1980-81, this was followed by transit Neptune in the 5H of pleasure at 22 Sagittarius, inconjunct solar-arc Jupiter and natal Uranus at 22 Cancer.

    Then in 1982-83, transit Neptune moved back and forth opposite natal and progressed Jupiter at 25-26 Gemini. During this period of his addiction, he caught the Hep-C virus.

- 1984. He "went cold turkey" on 21 January 1984. The ascendant, "soul purpose", had just progressed into Virgo and the 2nd house - it was time to begin a new phase in life, develop a new and higher set of Christ values to live by. He had the will to do it - Saturn, ruler of the 6H of health and of healing, was transiting over the progressed Sun at 13 Scorpio. He persevered and broke the addiction.

- In 2012, tests showed the liver was close to developing cirrhosis. By now, solar-arc Pluto had reached natal Neptune at 23 Libra, triggering the infection in a malignant way. Simultaneously, solar-arc Jupiter (the liver) was moving over natal Pluto (potential cirrhosis); and solar-arc Neptune was at 22 Sagittarius inconjunct natal Uranus (energising the virus).

- In 2013, February, he started 7 months of chemotherapy. Pluto rules death and it killed the virus. The natal aspect (Pluto in Leo {which rules cell life}, sextile Jupiter), promised treatment would go well and that his liver could be "reborn" and it has. During this period, he went through his second Saturn return - a new cycle started. He also had a Jupiter return which boosted his liver health.

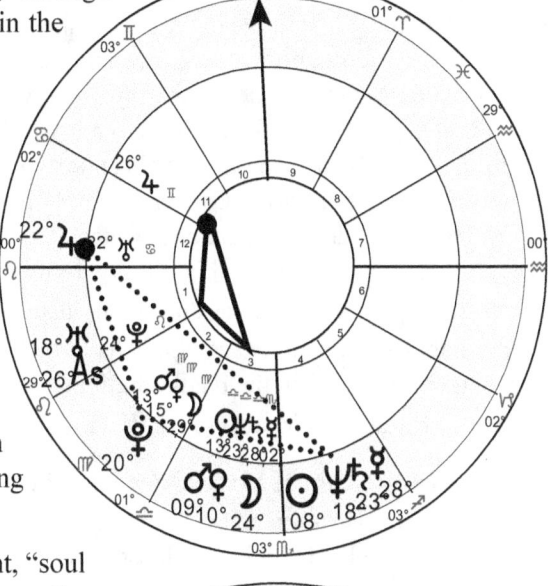

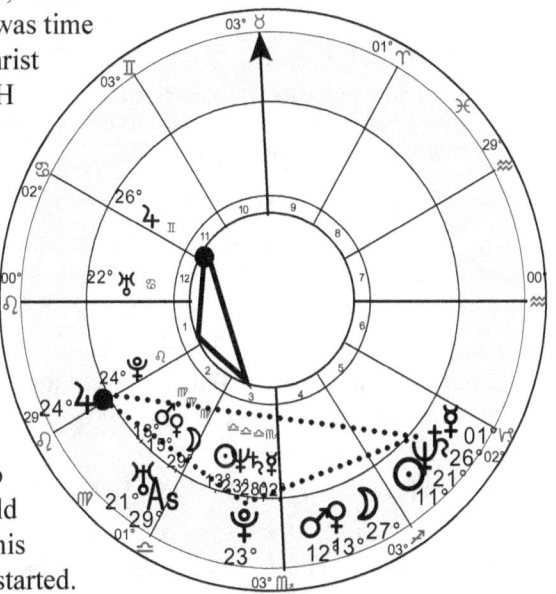

Higher chart, natal; outer solar-arc directions 1st chart 1979, lower chart 2012.

4e.4. Pancreas

a. Diabetes

Common type-2 diabetes is commonly linked to a diet high in fats or sugars so that the body's ability to use insulin to regulate blood sugar levels is impaired. However, Djwhal Khul said that "diabetes is more definitely the result of wrong inner desires and is not so definitely the result of wrong outer desires". [1] This means it is the inner desire and craving for love or other form of inner satisfaction, which then usually manifests as eating "comfort" food that is the cause of common diabetes. Khul goes on to say that "Cancer and diabetes are more definitely in the class of diseases which are connected with inner emotional desires and the violent suppressed wish-life". [2] This seems to fit type-1 diabetes where the immune system violently attacks and destroys insulin-producing cells.

Linda Goodman (9 April 1925, 06:05, Morgantown WV).
Goodman was the astrology author of 'Sun Signs', which sold paperback rights for a record-breaking $225 million. But she was bankrupt when she died on October 21 1995, from complications of diabetes.

Cause: emotional. Goodman's Moon is in Libra, in the 7H of intimate relationships. She was paranoid about her relationships (opposite Venus in Aries, in the 12H of hidden things. Venus squares Pluto). Friends said she would ask them to spend the night so that she did not have to be alone.

The fact Goodman died bankrupt and developed diabetes tells us she did not value herself as being worthy for love. Money, love, values and diabetes are all ruled by Venus. Perhaps a lover abandoned her, reinforcing a negative belief about being unlovable and triggering a violent suppression of her wish/ love life (Pluto in Cancer square Venus). This, and the foods she ate, contributed to the development of diabetes. People who feel deprived of love often seek comfort by eating foods high in sugar and carbohydrates, which Venus rules.

Organ: solar plexus - pancreas the Moon, insulin by Venus.

Effect: diabetes. At some stage, the cells in the pancreas were unable to absorb insulin (Venus), because of serious trouble (square Pluto) in the regulating function (Moon in Libra opposite Venus), and diabetes developed.

▲ (C) Moon. (O) Moon, Venus. (E) Pluto in Cancer.

Halle Berry (14 August 1966, 23:59, Cleveland OH) Type 1
Beautiful African-American actress has type-1 diabetes. During the taping of the TV series 'Living Dolls' in 1989, she lapsed into a diabetic coma. Shortly afterwards she was diagnosed and is insulin-dependent.

Cause: emotional. With the Moon in Leo, Berry was born with a natural self-confidence. But virulent criticisms directed at her in her childhood left their mark on her psyche (Moon in the 4H of family, semi-square Uranus and Pluto in Virgo), to resurface later as an autoimmune attack.

Organ: solar plexus - pancreas the Moon, insulin Venus.

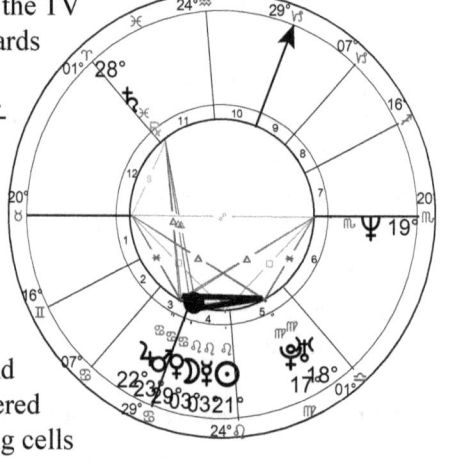

Effect: diabetes. The disease appeared when she was an adult - perhaps a lover (planets in the 5H of romance), repeated the abuse that occurred when she was a child, triggering a negative core belief that she was unworthy and unlovable (Moon-Venus > Pluto-Uranus). The subliminal self-attack triggered an autoimmune attack (Mars) that targeted the pancreas and insulin producing cells (Mars is in Cancer, conjunct Venus and the Moon). Diabetes developed (Venus rules the 6H of health with Libra on the cusp).

▲ (C) Moon, Virgo. (O) Moon, Venus. (E) Mars, Uranus, Pluto.

- In 1988 and early 1989, solar-arc Venus had moved onto the natal Sun at 21 Leo, triggering her emotional and self-hate issues. This is when diabetes surfaced.

---

[1] Bailey, Alice A; Esoteric Healing, 311.
[2] Bailey, Alice A; Esoteric Healing, 312.

b. Hypoglycaemia

Nicole Richie (21 September 1981 04:10, Berkeley CA)

American TV personality diagnosed with hypoglycaemia while filming the reality show The Simple Life in early 2007. The condition occurs when sugar levels are too low. She has been treated for drug addiction, which is a known cause.

Cause: emotional. Richie is super-sensitive emotionally (a Cancer Moon that is quindecile Neptune) and insecure in love (Neptune semi-squares Venus). Her childhood was very unstable (Uranus in the 4H), and there could have been hidden abuse (Mars that rules the 4H, is in the 12H of hidden things square Venus). Life stabilised and became more exciting, when pop-star Lionel Richie adopted her (Uranus sextile the Sun).

Organ: solar plexus - pancreas, Venus and the Moon.

Effect: hypoglycaemia. Richie self-medicated with drugs and alcohol (Moon > Neptune) and developed hypoglycaemia (Moon trine Venus that is afflicted in Scorpio).

▲ (C) Moon, Neptune. (O) Moon, Venus. (E) Neptune.

c. Pancreatitis

Pancreatitis is severe pain caused by an inflamed pancreas. Heavy alcohol consumption is a known cause of the trouble. Anger over the loss of love or sweetness in life is related.

Ernst, Prince of Hanover (26 February 1954 07:22, Hanover Germany)

Husband of Princess Caroline of Monaco, Ernst has been described as "a drunken, thuggish brawler". In April 2005, he suffered acute pancreatitis.

Cause: emotional. With the Moon in Sagittarius conjunct Mars, Ernst' natural impulse when he feels threatened is to strike out, to get others before they get him, and this is at the root of his problem. He is a sensitive Pisces personality who drinks alcohol to relieve anxiety and fear; who strikes out at life to protect himself.

Organ: solar plexus - pancreas, the Moon.

Effect: pancreatitis. Anxiety contributes to excessive drinking (Mars opposite Jupiter), which inflames (Mars) the pancreas (Moon).

▲ (C) Moon, Mars. (O) Moon. (E) Mars, Jupiter.

• When Ernst collapsed in 2005, solar-arc Uranus had reached 10 Virgo, squaring the natal Moon, symbolising the attack on the pancreas.

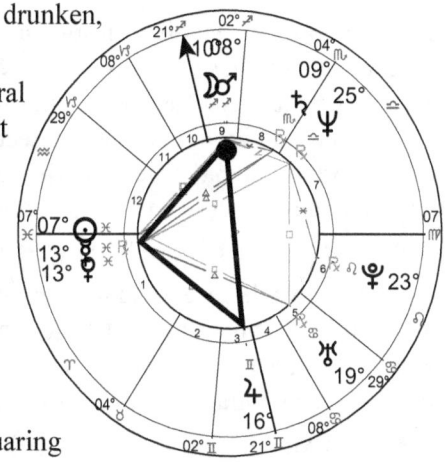

Freddie King (3 September 1934 12:00, Gilmer TX)

Freddie King was an American blues guitarist and singer, one of the "Three Kings" of electric blues guitar, along with Albert and B. B. King. Described as "living hard and drinking copiously", he died on December 28 1976, from acute pancreatitis.

Cause: emotional. King was a hyper-sensitive Cancer Moon person who masked his insecurities with alcohol (the Moon is sextile Neptune, and Mars is conjunct Pluto in Cancer).

Organ: solar plexus - pancreas, Venus.

Effect: pancreatitis. Alcoholic poisoning (Neptune in Virgo), seriously damaged his pancreas (Venus that rules the 6H of health, is midpoint Neptune and Pluto in Cancer). It put him into hospital, where he died (Pluto rules the 12H of hospitals and is in the 8H of death).

▲ (C) Moon, Mars. (O) Venus. (E) Neptune, Pluto

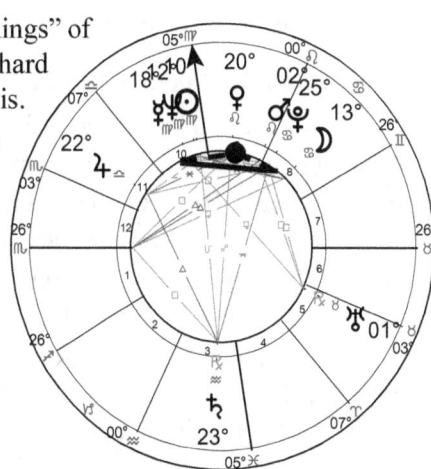

4e.5. Intestinal, Bowel

a. Colitis

The autoimmune system attacks the inner lining of the colon.

John F. Kennedy (29 May 1917 15:00, Brookline MA)

Charismatic USA president, Kennedy was diagnosed with colitis in 1934.

Cause: emotional. Kennedy was born with a self-criticising pattern (a Virgo Moon), which caused the trouble. He felt unloved by his father (the Moon rules the 10H, and is semi-square Neptune, which conjuncts Saturn), and resented having to enter politics to further his family's political (Uranus) ambitions (Mercury conjunct Mars square Uranus in the 4H of family).

Organ: solar plexus - colon, Mercury and Mars.

Effect: colitis. In response to his inner unhappiness, the immune system turned rogue (Mars in detriment in Taurus), and attacked the bowel (conjunct Mercury), causing diarrhoea, abdominal cramping and spasms (Mars > Uranus).

▲ (C) Moon. (O) Mercury, Mars. (E) Mars, Uranus.

b. Crohn's disease

A chronic inflammatory bowel disease of the digestive tract lining. An abnormal response from the immune system is the possible cause. Anal retention, holding onto one's "shit" is the psychological cause.

Mary Ann Mobley (17 February 1937, 16:00, Biloxi MS)

American beauty queen, diagnosed with Crohn's disease in 1962.

Cause: emotional. Mobley's instinctual impulse is to stand stubbornly firm and not give in - she has a Taurus Moon. While she needed inner strength to rise above secret family abuse (easy-opposition Moon-Mars-Pluto, touching the 4th and 10th family houses and the secretive 12th); it also meant she would hold onto the trauma of her experiences and find it hard to move on. This pattern underlies her bowel trouble. She holds onto her "shit".

Organ: solar plexus - bowel, Mars, Pluto.

Effect: Crohn's disease. Like so many victims, Mobley blamed and attacked herself for her family traumas, triggering an immune attack (Mars). Her inner pattern manifested as an attack on the walls of the bowel (Moon > Pluto and Mars), causing inflammation and diarrhoea.

▲ (C) Moon. (O) Mars, Pluto. (E) Mars, Pluto.

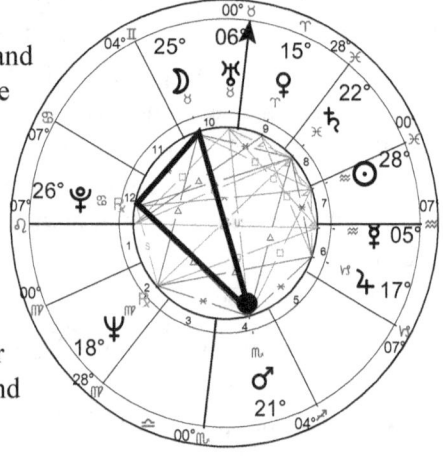

c. Diverticulitis

Constipation can lead to the development of diverticula, small sacs or blisters in the lining of the colon. If they are infected, it's called diverticulitis, causing pain and disturbed bowel function.

Jack Nicklaus (21 January 1940, 03:10, Columbus OH)

Golf great Jack Nicklaus was hospitalized in October 2010 for severe abdominal pain and was diagnosed as having diverticulitis.

Cause: emotional. With Scorpio rising and Pluto in a t-square with Saturn, the Sun and Mercury, Nicklaus faces life defensively. He stubbornly holds on to issues and absorbs anger and this is related to his bowel trouble.

Organ: solar plexus - bowel, Pluto.

Effect: diverticulitis. Stubbornness translated into constipation. Diverticula blisters developed in bowel walls (Pluto trines Jupiter and Mars in Aries) and became infected (Jupiter semi-squares Uranus).

▲ (C) Scorpio ascendant. (O) Pluto. (E) Saturn, Sun, Mars.

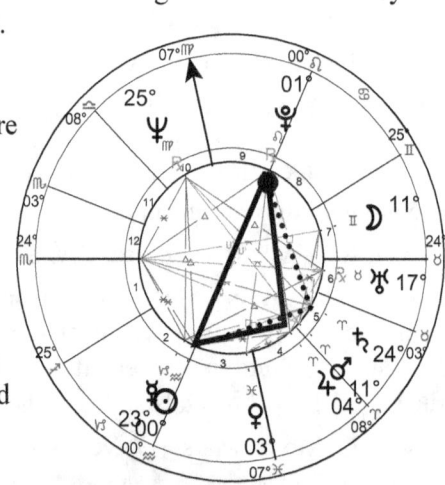

d. Haemorrhoids

Haemorrhoids are swollen or bulging veins around the anus. They can develop from straining during bowel movements, particularly as we age.

Karl Marx (5 May 1818, 02:00, Trier Germany)

Prussian-German revolutionary socialist, Marx had haemorrhoids. Writing to his friend Friedrich Engels he said, "To finish 'Das Kapital' I must at least be able to sit down. I hope the bourgeoisie will remember my carbuncles."

Cause: emotional. Marx was a fighting idealist (Mars in Cancer), a stubborn Taurus personality who was angry about the injustices suffered by the masses (Mars opposite Jupiter in the 11H of social affairs). Through his writings (semi-square Mercury, he argued for social change, for greater fairness and equality (Mars is septile Venus).

Organ: solar plexus - veins Venus, anus Mars.

Effect: haemorrhoids. Marx's stubbornness caused high blood pressure (Saturn-Pluto in Pisces square Uranus-Neptune), and congestion in the lower digestive region (Mars in Cancer). He developed inflamed haemorrhoids (opposite Jupiter), in veins (septile Venus) around the anus (Mars for Scorpio).

▲ (C) Mars in Cancer. (O) Venus, Mars. (E) Mars, Jupiter.

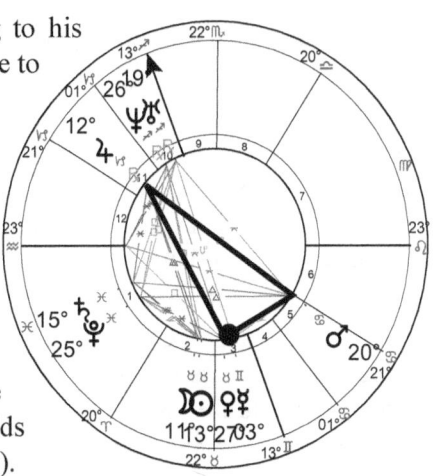

e. Cholera

Cholera is an infectious disease caused by consuming food and water contaminated by the faeces of people infected with the bacteria (Uranus). It strikes the gut causing severe diarrhoea (Mars) and dehydration (Saturn).

President Zachary Taylor (24 November 1784 10:57, Barboursville VI)

American politician who was the 12th President of the United States of America. After 16 months in office he died suddenly on 9 July 1850, from cholera

Cause: karmic. It was likely that the epidemic which claimed Taylor was group karma rather than individual. Lord of Karma, Saturn, is in the 12H of the masses, opposite Uranus in Cancer a sign that is also related to the masses. He picked it up while attending to his political responsibilities.

Organ: solar plexus - intestines, Mercury.

Effect: cholera. Taylor caught cholera (Uranus), spread through contaminated food and water (in Cancer, in the 6H of diet and health). It attacked his intestines (sesquiquadrate Mercury). Dehydrated (Saturn), and suffering with diarrhoea (Uranus in Cancer), he died (Mercury rules the 8H of death with Virgo on the cusp).

▲ (C) Saturn. (O) Mercury. (E) Saturn, Uranus.

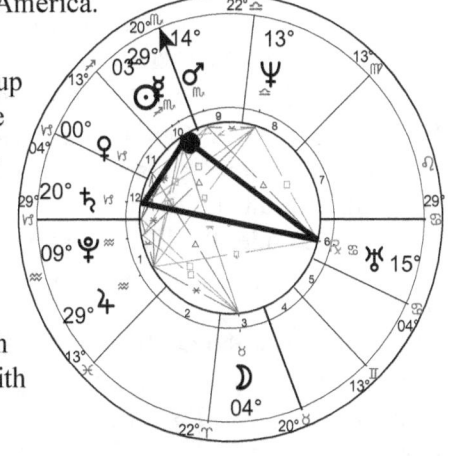

Victor Jaquemont (8 August 1801 23:00, Paris FR)

French botanist and geologist who went to India in 1828. He died of cholera in Bombay on 8 December 1832.

Cause: epidemic. Jaquemont's work took him to places and amongst people where viruses and epidemics flourished (Neptune in the 6H of work semi-square Uranus).

Organ: solar plexus - intestines, Mercury.

Effect: cholera. He caught cholera, a bacterial infection of the gut (Uranus in Virgo), by drinking water (semi-square Neptune in the 6H of health), contaminated by faeces (Neptune in Scorpio). The infection killed him (Neptune square Jupiter, ruler of 8H of death).

▲ (C) Uranus. (O) Mercury. (E) Uranus, Neptune.

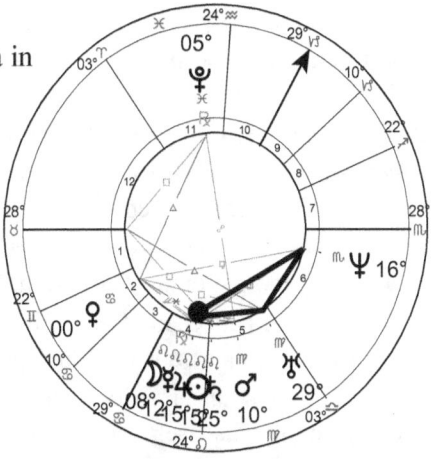

4e.6. Cancer in the Solar Plexus Organs

a. Breast cancer

Breast cancer primarily affects women, but men can get it too. Associated negative core beliefs are those of a belief in being unlovable, of not being worthy to receive love or emotional nourishment.

Jill Ireland (24 April 1936 19:00, Hounslow UK)

Ireland was a British actress who was diagnosed with breast cancer in 1984 and died of the disease on 18 May 1990.

Cause: emotional. Ireland suppressed her emotions (t-square: the Moon squares Saturn and Neptune), and rationalised her feelings (the Moon is in cerebral Gemini), to avoid a negative belief that she was unlovable (Neptune inconjunct Venus afflicted in Aries). This pattern underlies her illness.

Organ: solar plexus - breasts, the Moon and Venus.

Effect: breast cancer. Congestion (Saturn) in the solar plexus chakra (in Pisces), caused carcinogenic changes (opposite Neptune) in breast tissue (Moon, Venus in the 6H of health). She developed cancer, which killed her (the Moon is in the 8H of death).

▲ (C) Moon, Saturn, Neptune. (O) Moon, Venus. (E) Neptune.

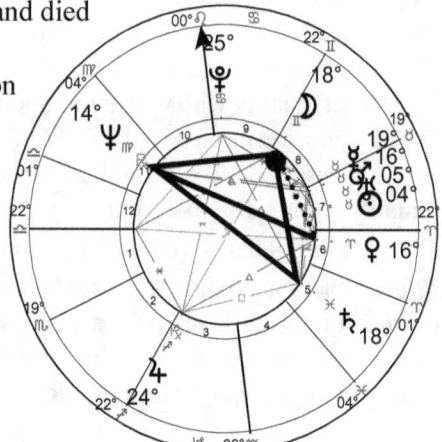

Linda McCartney (24 September 1941 10:00, New York NY)

Married to rock star Paul McCartney, Linda was diagnosed with breast cancer in 1995. It quickly spread to the liver and she died 17 April 1998.

Cause: emotional. McCartney was very intense emotionally (the Moon conjunct Venus in Scorpio), and her chart shows she harboured a negative belief about love causing pain and destruction (Venus square Pluto). In spite of a happy marriage, the fact that she developed breast cancer shows that she repressed this fear rather than healed it.

Organ: solar plexus - breasts, the Moon and Venus.

Effect: breast cancer. Carcinogenic (Neptune) changes occurred in breast tissue (semi-square Venus and septile the Moon, both of which are afflicted in Scorpio). It resulted in malignant cell growth and cancer (Neptune and Pluto in Leo. Venus rules the 12H of major illnesses).

▲ (C) Moon, Pluto. (O) Moon, Venus. (E) Pluto, Neptune.

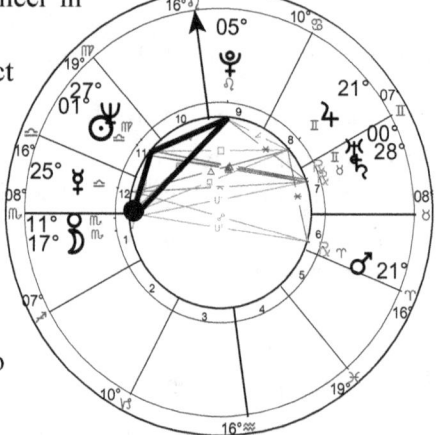

Olivia Newton John (26 September 1948 06:00, Cambridge UK)

Pop star and movie actress, John was successfully treated for breast cancer in July 1992, which included a mastectomy. In May 2017 it was announced she had stage 4 breast cancer that had spread to her lower spine.

Cause: emotional. Emotionally fragile (the Moon conjuncts Uranus in Cancer), John was (is) terrified that she would lose love, and if love died or left her, she could not survive the hurt (the Venus-Pluto conjunction is midpoint the Moon and Uranus on one wing and Neptune on the other).

Organ: solar plexus - breasts, the Moon and Venus.

Effect: breast cancer. Disruption in the solar plexus chakra (Uranus-Moon in Cancer > Neptune), caused carcinogenic changes (Neptune) in breast tissue (Moon in Cancer), and a malignant cancerous growth formed (Pluto, Neptune).

▲ (C) Moon, Uranus. (O) Moon, Venus. (E) Pluto, Uranus, Neptune.

- The onset of cancer in 1992 is shown by solar-arc Moon moving over natal Pluto at 15 Leo. Jupiter transiting through the 12th and 1st houses in this period helped her heal.
- In 2017, the solar-arc Moon-Uranus point had reached 9-11 Virgo, midpoint Venus-Pluto and the Sun. This re-energised the disease pattern. The Sun rules the spine, to which cancer has spread.

b. Bowel/ Colorectal and Rectal Cancer

Robin Gibb (22 December 1949, 03:15, Douglas, Man of Isle)

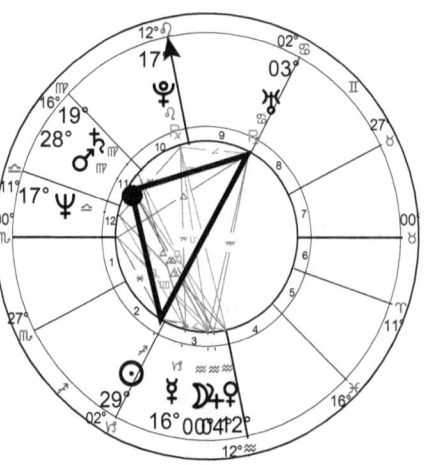

Gibb was a member of the pop group The Bee Gees. He died 20 May 2012, from liver and kidney failure brought on by colorectal cancer.

Cause: emotional. Mars in Virgo is a classic symbol for holding onto one's "shit" because of an anal/ narrow/ critical view of the world. This pattern underlies Gibb's trouble. Mars rules the 6H of health.

Organ: solar plexus - colon, Mars.

Effect: colon cancer. T-square: colon (Mars) cells (Sun), turned aberrant (opposite Uranus), began to rapidly multiply (Sun in Sagittarius), and he died from cancer (Sun semi-square Venus, ruler of the 8H of death).

▲ (C) Mars. (O) Mars. (E) Sun, Uranus.

Tammy Bakker (7 March 1942, 03:27, International Falls MN)

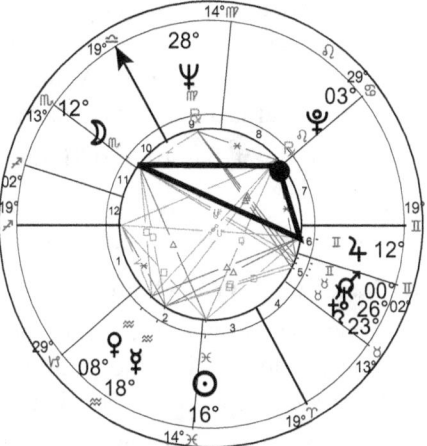

American Christian evangelist had rectal surgery on 6 March 1996.

Cause: emotional. Bakker held onto the rage she felt when her televangelist husband was convicted of fraud in 1989 and accused of sexual indiscretion (Moon square Pluto in Leo in the 8H of sex).

Organ: solar plexus - colon, Moon in Scorpio and Pluto.

Effect: colon cancer. Emotional conflict congested the solar plexus, causing carcinogenic changes in tissue in the rectum (Moon in Scorpio > Pluto), causing cancer (inconjunct Jupiter 6H). She had surgery and lived for another 8 years, dying July 20 2007.

▲ (C) Moon, Pluto. (O) Moon in Scorpio, Pluto. (E) Pluto, Jupiter.

Ada Phillips (4 May 1908 16:30, Brighton UK)

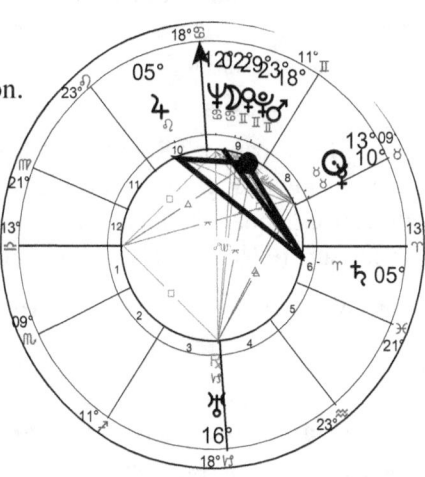

British astrologer, who died 9 December 1996, from rectum cancer.

Cause: emotional. The 5-planet stellium can be read as a group conjunction. In the 9H of higher mind we get the sense of mental congestion (3 planets are in Gemini), and emotional repression (Moon square Saturn in the 6H of health). With the rulers of the bowel involved (Mars, Pluto and the Moon), congestion occurred, causing cellular trouble in that region.

Organ: solar plexus - rectum, Pluto and Mars.

Effect: rectum cancer. Carcinogenic changes in bowel tissue (Pluto-Mars, Saturn square the Moon), migrated into rectal cancer (Jupiter semi-square Pluto, trine Saturn).

▲ (C) Moon, Saturn. (O) Pluto, Mars. (E) Jupiter.

c. Gallbladder Cancer

Iain Banks (16 February 1954, 04:10, Dunfermline UK)

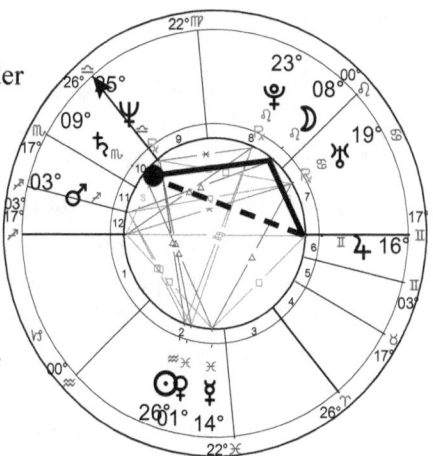

Scottish author, who on 3 April 2013, announced he had inoperable gall bladder cancer. He died 9 June, of that year.

Cause: emotional. Bank's chart shows great disappointment and resentment over failed career and life opportunities (the Moon squares Saturn in the professional 10H), which bred bitterness and toxicity. It caused congestion (Saturn) in the solar plexus chakra (Moon) and this affected the gallbladder.

Organ: solar plexus - gallbladder, the Moon and Saturn.

Effect: cancer. Cells (Moon in Leo), in the gallbladder (square Saturn), began to overbuild, resulting in cancer (the Moon is septile Jupiter in the 6H of health), which killed him (the Moon is in the 8H of death).

▲ (C) Moon, Saturn. (O) Moon, Saturn. (E) Jupiter.

d. Pancreatic Cancer

Pancreatic cancer is highly dangerous because there are often no symptoms until it is advanced. It kills most people by spreading to the liver, which then fails.

Donna Reed (27 January 1921 14:00, Denison Iowa)

American movie actress, Reed was diagnosed with pancreatic cancer in 1985, dying a few weeks later of the disease on January 14 1986.

Cause: emotional. The arc of trouble in Reed's chart is the 5-planet opposition group from the 10th to the 4th houses. It contains two rulers of the pancreas (Moon and Venus). Repression of emotion was the cause of the trouble (Saturn conjunct the Moon, and both opposing Venus in Cancer).

Organ: solar plexus - pancreas, the Moon and Venus.

Effect: pancreatic cancer. Congestion in the solar plexus caused carcinogenic changes in pancreatic cells (the Moon opposing Venus in Pisces); causing cell over-growth and cancer (Venus opposes Jupiter that is afflicted in Virgo, and semi-squares the Sun that carries the "over-building" ray 2).

▲ (C) Moon, Saturn. (O) Moon, Venus. (E) The Sun, Jupiter.

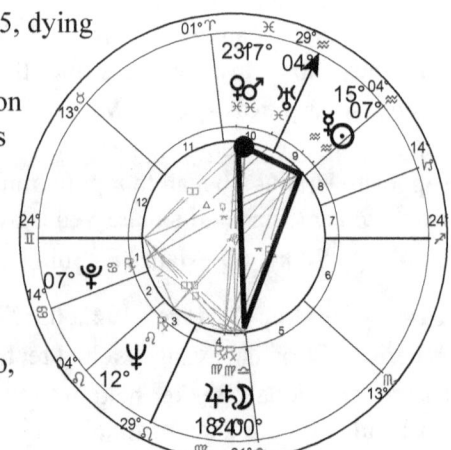

e. Liver cancer

Michael Landon (31 October 1936, 12:12, Jamaica NY)

American star of the TV programme 'The Little House on the Prairie'. In February 1991 he was told he had inoperable pancreatic cancer, which had metastasized to his liver and lymph nodes. He died 1 July 1991.

Cause: emotional. Self-criticism and repression of anger (t-square: Jupiter square Neptune-Mars and Saturn), caused trouble in the abdominal organs (Mars and Neptune in Virgo).

Organ: solar plexus - liver, Jupiter.

Effect: liver cancer. Repression coupled with heavy drinking, caused carcinogenic changes (Mars conjunct Neptune) in liver cells that migrated into cancer (square Jupiter). The cancer had metastasized from the pancreas (Venus square Neptune), spreading also into the lymph nodes (Neptune).

▲ (C) Mars, Saturn. (O) Jupiter. (E) Jupiter, Neptune.

f. Stomach Cancer

George Santayana (16 December 1863, 21:00, Madrid Spain)

Spanish-American philosopher and poet who died of stomach cancer in September 1952. He had a lifelong, unrequited passion for a straight man.

Cause: emotional. Santayana was a homosexual (Uranus), who hid his sexual preference from the public (square the Moon that rules the 12H of hidden things). This and his unsatisfied desire for the man he loved caused the trouble.

Organ: solar plexus - stomach, the Moon.

Effect: stomach cancer. Emotional-sexual repression and frustration for not being able to slake his sexual appetite for the one he desired (Uranus > Moon in the 8H of sex, inconjunct Saturn); manifested as carcinogenic tissue growth in the stomach and cancer (Moon in Pisces). It killed him (the Moon is in the 8H of death).

▲ (C) Moon, Saturn. (O) Moon. (E) Uranus, Pisces.

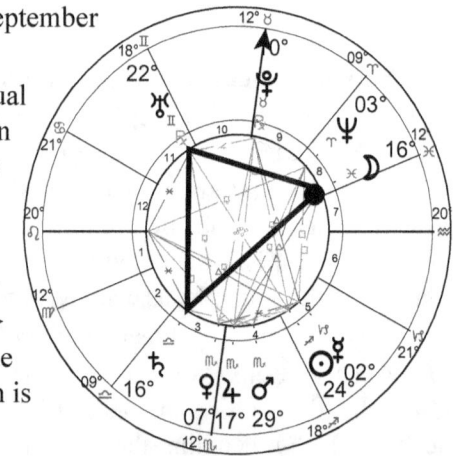

4e.7. Psychological Disorders

The nervous system is controlled principally today from the astral body, via the etheric, and the basis of all nervous trouble lies hidden in the emotional body. [1]

a. Anorexia Nervosa

The psychological problem associated with anorexia is "glamour", a condition where troubled emotions distort perception. When we have a glamour problem, we see and believe whatever we want to see and believe. In anorexia, body-image is distorted. The anorexic person has an obsessive desire to lose weight and achieves this by refusing to eat. It is an unhealthy way of trying to cope with emotional problems.

Karen Carpenter (2 March 1950 11:45, New Haven CT).

American member of the Carpenters singing duo in the 1970's, Karen developed anorexia and died from heart failure caused by complications related to the illness on 4 February 1983.

Cause: emotional. Carpenter was deeply emotional and intense and because she developed terminal anorexia, we know was also deeply troubled (menacing Pluto sitting on the Moon). We do not know the circumstances but there may have been abuse in the family (retrograde Mars is in the 4H of family, in detriment in Libra, square Uranus). Emotional trauma connected with her childhood lay at the root of her anorexia trouble (Moon > Pluto).

Organ: solar plexus - emotions, the Moon.

Effect: anorexia. As part of her disorder, Carpenter's self-worth was tied to her appearance, her body image (Moon, ruler of the 2H of values, semi-square the ascendant). She wanted to lose weight to look better, to gain people's approval so that she would be loved. To this end she used her will to suppress her appetite (Pluto that rules the 6H of health and diet, is conjunct the Moon).

▲ (C) Moon, Pluto, Mars. (O) Moon. (E) Pluto, Uranus, Mars.

Carpenter's heart was damaged (Pluto in Leo, Saturn opposite the Sun) and she died. Saturn rules the 8H of death.

Gelsey Kirkland (29 December 1952 09:36, Fountain Hill PA).

American ballerina who was top of the ballet world in the mid-70's. It ended with emotional problems, anorexia and addiction to cocaine. Trouble started at age 8, when she was unfavourably compared to her sister. She said "It made me withdraw. I developed a lot of inhibitions, complexes about my eyes, my nose, my complexion".

Cause: emotional. Kirkland intellectualised her emotions (Moon in Gemini). She brushed aside hurt feelings and determined to work as hard as she could to ensure people would think she was as pretty and talented as her sister (the Moon trines Venus and Mars in the 1H of appearances).

Organ: solar plexus - emotions, the Moon.

Effect: anorexia. Obsessed with her "unattractive" looks (Pluto opposite Venus in the 1H), she had cosmetic surgery (Mars in the 1H of appearances), she took drugs (Mars trine Neptune), and stopped eating (Pluto > Moon and Cancer on the 6H of diet). Controlling what she ate helped her feel she was in control of her life.

▲ (C) Moon, Pluto. (O) Moon. (E) Mars, Pluto.

Kirkland made peace with herself and in 2017 was in a happy relationship and back in New York running a successful ballet school.

1 Bailey, Alice A; Esoteric Healing, 107

b. Attention-deficit/hyperactivity disorder (ADHD)

ADHD is a combination of problems such as inattention, hyperactivity and impulsive behaviour

Russell Brand (4 June 1975, 0:00, Grays UK).

British comedian and actor who was diagnosed with ADHD and bipolar. In his earlier years he drank excessively and took drugs.

Cause: emotional. Chronic hyperactivity stems from emotional instability and volatility (Moon-Mars in Aries, Mars is quindecile Uranus). His energies were chaotic and needed grounding. Brand has no natal planets in earth signs and drugs made things worse (the Aries planets trine Neptune).

Organ: ajna - the nervous system, Mercury.

Effect: ADHD. Brand's over-stimulated nervous system kept his body hyper-active and on constant over-drive. His liking for sugary foods (Venus in Cancer, the sign ruling the 6H of diet), exacerbated the problem.

▲ (C) Moon, Mars, Uranus. (O) Mercury. (E) Uranus.

Brand says he has quietened down and is trying to live a decent, spiritual life. He is guided by Neptune in the 10H, a sort of North Star influence that continually encourages him to refine his energies and life expression. Additionally, five of his planets by solar-arc are slowly moving through earth signs, providing a counterbalance of stability to his fire-air, yang force.

c. Alcohol and Substance Abuse

Richard Burton (10 November 1925 15:00, Pontrhydfendigaid Wales)

Celebrated British actor who was a long term alcoholic.

Cause: emotional. Burton had a tough childhood. He was the twelfth child of an impoverished coal-miner and lost his mother when he was two years old (Pluto in the 4H). Criticised and bullied, he was unable to grieve his loss (the Sun-Saturn conjunction squaring Neptune). There was no soft place for him to fall and no kind words to encourage him (Mercury square the Moon). Consequently, he grew up with unresolved emotional trauma that was never attended to.

Organ: solar plexus - emotions, Neptune.

Effect: alcoholism. Burton self-medicated with alcohol (Neptune in the 6H), seeking oblivion from life's hardships (square the Saturn-Sun point), and painful emotions (inconjunct Uranus in Pisces in the 12H of hidden things).

▲ (C) Neptune, Saturn. (O) Neptune. (E) Sun-Saturn, Uranus.

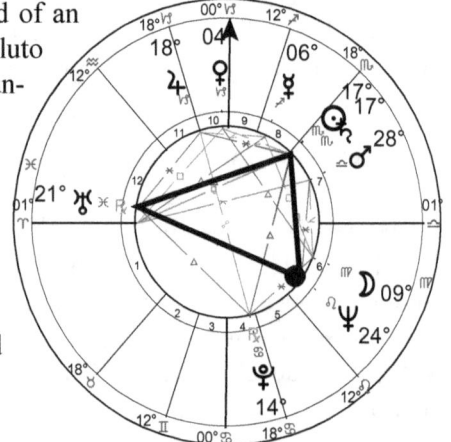

d. Bipolar (manic depression, mood swings)

Mood-swing disorders arise when the 4th Ray of Conflict, goes awry.

Vivien Leigh (5 November 1913, 17:16, Darjeeling India).

English actress best known for her Oscar-winning role as Scarlett O'Hara in the classic film 'Gone with the Wind'. Mild symptoms of bipolar were evident when she was at school in the 1920's. At 39, while filming 'Elephant Walk', she had a full breakdown.

Cause: emotional. Leigh was emotionally unstable and insecure (Moon conjunct Uranus) quite likely an inherited family pattern (quindecile the Mars-Neptune point in Cancer, which conjunct the 4H family cusp). The fact that she descended into insanity is an indication she was unable to find inner stability.

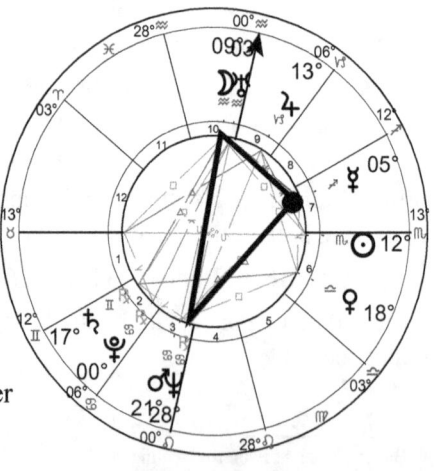

Organ: ajna - nervous system, Mercury.

Effect: solar plexus. As her star rose, Leigh's fragile grip on reality frayed. She sparkled with brilliance and wit when things were going well (Moon-Uranus on the MC, sextile Mercury), but would swing into depression when they were not and throw violent rages (Mars-Neptune). When Mercury and the Moon, which both carry ray 4 are involved in a conflict pattern, it exacerbates mood swings in emotionally susceptible people.

▲ (C) Moon-Uranus opposing Mars-Neptune. (O) Mercury. (E) Moon.

e. Bulimia Nervosa

A cycle of overeating and purging that can become an obsession if it is used to handle emotional distress.

Princess Diana 1 July 1961 19:45, Sandringham UK)

Princess Diana said in an interview, "I had bulimia for a number of years. You inflict it upon yourself because your self-esteem is at a low ebb, and you don't think you're worthy or valuable. You fill your stomach up four or five times a day - and it gives you a feeling of comfort."

Cause: emotional. Diana's troubles can be traced to her childhood. It is likely she never recovered from her mother's "abandonment" of her (Moon opposite Uranus), when she divorced Diana's father and remarried. Though she was a very emotional person (Sun in Cancer), to cope, she could split off from her feelings, compartmentalising those she did not want to deal with and lock them away (the Moon is in Aquarius, which carries the 5th ray that dissociates). But repressed emotions prevent us from developing healthy emotional expression and Diana was very shy and immature when she married sophisticated Charles. As we know now, it was a total mismatch (Jupiter, ruler of Diana's ascendant is inconjunct the 7H ruler of marriage, Mercury).

Organ: solar plexus - emotions, the Moon.

Effect: bulimia. The emotional hurts she stuffed away came up anyway - via her food. Diana would eat for comfort, then vomit it all up (Uranus > Moon; the Moon disposits Mercury that rules the 6H of diet and is inconjunct Jupiter).

▲ (C) Moon, Uranus. (O) Moon. (E) Sun, Mercury, Uranus.

- When Diana died in the infamous car crash in Paris on 31 August 1997, progressed Mercury, one of the rulers of the 8H of death, was in the 8th house at 5 Leo. Mercury rules transport and the suddenness of the accident is shown by transit Uranus at 5 Aquarius, opposing Mercury.

f. Cutting

Self-injury is an unhealthy way to cope with emotional pain, anger and frustration.

Amy Winehouse (14 September 1983 22:25, Enfield UK)

Talented English rocker and soul singer who had "criss-cross scars and scratches" up and down her left arm, 'People' magazine reported. A video showed her scratching her exposed midriff with a shard from a broken mirror.

Cause: emotional. Winehouse's feelings of emotional deprivation, of being without comfort, are shown by the Moon's location in the cold and icy realm of Capricorn. She felt lost (conjunct Neptune), unloved and abandoned (the Moon and Neptune square the Sun-Mercury point in Virgo in the 5H of romance). She perpetuated the problem with negative self-talk and criticism.

Organ: solar plexus - emotions, the Moon.

Effect: self-harm. Winehouse self-medicated with alcohol and drugs (Neptune); she cut herself because at the time it felt good (trine Mars conjunct Venus).

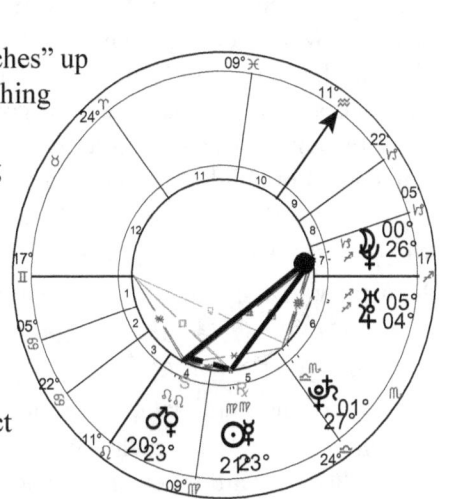

▲ (C) Moon, Neptune. (O) Moon. (E) Mercury, Neptune, Mars

- When Winehouse died in 23 July 2011, her progressed Moon was at 6 Capricorn and had just entered the 8H of death and transformation. Simultaneously, Saturn, the ruler of the 8H of death, had transited to 11 Libra in the 5th house of "pleasure". She died of an overdose while seeking "a high".

g. Obsessive compulsive disorder (OCD)

OCD is an anxiety disorder. Sufferers feel compelled to take certain actions, to repeatedly do something to avoid something bad happening. This helps to alleviate anxiety.

Astro.com 37914 (26 August 1958 14:30, 37S55, 145E Australia)

Australian female with OCD. "She has sought professional help over a period of many years from a variety of medical and alternative practitioners and is becoming suicidal in her desperation to find a cure or satisfactory means of controlling her disorder, a sad and desperate woman."

Cause: emotional. The Moon/ the astral nature, dominates perception (the Moon is conjunct the ascendant). She sees life through a prism of negativity, pessimism and despair (the Moon is in detriment in Capricorn). This is at the root of the problem - the Moon co-rules the 6H of health.

Organ: solar plexus - emotions, the Moon.

Effect: OCD. Driven by an anxiety disorder (Moon square Neptune), she is compelled to take action (trine Mars), to avoid something bad happening (Mars inconjunct Saturn on the 12H cusp of the unknown).

▲ (C) Moon, Neptune. (O) Moon. (E) Mars.

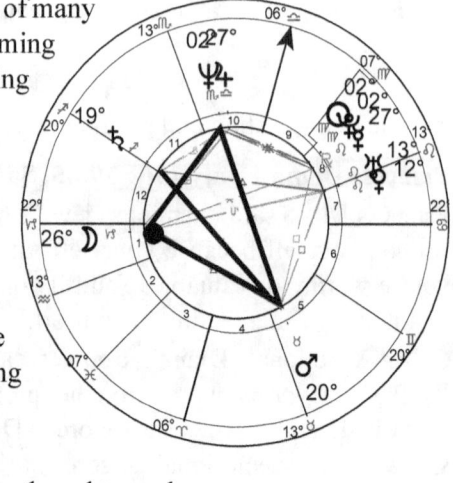

Stabilising the emotional nature. This woman is captive to her neurotic thoughts and feelings and needs help to break the negative cycle. Cognitive therapy or esoteric counselling from a kind and skilled practitioner to help expose untruths she believes about herself or unresolved emotional wounds that require healing, would help relieve tension and stabilise the nature. An active physical life with outdoor walks, swims and gentle Sun exposure will strengthen the etheric body and vitality. The home should be kept clean, bright and airy with beautiful music played. If marked improvement is made, then a simple meditation like building a beautiful garden would help restore emotional balance and bring inner quietness.

h. Panic-attack - Agoraphobia

A panic attack is a sudden overwhelming feeling of acute and disabling anxiety. Accompanying physical symptoms are sweating and a racing heart.

Susan, Astro.com 44645 (13 December 1958, 23:05, Scunthorpe UK)

British woman who has panic attacks that last for minutes. After an attack, she is afraid to go out for several days. Her symptoms began after her son was born and she suffered post-partum depression. By 1996, her attacks became too overwhelming for her to handle even with medication.

Cause: emotional. Susan disconnects from her emotions, from her deeper feelings (Moon in Aquarius square Neptune), and trauma (inconjunct Pluto in the 12H of self-undoing). This means she drags these unresolved emotions around like baggage. It is possible that her pregnancy triggered a past life memory of pain and suffering connected with childbirth (the Moon is in the 5H of children, inconjunct Pluto), hence her reaction.

Organ: solar plexus - emotions, the Moon.

Effect: panic attack. Until Susan gets in touch with her deeper feelings and heals them she will continue to suffer from panic attacks.

▲ (C) Moon, Neptune, Pluto. (O) Moon. (E) Pluto.

- During 1994 and 1995, solar-arc Neptune was passing over natal Mercury at 12 Sagittarius. This indicates the power of the astral nature over the mind, clouding rationality and enhancing emotionalism.
- Solar-arc Pluto had reached 10 Libra, conjunct the progressed ascendant at 11 Libra, and for a few years they travelled forward together. This added serious paranoia to her perception and accentuated her belief she was in serious physical and psychological danger.
- By 2002 as solar-arc Pluto moved away from the progressed ascendant, things should have started to improve, her perceptions of life had a chance to stabilise.

i. Post-traumatic stress disorder (PTSD)

PTSD is triggered by a terrifying event, with symptoms that may include flashbacks, nightmares and severe anxiety about the event. During an episode, researchers have found that the amygdala part of the brain that is key to the normal expression of emotions - especially fear, is highly active. At the same time the rationalising part seems ineffective.

John Mulligan (2 June 1950, 05:00 BST, Kirkintilloch UK).

Scottish-American ex-soldier who wrote about the horrors he witnessed in Vietnam. He came away with severe post-traumatic stress disorder.

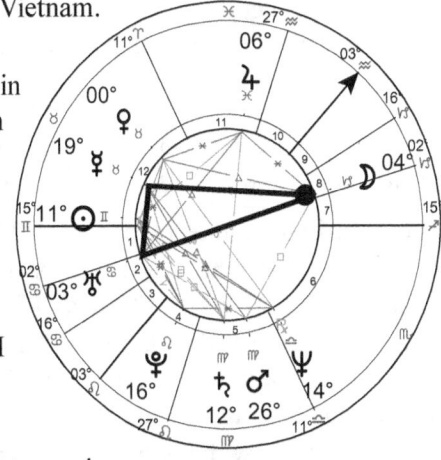

Cause: emotional. Mulligan was born with a depressive pattern (Moon in Capricorn) and emotions that react violently to trauma (opposite Uranus in Cancer). So it is not surprising he suffered from PTSD as a consequence of his experiences in the Vietnam War.

Organ: solar plexus - emotions the Moon; ajna - mind Mercury.

Effect: PTSD. During an attack, the emotion producing amygdala (the Moon), becomes highly active (opposite Uranus). Simultaneously, the rationalising mind is rendered ineffective, neutered by the emotions (Mercury in the 12H of hidden things is sesquiquadrate the Moon and semi-square Uranus).

▲ (C) Moon, Uranus. (O) Moon, Mercury. (E) Uranus.

- In the first few years Mulligan was in Vietnam, the solar-arc ascendant was in Cancer, moving over natal and progressed Uranus and opposite natal Moon. This emphasises the shattering effect that the horrors he was experiencing had on his psyche.

- In the final months in Vietnam, his progressed Sun had reached Uranus, indicating the complete change in his personality due to his war experiences.

j. Schizophrenia and Psychosis

Schizophrenia involves a breakdown between thought, emotion and behaviour. The result is a withdrawal into delusion. It usually appears in teenage years or early adulthood.

Vincent Van Gogh (30 March 1853 11:00, Zundert Netherlands)

Brilliantly talented Dutch artist, Van Gogh lived his brief life in misery and poverty. Disappointed in love and religion, he was intense, difficult and unhappy. In October 1889, he was put in an asylum. His doctor encouraged him to keep painting and flying into a creative frenzy he completed 70 canvases in 70 days. Six months later, while painting in a wheat field, he shot himself and died two days later on 29 July, 1890.

Cause: emotional. Van Gogh's violent and unstable emotional body (Moon in Sagittarius conjunct Jupiter, square Mars in Pisces) dominated his nature and his approach to life (the Moon carries the 4th ray of conflict and it rules the ascendant). The personality was not integrated or developed (an unaspected Sun), which means his personal will was not strong enough, nor was his intellect, to bring a moderating influence to his emotional swings and excesses.

Organ: solar plexus - emotions the Moon and Mars; ajna - mind Mercury.

Effect: schizophrenia. Dominated by his emotional life, it was easy for Van Gogh to believe that the dark, phantom images rising from his unfettered imagination (Pluto is conjunct Mercury, the ruler of the 12H of self-undoing), were real. He lived in delusion.

▲ (C) Moon, Mars. (O) Moon, Mars, Mercury. (E) Pluto.

- When Van Gogh shot himself, he could no longer cope with his inner demons. His progressed Moon was at zero degrees Taurus, conjunct natal Pluto.

4f. Sacral Chakra Diseases

The sacral chakra rules the reproductive glands, sex and reproduction. It receives energy primarily from rays 7 and 6, also ray 3. Sagittarius, Scorpio, Mars and Uranus are the main rulers while the Moon and Venus are influential for female reproduction and sex.

4f.1. Genetic Diseases

A genetic disorder is caused by an abnormality in DNA, especially a condition that is present from birth (congenital). DNA is the genetic or karmic map on which the foetus is modelled. It reflects any diseases or defects being passed on by parents. Ray 7 that flows via Uranus, rules DNA.

a. Achondroplasia: disproportionate Dwarfism

Achondroplasia, or disproportionate dwarfism (usually abnormally short legs), accounts for about 75% of all dwarfism. Cartilage does not convert to bone in this genetic bone growth disorder.

Peter Dinklage (June 11 1969, 01:37 Point Pleasure NJ)
American actor who has lately been acclaimed for his portrayal of Tyrion Lannister in the TV series 'Game of Thrones'.
Cause: genetic-emotional. Jupiter that represents growth is afflicted in Virgo. This suggests that in a previous life, Dinklage was emotionally stifled and stunted due to virulent and demeaning criticism (Moon conjunct Saturn).
Organ: ajna - growth hormone Venus; heart - growth, the Sun, Jupiter.
Effect: dwarfism. His physical growth was affected. A corrupted gene (Pluto conjunct Uranus), inhibited the pituitary growth hormone (sesquiquadrate Venus that is conjunct Saturn). Consequently bone (Saturn) growth was stunted (semi-square the Sun; Pluto is conjunct Jupiter and squares the Sun).

▲ (C) Uranus; Moon-Saturn. (O) Venus, Sun, Jupiter. (E) Pluto, Saturn.

b. Cystic Fibrosis

A protein that controls how salt and water move through cells is flawed. Thick mucus clogs organs and airways. There are constant respiratory infections.

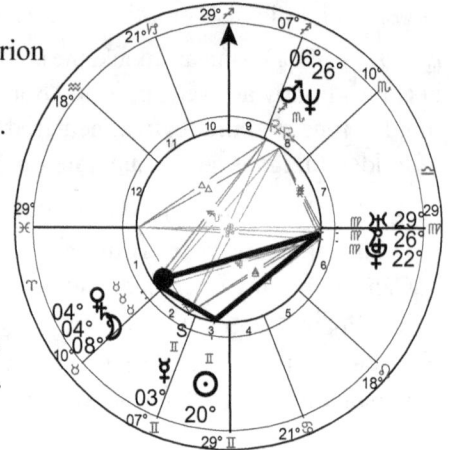

Annie Tulcin (14 June 1953 17:36, New York NY).
American woman born with cystic fibrosis.
Cause: genetic-emotional. Impaired water movement in the body suggests emotional congestion that drowns (Saturn-Neptune).
Organ: throat - airways, represented by Mercury and Gemini.
Effect: cystic fibrosis. The protein (Saturn) that controls salt-water balance was perverted, mucus was too thick (Neptune conjunct Saturn in Libra, sesquiquadrate Jupiter), clogging the airways (Jupiter in Gemini; and the Saturn-Neptune point squares Mercury in Cancer).

▲ (C) Uranus, Saturn-Neptune. (O) Mercury, Gemini. (E) Saturn-Neptune, Jupiter.

Greg Lemarchal (13 May 1983 05:08, La Tronche France).
French singer who won a TV competition. Born with cystic fibrosis, in 2007 he died while waiting for a lung transplant.
Cause: genetic. Emotional congestion (Moon conjunct Mars, inconjunct Pluto conjunct Saturn), underlies the problem.
Organ: throat - lungs, Mercury; heart - the Sun.
Effect: cystic fibrosis. A flawed salt-water regulating protein (Saturn-Pluto in Libra), thickened body fluids (Moon-Mars in Taurus) and produced mucus that clogged the lungs (Moon conjunct Sun-Mercury quindecile, Uranus-Jupiter).

▲ (C) Uranus, Moon-Mars. (O) Sun, Mercury. (E) Saturn-Pluto, Jupiter.

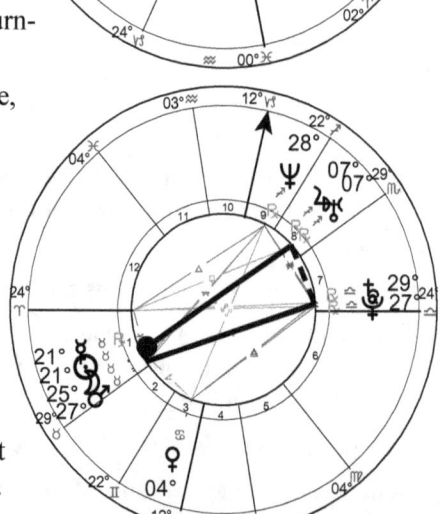

c. Down's Syndrome

A gene is composed of tiny chromosomes, each of which determines a particular characteristic. There is an extra chromosome in Down's syndrome. There may be mental disability, atypical facial structure and physical defects. Look for connections between Uranus (DNA) and Jupiter (extra). Here is a search over several Astro.com charts.
- 10068 (13 November 1945 22:01) Uranus trine Jupiter.
- 12437 (10 June 1953 02:30) Uranus semi-square Moon conjunct Jupiter
- 12768 (2 December 1954 08:22) Uranus conjunct Jupiter.
- 13234 (11 December 1957 06:14) Uranus trine Sun in Sagittarius.
- 13650 (20 March 1961 08:05) Jupiter in Aquarius.
- 13748 (4 February 1962 13:38) Jupiter in Aquarius.

Baby Doe (9 April 1982 20:18, Bloomington IL)
Cause: genetic. Uranus in Sagittarius represents the extra chromosome.
Organ: ajna - consciousness, the Sun and Mercury.
Effect: Down's. Because of the mutation, consciousness (Mercury conjunct the Sun) could not work effectively through the brain (opposite Saturn).
▲ (C) Uranus. (O) Sun-Mercury. (E) Saturn.

The baby was born with a throat fistula that blocked the alimentary tract so it could not eat. Instead of making a surgical correction, a hard-hearted hospital obstetrician advised the parents to let the baby die because its life was "not valuable". They let it starve to death.

d. Muscular Dystrophy (Duchenne)

It is caused by a faulty gene, which inhibits an essential protein for muscle growth so that muscles waste away.

Rona Barrett (8 October 1936, 04:15, New York NY)
American gossip columnist and businesswoman. As a child, she had muscular dystrophy and wore leg braces.
Cause: genetic-emotional. Uranus falls in Taurus, representing the mutated gene. It is trine Mars, the muscles, located in the 12H of self-undoing. On an emotional level this suggests a belief in being unable to cope with life. This is reinforced by the Moon-Pluto conjunction that is semi-square Mars.
Organ: base - muscles Mars.
Effect: muscular dystrophy. The gene inhibits a protein (Saturn in a t-square, in the 6H of health), so that movement is restricted (Jupiter) because muscles waste away (Neptune, wide conjunct to Mars).
▲ (C) Uranus, Mars. (O) Mars. (E) Saturn, Jupiter, Neptune.

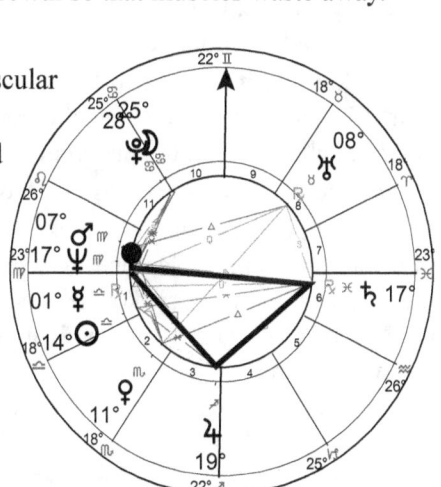

e. Progeria

Progeria is caused by a gene mutation that makes the nucleus of cells unstable, leading to premature ageing.

Peedie Snipes (10 May 1977 17:15, Burlington NC)
Snipes' hair began to fall out at age 1, he had age spots and cataracts at 3, arthritis at 13 and died of old age at 14, on 8 March 1992.
Cause: karmic: Saturn is the most exalted planet in the chart. It represents ageing and is in Leo that rules cells, square Uranus - the defective gene.
Organ: heart - cell life, the Sun, Leo.
Effect: progeria. Cell life is represented by the Sun, but it is unaspected, indicating a lack of nurturing from the life aspect. Perhaps this has something to do with the fact that it is conjunct the "evil" star Algol, the head of the Medusa at 26 Taurus. To look on it would turn the observer to stone.

Venus disposits the Sun. Afflicted in hasty Aries, trine Saturn and opposed by 1st ray Pluto; it represents the unnaturally accelerated life-span of cells.
▲ (C) Saturn. (O) Sun, Leo. (E) Venus, Pluto, Saturn.

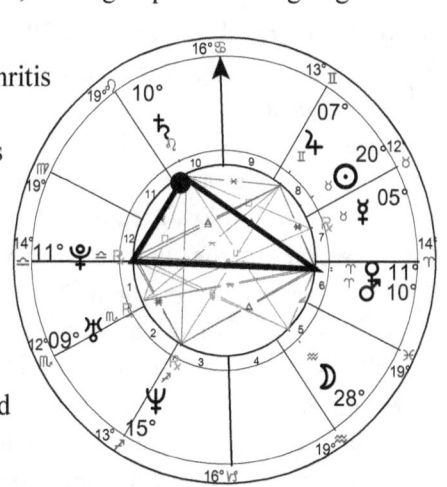

4f.2. Reproduction Problems

a. Abortion

Anais Nin (21 February 1903, 20:25, Paris France)
French female activist who had an abortion (August 21 1940), because financial circumstances were unfavourable. She was 3 months pregnant.
Cause: the mind. Although Nin was a Pisces Sun personality, her emotions were ruled by her intellect and expediency. She was non-maternal (the Moon is in chilly Capricorn conjunct individualistic Uranus).
Organ: sacral - foetus, the Moon.
Effect: abortion. The foetus was aborted (Moon conjunct Uranus opposite Pluto. Uranus rules the 5H of children). It was a clinical decision for financial reasons (Uranus square Venus that rules the 2H of money).
  ▲ (C) Venus. (O) Moon. (E) Venus, Uranus, Pluto.
• On the day of the abortion, transit Mars (the abortion), was at 1 Virgo, opposite natal Jupiter-Sun in the 5H of children.

b. Ectopic Pregnancy

The most common reason for an ectopic pregnancy is a damaged fallopian tube, causing a blockage or narrowing which prevents the egg from reaching its destination. Instead, it settles in the tube wall.

Sophie Rhys-Jones (20 January 1965, 12:46, Oxford UK)
Wife of Prince Edward, the son of Queen Elizabeth. On 6 December 2001, Sophie miscarried a two-month ectopic pregnancy.
Cause: karmic. It is difficult for Rhys-Jones to conceive or carry a baby full term. She has karma involving children - there are three malefics in the 5H of children, all crowding the maternal Moon.
Organ: sacral - fallopian tubes, the Moon, Mercury.
Effect: ectopic pregnancy. A blocked and diseased fallopian tube (Mercury in Capricorn, septile Neptune in Scorpio), caused the embryo to attach to the tube wall. It miscarried (trine Moon conjunct Uranus and Pluto). Luckily, the Moon is in a grand-trine with Jupiter. With assistance and care she now has two children.
  ▲ (C) Capricorn. (O) Moon, Mercury. (E) Neptune, Uranus, Pluto.

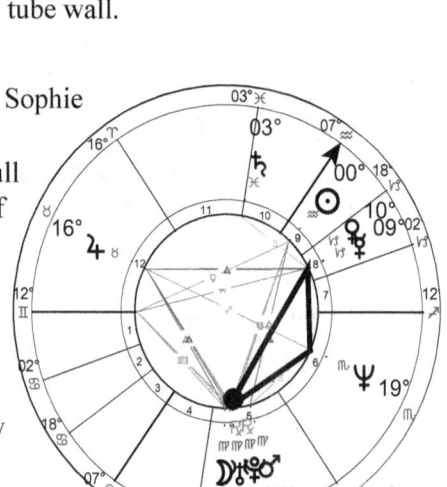

c. Endometriosis

The endometrium (inner tissue-surface of the uterus) grows outside the uterine cavity. Irregular menstrual blood flow is given as the likely cause. It results in painful periods and fertility problems.

Dolly Parton (19 January 1946, 20:25, Sevierville TN)
American singer-songwriter and actress. In 1982, Parton had a partial hysterectomy due to endometriosis.
Cause: emotional. Parton rejected her maternal side, said she was too selfish to have children (the Moon is in hyper-critical Virgo, and Saturn is in Cancer). Her attitude had a physical effect.
Organ: sacral - uterus the Moon, periods Venus.
Effect: endometriosis. Parton had very painful menstrual cycles (the Moon disposits Mars conjunct Saturn in Cancer; and Saturn opposes Venus). To remedy the problem she had a partial hysterectomy.
  ▲ (C) Moon. (O) Moon, Venus. (E) Mars, Saturn.
• In 1982, solar-arc Uranus had reach 20 Cancer and was on the natal Saturn-Mars point. This was when she had the partial hysterectomy.

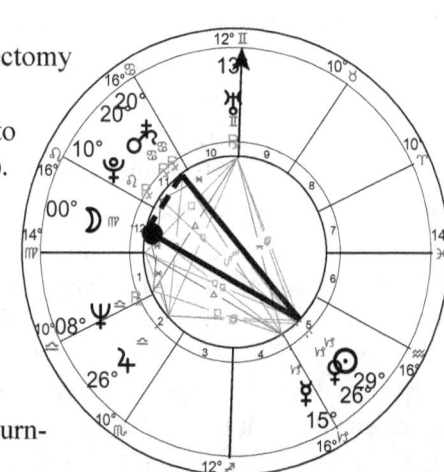

d. Hysterectomy

Althea Flynt (6 November 1953, 17:45, Marietta OH)
American publisher of Hustler magazine with her husband Larry Flynt. In 1982, she had a hysterectomy.
Cause: emotional. Flynt had deep emotional problems, a consequence of abuse suffered in her early years (the Moon is afflicted in Scorpio, in the 6H of health, square Pluto in the 4H of home). The same pattern showed serious obstacles for Flynt's hopes of motherhood.
Organ: sacral - womb, the Moon.
Effect: hysterectomy. All was not well with Flynt's uterus (Moon > Pluto), and eventually she was forced to have it removed (surgical Mars in the 5H of children, semi-squares the Moon).
▲ (C) Moon, Pluto. (O) Moon. (E) Pluto, Mars.

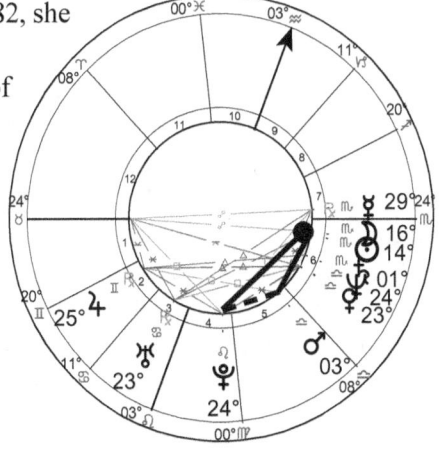

e. Infertility

Soraya (22 June 1932, 22:30, Isfahan Iran)
The second wife of the Shah of Iran. Her childless plight and divorce so the Shah could have children captured the attention of the world in the 1950's.
Cause: emotional. Conception requires a healthy and happy Moon, especially since in Soraya's chart it sits on the ascendant, a point that is also related to birth. Soraya was cool emotionally (Moon in Aquarius) and may also have been cool to the idea of having children (the Moon rules the 5H of children). Cancer planets located there include Pluto, which is hostile to children.
Organ: sacral - reproduction, the Moon.
Effect: infertile. The fallopian tubes (Mercury in Cancer), were blocked or irreparably damaged (conjunct Pluto), so that eggs (Moon), could not travel to the uterus (Moon sesquiquadrate Mercury) to be fertilised (square Mars).
▲ (C) Moon. (O) Moon. (E) Cancer planets, Mars.

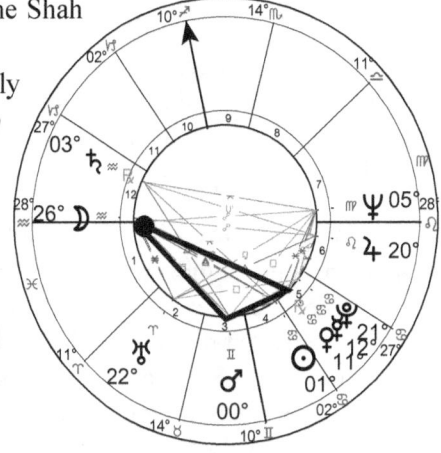

f. Miscarriage

Sophia Loren (20 September 1934, 14:10, Rome Italy)
Loren said "Always, in the third month, I was losing my babies—I had a lack of estrogen. Losing two babies made me feel such a failure as a woman".
Cause: emotional. Loren's maternal problems are linked to the Moon-Saturn conjunction versus Mars polarity in the chart.
Loren was illegitimate and the family impoverished, causing great hardship when she was growing up (Moon conjunct Saturn in the 2H of values). She fought her way to a better standard of living and towards respectability. But planet Mars, which represents this ability to fight hard, is also related to her miscarriages.
Organ: sacral - female sex hormone, the Moon.
Effect: miscarriage. Estrogen, the female sex hormone, is essential for the growth and delivery of a healthy baby. But Loren had a deficiency (Moon > Saturn), and this is given as the cause of her many miscarriages.
From her chart, it appears her testosterone levels were too high (Mars in Leo, sextile Jupiter). This destabilised and weakened the natal processes, causing irregularities (sextile Mercury ruling the 6H of health, opposite the Moon) and is linked to miscarriage and recurrent incidents of miscarriage.
▲ (C) Moon, Saturn. (O) Moon. (E) Saturn, Mars, Mercury.

g. Ovarian Cyst

Anne Elliot (7 July 1946 07:00, Melbourne Australia)
Australian astrologer. In October 1978 she required surgery for a ruptured ovarian cyst.
Cause: emotional. Elliot is a sensitive Cancer personality who tries to keep the peace and get on with everyone (Sun square Moon conjunct Jupiter in Libra). But she also tends to nurse hurts and disappointments from the past (the Moon squares Saturn in Cancer), which builds up emotional congestion. An ovarian cyst is a manifestation of this.
Organ: sacral - ovaries, the Moon.
Effect: ovarian cyst. A cyst, a fluid filled sac (Moon-Jupiter), developed in an ovary when an aberration (Uranus) occurred during egg release. It ruptured, requiring surgery (Mars semi-square Moon)

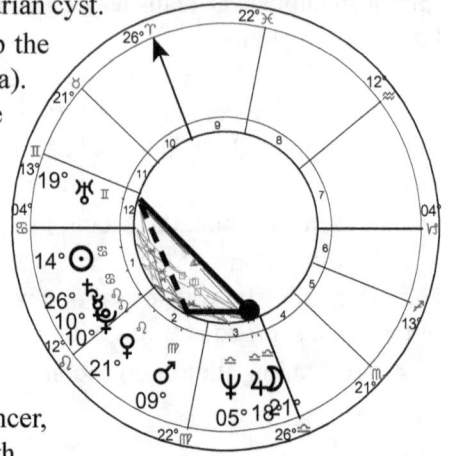

- ▲ (C) Moon, Saturn. (O) Moon. (E) Jupiter, Uranus, Mars.
- The rupture and surgery occurred when solar-arc Uranus reached 20 Cancer, square natal Moon and inconjunct the progressed Moon in the 6H of health.

h. Conjoined Twins

The condition is not genetic but occurs randomly. Trouble occurs very shortly after a single embryo has been fertilised. It does not properly split, so that instead of two identical twins being born, the twins are attached. The etheric web is the model upon which the physical body is constructed, so the problem lies there. It does not divide correctly. Look for afflictions to the signs that rule the etheric - Gemini and Aquarius.

Nolan Twins (3 May 2001, 09:43, Brisbane Australia)
Australian craniopagic twin sisters Alyssa and Bethany Nolan were born joined at the top of their heads. They had separate brains, but shared cranial draining vessels - veins that drain blood from the brain, emptying into the jugular vein. In addition, Alyssa was born with one kidney; Bethany had no kidney and no bladder. In less than a month, Bethany's health suddenly deteriorated and on 26 May 2001 doctors tried to separate them and Bethany died. Alyssa survived but has continuing health complications including 40 operations by age 8.
Cause: karmic. Uranus, ruling aberrations, is in the 8H of inheritances, square Saturn. This indicates that karma was involved in the condition.
Organ: sacral - etheric web, Gemini and Aquarius.
Effect: conjoined twins. A mutation occurred during the form-building process. Division of the etheric web upon which the physical body is constructed, was incomplete - Uranus in Aquarius governs the etheric and also the sacral chakra that manages the building of the form. It squares Saturn in Gemini that governs twins. Building work by the nature elementals went awry in the head (Mars inconjunct Saturn, sextile Uranus). Mars rules the lunar elementals that build the body [1] and it also rules the head via Aries. With a flawed design, the completed physical structures were also flawed - joined at the head (Mars quindecile Jupiter that "fuses").

The specific trouble involves Venus' function. It carries de-oxygenated blood back to the heart via the cranial veins to the jugular veins. The twins shared these veins. Lower in the body via Libra, Venus governs the kidneys and bladder, which Bethany lacked. Impairment in these functions is shown by afflicted Venus in the sign ruling the head - Aries, forming an easy-opposition with Saturn and Mars.

- ▲ (C) Saturn, Uranus. (O) Gemini, Aquarius. (E) Saturn, Uranus, Mars, Venus.

At 13, Alyssa was attending high school and although more operations were scheduled, photos taken of her in that period show her to be a happy teenager.

---

[1] Bailey, Alice A; Esoteric Astrology, 186.

4f.3. Sexually Transmitted Diseases (STD's)

Syphilis

Randolph Churchill (13 February 1849, 00:01, Oxfordshire, UK)
British peer, who entered Parliament in 1874 and was the father of Sir Winston. He is reported as dying of syphilis on 24 January 1895.

Cause: sexual karma. With the Moon in Scorpio, Churchill had sexual issues from a past life to deal with. He was a sensual man with powerful carnal habits (Mars is exalted in Capricorn).

Organ: sacral - sex organs, Mars and Uranus.

Effect: syphilis. Churchill caught syphilis (Mars square Pluto and Uranus in the 6H of health). The opposition from Pluto to the Moon in Scorpio in the 12H of hidden things, points to the point of infection coming from a back-street assignation or brothel, possibly in a foreign country (the Moon rules the 9H of foreign countries). Mars and Pluto disposit the Moon. After a lengthy fight against the disease he died in 1895 (the Moon co-rules the 8H of death).

▲ (C) Moon, Pluto. (O) Mars, Uranus. (E) Uranus, Pluto.

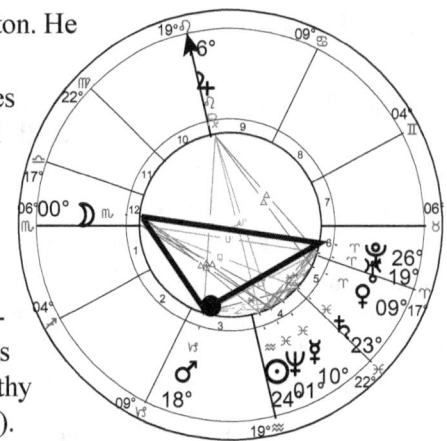

Gonorrhea

Laurie (24 February 1961, 08:47, Portland Maine)
(From Millard 'Case notes of a Medical Astrologer' page 109). Raised in religious family, Laurie was diagnosed with gonorrhea at 13, had a baby at 15 and a year later became sterile through another bout of gonorrhea.

Cause: emotional. Laurie was a malleable and emotional Pisces Sun and Cancer Moon girl, who was preyed upon sexually by predators from her church or cult at a young age (Mars conjunct the Moon; Saturn - and Jupiter that rules the 9H of religion, both square Venus in the 12H of hidden things). Consequently, Laurie grew up with loose morals and values (Venus afflicted) and poor sexual hygiene (Venus sesquiquadrate Pluto in Virgo).

Organ: sacral - sex organs, Venus.

Effect: gonorrhea. The result was several STD's (Venus, which is in detriment in Aries and co-rules the 6H of health, is trine Uranus). Uranus rules the sacral chakra and bacterial infections. Her reproductive organs were damaged and she was rendered sterile (Uranus in Leo, the sign ruling children, is in the 5H of children, septile the Moon).

▲ (C) Moon, Mars. (O) Venus. (E) Uranus.

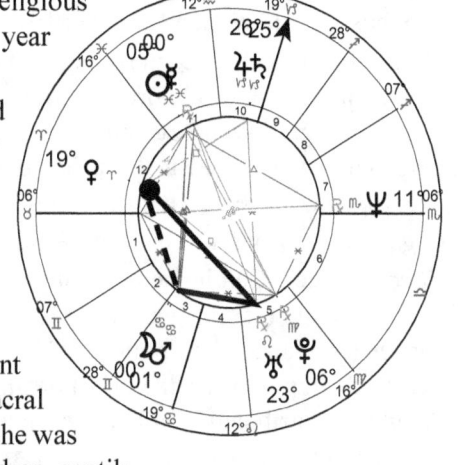

Herpes

Astro.com 5976 (30 June 1925, 07:00, Canton OH).
American insurance credit counsellor, married four times. She had a hysterectomy at an early age, breast cysts and herpes - a virus causing contagious sores, most often around the mouth or on the genitals

Cause: emotional. Our subject was an emotionally needy woman (a Cancer stellium in the 12H), who sought happiness through a succession of relationships and affairs (the Moon in Libra squares Venus that is conjunct Mars on the ascendant). Her sexual escapades contributed to health problems (Venus opposite Jupiter in the 6H of health), and the break-down of important intimate relationships.

Organ: sacral - sex organs, Mars and Venus.

Effect: herpes. She caught genital herpes (Mars-Venus > Jupiter inconjunct Neptune), causing blistering on her genitals (Mars-Venus).

▲ (C) Moon. (O) Venus, Mars. (E) Jupiter, Neptune, Mars.

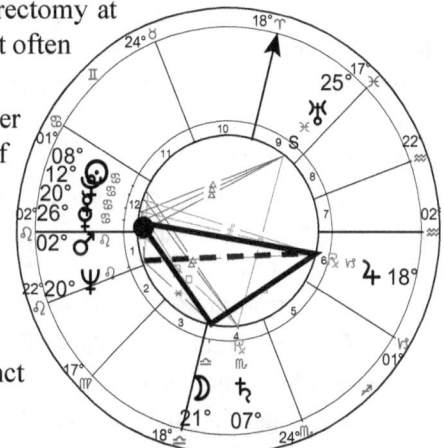

4f.4. Cancer in the Sacral Chakra Organs

a. Cancer of the Cervix and Uterus

Mirka Mora (18 March 1928 15:00, Paris France)

French-Australian artist, who led a bohemian and unconventional lifestyle. In 1993 she had a hysterectomy because of cancer in the cervix and uterus.

Cause: emotional. Mora was a sexually liberated woman (Mars in Aquarius), and likely caught the human papilloma virus, which causes most cases of cervical cancer through casual sex (Mars semi-square the Sun that is inconjunct Neptune on the ascendant. Neptune rules the 8H of sex).

Organ: sacral - the uterus and cervix, the Moon.

Effect: cancer. The HPV virus (Neptune), caused malignant changes in uterus and cervix tissue (semi-square Pluto in Cancer; Pluto is inconjunct the Moon and Mars), and cancerous cells developed. It required a hysterectomy (Mars conjunct the Moon in the 6H of health).

▲ (C) Moon, Mars. (O) Moon. (E) Mars, Neptune, Pluto.

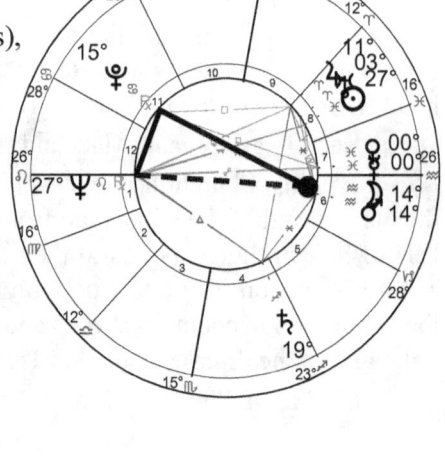

b. Ovarian Cancer

Patsy Ramsey (29 December 1956 14:00, Parkersburg WV)

Mother of JonBenet Ramsey, the child beauty pageant queen murdered in 1996. Diagnosed with ovarian cancer in 1993, she died from it on June 24 2006.

Cause: emotional. The unexplained murder of JonBenet is shown by Pluto (death) in the 5H of children, sesquiquadrate Mars (murder) in the 12H of hidden things. Psychologically, Ramsey was a very disciplined Capricorn personality who liked to keep her emotions controlled (Saturn conjunct Moon), and this repression as we have seen, so often leads to cancer.

Organ: sacral - ovaries, the Moon and Venus.

Effect: cancer. Carcinogenic changes (Neptune in the 6H of health), in ovarian tissue (semi-square the Moon), led to the development of ovarian cancer (Neptune is midpoint the Venus-Moon point and Jupiter). It caused her death (Jupiter rules the 8H of death). Grief over the tragedy surrounding her daughter contributed greatly to her illness (Neptune in Scorpio, sextile Pluto).

▲ (C) Moon, Saturn. (O) Moon, Venus. (E) Jupiter, Neptune.

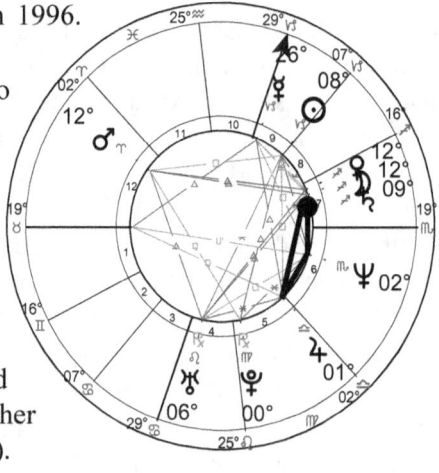

c. Prostate Cancer

Harry Secombe (8 September 1921, 12:00, Swansea UK)

Welsh comedian famous from the British radio comedy programme 'The Goon Show'. He died on April 11 2001, of prostate cancer.

Cause: ageing. Secombe's disease was age related - he got it in his late 70's. Body resilience and immunity wind down as we age. Secombe's Moon is in Sagittarius, the sign that rules the sacral chakra, pointing to potential trouble at some time in the sex organs.

Organ: sacral - prostate, Mars.

Effect: cancer. Tissue malignancies occurred in the prostate (Moon inconjunct Pluto in Cancer, semi-square Mars, the ruler 6H of health). It migrated into full blown cancer that killed him (the Moon is in Sagittarius that expands inconjunct Pluto in the 8H of death).

▲ (C) Moon, Pluto. (O) Mars. (E) Moon in Sagittarius, Pluto.

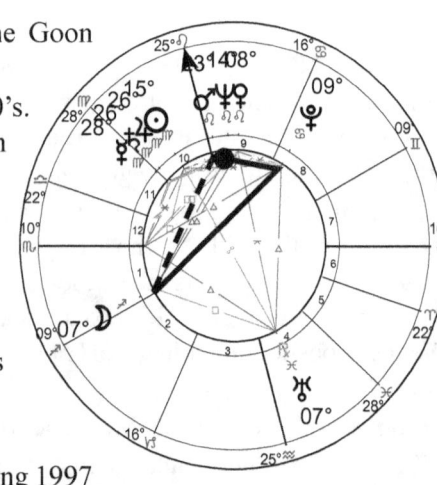

- Solar-arc Moon moved through 22 - 23 Aquarius, opposite natal Mars during 1997 to 1999, triggering the disease. When he died, solar-arc Mars was passing over the ascendant.

4g. Base Chakra Diseases

The base rules the adrenal glands, urinary system, physical body tissue generally and the skeleton. It receives energy primarily from rays 1 and 3, from Capricorn, Aquarius, Pisces, Pluto and Saturn.

4g.1. Adrenal Glands

a. Addison's Disease (underproduction of hormones)

Addison's is caused mainly by an autoimmune attack upon the adrenals, impairing hormones that deal with stress (cortisol) and salt-water regulation (aldosterone). Symptoms include fatigue, nausea and dizziness.

John F. Kennedy (29 May 1917 15:00, Brookline MA)
Popular US President, in 1947 he was diagnosed with Addison's disease.
Cause: emotional. In this chart, the adrenals are represented by Mars, which is afflicted in Taurus. Since Kennedy was born with the aspect, we know he had a latent weakness in his adrenals, which emerged as a disease just after his brother died and he was elected into congress.

Self-attack is always involved in an autoimmune disease and his chart shows that he felt threatened from affairs at home (Uranus in the 4H of family). He felt emasculated; perhaps felt attacked or attacked himself (square Mars) for not being able to measure up to his father's political aspirations. This may explain his promiscuity - trying to prove he was a man by having sex with many women.
Organ: base - adrenals, Mars and Venus.
Effect: Addison's disease. The immune system attacked (Mars) the adrenals and the salt-water regulating function was unbalanced (Venus disposits Mars). Mars represents the adrenals, the immune system and the attack on the adrenals and co-rules the 6H of health.

▲ (C) Mars. (O) Mars, Venus. (E) Uranus.

b. Adrenal disease

Dane Rudhyar (23 March 1895 01:00, Paris France)
Famed astrologer Rudhyar, his youth was marred by ill health. In 1908 when he was just 13 years of age, he had a life-threatening operation that removed his left kidney and adrenal gland.
Cause: emotional. Rudhyar had a busy and active mind (planets in Gemini) and could lose himself in his world of thought (Aquarius Moon), which could be negative and self-critical. This contributed to ongoing respiratory trouble when he was young (Mercury is afflicted in the 2H of values, and squares Mars and Pluto in the 6H of health).
Organ: base - adrenals, Mars and Venus.
Effect: adrenal disease. Malefics in Gemini, the sign that rules oxygenation, indicates difficulty with this function and consequent toxicity in the blood (Mars, the blood, conjunct Neptune, the bloodstream). Inflammation and an infection (Mars) occurred in the left-hand side upper urinary tract, in the ureters (square Mercury). It resulted in the left kidney and adrenal gland becoming diseased (Venus is afflicted in Aries and is semi-square Mars, Pluto and Neptune), requiring their surgical removal (Mars).

▲ (C) Mars. (O) Mars, Venus. (E) Mercury, Pluto, Neptune.

- In 1908, progressed Mars was at 19 Gemini, inconjunct natal Uranus in Scorpio. This represents the onset of the bacterial infection that struck the left side urinary tract and adrenal gland. Solar-arc Saturn, which is a ruler of the base chakra via the 3rd ray, was at 19 Scorpio conjunct natal Uranus. The disease was chronic and eventually the organ failed.

4g.2. Bladder, Kidney problems

a. Bladder infection and kidney stone

Una Chiodini (21 November 1936 10:58, Chicago IL)

American numerologist, palmist and astrologer. On 3 June 1993, she had a bladder infection and passed a kidney stone, starting after 1:30 PM.

Cause: emotional. Chiodini is an intense Scorpio, but when she gets angry or "pissed off", her natural impulse is to hold onto the aggravation and brood over things (ruler Mars that is emasculated in Libra, squares Venus in Capricorn in the 12H of hidden things). This breeds inner toxicity.

Organ: base - kidneys, bladder, Venus and Mars.

Effect: bladder infection. Chiodini is susceptible to urinary tract infections (Venus > Mars sextile Pluto in Cancer, the sign ruling the 6H of health).

- The infection she caught on June 3, occurred when solar-arc Mars was at 1 Sagittarius, conjunct natal Mercury, square the Moon. It triggered the natal infection-breeding circumstances. The transit Moon passed over these two points between 8 am and 12 noon, indicating the fertile period for the infection.

- Venus in crystallising Capricorn symbolises the kidney stone. Solar-arc Venus was at 3 Pisces, inconjunct Mars at 4 Libra, when the stone passed in 1993.

   ▲ (C) Mars. (O) Venus, Mars. (E) Pluto.

b. Kidney stone

Billy Joel (9 May 1949 09:30, Bronx NY)

American singer and writer of popular ballads. He went to a New York Hospital on 24 September 1989, for the removal of kidney stones.

Cause: emotional. Joel's instinct is to keep the peace and avoid conflict (Moon conjunct Neptune in Libra). He would rather gloss over problems than deal with them head on, something he learned at home (the Moon in the 4H of family rules the ascendant). But this built up inner tension and stress and led to health problems (the Moon is sesquiquadrate Venus, which in turn squares Saturn, the co-ruler of the 6H of health with Capricorn sharing the cusp).

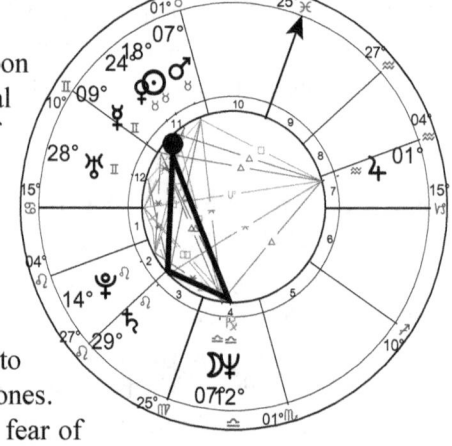

Organ: base - kidneys, Venus.

Effect: kidney stones. Joel developed kidney stones during his marriage to model Christie Brinkley. Venus square Saturn is a classic aspect for these stones. The marriage supposedly failed because of his drinking and infidelity. But fear of rejection and insecurity - the Venus > Saturn factor; really did the damage.

   ▲ (C) Moon. (O) Venus. (E) Saturn.

- On the day of surgery, transit Mars was at 3 Libra, square solar-arc Venus in the 12H of hospitals at 3 Cancer.

c. Kidney failure

Sarah Bernhardt (23 October 1844 20:00, Paris France)

French stage actress, the star of her day, who had a "larger than life personality". She was riddled with ill health from childhood into adulthood and died of kidney failure on March 26, 1923.

Cause: emotional. Bernhardt was emotional, volatile and expressive as actors tend to be (t-square: Cancer ascendant square the Moon and Uranus in Aries and Mars in Libra). This contributed to her ongoing health problems.

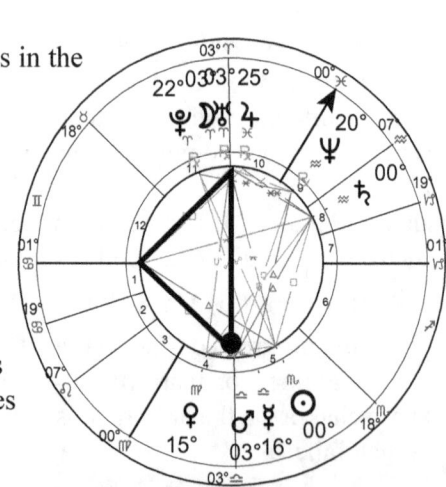

Organ: base - kidneys, Mars.

Effect: kidney failure. Kidneys are the cleansers of our system and Bernhardt's had a weakness (Mars afflicted in Libra opposite Uranus and the Moon). As her body started to age, they could no longer cope. Blood quality deteriorated affecting kidney health and a serious infection developed (Uranus > Mars that rules the 6H of health). The kidneys became diseased, they failed and she died (Mars trine Saturn in the 8H of death.

▲ (C) Moon, Uranus. (O) Mars. (E) Ascendant, Uranus.

- When she died, solar-arc Saturn, ruler of the 8H of death, was at 20 Aries moving over progressed Pluto (Lord of Death), at 21 Aries.

d. Kidney disease (Bright's disease, nephritis)

The kidneys become inflamed. It can lead to kidney failure if left untreated.

Georges Vallerey (21 October 1927 03:30, Amiens France)

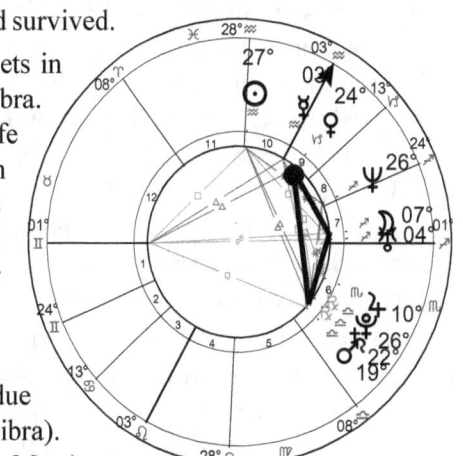

French champion swimmer. In 1950 he was diagnosed with nephritis (inflammation of the kidneys). After four years of very painful treatments he died on October 4 1954. He was just 27.

Cause: emotional. Mars and Venus rule the kidneys and they are both afflicted by sign, indicating both psychological and physical problems. Vallerey had low self-esteem. He was self-critical and tended to dwell on his problems, holding tension and stress in rather than releasing it (Venus in Virgo, ruling the 2H of values, in the 12H of self-undoing). This generated toxins in the blood (Venus semi-square Mars in Libra) making it harder for the kidneys to do their job.

Organ: base - kidneys, Venus and Mars.

Effect: Bright's disease. The kidneys picked up a bacterial infection and because of their poor condition it spread rapidly (Venus quindecile Uranus; Mars inconjunct Jupiter that rules the 6H of health). He died (Mars rules the 8H of death).

▲ (C) Mars. (O) Venus, Mars. (E) Uranus, Jupiter.

- In 1950, solar-arc Moon reached 0 Libra opposite Uranus at 0 Aries and the disease took hold.
- In 1953, solar-arc Uranus was in the 8H of death at 26 Aries, moving opposite natal Mars at 26 Libra. In this period the kidneys were irreparably damaged.
- In 1954 when he died, solar-arc Moon had reached 4 Libra, the midpoint between natal Venus > Mars. This was the virulent core of the disease pattern. Transit Uranus was at 27 Cancer, square solar-arc Uranus at 27 Aries, in the 8H of death.

Astro.com 14834 (16 February 1982 10:45, Redmond WA).

American baby born with a severe kidney defect. We do not know if the child survived.

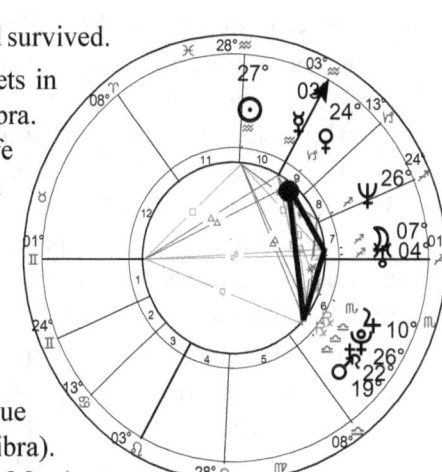

Cause: karmic. The danger to the kidneys is shown by three malefic planets in Libra that rules the kidneys, in the 6H of health that is also ruled by Libra. Saturn is one of the planets, pointing to kidney trouble in a previous life caused by the person's own choices and actions. All chronic illnesses in babies are karmic (Saturn conjunct Mars in this case). Parents who will pass the condition onto the child via their DNA are carefully chosen by the soul with this end in mind. These learning experiences teach us to take better care of the body.

Organ: base - kidneys, Venus and Mars.

Effect: kidney disease. The kidneys could not do their task of filtering urine due to a chronic defect in the organ (Venus in Capricorn square the planets in Libra). He was susceptible to kidney infections (Uranus septile Venus, semi-square Mars).

▲ (C) Saturn. (O) Venus, Mars. (E) Libra afflictions, Uranus.

4g.3. Skeletal, Spine, Joint, Muscle Diseases

a. Arthritis - Osteoarthritis

Psychological friction that translates into physical friction can cause early onset osteoarthritis. In most cases, simple ageing is the cause. Cartilage wears away as bone rubs against bone.

Carole Hemstreet (6 July 1938, 06:21, Los Angeles CA)

American woman who in her 40's began to develop early onset osteoarthritis.

Cause: emotional. Difficulty with joints, especially when it occurs at a relatively early age (mid-40's), suggests rigidity in attitude. Hemstreet was an emotional Cancerian who repressed her feelings (Cancer planets in the 12H of self-undoing square Saturn). She could be fixed and stubborn and this pattern underlies her arthritic condition. Saturn rules the 6H of health.

Organ: base - cartilage, bones, Saturn.

Effect: arthritis. Over time, cartilage (Saturn) wore away through friction (square Mars), and arthritis set in, restricting movement (Saturn semi-square Jupiter, and Mars sesquiquadrate Jupiter).

▲ (C) Mars, Saturn. (O) Saturn. (E) Saturn, Jupiter.

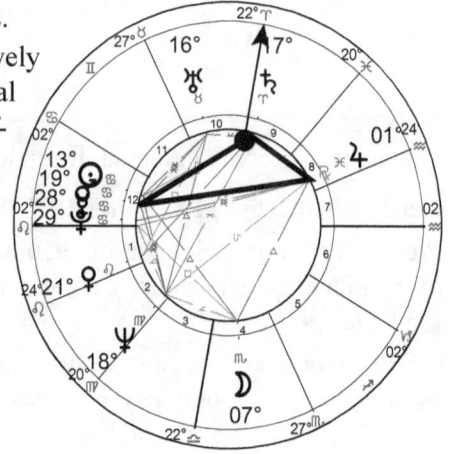

b. Bone - Osteoporosis

Sally Field (6 November 1946 04:23, Pasadena CA)

Popular American TV/ film actress, diagnosed with osteoporosis.

Cause: ageing. Trouble did not manifest until Field approached her 60th birthday indicating an age related disease. She could be tough when she needed to be (Saturn-Pluto in Leo square Sun-Jupiter in Scorpio in the 1H), but she had an easy way about her that helped good energy flow in the body overall (grand-trine configuration - Saturn, Moon and Mercury-Venus).

Organ: base - bones, Saturn.

Effect: osteoporosis. 1st ray Saturn and Pluto in 1st ray Leo points to skeletal rigidity at some point in time (as well as future heart trouble). As she aged, minerals were leached from the bones (Uranus semi-square Saturn) and they became dry and brittle, impairing her mobility (sesquiquadrate Jupiter).

▲ (C) Saturn. (O) Saturn. (E) Uranus, Pluto, Jupiter.

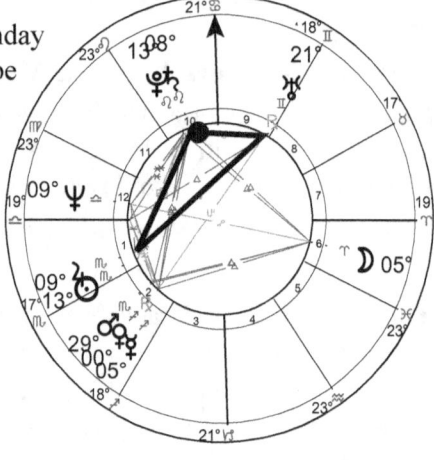

c. Arthritis - Rheumatoid Arthritis

In rheumatoid arthritis, the immune system attacks the joints, resulting in painful deformity and immobility.

Elsie Wheeler (3 September 1887 21:45, Norris City IL)

American spiritualist psychic who worked with Marc Edmund Jones to create the Sabian symbols - impressions for each degree of the zodiac. Wheeler was an astral psychic who worked through her solar plexus chakra (Moon in Pisces).

Cause: karmic-emotional. Crippled with arthritis and wheelchair bound from age 3, Wheeler was born with a powerful and destructive psychological pattern brought through from a previous life. The nature of her illness suggests she hated her body and thought it ugly (the Sun in critical Virgo squares the ascendant that governs the appearance).

Organ: base - bones and joints, Saturn.

Effect: rheumatoid arthritis. The toxicity generated by her negativity, triggered the immune system (Mars in Leo). It attacked the bones and joints (Saturn), twisting the body until it matched her thoughts and she was immobilised (square Jupiter in the 6H, and Jupiter inconjunct the ascendant).

▲ (C) Saturn, Mars. (O) Saturn. (C) Ascendant, Jupiter.

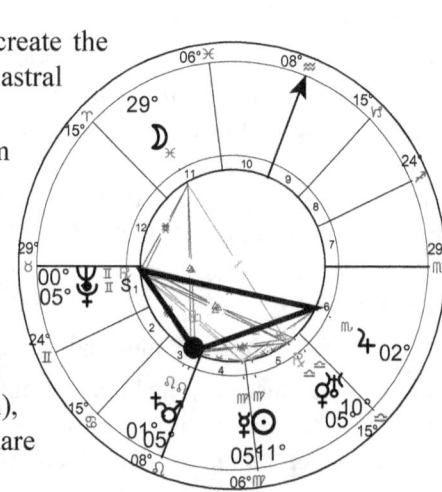

Jeanni (22 June 1949, 05:11, Bulawayo Zimbabwe)

Australian woman who contracted rheumatoid arthritis in 1988 and became partially crippled. But she managed to heal herself.

Cause: emotional. At the root of an autoimmune disease is a self-attack pattern and finding that pattern in the chart is vital.

Saturn is the key. It is the primary planet symbol of arthritis and its situation in the chart should reveal the attack pattern behind Jeanni's affliction. Saturn squares Mars - a classic pattern for arthritis.

Jeanni can be her own harshest critic (Mars-Mercury square Saturn in Virgo), something she learned from her mother (Mercury rules the 4H of mother with Virgo on the cusp). Her inner child just accepted the verbal abuse and repeated it to herself because she was "bad and deserved to be punished." This pattern and Mars rose to the forefront in the late 1980's when she went through a crisis in a personal relationship.

Organ: base - bones and joints, Saturn.

Effect: rheumatoid arthritis. The immune system attacked her joints (Mars square Saturn), crippling and impairing her movement (Saturn inconjunct Jupiter in Aquarius). Mars rules the 6H of health.

▲ (C) Mars, Saturn. (O) Saturn. (E) Saturn, Jupiter.

Two important factors to consider:

1. Healing the self-attack pattern was an important spiritual goal for Jeanni. This is because Mars and Mercury are parked on the ascendant and the ascendant sign (Gemini in this case) and its higher esoteric ruler (Venus), represent the purpose of the soul in the current incarnation. Venus in Cancer tells us that healing the pattern will release Jeanni from deep grief concerning betrayal by loved ones (square to Neptune), and help restore her self-worth and self-esteem (in the 2nd house of values).

2. Saturn is a wing in a Yod pattern (Jupiter is at the apex of the Yod, inconjunct Sun-Uranus and Saturn). A Yod highlights the need for a change of perception so that an inner integration can be achieved. The message from Jupiter in Aquarius in the 8H, is for Jeanni to study the wisdom philosophies, develop a more inclusive and spiritually oriented perception of life; then use what she has learnt to free her from the self-judging pattern.

Chart set for March 1989.

By 1988, Jeanni was ready. She had obtained a degree in psychology and wrote a thesis on psychosomatic illnesses. She was also exploring alternative and spiritual healing approaches.

- A crisis was initiated by her soul when solar-arc Mars and the ascendant made conjunctions to natal Venus.

- Transit Pluto moved into the 6H of health - which it rules with Scorpio on the cusp and squared its natal position; initiating a midlife crisis connected with health.

- At the same time, solar-arc Jupiter reached 8 Pisces (square natal Mars at 8 Gemini). This brought the 2 patterns - the health-triangle and the Yod, into a collision.

- Jupiter rules the 7H and Jeanni's important relationship was in trouble. Up came the attack pattern and arthritis struck. At the worst of it, she could only walk with assistance.

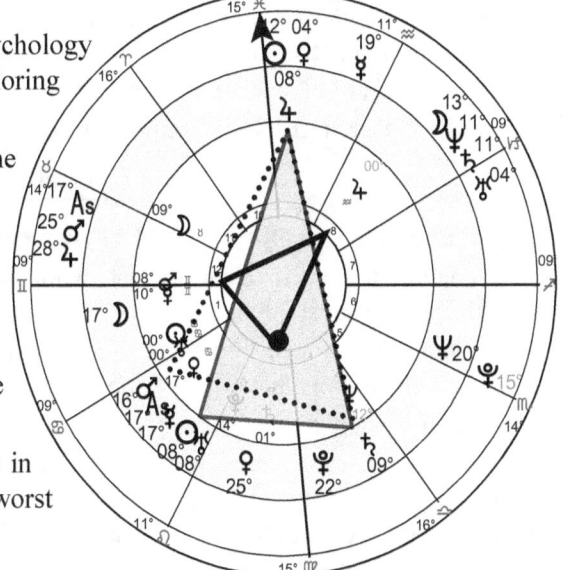

What did she do? Jeanni who is an astrologer, tells her story:

"A specialist told me I could end up in a wheel chair, but I refused to accept this and set out to heal myself. A deep tissue massage therapist would ask me to go into the physical pain in my body to retrieve painful emotional memories. As I recalled unhappy incidents, I cried a lot, releasing painful emotions through my tears. My naturopath put me on a cleansing program including juice fasting and I followed Jane Fonda's exercise video.

But the most important part of what I did was to meditate. I followed a taped, guided meditation where I visualised healing light and love flowing to my joints, restoring them to good health. In April 1990, the progressed Moon entered the 6H of health, allowing me to heal hidden issues with my mother and to work on the emotional body in a deeply purging way. In May 1990 the progressed Moon conjuncted transit Pluto. This was the catalyst for the healing. Within a year my body healed quite radically and I was walking normally, even running with joy on the beach again with my children."

d. Bursitis

Barry Manilow (17 June 1943 09:00, Brooklyn NY)
Popular singer and songwriter had surgery for bursitis (inflamed bursa) in his hips. Bursa are sacs of fluid around joints that provide cushioning.
Cause: emotional. One side of Manilow wants to be free to enjoy life (the Moon is in Sagittarius in the 5H of pleasure); but another side fears moving forward in life in case something bad happens or he gets attacked and is hurt (an easy-opposition pattern with Mars, Saturn).
Organ: base - the bursa, the Moon.
Effect: bursitis. The stress this inner conflict generated accentuated normal wear and tear on the body (Saturn). Friction (Mars) in the hip bursa (the Moon in Sagittarius), resulted in inflammation and pain (Mars).
▲ (C) Moon, Saturn. (O) Moon. (E) Saturn, Mars.

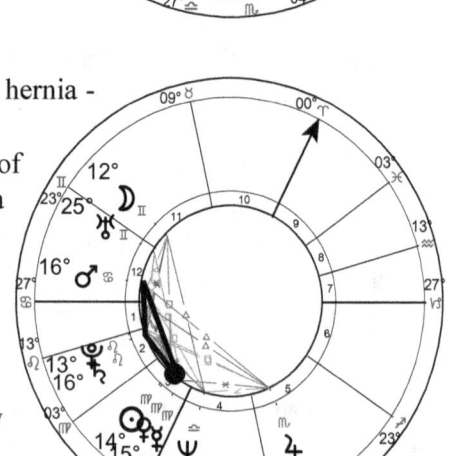

e. Hernia

L1010 (8 September 1947 01:55 BST, Hawkwell UK)
Australian car mechanic who had an operation in 2009 to repair a stomach hernia - intestines had protruded through the abdomen lining.
Cause: emotional. Our subject was struggling to deal with the weight of emotional problems in his marriage at the time the hernia occurred. On a physical level, lifting heavy objects caused the problem.
Organ: base - intestines and the abdomen, Mercury and Virgo.
Effect: hernia. There was a weakness in the wall of the abdomen (Venus that weakens, is afflicted in Virgo, conjunct Mercury). Pressure (the Saturn-Pluto, aspect is midpoint Mars and Venus), caused a tear (Mars) and the intestines protruded through. It required corrective surgery and a short hospital stay (Mars in the 12H of hospitals). He has had many auto accidents in his life.
▲ (C) Mars, Saturn. (O) Mercury, Virgo. (E) Venus, Saturn-Pluto, Mars.

f. Sciatica

Jeannie Longo (31 October 1958 15:00, Annecy France)
World champion French racing cyclist, who was plagued with sciatic nerve pain while racing in August 2008.
Cause: emotional. Longo thrives on mental and emotional tension. It helped make her a champion athlete (Mars opposite Mercury).
Organ: ajna - sciatic nerve, Mercury.
Effect: sciatica. During strenuous competition in 2008, Longo experienced excruciating pain in the sciatic nerve (Mercury opposite Mars and square Uranus in the 6H of health. Uranus squares Jupiter).
▲ (C) Mars. (O) Mercury. (E) Uranus, Jupiter.
- When the trouble happened in August 2008, transit Jupiter (which is related to the sciatic nerve), was at 12-13 Capricorn, moving over solar-arc Mercury at 13 Capricorn. At the same time transit Mars moved over solar-arc Uranus at 6 Libra.

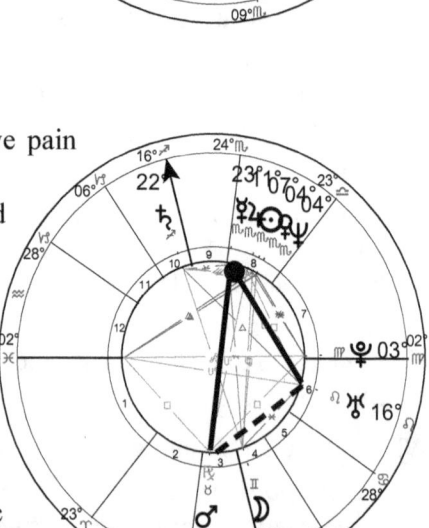

g. Scoliosis

Rowena Wallace (23 August 1947 08:10, Coventry UK)
Australian actress of TV and theatre. At 19, she was diagnosed with scoliosis, a curve of the spine. She has required painkillers almost continuously since.
Cause: emotional. A stellium of 5 planets in Leo draws attention to the spine, which Leo rules. Positively, Leo represents our ability to stand erect and strong in life. The fact that the spine weakened indicates that Wallace wilted due to painful incidences in her teens. She was born with a morose and suspicious side (Moon falling in Scorpio). Perhaps she was bullied at school (Sun square Moon the 3H of formal education) and this started the damage.
Organ: base - spine, the Sun and Leo.
Effect: scoliosis. The spine (Sun in Leo), weakened (conjunct Venus), and became distorted, deviated from the norm (square the Moon in Scorpio and sextile Uranus). Scoliosis developed.

▲ (C) Moon. (O) The Sun, Leo. (E) Venus, Uranus.

- In the year prior to diagnosis, trouble started. The progressed Sun was in the 12H of hidden things at 16 Virgo, when transit Uranus and Pluto crossed it.
- Simultaneously, solar-arc ascendant was at 9 Libra, moving over natal Neptune. On a psychological level, it shows she was feeling vulnerable, weak and unsupported at that time in her life. The inherited weakness in the spine manifested.

h. Spina Bifida

Spina bifida is incomplete closure of the vertebra around the spinal canal, leaving nerves exposed. Severe forms of the condition are accompanied by nerve defects and damage that impairs mobility, bowel and bladder function. The Sun, Leo and Saturn rule the spine.

Samuel Reynolds (22 November 1967 13:20, Buffalo NY)
American male, born with spina bifida, he endured 25 surgeries before age 21. The pain and suffering he experienced caused him to seek spiritual answers for his life. This is not surprising, mystical Neptune is conjunct his Sun. At age 12, he became a minister of his church and preached his first sermon in 1980. Then in 1990, after receiving counselling from an astrologer, he studied the science and became a dedicated student and teacher of astrology (Sun sextile Uranus).

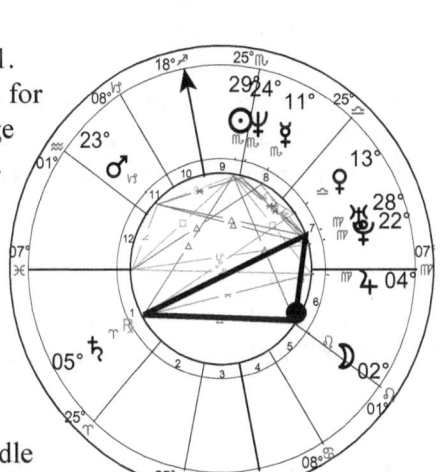

- At that time in 1990, solar-arc ascendant had reached 28 Pisces and solar-arc Jupiter 27 Virgo. They made contact with the astrologer's planet Uranus at natal 28 Virgo. This encouraged him to make astrology his profession - Jupiter rules the 10H of career.

Cause: karmic. Saturn dominates the chart from the point of view it is the handle of a "bucket" planetary pattern. This makes its message powerful. It is afflicted, falling in Aries, retrograde and in an easy-opposition pattern with Uranus and the Moon in Leo in the 6H of health. On a physical level, the pattern represents the unfinished (Saturn) state of the spine and nerve endings. But on a metaphysical level, Saturn informs us that this affliction is karmic and provides opportunities to overcome adversity and make progress in life. With his achievements, he can show others (Saturn is in the 1H of the appearance), how they too can rise above their disabilities. He may have a physically damaged spine, but his psychic spine is dignified and erect (Saturn is in a grand-trine with the Sun and Moon in Leo).
Organ: base - spine, Leo and Saturn.
Effect: spina bifida. There was a serious aberration in the pattern of the etheric web (Uranus conjunct Pluto). Spinal closure work was incomplete and nerves were left exposed (easy-opposition pattern). Consequently, in his early years he spent a lot of time in hospital (Uranus rules the 12H of hospitals with Aquarius on the cusp), to fix the spine, nerves and associated health complications.

▲ (C) Saturn. (O) Leo, Saturn. (E) Uranus, Pluto.

4g.4. Skin and Hair

> Violent emotion.. If suppressed .. results in the poisons which.. find their outlet in certain cases of septic poisoning, in skin diseases.. [1]

a. Alopecia areata

Alopecia areata is hair loss that occurs when the immune system mistakenly attacks hair follicles.

L1006 (6 April 1951, 13:51, London UK)
Australian woman whose hair fell out at age 7 - shortly "after I fell off a swing". At 14 it grew back, only to fall out again at 21, then grew back at 28. Since then, only occasional patches fall. Saturn, which every 7 years makes a challenging aspect to its natal position, is involved.

Cause: emotional. Our subject can quickly fly into a panic when something unfortunate happens or she is criticised (the Moon and Sun are in Aries quindecile Saturn in Virgo; and Mars is in Aries inconjunct Saturn). The fact that she got alopecia, which drastically affects the appearance, suggests sensitivity about her appearance - the Sun rules the Leo ascendant.

Our subject confirmed that before age 7, she came to believe she was unloved because she was unattractive. She recalls vividly her mother telling her she was going to be adopted, and her uncle calling her "tubs". Falling off a swing was a metaphor for her feeling that she was unsupported.

Organ: base - the hair, Aries and Saturn.

Effect: alopecia areata. Unhappiness and self-criticism about her appearance sets off a panic attack (Uranus in Cancer that is disposited by the Moon). This in turn caused an autoimmune attack (the Sun and Mars) on hair follicles (Aries), and her hair fell out (Mars inconjunct Saturn).

▲ (C) Moon. (O) Aries, Saturn. (E) Mars, Uranus.

- At age 7, transit Saturn squared its natal position. This forced her to confront the "truth" she had formed about herself "that she was unattractive", and believing it, her hair fell out.
- At age 14, transit Saturn opposed its natal position and the Sun progressed into Taurus - a stabilising and maturing period for our subject. She felt stronger and more confident and her hair grew back.
- At age 21, transit Saturn squared its natal position. A failed relationship caused the negative belief to surface again. Solar-arc Mars had reached 19 Taurus and was moving over Venus. The immune system attacked and her hair fell out.
- At age 28-29, Saturn returned to its natal position. This is a maturing period, when a serious assessment of the life is made. With Saturn in the 2nd house, our subject learned to appreciate and value herself for the fine and accomplished woman she is and the problem virtually disappeared.

b. Eczema

Skin becomes rough and inflamed with blisters, causing itching and bleeding.

Jean Didier Wolfromm (21 May 1941 21:00, Paris France)
French novelist and literary critic who had chronic eczema.

Cause: emotional. Eczema is caused by an emotional disturbance. Wolfromm had fiery and irritable emotions, bubbling resentment and anger (Moon in Aries semi-square Uranus; Mars square Uranus).

Organ: base - skin, Saturn.

Effect: eczema. Emotional toxicity poisoned the blood (Mars in Pisces > Uranus), causing his eczema, skin eruptions and bleeding (Uranus conjunct Saturn that is in the 6H of health). Consequently, his appearance was marred (Saturn-Uranus opposite the ascendant).

▲ (C) Moon, Mars. (O) Saturn. (E) Uranus, ascendant.

---
1 Bailey, Alice A; Letters on Occult Meditation, 159.

c. Leprosy

Leprosy is a bacterial infection that damages nerve endings causing numbness. Scaly white skin crustaceans make sufferers look like corpses. It is caught after repeated contact with a carrier of the disease.

Heindel: 305, (19 March 1896 19:50, Calcutta India)

This case is from Max Heindel's 'Astro-Diagnosis' page 305. He put the cause of leprosy in this case as "moral depravity".

Cause: karmic. Our subject had karma associated with the misuse of sex (Saturn in Scorpio: conjunct Uranus the ruler of the sacral chakra, square Mars, and opposite the Moon in Taurus in the 8H of sex).

Organ: ajna - nerves Uranus, Gemini and Aquarius; base - the skin Saturn.

Effect: leprosy. The leprosy bacteria (Uranus), infected the subject during sexual contact (Mars co-rules the 6H of health with Aries sharing the cusp). Nerve endings were damaged (Saturn conjunct Uranus, Neptune-Pluto in Gemini, and Pluto quindecile Uranus). White crustaceans covered the skin - the Moon's colour is white and it rules soft tissue.

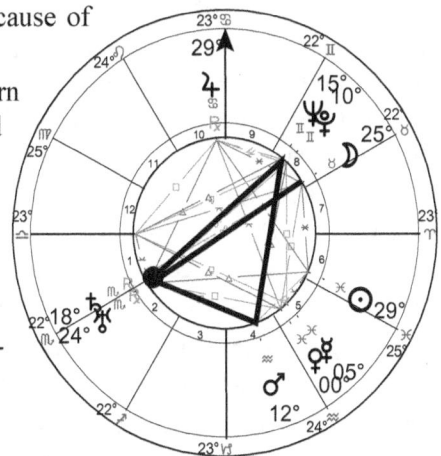

▲ (C) Saturn, Mars. (O) Aquarius, Gemini; Saturn. (E) Mars, Uranus, Pluto.

Father Damien (3 January 1840, 12:30, Tremelo Belgium)

Roman Catholic priest. He caught leprosy after sixteen years of working in a Hawaiian leper colony and died from the disease 15 April 1889.

Cause: karmic. Damien had karma to do with sex and hygiene. (Saturn in the 8H of sex is conjunct Mercury that rules hygiene and the 6H of health. Mercury is afflicted in Sagittarius, is sextile Mars and square Uranus). Perhaps he thought he was immune to the disease because for years he never caught it.

Organ: ajna - nervous system Mercury, base - the skin Saturn.

Effect: leprosy. Damien was infected with the leprosy bacteria (Uranus), which damaged nerve endings (square Mercury), causing numbness (Mercury-Saturn). Eventually his skin became covered with unsightly white crustaceans (Saturn and Mercury, conjunct the Moon).

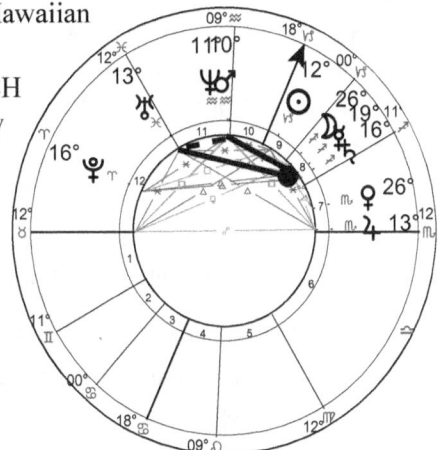

▲ (C) Saturn. (O) Mercury, Saturn. (E) Uranus.

d. Lupus

Seal (19 February 1963 15:34, London UK)

English singer of African descent, Seal has extreme scarring on his face, the result of a cutaneous lupus that attacks the skin. He had it as a teenager. Lupus is an autoimmune attack that can affect any part of the body.

Cause: emotional. Seal's self-attack pattern is represented by a t-square, headed by Mars on the ascendant. This shows anger, simmering closely on the surface, caused by strange and unstable home-life conditions (square Neptune in the 4H), also cruelty and hardship (opposite Saturn, ruler of the 6H of health). Perhaps he was told that he was ugly or unworthy and believing it triggered the autoimmune attack on the face.

Organ: base - skin, Saturn.

Effect: lupus. The immune system attacked his face (Mars conjunct ascendant), causing scarring (Saturn).

▲ (C) Mars, Saturn. (O) Saturn (E) Mars, Saturn, Neptune.

- When he was 14, solar-arc Saturn was at 0 degrees Pisces, conjunct the natal Sun, the immune system. This is either the start of the attack or an acceleration of its attack on the body. Solar-arc Neptune was at 0 degrees Sagittarius, square the Sun.

e. Proteus Syndrome

A rare congenital disorder that causes skin overgrowth and atypical bone development, often accompanied by tumours over half the body.

Joseph Merrick, "Elephant Man" (5 August 1862 Leicester UK)

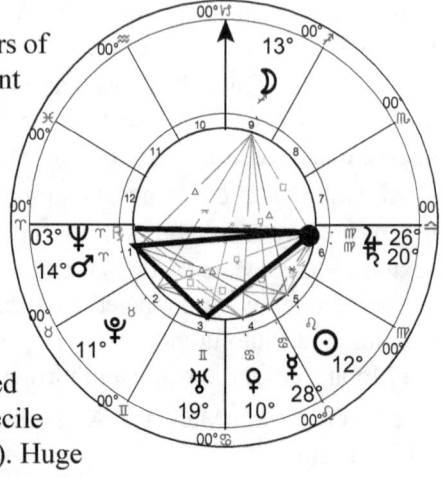

Unknown time, 12 PM midday used and the 0 degrees Aries House System. Born normal, Merrick's skin became thick and lumpy during the first few years of his life until he was grossly deformed with skin hanging off his head. He spent time in a workhouse, then as a professional "freak" in side-shows, called "the Elephant Man".

Cause: karmic. We do not have a birth time so cannot use the ascendant, the appearance, to help us find the disease pattern. Merrick had karma (Saturn) to do with sexual excess (conjunct Jupiter, square Uranus that rules the sexual, sacral chakra). Saturn is in Virgo, the natural ruler of the 6H of health.

Organ: base - skin Saturn, cells the Sun.

Effect: proteus syndrome. The growth factor (Jupiter) in the body was subverted (Jupiter afflicted in Virgo, conjunct Saturn, opposing Neptune, and quindecile Mars), so that cell-building (semi-square the Sun) went wild (square Uranus). Huge and freakish protuberances appeared on his head (Aries planets > Jupiter > Uranus; sesquiquadrate to Pluto). He went into a trade as a freak (Uranus is in Gemini and in the 3rd house that rules trade).

▲ (C) Saturn. (O) Saturn, Sun. (E) Jupiter, Uranus, Neptune, Pluto.

• Merrick's karma was exhausted before he died. He was befriended by a surgeon who was sympathetic to his plight and from 1886 until his death in 1890, lived quietly in a London Hospital with his friend.

f. Scleroderma

Scleroderma results from an overproduction of collagen in body tissues, caused by an autoimmune malfunction. There is chronic hardening and contraction of the skin and connective tissue throughout the body.

Alice Lon (23 November 1926 10:00, Kilgore TX)

American singer and dancer on The Lawrence Welk Show during its early years on television. She died "after a long battle" with scleroderma, on 24 April 1981.

Cause: emotional. Saturn rules the professional life and the disease surfaced sometime after Lon was fired from the Lawrence Welk show and had a vitriolic, public brawl with him. Lon must have been deeply embittered (Saturn in unforgiving Scorpio), because the disease appeared. Saturn rules the skin, scarring and hardening and co-rules the base chakra. It is central to the trouble.

Lon's health-triangle includes the Moon, which always represents the "prison of the soul" pattern, or in modern psychological terminology, a negative core belief. Moon conjunct Pluto suggests a belief such as "I am bad and deserve to die"; opposite the ascendant - "Dangerous people want to hurt me". The public death (Moon-Pluto), of her employment (Pluto sesquiquadrate Saturn), was simply the proof that her beliefs about herself were true.

Organ: base - collagen, Saturn; connective tissue Mercury.

Effect: scleroderma. The immune system attacked (Mars afflicted in Taurus and retrograde) the body's collagen and connective tissue (inconjunct retrograde Mercury that is in detriment in Sagittarius. Mercury in turn conjuncts Saturn and rules the 6H of health, with Gemini on the cusp). Gradually hardened and scarred tissue (Moon-Pluto > Saturn), formed a tightened prison around organs and she died (the Sun rules the 8H of death with Leo on the cusp).

▲ (C) Moon, Pluto. (O) Saturn, Mercury, (E) Mars, Saturn, Pluto.

4g.5. Cancer in the Base chakra Organs

a. Adrenal Cancer

Gary Betty (4 March 1957, Atlanta Georgia)
Unknown time, 12 PM midday used and the 0 degrees Aries House System.
President and CEO of internet provider EarthLink, who was diagnosed with adrenal cortical cancer late 2006, dying January 3 2007.
Cause: emotional. Betty would hold in his frustration and anger until he exploded (Mars afflicted in Taurus, square Pluto). This pattern impacted negatively on his relationships (Pluto opposite Venus) and health.
Organ: base - adrenals, Mars.
Effect: cancer. Trouble in the solar plexus (Mars) and base (Pluto) chakras affected cells (Pluto in Leo) in the adrenals (Mars). Dangerous carcinogenic changes (ray 6 via Mars), led to adrenal cancer (Mars trine Jupiter afflicted in Virgo, the natural ruler of the 6H). He died - Pluto rules death.
  ▲ (C) Mars. (O) Mars. (E) Pluto.
- In late 2006 when the cancer made its rapid appearance, solar-arc Neptune, was at 21 Sagittarius inconjunct natal Mars, ruler of the adrenals. The cancer grew vigorously.

b. Bone Cancer

George Estregan (10 July 1939 12:25, Manila Philippines)
Filipino film actor and younger brother of former Philippine President Joseph Estrada. He died on 8 August 1988 of bone cancer.
Cause: emotional - karmic. Bone cancer indicates deep seated anger and pain from the past that is held onto and not released. Saturn rules the skeleton and it is in a grand-cross. Estregan was bullied at home (Mars in the 4H of family), by carers (square Saturn, opposing Pluto in the 10H of father). Unable to fight back against his all-powerful tormentors (Pluto), he suppressed his rage and despair (Saturn square Mars) and it settled in his bones (Saturn).
Organ: base - bones, Saturn.
Effect: cancer. Homoeostasis (Libra ascendant) was destroyed (Saturn, Pluto). Bone (Saturn) cells turned malignant (square Pluto in Leo), and began to rapidly overbuild (Jupiter forms an easy-opposition pattern with Mars and Pluto). Within 8 months of diagnosis, he was dead (Jupiter square Venus, ruler of the 8H of death).
  ▲ (C) Mars, Saturn. (O) Saturn. (E) Pluto, Jupiter.

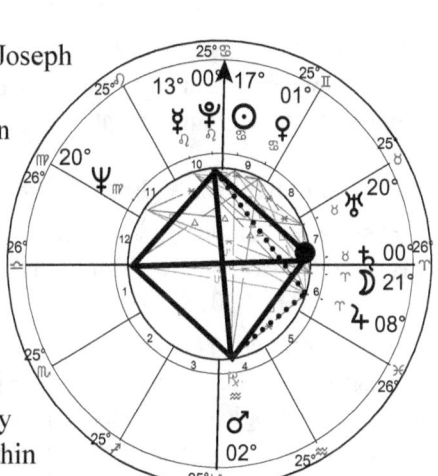

c. Bladder Cancer

Jon Hall (26 February 1915 22:00, Fresno CA)
Handsome Tahitian actor, who had surgery for bladder cancer in February of 1979, but shot himself on the 13th December 1979.
Cause: emotional. Venus and Mars both rule the bladder and both are in triangles that indicate the trouble. Hall may have felt "pissed off" (Moon opposite Mars) and guilty (conjunct Neptune), because of "sexual" things he did to further his career (Venus is in the business sign Capricorn, in the bartering 3H, opposite Neptune conjunct the MC).
Organ: base - the bladder, Venus and Libra.
Effect: cancer. There were carcinogenic (Neptune, Moon) changes in bladder cells (Venus, Mars), and surgery left him impotent and incontinent (Mars rules the 6H of health; Venus rules the 8H of sex and death); which would explain why he killed himself a year later, being unable to deal with the infirmity.
  ▲ (C) Moon. (O) Venus, Mars. (E) Neptune, ascendant.

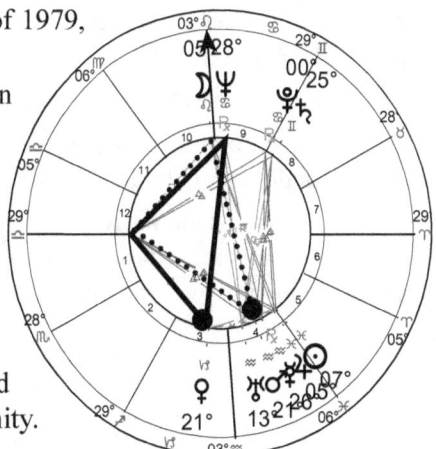

d. Melanoma (Skin Cancer)

John McCain (29 August 1936, 18:25, Colon Panama)

American politician and Senator from Arizona. He has had melanomas, on his back (1993), arm (2000), and nose (2002). In 2017, he was diagnosed with a glioblastoma, an aggressive brain cancer.

Cause: emotional. Saturn represents the skin. It is located in the 1st house that governs the body generally, and in Pisces that carries the 2nd ray that causes cell over-building. Further, it is in a stressful t-square, opposing Neptune (in detriment in Virgo), which represents potential carcinogenicity. We have the base arm of the health-triangle.

Psychologically, the aspect represents a disciplined (Saturn), clamping down on any form of inner vulnerability or weakness (Neptune), in order to survive life challenges (Jupiter in Sagittarius). He grew a "tough skin". This helped him through his war years, but repression is a recipe for disease in the long term.

Organ: base - skin, Saturn.

Effect: cancer. Repression of emotional sensitivity and unexpressed grief (Neptune) as well as over-exposure of skin to the Sun (Sun opposite ascendant), led to insidious cell changes (Neptune), and skin cancer developed (t-square: Saturn-Neptune-Jupiter).

▲ (C) Neptune. (O) Saturn. (E) Jupiter, Neptune.

- In 2017, McCain announced he had an aggressive brain cancer. The transference of malignancy from the base to the crown chakra brings Pluto into play - see the lower triangle in the chart. It is in Cancer, which rules the brain mass. At the announcement - by solar-arc, Pluto was at 18 Libra in the 8H of death.

Colin Bloomfield (22 February 1982 19:30, Montford Bridge UK)

English radio personality and sports commentator. In 2001, a malignant melanoma was removed from his leg. But it returned in 2013 and metastasised into his lungs. He died 25 April 2015.

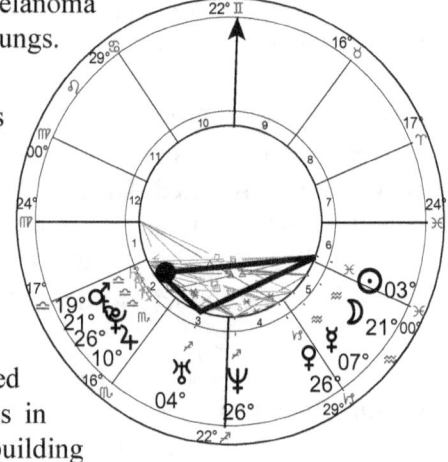

Cause: emotional. There are two candidates for the skin - Saturn and Venus because it is in Capricorn. They are in mutual reception and square each other. Psychologically, Venus-Capricorn-Saturn people are very cautious in love. They fear showing their feelings, because to do so would expose them to rejection and emotional pain. Repression of affection has health repercussions.

Organ: base - skin, Saturn.

Effect: cancer. Scorching of the skin (Sun sesquiquadrate Saturn), caused aberrant (square Uranus) cell conditions in the skin of his thigh (Uranus in Sagittarius), which became cancerous (the Sun that carries the 2nd over-building ray, is in the 6H of health).

▲ (C) Pisces. (O) Saturn. (E) Sun, Uranus.

- In 2000, overexposure of the skin to the Sun triggered the malignant skin cells (the progressed Sun was at 21 Pisces inconjunct natal Saturn at 21 Libra.

- In 2012, the melanoma reappeared (progressed Sun was at 4 Aries, trine natal Uranus at 4 Sagittarius), and cancerous cells metastasised (Neptune, ruler of the bloodstream and lymph system, which spreads cells, was in Pisces transiting over the Sun). Cancer appeared in his lungs (the Sun co-rules the lungs).

5. STEPS TO GOOD HEALTH

The healer must understand also how to radiate, for the radiation of the soul will stimulate to activity the soul of the one to be healed and the healing process will be set in motion; the radiation of his mind will illumine the other mind and polarise the will of the patient; the radiation of his astral body, controlled and selfless, will impose a rhythm upon the agitation of the patient's astral body, and so enable the patient to take right action, whilst the radiation of the vital body, working through the splenic centre, will aid in organising the patient's force-body and so facilitate the work of healing. Therefore, the healer has the duty of rendering himself effective, and according to what he is, so will be the effect upon the patient. When a healer works magnetically and radiates his soul force to the patient, that patient is enabled more easily to achieve the end desired—which may be complete healing, or it may be the establishing of a state of mind which will enable the patient to live with himself and with his complaint, unhandicapped by the karmic limitations of the body. Or it may be enabling the patient to achieve (with joy and facility) the right liberation from the body and, through the portal of death, to pass to complete health. [1]

---

1 Bailey, Alice A; Esoteric Healing, 7-8.

1. The link between psychology and disease

Traditional medicine is slowly making the link between psychology and disease, between our mental and emotional states and the many disorders that plague us. For instance, there is a general acceptance that unrelieved mental and emotional stress contributes to high blood pressure and that depression weakens the effectiveness of the immune system. But generally, medicine looks to external factors as a cause of disease.

The esoteric view is that most complaints in individual average man are based upon an emotional cause or a clearly defined desire. These compel people to act in ways or do things that result in disease. For instance, emotional anxiety may compel people to take drugs to alleviate anxiety, so they become addicted. Unresolved anger may cause a person to rant and rave so he or she has a stroke. Sexual promiscuity may result in catching an STD.

Well-established emotional and mental attitudes, habits and preferences that produce disease, stem from previous incarnations. Until expunged, they follow us karmically from life to life in our genetic make-up. When the foetus is being built in the womb, the building devas follow the inherited genetic blueprint for the physical body and hypothetically download into the Limbic System in the brain, our preferences and desires.

Astrologers are esotericists and medical astrologers lead the way in making the link between psychology and disease. In the future, perhaps within a century, it is feasible to think that astrology will be a respected part of orthodox medicine. Practitioners will identify mental-emotional patterns that have led to disease and monitor psycho-spiritual practises to help straighten them out. Preventative work will identity negative emotions in children that could potentially lead to disease and recommendations made to balance these. But at present, to mainstream medicine, astrology remains bunkum with no credibility. This will change. Khul said:

> the astrology of the future, some day will be lifted up to a higher plane. True interpretation will come and true healing in all departments of human living through a proper understanding of the available potencies and energies pouring into the planet at any particular time. [1]

The core essential information, on which this medical astrology book is based, has been drawn from Alice A. Bailey books: *Esoteric Psychology II* and *Esoteric Healing*. The author recommends these books to all medical astrologers who are trying to make the link between our inner states and disease. Certain rules for esoteric healing - of which medical astrology is a branch are given in the Esoteric Healing book. The first rule is:

> Rule I. Let the healer train himself to know the inner stage of thought or of desire of the one who seeks his help. He can thereby know the source from whence the trouble comes. Let him relate the cause and the effect and know the point exact through which relief must come.

To find the inner source of trouble, astrologers look into the world of energies. Here they are the masters. A trained, professional astrologer is more skilled at diagnosing the originating cause of a disease than traditional medical practitioners. This is because mainstream medicine deals primarily with the effects of a disease rather than the originating, energetic cause. As the Master Djwhal Khul said:

> Astrology is essentially the purest presentation of occult truth in the world at this time, because it is the science which deals with those conditioning and governing energies and forces which play through and upon the whole field of space and all that is found within that field. [2]

> astrology which is in many ways the science of sciences. [3]

Human beings are energy units functioning in a world of energies. Blockages within the mental, emotional and etheric bodies hinder the life-sustaining forces pouring in from the soul and Sun so that parts of the body become under-nourished. This results in disease. The job of the astrologer is to identify these blockages, where they lie, what is causing them and how to get rid of them. This involves finding a minimum of three planets in the natal chart.

- One planet represents the psychological cause of the disease.
- A second planet represents the affected organ.
- A third planet (with other linking planets), represent the disease itself and its debilitating effects.

These three steps build the health-triangle.

---

[1] Bailey, Alice A; Esoteric Astrology, 353.
[2] Bailey, Alice A; Esoteric Astrology, 5.
[3] Bailey, Alice A; Discipleship in the New Age I, 437.

2. Astrologers heal through counselling

Once the relevant patterns in the astrology chart have been found, the astrologer is ready to counsel. Astrologers heal through counselling. Astrology is governed by 3rd Ray of Intelligent-Activity,[1] which governs the communicative throat chakra. Counselling or psychotherapy is a 3rd ray art that heals through words of wisdom sent forth on the wings of love. The goal is to help people make healthy adjustments in the way they see themselves and their place in the world.

> **Central to the esoteric counselling approach is the concept of the soul. The counsellor's task is to shift the person's identification from the lower troubled self, from the diseased or broken down part of the body, up to the soul. This is the true self, the light-filled, radiant wisdom part of the nature.**

Using the astrology chart as the reference point, through skilled manipulation with words, energies and subtle suggestions, the astrologer impresses his soul charged personality onto the weakened energies of the client. He draws together the many frayed threads in the person's psyche and weaves them into a new life-tapestry with the person/ the soul, cast as the central figure. He retells the story of the life and the onset of the disease from a different perspective, brings into the light the positive side of the experience. Clarity is given, about the higher purpose of the incarnation and how to move positively into the future, that there will be future opportunities and incarnations in which to write a new life story. Any sense of guilt or sin should be eliminated. The notion that we are all here to learn and so-called "mistakes" or "failures" are a normal and natural part of the process of growing in spirit, is emphasised.

In other words, the person's life is reframed, giving it a higher and more meaningful interpretation. This helps to free people from any negative patterns they may be embedded in, so they can move forward. Bringing about an alignment with the soul allows healing light to flow through the mind into the body to facilitate the healing process.

> **The radiation of the soul-aligned astrologer stimulates to activity the soul of the one to be healed, triggering the healing process.**

While the counselling work is progressing, while the energies remain quiet and calm between the healer and the client, a vortex of whirling force is created around the two. Energetically, what the healer is doing, is lifting the client out of the stagnant pool of energies in which he or she has become mired. By bringing in new and higher forces, the astrologer promotes a condition to support the healing process.

a. The Health-Triangle

Discuss the negative psychological patterns found in the chart that underlie the disease and the link between these mental-emotional expressions and the trouble. Explain that the removal of these patterns will free up energy flow and if this is achieved to any degree, no matter what happens immediately in the physical body, life ahead will be more serene and peaceful. A positive side of illness, is that we are given time-out from ordinary life to focus on ourselves and change our life-trajectory if that is required.

In the chart, once a planet has been found to represent the cause of the disease, the sign it is in is noted and the negative traits of this sign that have contributed to the trouble are identified. The astrologer can then advise the person to neutralise these traits by cultivating the opposite positive qualities.

b. Change the way you think - "think an opposite thought"

Teach the Raja Yoga technique of "thinking an opposite thought" to clients. This technique that trains the mind to think positively requires continuous effort and commitment but the rewards are worth it.

> Whenever we catch ourselves thinking critically about someone, think an opposite positive kind or compassionate thought. Find something admirable in the person and acknowledge that. Alternatively, imaginatively hold the person in the light and love of their soul or God.

When successfully applied this technique improves health because it removes negative emotional-mental habits that cause most of our diseases. It also accelerates spiritual growth, because when we remove impediments to soul flow, increased light and wisdom flows through the mind and nature.

---

1 Bailey, Alice A; Esoteric Psychology I, 166.

3. Other means and ways to build good health

a. The cultivation of positive qualities to benefit health

Develop *goodwill*: it is the will of good intention and motive. Its development and expression will heal respiratory tract, lung and throat diseases. Goodwill stabilises brain cells, cures insanities and obsessions, establishes equilibrium, rhythm and leads to greater life longevity. [1]

Develop h*armlessness*: people should strive to be inclusive, kind and harmless, in thought, speech and action. Harmlessness purifies the centres, clears clogged channels, lets in higher energies and effectively arrests the progression of a disease. [2] Whenever a harmful thought appears in the mind, immediately practise the "think an opposite thought" technique.

b. Better health though diet and behaviour

> By the understanding of right methods of assimilation and elimination will come the healing of diseases connected with the bodily tissues, the stomach and bowels and the male and female organs of generation. [3]

A moderate and balanced lifestyle with adequate exercise, bathing, fresh air, sunlight, and a diet based largely upon clear water, fresh fruit and vegetables, nuts and grains will result in better assimilation of the pranic fluids, improving the vitality of the etheric body and physical organs. Salt sea bathing is beneficial - water absorbed through the skin and by the mouth helps to prevent disease. Minimal consumption of meat is recommended, especially when one is sick. Vegetarianism is preferred. On the sexual level, promiscuous or wrong intercourse is a means through which diseases are introduced into the body. Balance, moderation and cleanliness is required throughout.

c. Increase vitality

> By a comprehension of the laws of vitality.. the laws governing prana, radiation and magnetism - will come the healing of the diseases in the blood, of the arteries and veins, of certain nervous complaints, lack of vitality, senile decay, poor circulation and similar ills. This too will result in the prolongation of life. [4]

Sedentary and lazy lifestyle habits make the whole system sluggish, so that vitalisation of the body and circulation of nourishing life and prana to all cells in the body is diminished. The Tibetan points to this as being a factor related to a variety of diseases including dementia, where brain cells do not receive adequate vitalisation. Daily moderate exercise such as walking will keep circulation moving healthily.

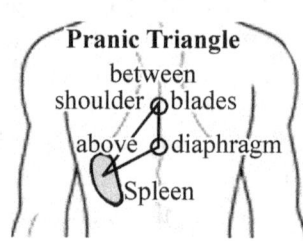

> The mind can be used to aid vitalisation through visualisation exercises.
>
> One technique is to visualise golden prana surrounding the spleen - not the physical organ, but the etheric area surrounding it and picture it as bathed in pure golden prana.
>
> Another is to visualise solar prana flowing into any point of the pranic triangle (which includes the etheric spleen), and circulating around it three times before being transmitted to all parts of the etheric vehicle and from then to the dense physical body.

d. Colour therapy

- Violet and orange light help the etheric body. Orange stimulates the action of the etheric body, removes congestion and increases the flow of prana.
- The colour gold strengthens the etheric web and its flow.
- Rose improves the nervous system, removes depression and its symptoms and increases the will to live.
- Green being the colour of nature has a general healing effect, especially on the dense physical body. It helps ease inflammation and fever.

---

1 Bailey, Alice A; Esoteric Healing, 108.
2 Ibid, 40.
3 Ibid, 109.
4 Ibid, 108.

e. Meditation

Meditation is calming and balancing. As we meditate on topics like the love and wisdom of God and the beauty of Mother Nature, our consciousness fills with beneficial energies and the consequent impact on the cells in our body is healing. The Raja Yoga meditation programme is recommended and there are also excellent Buddhist programs available. Here are some basic points.

- Try to meditate in a quiet spot.
- Early morning is the best time for meditation.
- Make your meditation space beautiful and fragrant.
  Use incense, flowers, a photograph or statue of an enlightened Master or Buddha.
- Burn a candle, to purify the atmosphere.
- Sit comfortably, spine erect - on a chair or floor. The goal is to forget about your body during meditation. Balance your head comfortably on your neck, ensure there is no tension in your jaw or body. Hold the head with the chin slightly dropped.
- Eyes are normally closed, though may be opened slightly (looking downwards) to help stay mentally alert.
- Unless you are doing specifically a relaxation meditation, keep your mind alert and aware. Avoid "spacing out". In mindfulness meditation, five minutes of wakeful alertness is of far greater value than twenty minutes dozing.

Garden Meditation
(It is very healing for those who are ill or depressed)

This meditation is very healing. .

1. Relax your body...
   Harmonise your emotions...
   Be alert in your mind.
   Align with your Soul

2. In your mind's eye, find a beautiful spot in nature and imaginatively create a garden. Select flowers, shrubs and trees, add rocks or water features to maximise its beauty. Each day return to your garden in meditation. Tidy it, do weeding if necessary, replanting and reconstructing if you wish to.

3. Find a peaceful spot in the garden and seat yourself. Imagine as you breathe in the fragrant beauty of your garden that every cell in your body is being filled with light.

4. Finally, send a blessing of peace and love to the world.

Balance the Chakras

This is an exercise to tone up the seven major chakras.

Chakra	*Colour*
base	red
sacral	orange
solar plexus	yellow
heart	gold
throat	pale blue
brow	indigo blue
crown	violet or white

Visualise your etheric body and the chakras. Then starting from the base chakra and working upwards:

1. Breathe in,
2. On the out-breath, sound an OM, directing the sound through the chakra.
   Simultaneously, colour that energy stream with the chakra colour, fading it out to pure white.
3. See the chakra healthy and vibrant.
4. Do the same for all the chakras.

4. In summary

From the esoteric perspective, we are souls having a physical incarnation. The health of the physical body we use today is inextricably linked to our karma from past lives. If we were a little older in our soul experience in the past, were reasonably balanced psychologically and lived a reasonably healthy life, we earned by right a reasonably healthy body - and vice versa. If we were younger in soul experience, unbalanced psychologically and abused the "temple of the Lord" as the Bible calls it; we inherit a damaged body.

Whatever type of body we start with, we can improve or degrade its performance in this life by how we treat it. Using a motorcar as a metaphor for the physical body is helpful. Modern cars that are run by computers are good examples of how our psychological states (the computer), can affect engine performance (the body). Just as a programming error in the car computer disrupts engine performance, disruptive mental and emotional states do the same in the physical body. Then, if we load the gas tank with the wrong type of fuel, we can expect its road performance to fall and for the engine eventually to fail. So it is with our physical bodies. If we fill them up with junk food, drugs and alcohol, eventually they too will fail.

If we inherit a broken down or diseased body in this life, we can improve its quality and performance by living a relatively clean life psychologically and by eating quality food, getting moderate exercise and holding a positive and balanced attitude to life. If the problems are such that an improvement is not possible in this life, we reap the rewards of a stronger and healthier body in the next incarnation.

Death and dying

Most people fear of death, but it is the commonest phenomenon upon the planet and we have died many times before - we just do not remember. When the soul deems the incarnation has run its usefulness, it initiates those processes that cause the physical body to die. This is the natural process of death by ageing and not by accident or murder.

People who are not familiar with the esoteric processes of life and death and who have not made a connection to their souls, usually fear death because they believe it represents annihilation and extinction. Even if carrying around the body has become a burden because it is heavy and crippled through disease, they fight to keep it alive. But to those who have made the inner connection or are sympathetic with the flow of nature, they intuitively know when it is time to depart this earthly life and in response, begin to tidy up loose ends. They face the process with inner quiet and acceptance because they know that it is a natural part of nature and look forward to a period of rest and restitution. Later, there will be a new incarnation and a new cycle of opportunity.

Pluto, bearer of the 1st Ray of Will and Power is the primary representative of death in its psychological aspects as well as physical death. Pluto is a healer and liberator, assisting our spiritual journey towards enlightenment through the death process.

One of the tasks of the astrologer-healer when death is inevitable, is to help the person meet this life conclusion positively. This is achieved by re-framing the death as one more step in our journey - as souls, towards future life opportunities and union with the Divine. Working with the ascendant sign, which represents the next incarnation,[1] and the ascendant's esoteric ruler; the healer can weave hypothetical images of new opportunities coming up in the next incarnation. This will help to lift the spirits and ease any concerns. It can greatly facilitate the cross-over process if it helps people let go of the mortal shards of the current life and move expectantly towards their next soul adventure.

> *We are all trying to live happy and successful lives and the breakdown of health cuts across that like a lightning bolt felling a tree. But often it is unnecessary. An adjustment in our nature to ease energy flow, a positive outlook and the concentrated practice of harmlessness may be all that is required to keep disease at bay. At least in the earlier stages. If the condition has progressed too far, these adjustments will ease the process of crossing over to the next life. Either way, by giving people the information they need in a helpful and supportive context so they can begin to move forward positively again in time and space, and boosting that process with soul light and love is the task of the medical astrologer.*

---

1 Bailey, Alice A; Esoteric Astrology, 18.

APPENDIX

Glossary

Angel (Deva)	The angelic or deva life stream runs parallel with the human life stream. The higher devas are called celestial beings, angels, or Greater Builders. The lower unconscious devas are the elementals of substance in all kingdoms, and are called Lesser or Lunar Builders, fairies and goblins. There are many grades of semi-intelligent devas between these two extremes.
Antahkarana	A bridge of mental essence between the higher and lower minds, that serves as a medium of communication between the two. When the higher reach of this bridge is constructed, man has access to his spiritual nature and is aware as a spiritual man. The thread anchors in the region of the pineal gland. This region in the head is the seat of consciousness, the seat of the soul. From there, the soul's job is to control human consciousness via the brain and nervous system. The antahkarana extends beyond the human worlds.
Asc	The ascendant in astrology. It forms the cusp of the first house.
Aspect	A part of the Trinity, the 1st, 2nd or 3rd aspect, or Spirit, Soul and Body.
Aspirant	Those who are aspiring to something higher and finer than ordinary material life.
Atma	The Universal Spirit or Spiritual will. This level of consciousness is located at the Atmic Plane level.
Bucket pattern	One or two planets stand alone on one side of the chart with the other planets arranged on the other half. The forces of the larger group of planets will try to find release through the planet handle planet(s).
Buddhi	The Universal Soul. Spiritual love, whose faculty is the intuition. This level of consciousness is located at the Buddhic Plane level.
Conjunction	Planet aspect - 2 planets within 8 degrees together. It represents the uniting of forces, intensity, emphasis.
Consciousness	The *consciousness thread*, the thread of intelligence, the responsive agent in all sentient reactions comes directly from the soul and anchors in the head in the region of the pineal gland. There is the seat of "soul" consciousness. However, in average man, consciousness is centred in one of the lower chakras in the body. The consciousness thread functions in connection with a stream of desire that enters the body via the solar plexus centre. In undeveloped/ average of man, the solar plexus is the focus of consciousness. *The consciousness thread the consciousness aspect or the faculty of soul knowledge, controls the brain, and through its medium it directs activity and induces awareness throughout the body by means of the nervous system.* [1]
DC	The descendant. In astrology it forms the cusp of the seventh house.
Deva	See "Angel".
Disciple	One who is pledged to a Master and who co-operates with the plans of the Masters as best he may. The personal task is to transform the nature, thereby taking initiation and become enlightened.
Egoic Lotus	The Causal Body. It is the centre of human or soul consciousness and is formed from the conjunction of buddhic and mental essence. All knowledge and wisdom accumulated throughout our incarnations is stored in the lotus, in its petals. Each petal in the lotus represents a quality. There are nine petals surrounding an inner bud, which is called the jewel in the lotus. Spiritual essence connects with that inner point. The lotus shatters at the 4th initiation when we become spiritually aware.
Elementals	See "Deva".
Enlightenment	In Bailey's work, enlightenment is associated with the 3rd initiation of Transfiguration, symbolised by Jesus on the mountaintop when he was flooded with spiritual light. In Buddhism, it seems to equal Monadic awareness, or esoterically, the 6th Initiation.
Esoteric	The words "esoteric" and "occult" signify "that which is hidden". They indicate that which lies behind the outer, the world of energies that produce appearance and effects. Occultists or esotericists are concerned with the subtler world of energies and forces which all outer forms veil and hide. Esotericism is the study and intelligent use of energies.
Etheric body	Man's physical body has two parts. The dense physical body, formed of matter of the lowest three subplanes of the Physical Plane, and the etheric body formed of the four higher etheric subplanes of the Physical Plane. The etheric body is the blueprint for the physical, and it receives and distributes energy to the body.
Grand-trine	Planet pattern with 3 planets trine, forming an equilateral triangle. It represents easy energy flow that usually benefits health. But not always. It can manifest as laziness that leads to disease.
IC	Imum coeli. Latin for "bottom of the sky". In astrology it marks the bottom of the chart, also the fourth house cusp in most house systems.

---

1 Bailey, Alice A; Education in the New Age, 92

Inconjunct	Planet aspect, also called quincunx - 2 planets 150 degrees apart. It represents stress and fighting forces.
Indigenous disease	Three diseases (tuberculosis, cancer and syphilis) that are indigenous to our planet and to the matter from which our physical bodies are constructed. This means they are in our physical body DNA.
Initiates	Higher than a disciple in consciousness, but beneath a Master. One in whom soul and personality have fused, and who rules the human worlds. He is a spiritual man, a blend of scientific and religious training, who is guided by the Monad.
Initiation	An expansion of consciousness. Each initiation enables us to function consciously on a higher level than before, and to express a greater proportion of wisdom.
Jewel in the lotus	See the "Egoic Lotus".
Karma	The law of cause and effect. It is the power that controls the behaviour of all things.
Kite	A planetary pattern that looks like a kite. A grand-trine has a another triangle formed on one of its sides. There is a planet on each of the points of the triangles.
Kundalini	The power of physical life, the fire of matter. It is centred in the base chakra and rises up the spine when man connects consciously with his spiritual nature.
Lemuria	A term first used by scientists and adopted by Theosophists to indicate a continent that, according to the Secret Doctrine, preceded Atlantis. It was the home of the third root race, primitive man.
Life-thread	Synonyms are sutratma, silver cord and thread soul. It originates from the Monad and via the soul, it anchors in the heart. Life force streams along the life thread.
Logos	Gk: the word of God, in some cases it can represent God. The divine Life behind the sun is the solar Logos. This level of God-consciousness is located at the Logoic Plane level.
Manas	Spiritual mind.
Master	A Master of the Wisdom has expanded His centre of consciousness to include the plane of spirit.
MC	The midheaven, medium coeli, or highest point of the chart. It represents our professional life, our highest life goals, status, power and rulership.
Monad	It is the spiritual Spark, the God aspect in our nature.
Mystic	One who senses divine realities from the heights of aspiration. Who contacts the mystical vision through prayer, adoration and worship, then longs ceaselessly for the constant repetition of the achieved ecstatic state. The mystic must eventually become an occultist.
Occult	See "Esoteric".
OM	A sacred word, sound or vibration. When we sound an OM with positive intent, the vibration purifies our nature and brings us into alignment with the soul.
Path (the)	An abbreviated term for the Path of Spiritual Development, also called the Path of Discipleship. We step onto the Path when we begin to aspire to something higher and finer than ordinary material life. It is the call or influence of the soul, of our spiritual nature that awakens this desire within us.
Permanent atom	There are five, one on each of the five planes of human evolution. The Monad appropriates them for the purposes of manifestation. Around them the various sheaths or bodies are built. They are small force centres that carry the "DNA" of a person's bodies from life to life.
Planet pattern	A recognised arrangement of planets that represent patterns of energy flow. Some such as a grand-trine represent an easy flow of energy, others such as the t-square represent blockages and disruptions.
Prana	The Life Principle, the breath of Life.
Quindecile	Aspects in 15 degree intervals, especially the 165 degree aspect, which represents disruption and separation.
Raja Yoga	The Royal Science of the Mind, or union with the Divine through mind. It involves the exercise, regulation and concentration of thought.
Ray	One of the seven fundamental energy streams of force in the universe, a ray of energy.
Rayology work	7 Ray Personality Profiling is a stand-alone science and is not included in this book. The technique is comprehensive; consciousness is examined at the soul, personality, mental, emotional and physical levels. There is a slight similarity with Myers-Briggs Type Indicator.
SA	Solar-arc directions. This system rotates the entire chart through the signs, at the same rate as the Sun, which is approximately 1 degree a year.
Septile	Planet aspect - 2 planets 51.5 degrees apart, the zodiac divided by 7. It is of the nature of the 7th ray and Uranus, representing fatality, something unexpected and in terms of health, cellular promiscuity.
Sesquiquadrate	Planet aspect - 2 planets 135 degrees apart. It represents confrontation and conflict.

Shamballa	The seat of world spiritual government, headed by Sanat Kumara.
Solar Angel	A member of the Kingdom of Souls, who control the evolution of humanity. We each have a Solar Angel.
Solar Logos	The ensouling life of the solar system.
Soul	The consciousness aspect in all living things. The human soul (egoic lotus or causal body) is the storehouse of man's expanding soul knowledge, love and wisdom. The Solar Angel mentors the human soul.
Souls old, young	From one angle, old soul/ young soul refers to the time period we have been cycling through incarnation on the Path of Evolution. Older souls started before younger souls. However, from another angle - since some souls travel faster on the Path because they make a greater effort, it refers to wisdom. Older souls have a more expanded consciousness, are wiser, more intelligent and compassionate than younger souls.
Square	Planet aspect - 2 planets 90 degrees apart. It represents blockages, challenges and disruption to energy.
Stellium	A group of planets located together in one sign or one house, or that connect to each other by at least 8 degrees so that a "super" conjunction of planets is formed. It represents a powerful source of energy.
Sutratma	See Life Thread.
Tables, Astrology	

Chart 9: Decanates

Sign	Decanate 1	Decanate 2	Decanate 3
Aries	Aries: Mars	Leo: Sun	Sagittarius: Jupiter
Taurus	Taurus: Venus	Virgo: Mercury	Capricorn: Saturn
Gemini	Gemini: Mercury	Libra: Venus	Aquarius: Uranus
Cancer	Cancer: Moon	Scorpio: Mars - Pluto	Pisces: Jupiter - Neptune
Leo	Leo: Sun	Sagittarius: Jupiter	Aries: Mars
Virgo	Virgo: Mercury	Capricorn: Saturn	Taurus: Venus
Libra	Libra: Venus	Aquarius: Uranus	Gemini: Mercury
Scorpio	Scorpio: Mars - Pluto	Pisces: Jupiter - Neptune	Cancer: Moon
Sagittarius	Sagittarius: Jupiter	Aries: Mars	Leo: Sun
Capricorn	Capricorn: Saturn	Taurus: Venus	Virgo: Mercury
Aquarius	Aquarius: Uranus	Gemini: Mercury	Libra: Venus
Pisces	Pisces: Jupiter - Neptune	Cancer: Moon	Scorpio: Mars - Pluto

Chart 10: Aspects

Aspect name	Angle	Symbol	Nature
Conjunction	0	☌	Unites for good or ill
Opposition	180	☍	Opposes, fights, conflict
Trine	120	△	Flows with, harmonious
Square	90	□	Blocks, congests
Sextile	60	✶	Compatible, harmonious
Semi-square	45	∠	Irritates, hinders
Quincunx	150	⚻	Imbalance
Sesquiquadrate	135	⚼	Disruption
Quindecile	165	QD	Upheaval, disruption, separation

Trine	Planet aspect - 2 planets 120 degrees apart. It represents an easy and beneficial flow of energy.

Bibliography

Bailey, Alice. A. *A Treatise on Cosmic Fire.* Lucis Press, London, fifteenth printing 1999.

Bailey, Alice. A. *A Treatise on White Magic.* Lucis Press, London, nineteenth printing 2001.

Bailey, Alice. A. *Destine of the Nations.* Lucis Press, London, third printing 1968

Bailey, Alice. A. *Discipleship in the New Age I.* Lucis Press, London,

Bailey, Alice. A. *Discipleship in the New Age II.* Lucis Press, London, fifth printing 1979.

Bailey, Alice. A. *Esoteric Astrology.* Lucis Press, London, eighteenth printing 2016.

Bailey, Alice. A. *Esoteric Healing.* Lucis Press, London, eighth printing 1977.

Bailey, Alice. A. *Esoteric Psychology I.* Lucis Press, London, ninth printing 1979

Bailey, Alice. A. *Esoteric Psychology II.* Lucis Press, London, eighth printing 1981.

Bailey, Alice. A. *Externalisation of the Hierarchy.* Lucis Press, London, seventh printing 1982.

Bailey, Alice. A. *From Intellect to Intuition.* Lucis Press, London, sixth printing 1965.

Bailey, Alice. A. *Glamour: A World Problem.* Lucis Press, London, third printing 1967.

Bailey, Alice. A. *Initiation, Human and Solar.* Lucis Press, London, sixth edition 1951.

Bailey, Alice. A. *Letters on Occult Meditation.* Lucis Press, London, eleventh printing 1973.

Bailey, Alice. A. *The Soul and its Mechanism.* Lucis Press, London, fifth printing 1971.

Bailey, Alice. A. *Telepathy.* Lucis Press, London, sixth printing 1971.

Carter, C.E.O. *An Encyclopaedia of Psychological Astrology,* Theosophical Publishing House London, 1963

Cornell, H. L., M.D. *The Encyclopaedia of Medical Astrology.* third edition, 1972.

Cramer, Diane. L. Dictionary of Medical Astrology. American Fed. Astrologers, 2003.

Daath, Heinrich. *Medical Astrology.* Cosimo Classics, NY. 2005.

Hay, Louise. L. *Heal your Body.* Published by Louise L. Hay. Revised edition 1984.

Heindel, Max. *Astro-Diagnosis. A Guide to Healing.* Rosicrucian Fellowship, tenth edition, 2011.

Hodgson, Leoni, Ph.D. *Journey of the Soul.* Published by Leoni Hodgson, fifth edition 2013.

Hodgson, Leoni, Ph.D. *OM, Union through Astrology.* Published by Leoni Hodgson, fifth edition 2014.

Jacka, Judy. N.D. *Synthesis in Healing.* Hamptons Roads Publishing Company, Inc. 2003

Jacka, Judy. N.D. *Esoteric Healing workbooks 1-4.* Published by Judy Jacka.

Jansky, Robert. C. *Modern Medical Astrology.* Astro-Analytics Pub. CA., second revision 1978.

Lansdowne, Zachary, F. Ph.D. *The Chakras and Esoteric Healing.* Samuel Weiser, Inc. 1986.

Millard, Margaret. M.D. *Casenotes of a Medical Astrologer.* Samuel Weiser, Inc. 1984.

Tansley, David. V. D.C. *Radionics and the Subtle Anatomy of Man.* Penguin Random House. 1972.

Tansley, David. V. D.C. *Chakras - Rays and Radionics.* C.W. Daniel Co. Second impression 1985.

Tyl, Noel. *Astrological Timing of Critical Illness.* Llewellyn Publications. First edition 1998.

INDEX

Symbols

1 Charts
    Chart 1: Planet rulers of the Signs 6
    Chart 2: Seven Rays and Astrology 13
    Chart 3: Sign rulerships in the Body 27
    Chart 4: The 7 Major Chakras 77
    Chart 5: Chakras and Psychology 101
    Chart 6: Planetary Strengths 102
    Chart 7: Rays, Psychology, Disease 108
    Chart 8: Chakras and the Body 109
    Chart 9: Decanates 206
    Chart 10: Aspects 206
2 Diagrams
    Astrology - Chakra Divisions 92
    Chakras and the Glands 77
    Rays in the solar system 12
    Seven Rays and Astrology 13
    Spirit, Soul, Body 2
    The Path and Consciousness 3

A

Aadland, Florence 164
Abdomen 19, 35, 39, 57, 87
Abortion 25, 35, 43, 57, 63, 69, 73, 89, 180
Abscesses 23, 63, 71, 87
Abstract mind 5, 68
Accidents 25, 29, 63, 105, 117, 118
    defined 99, 137
    horse-riding 45
Aches 15, 47, 67, 91
Achondroplasia 15, 47, 61, 67, 81, 178
Acidosis 19, 23, 35, 63, 87
Acid reflux 19, 23, 35, 63, 87, 163
Acne 23, 63, 87
Acromegaly 17, 61, 65, 81, 139
Adadevoh, Ameyo 159
Adam's apple 19, 31, 61, 83
Adams, John Quincy 121
ADD: attention deficit disorder 19, 33, 59, 63, 83
Addictive susceptibility 50, 70
Addison's disease 15, 41, 43, 61, 63, 91, 185
Adenoids 19, 31, 51, 61, 83
ADHD: Attention-deficit/hyperactivity disorder 19, 33, 59, 63, 83, 101, 174
Adrenaline 15, 43, 62–63, 73, 90–91
Adrenals 14–15, 40–43, 61–63, 72–73, 90–91, 185
Ageing 15, 47, 67, 91
AIDS 15, 37, 55, 63, 85, 157
Airways 19, 33, 59, 83
AJNA chakra 80–81
    Case Studies 126–143
Alcoholism 23, 51, 57, 63, 71, 87
Aldosterone 15, 41, 43, 61, 63, 91
Alimentary canal 19, 31, 83
Ali, Muhammad 137
Allergies 17, 19, 23, 33, 35, 37, 55, 57, 59, 63, 83, 85, 87, 161
    anaesthetics 161
    bee stings 161
    gluten 162
Alopecia 15, 29, 63, 67, 87, 192
ALS: amyotrophic lateral sclerosis 15, 33, 59, 63, 69, 81
Alta-major 19, 33, 59, 67
Alveoli 19, 33, 59, 83
Alzheimer's 15, 29, 51, 57, 67, 71, 73, 79, 122, 124
Amputation 15, 63, 73
Amygdala 31, 61, 81
Anaemia 25, 37, 49, 55, 69, 85, 151, 152
Anaesthetics 23, 51, 71
Anal fissure 19, 43, 63, 73, 87
Anaphylaxis 161
Aneurysm 17, 37, 55, 65, 85, 116
Angel, angels 16, 60
    Solar Angel 60–61, 206
Angina 25, 37, 49, 55, 85, 153
Ankles 25, 48–49, 68–69, 91
Ankylosis spondylosis 15, 37, 55, 67, 91
Anorexia 35, 57, 67, 87, 173
Antahkarana 2, 17, 33, 58, 59, 79, 204
Anti-social 20–21, 23, 57, 63, 87
Anus 19, 43, 63, 73, 87
Anxiety 20, 23, 35, 57, 87
Aorta 17, 37, 54–55, 65, 85
Aphasia 19, 33, 59, 83
Appearance 4
Appendicitis 23, 39, 59, 87
Appendix 19, 39, 51, 59, 87
Appetite 19, 31, 61, 83
Aquarius 21, 24, 48–49
Aries 14, 24, 28–29
Arms 15, 25, 32, 38, 45, 59–60, 82, 91, 153
Arrested development 15, 55, 59, 79
Arrhythmia 25, 37, 55, 69, 85
Arrow of God 73
Arteries 14, 17, 19, 30, 31, 37, 49, 54, 55, 61, 64–65, 70, 83, 83–85, 116, 121, 153, 155–156
Arteriosclerosis 25, 37, 85, 153
Arthritis 15, 47, 67, 91, 188
Asc Ascendant 4, 204
Asperger's 21, 33, 59, 61, 81
Asphyxia 15, 43, 73, 83
Aspirant 74, 100
Asthma 19, 33, 59, 83, 144
Astigmatism 25, 29, 55, 57, 81
Astral body 5, 22, 76, 86, 148, 173
Astral maniac 23, 63, 71, 87
Astral Plane 4, 22, 50, 62, 70, 72, 79, 86, 99
Astrologer 12, 129, 135, 145, 149, 171, 182–183, 185–186, 191, 198–199
ASTROLOGY 27–74, 53–100, 198
    of the future 198
Ataxia 15, 29, 63, 79
Athlete's foot 23, 35, 57, 87, 91
Atlas axis 25, 61, 91
Atma 2, 204
Atoms 7, 36, 49, 55, 73, 84
    permanent 98
Atrial fibrillation 25, 37, 55, 69, 85
Attrition 15, 47, 67, 91
Aura 204
Autism 21, 33, 59, 61, 81, 141
Autoimmune diseases 15, 37, 55, 63, 85

B

Babies 19, 35, 57, 89, 128
Baby Doe 179
Back pain 15, 37, 47, 55, 67, 91
Bacteria 25, 35, 57, 68, 119, 133, 163, 169, 193
Bacterial infection 25, 35, 57
Bad breath 19, 59, 67, 83
Bailey, Alice A. iii, 4, 29, 60, 76, 82, 140, 198
Bakker, Tammy 171
Balance, equilibrium 25, 41, 61, 81, 106
Baldness 19, 29, 63, 91
Banks, Iain 171
Barrenness 19, 25, 35, 57, 67, 89
Barrett, Rona 179
BASE chakra 90–91
    Case Studies 185–196
Becker, Cacilda 116
Beethoven, Ludwig van 126
Bells Palsy 25, 33, 59, 69, 81
Berlusconi, Silvio 133
Bernhardt, Sarah 186
Berry, Fred 134
Berry, Halle 166
Betty, Gary 195
Biceps 19, 33, 63, 91
Biden, Joe 116
Bile 19, 35, 63, 87
Biliousness 19, 23, 35, 57, 87
Bipolar 20, 57, 59, 87, 174
Birth 19, 25, 35, 57, 89
Birthmark 19, 47, 67, 91
Bladder 15, 40–41, 43, 60–61, 63–64, 72–73, 90–91, 161, 171, 186, 191, 195–196
Blindness 15, 29, 55, 57, 81, 128–130
Blister 63
Blood 24–25, 36, 41–42, 49, 51–52, 60, 62, 64, 68, 83, 85–86
    cancer 17, 25, 37, 49, 55, 69, 85
    cells 151, 159
        red 17, 37, 55, 62, 83, 151–152
        white 35, 51, 54, 57
    circulation 17, 24–25, 49, 51–52, 68, 151–153
    poison, poisoning 23, 63, 71, 85
    pressure 14–15, 17, 29, 37, 41, 55, 63, 65, 78–79, 85, 153, 156
    quality 17, 37, 49, 69, 85, 106, 158
    stream 51, 55, 70, 85–86, 151
Bloomfield, Colin 196
Bocelli, Andrea 131
Body 202
    containers 19, 57, 91
    fat 17, 65, 91
    fluids 23, 34, 35, 43, 50–51, 71
    intelligence 18–19, 35, 47, 57, 67, 91
    warmth 19
Boils 23, 63, 71, 87

Bone 25, 47, 50, 67, 91
    deformities 15
    fractures 15, 45, 59, 67
    marrow 19, 35, 47, 51, 57, 67, 91
    spinal fractures 55, 67
Bono, Sonny 117
Booth, Evangeline 153
Borkowski, Georgie 129
Bowel 19, 39, 43, 63, 73, 87, 168, 171
Boyle, Susan 142
Brain 15, 19, 21, 25, 29–30, 49, 57, 61, 63, 67, 73, 79, 116–117
    aneurysm 116
    cancer 117
    cells overactive 15, 29, 63, 73, 79
    congenital disorders 25, 29, 57, 79
    haemorrhage 15, 29, 63
    inflammation 15
    lesion 21, 49, 61, 79
    mass 19, 29, 57, 67, 79, 196
    stem 19, 33, 59, 83
    trauma 117
    tumour 15, 29, 63, 73, 79, 117
Brand, Russell 174
Breasts 19, 25, 35, 57, 89
Breathing 15, 18, 33, 59, 83, 144
    problems 144
Breivik, Anders 143
Bright's disease, nephritis 15, 41, 43, 61, 63, 73, 91, 187
Bronchial
    tract 33, 160
    tree 19, 33, 58–59, 83–84
Bronchitis 19, 33, 59, 83, 144–145
Bronte, Charlotte 140
Brow 17, 29, 63, 80–81
Brown, Melanie 129
Bruises 17, 37, 55, 85
Buboes, plague 19, 25, 35, 51, 57, 71, 83
Bucket pattern 204
Buddha, Buddhi, Buddhic 2, 7, 31, 79–80, 204
Bulimia 19, 23, 35, 57, 87, 175
Bunions 19, 51, 71, 91
Bursitis 15, 47, 67, 91, 190
Burton, Richard 174
Bush, George HW 148
Buttocks 19, 45, 65, 91

C

Calcification 15, 47, 67, 91
Calcium 25, 47, 67, 91
Calf problems 49, 69, 91
Calves 19, 49, 68–69, 91
Campbell, Glen 123
Cancer (disease) 15, 17, 25, 35, 37, 49, 55, 57, 63, 65, 69, 71, 73, 79, 85, 87, 117, 149–150
    adrenal 195
    bladder 195
    blood 17
    bone 195
    bowel 171
    brain 117
    breast 170
    cervical 184
    gallbladder 171
    leukaemia 158
    lung 160
    melanoma 196
    ovarian 184
    pancreatic 172
    prostate 184
    stomach 172
    testicular 111
Cancer (sign) 18, 24, 34–35
Candida 23, 35, 57, 87
Capillaries 17, 37, 55, 85
Capricorn 14, 18, 24, 46–47
Carbohydrates 19, 61, 87
Carcinogenic 23, 51, 57, 65, 71, 170
Carcinoma 17, 57, 65, 71, 87
Cardiomyopathy 17, 37, 55, 85
Cardiovascular system 16–17, 24–25, 36–37, 54–56, 64, 79, 85, 104, 151
    diseases 153
Carotid 19, 30, 31, 61, 83
    carotid gland 83
Carpal 17, 25, 33, 59, 83, 91
Carpenter, Karen 173
Cartilage 19, 46, 47, 67, 91, 188
Case Studies
    1. Crown 116–126
    2. Ajna 126–143
    3. Throat 144–150
    4. Heart 151–160
    5. Solar Plexus 161–176
    6. Sacral 178–184
    7. Base 185–196
    astro.com
        3118 146
        5976 183
        6814 162
        7221 159
        12077 120
        12561 126
        13842 126
        14115 127
        14834 187
        37914 176
        Karen 161
    Heindel 305 193
    L1001 136
    L1004 164
    L1005 165
    L1006 192
    Millard: Laurie 183
Castration 25, 43, 63, 73, 89
Catalysts, body 15, 69, 73, 91
Cataracts 15, 29, 55, 57, 81, 131
Causal body 204
    defined 77
Celiac disease 162
Cells
    cell life 17, 37, 54, 55, 85
    malignant 170, 195, 196
    red blood 17, 37, 55, 62, 63, 83, 85, 151, 152
    stem 17, 55, 57, 85
    white blood 17, 37, 51, 54, 158
Cellulite 17, 65, 87
Central nervous system 17, 32–33, 69, 119, 137
Cerebellum 19, 33, 59, 81, 83
Cerebral cortex 15, 29, 59, 81
Cerebral palsy 25, 33, 59, 69, 81, 134
Cerebral-spinal meningitis 15, 29, 63, 79
Cervical osteoarthritis 15, 47, 67, 83, 91
Cervix 19, 25, 35, 42, 57, 89, 184
Chakra 13
    Balancing 201
    Base or Muladhara Chakra 90–91
    Brow or Ajna Chakra 80–81
    Crown or Sahasrara Chakra 78–79
    Heart or Anahata Chakra 84–85
    Sacral or Svadhisthana Chakra 88–89
    Solar Plexus or Manipura Chakra 86–87
    Throat or Vishudda Chakra 82–83
Chaplin, Charles 154
Cheek, James 131
Chemical medicines, drugs 21, 69
Chemotherapy 15, 21, 25, 69, 73, 149
Chevenement, Jean-Pierre 161
Chicken pox 19, 33, 59, 71, 83
Chin 19, 29, 63, 91
Chiodini, Una 186
Chlamydia 19, 23, 43, 63, 73, 89
Cholera 19, 33, 59, 69, 83, 169
Cholesterol 17, 65, 87, 156
Christ 3, 7, 38, 48, 65, 165
Christian 171
Chromosome 25, 49, 69, 89
Chronic diseases 15, 47, 67, 91
Chronic fatigue 20, 57, 59, 87
Churchill, Randolph 183
Chyle 19, 35, 39, 57, 87
Circadian rhythm 15, 69, 78, 79, 120
Circular fluid waterways 70
Cirrhosis, liver 15, 65, 67, 87
Clapton, Eric 163
Clavicle 25, 33, 59, 91
Cleavage 61, 141–142
Clitoris 19, 25, 43, 61, 89
Clooney, Rosemary 160
Coccyx 25, 40, 42, 45, 47, 65, 67, 91
Coeliac disease 19, 23, 35, 39, 57, 87
Cognition 17, 33, 59, 61, 69, 81
Colds 20, 33, 59, 71, 83
Cole, Nat King 163
Colic 23, 39, 59, 87
Colitis 17, 43, 63, 73, 87, 168
Collagen 25, 47, 67, 91
Colon 19, 39, 43, 63, 72, 73, 87, 196
Colour therapy 200
Coma 15, 29, 59, 79, 119, 161, 166
Compassion 4, 16, 21, 72, 98, 206
Conception 19, 25, 35, 43, 57, 63, 89, 181
Concrete mind 12, 21, 48, 60, 68
Concussion 15, 29, 63, 79
Congenital diseases 25, 49, 69, 89
Congestion 34, 200
    chakra 16, 77, 195
    crown 122
    digestive 169
    emotional 35
    etheric 76, 86

solar plexus 150, 170
throat 144, 150
Conjoined twins 182
Conjunction 102, 204
Conjunctivitis 17, 29, 55, 57, 81
Con-men 67, 71, 83
Consciousness 2, 3, 17, 59, 65
    defined 2, 16, 32, 46
    development of 58
    dual 32
    expanding 64
    heart-centred 70
    obscured, oblivious 122
    personality 30, 54, 81
    Pluto never destroys 72
    radiant 28
    ray 2 54
    self 16, 55, 59
    stream 142
    thread 17, 33, 58–59, 72, 79, 135, 204
    unfoldment of 6
    universal 48
    victim 50, 70
Constipation 23, 39, 43, 87, 168
Constitution 17, 37, 55, 63, 65, 85
Constrictions 15, 47, 67, 91
Contagious
    diseases 25, 57, 59, 68
    infections 20, 25, 35, 57, 59
Convulsions 15, 29, 63, 69, 79
Cornea 17, 29, 55, 59, 81
Corpses 19, 57, 67, 91
Cortesi, Anita 135
Cortisol 15, 41, 43, 61, 63, 91
Cosby, Ennis 118
Counsellor, counselling 30, 199
Cowper's glands 43, 63, 89
Crabs, pubic 19, 23, 43, 63, 89
Cramps 19, 63, 69, 91
Cranium 25, 29, 63, 91
Crawford, Michael 157
Crippled 15, 45, 47, 65, 67, 91
Crohn's disease 23, 39, 43, 63, 73, 87, 168
Croup 19, 33, 59, 83, 145
CROWN chakra 78–79
    case studies 116–125
Curie, Marie 151
Cushing's syndrome 15, 41, 43, 61, 63, 91
Cuts, cutting 23, 35, 51, 57, 63, 71, 87
Cyber-bully, stalker, troll 67, 71, 83
Cystic fibrosis 19, 35, 51, 57, 71, 83
Cystitis 15, 41, 43, 61, 63, 73, 91
Cysts 17, 35, 51, 57, 71, 87

D

Daumier, Sophie 123
DC Descendant 204
Dead things 19, 57, 67, 91
Deafness 15, 33, 59, 81, 83
Death 72–73, 79, 84, 91, 202
Debilitation 20, 76
Debility 20, 42
Decay 19, 57, 67, 91
Decile 102

Deep vein thrombosis 25, 49, 61, 85
Defecation 19, 43, 63, 73, 87
Deformity 15, 47, 67, 91
Delirium, delusory 23, 35, 51, 57, 71, 87
Dementia 15, 25, 29, 43, 51, 57, 67, 69, 71, 73, 79–80, 122–125
Dengue fever 19, 33, 59, 71, 83
Dental 25, 47, 67, 91
Depression 14, 20, 23, 57, 59, 67, 79, 87, 104, 117, 124, 174, 176
Dermatitis 23, 47, 63, 67, 71, 87
Desire 2, 4, 5, 20–23, 29–31, 41–42, 44, 46, 48, 50, 54, 60, 62, 65–66, 72, 77, 84, 86, 88–89, 106, 119, 165, 198
Deva, devas 16, 204
Devitalisation 20, 57, 59, 87
Diabetes 23, 31, 35, 41, 60, 61, 87, 166
DIAGNOSING DISEASE 95–110
    via astrology 102
    via chakras, consciousness 100
Diaphragm 19, 33, 59, 83
Diarrhoea 23, 39, 43, 63, 73, 87
Diet 200
Digestion 18–19, 34–35, 39–40, 56–57, 60, 83, 86
Digestive tract 23, 31
Dinklage, Peter 178
Dionne Quintuplets 135
Diphtheria 19, 33, 59, 83, 145
Disciple 7
    defined 204
Disease
    caused by excess 17, 51, 65, 71, 87
    cause of 96
Dissociative mental disorder 141
Diverticulitis 23, 39, 43, 63, 73, 87, 168
DNA 24–25, 31, 43, 48–49, 68–69, 87–89, 98, 118, 123, 155, 158–159
Doolittle, Hilda 121
Dopamine 31, 61, 81
Douglas, Michael 150
Dreams 23, 35, 51, 57, 71, 87
Drowns 15, 51, 71, 83
Drug addiction 23, 35, 51, 57, 71, 87
Duodenum 19, 39, 59, 87
Du Pre, Jacqueline 113–114
Dwarfism 15, 47, 61, 67, 81, 139, 178
Dysentery 23, 39, 43, 63, 73, 87
Dyslexia 19, 33, 59, 83
Dyspepsia 19, 23, 35, 39, 57, 87
Dysplasia 19, 45, 65, 91

E

Ears 17, 29, 33, 59, 80, 83, 126
Earth 13, 18, 74
Easy-opposition 103, 204
Eating disorders 19, 23, 35, 57, 87
Eben, Alexander 119
Ebola virus 15, 37, 55, 63, 85, 159
Eczema 23, 47, 63, 67, 71, 87, 192
Egg ovum 19, 25, 35, 57, 89
Egoic Lotus 3, 77, 78, 80, 82, 84
    defined 204
Egomania 15, 21, 54, 73, 81, 91
Einstein 18

Eisenreich, Jim 138
Elbow 25, 33, 59, 91
Electrification 25, 69
Elimination 14, 41, 43, 61, 73, 90
Elliot, Ann 182
Embryo 19, 25, 35, 57, 89, 182
Emotionalism 87
Emotions, emotional 5, 22–23, 35, 39, 50, 56, 98, 105–107, 176
    body 4
    brain 29, 31
    congestion 35, 178
    disturbances 76
    expression 105
    nature 7, 176
    repression 116
    transmute 50
    trouble 23
    violent 192
Emphysema 19, 33, 59, 83, 145
Enamel 25, 47, 67, 91
Encephalitis 15, 29, 63, 79
Endocrine system 18–19, 59, 66–67, 77, 82–83
Endometriosis 19, 25, 35, 57, 61, 89, 180
Energies 4, 9, 75–78, 76, 81, 174, 198
    pineal and pituitary glands 49
Enlightenment 44, 46, 72, 96, 202
    defined 3, 204
Enteric nervous system 17, 39, 59, 87
Enteritis 25, 39, 59, 87
Enzymes 15, 68–69, 73, 91
Epidemics 20, 25, 35, 57, 59, 169
Epididymis 43, 63, 88–89
Epilepsy 25, 33, 59, 69, 81, 135
Epstein-Barr virus 19, 35, 51, 57, 71, 83
Esoteric 204
    astrology 6
    counselling approach 199
    planets 6
Estregan, George 195
Estrogen 19, 25, 35, 57, 61, 89, 181
ETHERIC WEB & CHAKRAS 4, 16, 24–25, 33, 48–49, 57, 68, 75–94, 89
    defined 204
    web 75, 76
Evolution 5 planes 205
Evolutionary
    path 38, 54
Excretion 19, 43, 62–63, 73, 87
Exoteric astrology 6
Extra body parts 17, 55, 65, 89, 91
Eyck, Charles 127
Eyes 17, 29, 55, 57, 59, 81, 128

F

Face 17, 28–29, 29, 63, 80
Faeces 19, 43, 63, 67, 73, 87
Fainting 17, 37, 55, 85
Fallopian tubes 19, 25, 35, 42, 57, 61, 89
Father Damien 193
Fatigue, exhaustion 15, 19, 20, 43, 57, 59, 63, 73, 87, 91, 157, 162
Fatness 17, 65, 87
Feet 19, 50–51, 70–71, 91

Feliciano, Jose 132
Female cycles 60
Femur 25, 44, 45, 65, 91
Fertility 19, 35, 43, 57, 63, 89
Fever 15, 17, 19, 25, 33, 35, 37, 39, 51, 55, 57, 59, 63–64, 67, 69, 71, 73, 83, 85, 87, 127, 145–146, 200
Fibrillation 25
Fibroids 25, 35, 57, 67, 89
Fibroids in womb 19
Fibula 25, 48, 49, 69, 91
Field, Sally 188
Fight or flight 15, 43, 63, 73, 91
Fingers 25, 32, 33, 58, 59, 82, 91, 114
Fistula 19, 43, 63, 73, 91
Flabbiness 17, 51, 65, 71, 87
Flatulence 19, 23, 35, 57, 87
Flesh 19, 34, 35, 47, 56–57, 67, 91
Flynt, Althea 181
Fonda, Henry 104
Food allergies 23, 35, 39, 57, 87
Food poisoning 25, 35, 57, 87, 163
Fractures 15, 33, 37, 45, 55, 59, 65, 67, 91
Fractures, bones 15, 47, 67, 91
Frigidity 25, 43, 61, 63, 67, 69, 89
Fry, Stephen 133
Fungus, fungi 23, 35, 57, 87

G

Gallbladder 19, 34–35, 63, 86–87, 163, 171
Gallstones 15, 35, 67, 87
Gambling addiction 23, 44, 89
Gangrene 25, 37, 49, 55, 85
Gastric 19, 23, 35, 39, 57, 87
Gastrointestinal 18–19, 30, 83
Gautama Buddha 7
Gemini 16, 32–33
Gene 25, 49, 69, 89
Genetic 24–25, 49, 69, 89
Genitals 19, 25, 41
    disorders 19, 23, 43, 63, 89
Geriatric 15, 47, 67
Germs 25, 68–69, 85
Gershwin, George 117
Gestation 19, 25, 35, 57, 89
Gibb, Robin 171
Gigantism 17, 61, 65, 81
Gingivitis 25, 47, 67, 91
Glamour 22–23, 51, 62–63, 70–71, 87
Glandular fever 19, 35, 51, 57, 71, 83
Glaucoma 15, 29, 55, 57, 81, 131
Glioblastoma 196
Glottis 19, 31, 61, 83
Glucose 19, 60–61, 87
Gluteus muscles 45, 65, 91
Gluttony 16–17, 30, 51, 54, 64–65, 71, 87
God, mind of 18
Goitre 17, 31, 61, 67, 83
Gonorrhea 19, 23, 43, 63, 89, 183
Goodman, Linda 166
Goodwill 200
Gout 23, 51, 65, 71, 87

Grand-cross 103
Grand-trine 103, 204
Grave's disease 15, 31, 61, 63, 83
Greene, Lorne 146
Growth 17, 91
    stunted 15, 47, 61, 67, 81
Growths 17, 51, 55, 57, 65, 71, 87, 112
Guillain-Barre syndrome 15, 33, 59, 81
Guilt 5, 66, 70, 195–196, 199
Gums 19, 31, 61, 91
Guthrie, Woody 124

H

Hadid, Yolanda 162
Haemoglobin 17, 37, 55, 62–63, 85
Haemorrhoids 23, 43, 61, 73, 87, 169
Hair 19, 29, 47, 61, 67, 91, 179, 192
Halitosis 19, 67, 83
Hall, Jon 195
Hallucination 23, 35, 51, 57, 71, 87
Hallucinatory 23, 35, 51, 71, 87
Hamilton, Scott 103, 111–112
Hamstrings 19, 45, 65, 91
Hands 15, 19, 24–25, 32–33, 45, 59–60, 82, 91, 137
Hardening, stiffening 15, 47, 67, 91
Harmlessness 87
Harris, Richard 149
Harvey, Charles 149
Hashimoto's 15, 31, 61, 63, 83, 148
Hawking, Stephen 134
Head 15, 28–29, 63, 79
    injuries 15, 29, 63
Headaches 21, 49, 61, 81
Heal, healers, healing 16, 22, 104–105, 115, 136, 189–190
Health-Triangle 23, 108–113, 198
Hearing 17, 33, 81, 83, 126
Heart 16, 36, 54–56, 70, 84–85, 98, 104
    attack 15, 37, 55, 85, 153, 155–156, 161
    centre, higher 84
    difficulties, disease 25, 36–37, 47, 67, 85, 98, 155
    disease 104
    failure 156
    fibrillation 25, 37, 69, 85
    valves 17, 37, 55, 85
Heartburn 19, 23, 35, 63, 87
HEART chakra 84
    case studies 151
Hegel, Friedrich 105
Hemstreet, Carole 188
Hepatitis 23, 65, 87, 164, 165
Hereditary diseases 19, 35, 57, 89
Hernia 19, 43, 63, 73, 91, 190
Herpes 19, 23, 43, 63, 89, 183
Hidden, obscure disorders 23, 51, 71
High blood pressure 17, 37, 55, 65, 85, 116, 153
Higher mind 80
High temperature 17, 37, 55, 63, 85
Hippocampus 31–32, 61, 81
Hips 25, 44–45, 65–66, 91

disease 25, 45, 65, 67, 91
Hitler, Adolf 90
Hodgkin's disease 15, 35, 51, 57, 71, 83, 149
Holiday, Billie 164
Homeostasis 25, 41–42, 61, 81
Hormonal trouble 19, 31, 61, 67, 83
Horse riding injuries 45, 65
Houses: 6th and 12th 107
Howard, John 104
Human love 22
Humbert, Vincent 129
Humerus 25, 33, 59, 91
Huntington's disease 15, 25, 29, 57, 67, 69, 73, 79, 124
Hydrocephalus 15, 29, 57, 67, 79, 118
Hyoid bone 25, 31, 61, 91
Hyperactivity 19, 33, 59, 83
Hyperglycemia 23, 35, 61, 87
Hypertension 15, 17, 29, 37, 55, 63, 65, 79, 85, 156
Hypertrophy 17, 51, 65, 87
Hyperuricaemia 15, 41, 43, 61, 73
Hypochondria 23, 39, 47, 67, 87
Hypoglycaemia 23, 61
Hypopituitarism 17, 59, 61, 81
Hypotension 17, 55, 85
Hypothalamus 17, 31, 59, 61, 81
Hysteria 23, 35, 51, 57, 71, 87

I

IC Imum Coeli 204
Ida 77
Ileum 19, 39, 59, 87
Ilium 25, 45, 65, 91
Illumination 5, 7
Imbecilities 33, 59, 61, 81
Immorality 25, 43, 61, 63, 69, 89
Immune attack 15, 37, 55, 63, 85, 135–136, 147, 151, 161–162, 162, 166–168, 185, 188–189, 192–194
Immune system 16–17, 23, 32, 35–37, 51–53, 104
    debility, devitalise 20, 35, 43, 57, 71
    over-reacts 161
Immunity 20, 57, 59, 87
Impetigo 23, 47, 63, 67, 71, 87
Impotency 25, 43, 63, 67, 89
Incarnation 14, 36, 43–44, 48, 56, 79, 98, 155, 198–199, 202, 204–205
Incest 23, 43, 63, 69, 89
Inconjunct 205
Indigenous diseases 57, 98, 105, 205
Indigestion 19, 23, 35, 39, 57, 86, 87
Infancy 19
Infectious diseases 25, 41, 59, 83, 147, 169
Infertility 19, 25, 35, 43, 57, 63, 89, 181
Inflammation 15, 17, 29, 37, 55, 63–64, 73, 79, 85, 106–107, 124, 133, 144–145, 168, 185, 187, 190, 200
Influenza 20, 33, 59, 71, 83, 146
Initiates 7, 14, 58, 69, 74, 205
Initiation 7, 204–205
Inner conflict 20, 57, 87, 152

Insanities 21, 33, 59, 61, 81
Insanity 15, 29, 30, 59, 79, 91
Insomnia 15, 71, 73, 79
Instinctual brain 29, 33
Insulin 19, 35, 60–61, 87
Integumentary system 19, 47, 67–68, 91
Intelligent, intelligence 4, 18, 36, 204
    activity, ray 3 18
    ajna 80
    endocrine system 18
    love 6, 60
    non-spiritual 100
    self-consciousness 17, 33, 59, 61, 81
    throat chakra 66
Intestines, Bowel 18–19, 39–40, 43, 58, 63–64, 73, 86–87, 137, 155, 162, 169, 190
Intuition 3, 5, 7, 78
IRA terrorist bombing 130
Ireland, Jill 170
Iris 17, 29, 55, 59, 81
Iron in the blood 17, 37, 55, 63, 85
Irritable bowel 23, 39, 43, 63, 73, 87
Ischium 25, 45, 65, 91
Islets of Langerhans 19, 35, 41, 60–61, 87

J

Jaquemont, Victor 169
Jaundice 23, 65, 87
Jaws 25, 91
Jejunum 19, 39, 59, 87
Jewel in the lotus 77, 204–205
Joel, Billy 186
John, Elton 154
Joints 15, 19, 47, 67, 91
Jugular vein 19, 31, 61, 83
Jupiter 16–17, 64–65

K

Karma, karmic 66, 98, 187
    collective karma 98
    defined 205
    diseases 89
    karmic diseases 15
    personal karma 98
Keith, Brian 160
Keller, Helen 130
Kennedy, John F 168, 185
Keratitis 17, 29, 55, 57, 81
Khan, Inayat 146
Khul, Djwhal iii, 5, 124
Kidneys 14–15, 40–41, 43, 60–61, 63, 72–73, 90–91, 106, 187–188
    failure 186
    infection 15, 41
    stones 15, 41, 43, 61, 63, 67, 73, 91, 186
Kindness 5, 87, 98, 107
King, Freddie 167
King, Larry 131
King, Stephen 132
Kirkland, Gelsey 173
Kite defined 205
Knatchbull, Timothy 130
Knees 15, 19, 46–47, 67, 91
Kudrow, Lisa 140
Kundalini 18–19, 62–63, 79, 90–91, 205

L

Labyrinthitis 25, 33, 41, 59, 81, 83
Lacteals 19, 35, 57, 89
Landon, Michael 172
Laryngitis 19, 59, 61, 83
Larynx 19, 31, 61, 83
Laser eye surgery 129
Laurie 183
Learning, difficulties 19, 32–33, 59, 83
Ledger, Heath 105
Left-brain 21
Left eye of manas 81
Leg bones 25, 47, 67, 91
Legs 25
Leigh, Vivien 174
Lemarchal, Greg 178
Leo 14, 21, 36
Leprosy 23, 47, 63, 67, 71, 87, 193
Lesions 19, 47, 67, 91
Lesser builders, devas 204
Letterman, David 138
Leukaemia 25, 49, 69, 85, 158
Leukocytes 17, 37, 55, 63, 85
Lewy body dementia 15, 25, 29, 57, 67, 69, 79, 122
Libido 25, 43, 61, 63, 89
Libra 18, 40–41
Life
    and death 14, 72
    defined 205
    force 17, 37, 55, 65, 84, 85
    stream 16
    thread 14, 15, 37, 55, 85, 205
Ligaments 19, 46, 47, 67, 91
Limbic system 29–32, 60, 61, 81, 198
Limbs 25, 49, 69, 91
Lincoln, Abraham 48, 118, 147
Lips 19, 31, 61, 83
Liver 15, 19, 34, 35, 39, 64, 65, 67, 86, 87, 164, 165, 170, 171, 172
    hepatitis 164, 165
Locomotion 19, 45, 65–66
Locomotive disorders 33, 45, 65, 89
Logoic 205
Logos 205
    Solar 65, 206
Lon, Alice 194
Longo, Jeannie 190
Lord
    of Death 73, 158
    of Love 65
Loren, Sophia 181
Lou Gehrig's disease 15, 33, 59, 63, 69, 81
Louis, Joe 153
Love 4, 16, 39, 84
    brotherly 16
    intelligent 21, 80
    is patient 84
    pure 65
    soul 81, 84
    spiritual 84
Lower brain 80, 82, 144
Lower mind 5, 82
Lumbago 15, 41, 61, 91
Lunacy 15, 57, 59, 79
Lungs 19, 33, 59, 83
    cancer 160
Lupus 15, 37, 55, 63, 85, 193
Lyme disease 162
Lymph 19, 35, 51, 57, 71, 83
    nodes 19
Lymphatic System 18, 19, 23, 34, 35, 50, 51, 56, 57, 70, 71, 83
Lymphoma 15, 35, 51, 57, 71, 83
Lynn, Loretta 140

M

MacLean, Paul D. 29
MacRae, Gordon 150
Macular degeneration 132
Malignant 160
    cancer 160, 170
    cells 170
    disease 158
    infection 165
Malnutrition 19, 35, 67, 87
Man
    average emotional 100
    Intelligent, non-spiritual 100
Manas 205
Manic depression 20, 57, 59, 87
Manilow, Barry 190
Manson, Charles 143
Marriage 24, 89, 112, 114, 136–137, 186
Mars 4, 22, 23, 62–63, 105
Martel, Linda 118
Martin, Billy 120
Martin, Dean 145
Marx, Karl 169
Mary Stuart 147
Masochism 23, 43, 63, 69, 89
Master 7, 198, 205
Maternity 19, 35, 57, 89
McCain, John 196
McCartney, Linda 170
McCullough, Colleen 132
Measles 19, 33, 59, 71, 83, 127
Medical astrologers 183, 198, 202
Medicine iii
    alternative 136
    modern 21, 69, 127–129
    traditional 67, 198
Meditation 201
Medulla oblongata 19, 33, 59, 83
Megalomania 15, 21, 73, 81, 91
Melanoma 17, 57, 65, 67, 71, 91, 196
Melatonin 15, 29, 73, 78, 79
Membranes 19, 47, 67, 91
Meniere's disease 25, 33, 41, 59, 81, 83
Meningitis 15, 29, 37, 47, 55, 63, 67, 79, 91, 119
Menstruation 19, 25, 35, 43, 57, 61, 89
Mental
    body 5, 77, 82
    disorders 20, 21

inflexibility 21
plane 5
unstable 59
Mercury 5, 20, 32, 58–59, 104
Merrick, Joseph 194
Messenger of God 32, 58
Metabolic 21, 31, 61, 83
problems 21
Metabolism 19, 31, 61, 83
Metacarpal 25, 33, 59, 91
Metastases 17, 57, 65, 71, 87
Metastasised 196
Middle ear problems 25, 33, 41, 81, 83
Migraine 21, 29, 49, 61, 81, 140
Mind 2, 5, 7, 12, 39, 42, 48, 76
4th ray 20
5th ray 21
abstract 5, 68
Aquarius 48, 106
concrete 21, 80
conscious 138
feeling 20
fixed, inflexible 21, 36, 48
Gemini 32, 106
Libra 40, 106
Mercury 58
of God 18, 21
Raja Yoga 139
scientific 36
Scorpio, deluded 106
Venus 60
Virgo, critical 106
wisdom types 16
Minerals 15, 25, 69
Minnelli, Liza 107
Miscarriage 19, 25, 35, 43, 57, 63, 69, 89, 181
Misdiagnosis 23, 51, 71
Misuse of sex 23
Mobility, movement 19, 33, 45, 47, 59, 64–66, 82, 113–114, 122, 134, 137
Mobley, Mary Ann 168
Moles 19, 47, 67, 91
Monad 36, 78, 84, 205
defined 205
Monadic
awareness 204
life stream 14
plane 3, 7
Mononucleosis 19, 35, 51, 57, 71, 83
Mood swings 20, 57, 59, 87
Moon 5, 20, 22, 24, 56–57, 105
Mora, Mirka 184
Mother Nature 18
Mother of the World 90
Mothers 19, 35, 57, 89
Mother Teresa 3
Motor nerves 17, 33, 59, 63, 81, 87
Motor neurone disease 15, 33, 59, 63, 69, 81
Mouth 19, 30, 31, 61, 83, 150
Mucus 19, 35, 51, 57, 71, 83
Mukpo, Tagtrug 141
Mulligan, John 177
Multiple personalities 15, 29, 59, 79
Multiple sclerosis 15, 37, 55, 59, 61, 63, 81
Mumps 19, 31, 61, 83
Murder 15, 43, 73, 91
Muscle spasms, cramps 25, 33, 59, 63, 69, 81
Myasthenia gravis 15, 37, 55, 63, 85
Myocarditis 25, 37, 55, 85
Myopia 15, 29, 55, 57, 81
Mystics 205

N

Nails 19, 47, 67, 91
Narcissism 54, 60, 143
Narcolepsy 23, 35, 51, 57, 71, 87
Nasal 19, 33, 59, 83
Nature spirit 73
Nausea 19, 23, 35, 57, 87
Neck 19, 30–31, 61, 83, 121
Negative core belief 5
Negro, Andrea 142
Neocortex 15, 28–29, 59, 81
Nephritis 15, 41, 43, 61, 63, 73, 91
Neptune 4, 22–23, 70–71, 105
Nerve
fluid 17, 33, 59, 81
spasms 25, 33, 59, 69, 81
synapse 17, 33, 59, 69, 81
Nervous
diseases 98
disorders 23
energy 69
Nervous system 17, 32, 49, 58, 60, 63, 68, 122
Neuralgia 20, 33, 59, 63, 81
Neurodegenerative 25, 33, 51, 59, 69, 71, 81
Neurons 17, 33, 59, 69, 81
Neurotics 23, 35, 51, 57, 71, 87
Newton John, Olivia 170
Nicklaus, Jack 168
Nicks, Stevie 133
Nightmares 23, 35, 51, 57, 71, 87
Nin, Anais 180
Nolan Twins 182
Nose 17, 29, 63, 81, 133
broken 133
cocaine damage 133
sinusitis 133
Nucleus accumben 31, 61, 81
Nureyev, Rudolph 157
Nutrition 19, 35, 39, 57, 87

O

Obesity 17, 45, 51, 65, 71, 87, 120
Obscure diseases 23, 51, 71, 87
Obsession 79, 175
Obsessive compulsive 23, 35, 51, 57, 63, 71, 87, 176
Occult
defined 205
Oedema 23, 35, 51, 57, 71, 87
Oesophagus 19, 31, 35, 57, 83, 87
Old age 15, 47, 67, 91
Olfactory bulb 31–32, 61, 81

Ollerenshaw, Dame Kathleen 127
OM 205
Online scammers 67, 71
Opposition 102
Osteoarthritis 15, 47, 67, 83, 91, 188
Osteoporosis 15, 47, 67, 91, 188
Ovaries 19, 25, 35, 42, 56–57, 61, 77, 89
Overgrowth 17, 37, 55, 85
Oxygen 17, 33, 59, 83, 85
Oxygenation 17, 33–34, 59–60, 85, 159

P

Paedophilia 23, 43, 63, 69, 89
Paget's disease 15, 47, 67, 91
Pain and suffering 20, 57
Palate 19, 31–32, 83
Palpitations 25, 55, 69, 85
Palsy 15, 25, 33, 59, 63, 69, 81, 134
Pancreas 19, 34–35, 39–40, 57, 60–61, 86–87, 161
Pancreatitis 23, 35, 57, 61, 87, 167
Panic attacks 23, 35, 51, 57, 71, 87
Paralysis 15, 33, 59, 63, 69, 81
Paranoia 23, 35, 51, 57, 71, 87
Paraplegic 15, 33, 59, 69
Parasites 19, 39, 59, 87
Parathyroids 19, 31, 61, 66–67, 83
Parkinson's disease 15, 33, 59, 63, 69, 81, 137
Parotid glands 19, 31, 61, 83
Parton, Dolly 180
Patanjali 141
Patella 25, 47, 67, 91
Pathogens 25, 69, 85
Path, the 3, 7, 74, 100, 205
evolution 3, 42, 45, 68
outgoing, return 54
spiritual development 3
Peary, Robert 151
Pedro, Afonso 135
Pelvic girdle 25, 45, 65, 91
Pelvis 25, 65, 91
Penis 19, 25, 43, 63, 89
Peptic ulcer 19, 23, 35, 57, 63, 87
Pericardium 17, 37, 55, 85
Periods 19, 25, 35, 57, 61, 89
Peristalsis 19, 57, 83
Peritoneum 19, 47, 67, 91
Peritonitis 25, 35, 39, 57, 87
Permanent atom 68, 89
defined 24, 48, 98, 205
Personality 5
Perverted, perversions 70, 89
Phalanges 25, 33, 59, 91
Pharynx 19, 31, 83
Phillips, Ada 171
Phlegm 19, 35, 51, 57, 71, 83
Phobias 23, 35, 51, 57, 71, 87
Physical body 4, 7, 34, 36, 45, 46–47, 49, 50, 56, 62, 66, 70, 76, 77, 90, 96, 120, 185
animal form 96
atoms 18, 73
Capricorn 47
Capricorn, Cancer 66

consciousness vacates 72
debilitation, tired 76
elemental 73
energy pattern 24, 48, 68, 89
etheric web 76, 88
intelligence 18
Mars rules 62
nature spirit 73
quality, energy 76
weakened, weakness 91, 98
will to live 14, 90
Physical power and strength 19, 45, 63, 89
Piles 23, 43, 61, 73, 87
Pimples 23, 63, 71, 87
Pineal gland 14–15, 28–29, 69, 81, 116, 120
Pingala 77
Pisces 16, 22, 50–51
Pituitary Gland 17, 21, 25, 32, 41–42, 43, 49, 58–61, 80–81, 103, 123, 126, 139
    acromegaly 139
    dwarfism 139
    migraines 140
    tumours 111
Placenta 19, 25, 35, 57, 89
Planet pattern 205
Plasma 17, 37, 55, 85
Pleasure centre 31, 61, 81, 165
Pleurae 19, 47, 67, 91
Pleurisy 19, 33, 59, 83
Pluto 7, 13, 72–73
    death 72–73, 158, 187, 202
Pneumonia 19, 33, 59, 83, 146
Poison, poisonous 25
    gas 23
    lead 15
    mineral 15
    plant 23
    radiation 15
Polio 15, 33, 59, 69, 137
Polyps 17, 51, 65, 71, 91
Pons 19, 33–34, 59, 83
Possession 15, 29, 59, 79
Postpartum blues 20, 31, 61, 67, 83
Prana 16–17, 37, 63, 65, 85, 205
Predatory behaviour 23, 89
Pregnancy 19, 35, 57, 89, 180
Premature ejaculation 25, 43, 63, 69, 89
Prince Alexei 152
Prince Ernst 167
Princess Alice 145
Princess Diana 175
Princess Mathilde 147
Prison of the soul 5
Procreation 19, 25, 35, 43, 57, 63, 69, 89
Progeria 15, 47, 67, 91
Progesterone 19, 25, 35, 57, 89
Prolapses 19, 41, 61, 91
Prostate
    gland 19, 25, 43, 63, 89
    trouble 25, 43, 63, 89
Protective power 45, 89
Protein 19, 47, 67, 91
Psychological disorders, trouble 21, 33, 59, 61, 81, 141
    ADHD 174

alcoholism 174
anorexia 23, 57, 67, 87
Asperger's 142
autism 141
bipolar 174
borderline personality disorder 23, 35, 51, 57, 71, 87
bulimia 175
cutting 175
dissociative disorder 141
insanity, mental 143
narcissism 142
narrow crystallised thinking 143
OCD 176
panic attacks 176
phobias 23, 35, 51, 57, 71, 87
PTSD 23, 35, 51, 57, 71, 87, 177
schizophrenia 177
Psychopath, sociopath 59, 67, 71, 83, 101
Psychotherapy 199
Puberty 25, 43, 61, 63, 89
Pubic bone 25, 43, 91
Pubis 25, 61, 65, 89, 91
Pulmonary
    circulation 17, 33, 59, 85
    tuberculosis 19, 33, 59, 83
Pupils 17, 29, 55, 59, 81
Pus 23, 63, 71, 87
Pylorus 19, 39, 59, 87
Pyorrhea 25, 47, 67, 91

Q

Quadriplegic 15, 33, 59, 69, 129, 137
Queen Elizabeth II 107
Queen Victoria 152
Quincunx 102
Quindecile 102, 205

R

Radius 25, 33, 59, 91
Raja Yoga 139, 205
Ramsey, Patsy 184
Rape 23
Rashes 23, 47, 63, 67, 71, 87
Ray 1, One: 13, 28, 36, 46, 72, 74, 78, 90
Ray 2, Two: 12, 13, 16–17, 32, 39, 50, 64, 84
Ray 3, Three: 13, 18–19, 34, 40, 46, 66, 74, 82, 90
Ray 4, Four: 13, 20–21, 30, 42, 44
Ray 5, Five: 12, 13, 21, 36, 40, 44, 48, 60, 80
    21–22
Ray 6, Six: 12, 13, 22–23, 39, 44, 50, 62, 70
Ray 7, Seven: 12, 13, 24–25, 28, 34, 46, 68, 88
Ray defined 205
Ray, Dixie Lee 144
Rays 13
    spiritual 3
    the seven 12
Reagan, Ronald 122
Recreational drugs 35, 51, 71, 87
Rectum 19, 43, 63, 73, 87

Recuperative power 17, 37, 55, 63, 65, 85
Reed, Donna 172
Reeves, Christopher 137
Reflux 19, 23, 35, 57, 63, 87, 163
Relationships 16
Repression 87, 144, 160, 172, 196
    cancer 35, 71, 103, 149
Reproduction 19, 24–25, 34–35, 41–43, 45, 56–57, 61–63, 69, 89–90, 106, 178, 180–181
Reptilian brain 19, 29–30, 33, 59, 83
Respiration 14–15, 58–59, 83–84
Respiratory organs 18
Retina 17, 29, 55, 59, 69, 81
Retrograde 103
Reward-pleasure centre, 31
Reynaud's disease 25, 49, 69, 85
Reynolds, Samuel 191
Rheumatic fever 15, 37, 55, 63, 67, 73, 85
Rheumatism 15, 47, 67, 91
Rheumatoid arthritis 15, 37, 55, 63, 67, 73, 91
Rhys-Jones, Sophie 180
Ribs 25, 47, 67, 91
Richie, Nicole 167
Rickets 25, 47, 67, 91
Right-brain 20
Right eye of buddhi 79
Rigor mortis 15, 47, 67, 91
Ringworm 23, 35, 57, 87
Robbins, Anthony 139
Rodden, Amy 145
Roles Triplets 128
Ronstadt, Linda 120
Roosevelt, Franklin D 137
Roosevelt, Theodore 144
Rubella 19, 33, 59, 71, 83, 127
Rudhyar, Dane 185
Rule 1 of healing 115, 198

S

Sachs, Andrew 125
SACRAL chakra 88–89
    Case Studies 178–182
Sacroiliac joint 25, 45, 47, 65, 67, 91
Sacrum 25, 44, 45, 65, 91
Sadistic 143
Sagittarius 20–22, 44–45
Saint-Laurent, Yves 117
Salivary glands 19, 31–32, 61, 83
Santayana, George 172
Sarcoma 17, 57, 65, 71, 87
SA Solar-arc directions 205
Saturn 18, 66–67
Scabies 23, 47, 63, 67, 71, 87
Scapula 25, 33, 59, 91
Scarlet fever 19, 33, 59, 69, 83
Schizophrenia 23, 35, 51, 57, 71, 87, 177
Sciatica 15, 41, 45, 89, 190
Sciatic nerve 17, 45, 65, 89
Sclera 17, 29, 55, 81
Scleroderma 15, 47, 67, 87, 91, 194
Sclerosis 15, 47, 67, 91, 136
Scoliosis 15, 37, 47, 55, 67, 91, 191

Scorpio 20, 23, 42–43
Scrotum 43, 63, 89
Scurvy 19, 47, 67, 87
Seal 193
Secombe, Harry 184
Secretions 19, 35, 57, 91
Seizures 25, 33, 59, 69, 81
Self-consciousness 17, 37, 55, 59, 81
Self-harm, self-injury 23, 35, 51, 57, 63, 71, 87
Sellers, Peter 156
Semen 19, 25, 43, 63, 89
Seminal vesicle 43, 63, 89
Semi-square 102
Senile decay 15, 57, 67, 79
Senses, the 29
Sentiency 16, 17, 55, 81
Separativeness 48, 60, 140
Sepsis 86, 106
Septicaemia 23, 63, 71, 87
Septile 102, 205
Serial killer 23, 43, 63, 69, 89
Serotonin 15, 29, 59, 69, 78–79
Sesquiquadrate 102, 206
SEVEN RAYS, the 12–27
Sex 24–25, 41, 43, 61–63, 68–69, 88–89
    development 25
    hormones 25, 43, 61, 63, 69, 89
    life 25
    relations 25
    STD's 182
Sex hormones, 19
Sextile 103
Sexual
    development 25, 43, 61, 63, 69, 89
    power 45, 63, 89
    problems, perversions 23, 25, 43, 63, 69, 89
Sexual power 19
Shackleton, Ernest 153
Shaw, Harry 163
Shingles 20, 33, 59, 63, 81, 138
Shock 37, 55, 85
Short sighted 15, 29, 55, 57, 81
Shoulders 15, 25, 30, 32–33, 45, 59–60, 82, 91, 153
SIDS: sudden death infant 15, 73, 79
Sight 17, 29, 55, 59, 81
Sigmoid flexure 19, 25, 43, 63, 89
Silver cord 14, 15, 37, 55, 85
Simmond's disease 15, 59, 61, 81
Sinuses 19, 33, 57, 59, 83
Sinusitis 19, 33, 57, 59, 83, 133
Skeleton, joints, muscles 14, 25, 46, 47, 66, 67, 91
Skin 19, 23, 47, 63, 67–68, 71, 192, 196
    eruptions, troubles 43, 63, 86, 138, 147, 192–194, 196
Skull 15, 25, 29, 63, 91
Sleep 14–15, 23, 35, 50–51, 57, 67, 70–73, 79, 83, 87
    apnoea 19, 67, 83
    disturbance 15, 71, 79
    troubled 79
    walking 23, 35, 51, 57, 71, 87
Sluggish organs 23, 35, 43, 51, 57, 71, 87

Smallpox 19, 33, 59, 71, 83, 147
Snipes, Peedie 179
Snoring 19, 31, 61, 83
Social diseases 23, 25, 43, 63, 69, 89
Solar
    Angel 6, 60, 206
    Logos 65, 205, 205–206, 206
SOLAR PLEXUS chakra 86–87
    Case Studies 161–177
Soraya 181
Sores 23, 63, 71, 87
Soul
    defined 16, 206
    eye of 81
    human 6, 55, 60, 206
    love 3, 46, 70, 81, 84
    older - younger 7–8, 39, 206
    prison of 5, 105, 119
    purpose 119, 165
    seat of 78–79, 204
Spanish Inquisition 143
Spasms 25, 33, 59, 69, 81
Spasticity 25, 33, 59, 69, 81
Speech 18–19, 32–33, 58–59, 59, 127, 144, 155
    organs 18
Sperm 19, 25, 43, 63, 89
Spina bifida 15, 37, 47, 55, 67, 91, 191
Spinal
    channels 77
    column 14–15, 25, 37, 55, 67, 91
    cord 17, 33, 37, 58–59, 69, 81–82, 86, 113, 136
    fluid 17, 33, 59, 81
    fractures 15
Spiritual
    man 22
    Path 3, 6, 77, 100
    workers 16
Spitz, Mark 163
Spleen 16–17, 37, 51, 55, 65, 85
Square 102, 206
Stalkers 59, 63, 67, 71, 83
Starvation 19, 35, 67, 87
STD: sexually transmitted diseases 18–19, 23, 25, 43, 63, 69, 73, 89, 183
Stellium 206
Stem cells 17, 35, 37, 55, 57, 85
Sterility 19, 25, 35, 43, 57, 63, 67, 69, 89
Stiffness 15, 47, 67, 91
Stomach 18–19, 34, 35, 39, 57, 83, 86–87, 163, 172, 175, 190
Stones 15, 47, 67, 91
Strangulation 15, 43, 63, 83
Stratton, Charles 139
Stroke 15, 29, 63, 79, 116, 121
Stuttering 19, 33, 59, 83
Subclavian veins 51
Submandibular glands 19, 31, 61, 81
Substance abuse 23, 35, 51, 57, 63, 71, 87
Suffocation 15, 43, 73, 83
Sugar, glucose 19, 41–42, 60–61, 64, 86–87, 166, 167
Suicidal thoughts 59, 63, 83
Suicide 124
Sun 16, 17, 54–55, 104

Sunburn 17, 37, 55, 85
Sunstroke 17, 37, 55, 63, 85
Suppress 15
Surgery 21, 63, 69
Survival instinct 15, 43, 63, 73, 91
Sushumna 77
Sutratma 14–15, 36–37, 55, 84–85, 206
Swellings 17, 51, 65, 71, 87
Swift, Jane 162
Sympathetic Nervous System 17, 33, 59, 63, 86–87
Synapse 17, 33, 59, 69, 81, 138
Syphilis 19, 23, 43, 63, 89

T

Tapeworm 19, 39, 59, 87
Taste 19, 31, 61, 83
Taurus 20, 30–31
Taylor, Elizabeth 156
Taylor, President Zachary 169
Tears 19, 35, 57, 91
Teeth 25, 47, 91, 133
Tendons 19, 47, 67, 91
Testes 19, 25, 43, 63, 89
Testicles 43, 63, 89
Testosterone 19, 25, 43, 63, 89
Thalamus 19, 31–32, 33, 59, 83
Thatcher, Margaret 125
Thighs 15, 19, 33, 44–45, 59, 65–66, 91, 106
    injuries 45, 65
Think an opposite thought 199
Third Eye 81
Thoracic duct 19, 35, 51–52, 57, 71, 83
Throat 15, 19, 30–31, 35, 43, 45, 57, 59–61, 63, 67
THROAT chakra 82–83, 144
    Case studies 144–150
Thrush 23, 35, 57, 87
Thymus 16–17, 32–33, 37–38, 51, 54–55, 84–85, 151
Thyroid 18–19, 25, 30–31, 60–61, 66–67, 74, 82–83, 105, 144, 148
Thyroxine 19, 30–31, 61, 83
Tibetan iii, 98, 199
Tibia 25, 48, 69, 91
Tics 25, 33, 59, 69, 81, 138
Tinea 23, 35, 57, 87
Tinnitus 25, 33, 41, 59, 81, 83
Tiredness 76, 148, 157
Tissue 19–20, 34, 35, 47, 51, 56–57, 67, 71, 87, 91, 150
    brain 43, 56, 79, 117, 122–125
    breast 170
    insidious 35
    lung 147
    scar 164
    unhealthy 103
Toes 19, 51, 71, 91
Tongue 19, 31, 61, 83
Tonsillitis 19, 31, 61, 83
Tonsils 19, 31–32, 51, 61, 83
Toothache 15, 47, 67, 83
Tourette's syndrome 25, 33, 59, 69, 81, 138

Trachea 19, 33, 59, 83
Trauma 20, 57, 59
Travolta, Jett 142
Tremors 25, 33, 59, 69, 81
Tricksters, con-men 67, 71, 83, 101
Trine 102–103, 206
Triune Brain 29
T-square 103
Tuberculosis 98, 147
Tubes 19, 33, 45, 58, 83
Tulcin, Annie 178
Tumours 17, 55, 57, 65, 71, 87, 111
Twitching 25, 33, 59, 69, 81
Typhoid fever 25, 39, 59, 69, 71, 87

U

Ulcers 19, 23, 35, 63, 87, 163
Ulna 25, 33, 59, 91
Undeveloped organ 15, 47, 67, 89
Upper brain 78
Uranus 4, 24–25, 68–69
Urea 15, 41, 43, 61, 63, 73, 91
Ureters 15, 41, 43, 61, 63, 73, 91
Urethra 15, 33, 40–41, 43, 61, 63, 73, 90–91
Uric acid 15, 41, 43, 61, 63, 73, 91
Urinary tract 14–15, 40–41, 43, 61, 63, 73, 91
Urine 14–15, 33, 41, 61, 90
Uterine troubles 25, 35, 57, 61, 89
Uterus 19, 25, 35, 42, 57, 61, 89, 184
Uvula 19, 61, 83

V

Vagina 19, 25, 42, 43, 61, 89
Vagus nerve 17, 33, 59, 61, 69, 85, 155
Vallerey, Georges 187
Van Gogh, Vincent 177
Vans deferens 19, 25, 43, 63, 89
Veins 17, 37, 49, 55, 61, 85
    varicose 25, 49, 61, 85
Vena Cava 17, 37, 55, 61, 85
Venereal disease 23, 43, 63, 89
Venous system 17, 37, 55, 60–61, 85
Venus 5, 21, 60–61, 104
Vertebrae 15, 25, 36–37, 40, 47, 55, 66–67, 91
Vertebral column 90
Vertigo 25, 41, 61, 81
Vetter, David 159
Victim of a thoughtform 143
Violent, violence 12, 23, 24, 62, 116, 127, 143, 161, 166, 175, 192
Virgo 16, 22, 39–40
Viruses 23, 63, 71, 87
Vision 17, 29, 55, 59, 81, 128
Vitalisation 16, 18, 36, 62, 85, 200
Vitalising 16, 54
Vitality 16, 29, 36–37, 55, 63, 65, 85
Vitamin 17, 55, 67, 85, 104, 151
Vocal cords 19, 33, 59, 83
Vomiting 19, 23, 35, 57, 63, 87
Vulcan 13–14, 74

W

Wallace, Rowena 191
Warren, Lavinia 139
Warts 19, 47, 67, 71, 91
Water retention 23, 35, 51, 57, 71, 87
Waterways 22
Watery systems in the body 35, 51, 57, 71
Watkins, Tionne 152
Weight gain 17, 23, 31, 51, 61, 65, 67, 71, 83, 87
Wheeler, Elsie 188
Wheel of Rebirth 4
White, Barry 156
Wilde, Oscar 119
Will
    to live 14–15, 43, 63, 73, 200
    to survive 90
Williams, Robin 124
Wilson, Harold 122
Wind 23, 39, 87, 174
Windpipe 19, 33, 59, 83
Winehouse, Amy 175
Winfrey, Oprah 148
Wisdom types 16
Wolfromm, Jean Didier 192
Womb 19, 25, 35, 57, 89
Wonder, Stevie 128
Worms 19, 39, 59, 87
Worry, agitation, inner suffering 56, 58–59
Wrinkles 19, 47, 67, 91
Wrist 19, 33, 59, 91

Y

Yeast infection 23, 35, 57, 87
Yod 103

Z

Zodiac 4

www.ingramcontent.com/pod-product-compliance
Lightning Source LLC
Chambersburg PA
CBHW081355290426
44110CB00018B/2379